GOOD TO GO

GOOD TO GO

The Life and Times of a Decorated Member
of the U.S. Navy's Elite SEAL Team Two

Harry Constance and Randall Fuerst

William Morrow and Company, Inc.
New York

Library of Congress Cataloging-in-Publication Data

Constance, Harry.
     Good to go : the life and times of a decorated member of the U.S.
  Navy's elite SEAL Team Two / Harry Constance and Randall Fuerst. —
  1st ed.
        p.   cm.
     ISBN 0-688-15249-X
     1. Constance, Harry.   2. United States. Navy. SEALs—History.
  3. United States. Navy—Biography.   I. Fuerst, Randall.
  II. Title.
  VG87.C65   1997
  359.9—dc21
  [B]   97-303
                                                                            CIP

Printed in the United States of America

First Edition

1 2 3 4 5 6 7 8 9 10

BOOK DESIGN BY PAUL CHEVANNES

PROLOGUE

HARRY CONSTANCE WAS MY NEIGHBOR. SOME MONTHS AGO, I started realizing he was more than the average, upbeat, "good guy" neighbor you said hello to a couple of times a week. We had our share of mindless conversations about the weather, kids, politics, and camping. Harry was always helpful and quick to offer assistance, and on this particular day he had volunteered to assist me in landscaping my yard. Unfortunately, he had to call and cancel due to a problem at work.

At the time, Harry was the Director of Security at the Sacramento Army Depot. The depot had been moving employees and weaponry out of the facility because it was in the process of being closed, and Harry was needed to provide security for a caravan of munitions on their way to the Concord Naval Weapons Station. An informant had given information that a local Crips gang had gotten word of the shipment and had made plans to hijack the weaponry. I was taken aback. This was Hollywood scripting—not local news.

When he returned, I quizzed Harry. "Did you use an Uzi or sawed-off shotgun? How about a bulletproof vest and riot gear? Were the local police brought in?" He shrugged his shoulders and smiled. "No," he said. "They changed the time of departure. I took my three-fifty-seven revolver and a twelve-gauge shotgun. No big deal.'' That was all.

"No big deal''! I watched the L.A. riots along with the rest of the world. I've seen reports on the gang epidemic—of drive-by shootings and other criminal activities—and all he could say was "No big deal." I remember thinking that this is someone who is either pretty stupid or overly macho. I commented something to this effect. Harry leaned his head back and recounted several stories about his time in Vietnam as a Navy SEAL. Stories of hand-to-hand, lethal combat. Stories about guns being placed to his head, and of other events that helped shape the character of a young man in war. The Vietnam War. A war that was not tidy and clean. Certainly not a war that was played by all the gallant rules of the Hollywood-sanitized, hero-filled World War II genre films of the 1950s and early '60s.

Harry killed people. Lots of people. He was trained and commanded to put himself in positions demanding he kill or be killed.

Harry came home after the war, served this country for several more years in less harrowing tours, was one of the first antiterrorist strike force members, went through hell, and today is the picture of the contented middle-aged family man. He likes to hunt and fish, is happily married, has his faithful dog he takes everywhere, and has not been plagued by post-traumatic stress disorder.

I think you will find the stories within the pages of this book to be fascinating. There is no embellishment. There is no need for it, as the true-to-life version is sufficient. This is not a Ramboesque persona that was larger than life. Instead, this is a story of an immature, oftentimes scared young man whose character was forged in a furnace most will never contemplate.

"No big deal," he said. And he meant just that. The Crips did not come to visit, but the driver was arrested for leaving the truck unguarded in a remote back lot. Harry was sorry he'd had to cancel me out.

I asked if the stress of this kind of event fatigued him much. "You know, the good Lord has watched over me time and time again. How else do I explain why I lived and others died? I'm happy to be alive, to ride my horses, to be with Barb and my family.''

This book is dedicated to the thousands of servicemen and servicewomen who came home to a country that did not want to repatriate them. Who returned to face people who, in their zeal, somehow equated the conscripted warriors with the political leaders who had sent them off to war. Who metamorphosed back from a world of war to a changed, civilized society. A world they quietly refit themselves into without complaint.

"I was paid to do a job and I did it. No big deal," says Harry. "Look at me. I have a roof over my head and a family I love. I'm good to go!"

ACKNOWLEDGMENTS

RANDALL FUERST AND I ARE GRATEFUL TO MANY PEOPLE WHO helped make this process go from fireside chat to printed page. First and foremost are Zach Schisgal, our editor at William Morrow, and assistant editor Anne Cole, for their patience and perseverance in working with us. We both wish to thank Nancy Jellison and Dave Marriner for their hours of dedication and keen insight in helping polish the rough edges.

I would like to thank my wife Barbara for her support. Also, many thanks to my daughter Carrie and her husband Paul for listening to all my war stories. To my son Darren, a computer wizard; my brother Charles; brother-in-law Frank Thornton; and my close friend Gary Chamberlin, for always being there.

Dr. Fuerst wishes to thank his family: his wife, Shirlene, along with Rachel, Ryan, and Marissa for supporting him through the many, many hours of research, writing, and editing. Marilyn Fuerst, his mother, gave tremendous support, which was greatly appreciated. He also wants to sincerely thank his partners, Drs. Fred Fuerst, Palmer Lee, and Scott Gittins. Dr. Kenji Hamada's encouragement deserves recognition, as well.

CONTENTS

GOOD TO GO

CHAPTER 1

SO THIS IS VIETNAM

SO THIS IS VIETNAM. MY FIRST GLIMPSES CAME THROUGH A BROken cloud cover while making our final approach into Tan Son Nhut Air Base near Saigon. The anticipation continued to gnaw at my gut. We'd prepared for this for almost two years, and here we were. I was the point man for SEAL Team Two, Seventh Platoon, and we were minutes away from our first exposure to warm temperatures, high humidity, foreign culture, foreign language, foreign foods—and a foreign war.

So this is Vietnam. The past two hours had seen a metamorphosis from bravado to introspection, each of us alone with our thoughts. *Could I kill? Would my reactions be as lightning quick as they were in training, or would I have the proverbial ''buck fever'' and ''freeze'' at the worst possible moment?* How could I know?

From twelve thousand feet, I pored intently over the topography of the land below us. The countryside was scarred by hundreds of pockmarked craters courtesy of our B-52s. Water was everywhere, rising and ebbing with the tide. It reminded me of the Mississippi Delta region back in the States. Sparkling like diamonds, sunrays danced upon the moving waters. The Mekong Delta spilled into the Vietnamese countryside as water, swampland, and dense, green vegetation all coalesced together. We'd soon be tromping through canals, streams, and rivers—loaded with dense jungle vegetation, leeches, mosquitoes, spiders, wasps, and sharks. Almost always during the dead of night.

"Prepare for landing. Get your gear ready. Five minutes," the co-pilot barked over the intercom. The mood on the plane quickly intensified. We'd trained in Virginia Beach at Little Creek Naval Amphibious Base. We spent many hours learning how to walk quickly, quietly, and with endurance through waist-deep water and the "ooze" of the Dismal Swamp that is part of the Intercoastal Waterway situated between Virginia and North Carolina. We also learned to acclimate to things that swam in the swamp and liked to crawl on you. We moved silently with sixty pounds of gear in and out of the water, all in an effort to simulate Vietnam. Now, we were five minutes away from the real deal.

There were many times in Virginia and Panama when we weren't even remotely quiet while sloshing through the vines and the muck. Now, we were going to face bullets that traveled easily and faster through the jungle landscape than we could. After a gun battle, where we obviously announced our presence to all creation, could we disappear in the enemy's backyard? *I don't know.*

We received intelligence briefings on what to expect in Vietnam. What its food, people, living conditions, climate, and geography were like. How political influences affected the country. A lot of time was spent on what the typical Viet Cong guerrilla looked like, their tactics in the jungle, as well as learning about punji pits and booby traps. At that point, it was all just book knowledge—and the nervous anticipation of waiting for our first taste of real action. We ranged in age from twenty to thirty-five years old (I was twenty-three). We were all about to age well beyond our years.

Flying to Vietnam was quite an experience. We were in a large prop-driven C-118 transport that carried *all* our gear. We had guns, guns, and more guns. All the grenades, knives, clothing, and rubber boats for our entire team were in this huge transport. After we left San Diego, we stopped in Hawaii, Guam, Wake, and everywhere else we could, it seemed, in order to drag it out. One hundred and sixty hours of dragging it out. . . . And now there we were, ready to touch down and begin a new chapter in each of our lives. *Could I kill?*

So this is Vietnam. Growing up, I'd never killed anything. I remembered shooting a rabbit with a BB gun once, but I'm still not sure if I killed it. I had gone camping a few times, and went hunting with my dad a few times—but I had never done more than go along. It is difficult to explain how I felt. I was expected to identify, kill, or abduct human beings, then wake up and do it again.

Here we are, ready to land in Vietnam. On the other hand, we truly believed we were the most highly trained, professional soldiers in the world. Navy SEALs are experts in stealth. Whether on land or in water, we prowled around in the dark exploiting the element of surprise. We used this tactic to perfection with small teams, surprising unsuspecting guerrillas and taking out larger forces as a result. We trained at remote locations all over the world, swimming for miles into tide pools and onto beaches in order to gain intelligence and placing lethal explosives. Whether parachuting behind enemy lines, or simply donning civilian attire and utilizing our foreign language skills, our training had been extensive and, hopefully, thorough.

Our abilities to travel in the dark were well honed. We were extremely quiet, well learned in recognizing sights and sounds with amazing clarity. We could discern a footfall from a leaf rustling in the breeze, and pick out silhouettes in the dead of night.

I was one of the best at this, and thus, I was point man. In Vietnam, the SEAL objective was to provide behind-the-lines terrorist attacks against the Viet Cong (VC) and North Vietnamese Army (NVA). The point man led the way, spotting trails, trip wires, and "bad guys" in order to keep the team alive. We were the best, and, as twenty-something-year-old men are apt to be, eager to prove it.

"Hey Constance, what're you looking at? I hope you don't get us all lost out there," said blue-eyed, blond-haired Curtis Ashton in his Texas drawl. Curtis, somewhat baby-faced, stood five feet ten inches tall, without an ounce of fat on his sinewy, tennis player physique.

"You stick close to me if you want to keep your ass alive," I retorted, as arrogantly as possible.

Everything up till then had been practice. Now, departing the plane, our senses heightened with anticipation. I didn't know if we might have to shoot our way off the tarmac after we landed, or what. The closer we got to shipping out, the more we paid attention to reports of snipers, ambushes, and casualties.

As we bounced onto the runway at Tan Son Nhut Air Base in Saigon, the copilot cackled over the intercom, "Welcome to Vietnam, fellas. Get your gear."

The fear, the anxiety, the cockiness, and the long plane ride coalesced into the sights, smells, and sounds of Saigon. As we disembarked with all of our gear and paraphernalia, I broke out in a perpetual sweat. We stepped into a sauna, engulfed by a tropical 95 degrees, 95 percent humidity. *Jeez, it's hot.* It was almost suffocating. The heat was more oppressive than any I had experienced in Puerto Rico, Guam, the Philippines, or Okinawa. It was hard to breathe.

The adrenaline ran high as our eyes darted back and forth from one new sight to another. We walked onto the tarmac.

"Whooa!" said Keener, his eyebrows raised and his lips forming a drawn-out "O." Fred Keener was the third member, along with Curtis Ashton and myself, of the "Three Amigos." All of us were about the same age and, with our blue eyes and sun-bleached blond hair, stood out in this Asian land. "This is hot! Man, I don't envy those Army guys at all. I'm sure glad we work at night. This heat is nuts."

We immediately left the tarmac and boarded another air transport that took us to the town of Can Tho (pronounced Can-toe). Can Tho was the Navy's headquarters, and we were processed there. After a two-hour flight, we disembarked for a briefing. It was your typical, *Welcome, men. You will enjoy yourselves here if you use the superior skills, training, and equipment we have provided you. You are USN, and this is what you trained for—Vietnam. You are here, the enemy is here, and . . . Tomorrow, you will travel by convoy for six hours to the provincial city of My Tho [pronounced Me-toe]. Good luck, and welcome to Vietnam.*

My Tho is a large city of several hundred thousand people, situated alongside the My Tho River. The My Tho River is large, with a width from between 200 to 400 yards, traveling from northwest to southeast before emptying into the ocean. The My Tho River is one of three major rivers that comprise the Mekong Delta region. All three rivers are altered by the changing tidewaters, rising and falling by as much as 10 to 20 feet over the course of the day.

We traveled in the six-by-"deuce-and-a-half" transport, big-eyed, surveying everything around us. This was considered hostile territory. Within two miles (four thousand meters), we could easily be killed—only five miles away was a "free-fire zone." (A free-fire zone was a war zone. Anyone caught in a designated free-fire zone could be shot.) While we, the North Vietnamese Army, and the Viet Cong understood it to be a free-fire zone, men and women who lived and worked there did not know of, or understand, this new designation. They attempted to fish, raise crops, and survive in the middle of a war. I felt sorry for these hardworking people who were caught, literally, in the crossfire.

We traveled the narrow road to My Tho, about 130 miles southeast of Saigon and 90 miles northwest of Can Tho, on our way to the Naval compound. There were peasants alongside the road—people everywhere. As we eased out of Can Tho, our guns held firmly in hand, we weren't sure what to expect. The adrenaline flowed as we continued to sweat profusely. As we traveled, Vietnamese people waved to us. They gave us friendly smiles. *Maybe this won't be so bad, after all,* I reasoned. From all the stories, I expected Viet Cong to pour out of the trees, screaming, "Look, here come a bunch of new guys, let's shoot 'em up!" Instead, I saw all these people, Americans and Vietnamese alike, intermingling as they strolled about. They didn't seem to care that we were there.

It can't be too bad; they're standing upright and not getting shot at. Suddenly, *paschaw!*—the sound of a gunshot—rang through the air. We all jumped, jerking our guns to our shoulders. We stared at other military personnel who'd been there awhile, and they acted like nothing had happened. Sheepishly, we looked at one another, shrugged our shoulders, and put our guns down. All of my group was big-eyed— looking to and fro, trying not to look as scared as we felt.

"Well, I guess it's not really coming close," I said to no one in particular.

Lumbering along in the big transport, we looked down on the people. Sure enough, they were smiling and waving up at us. Yet again, another gunshot rang out, sending us diving for cover. It was the strangest thing—wave some, take cover. Wave some, take cover. Two hours later, it didn't bother us quite as much. We started getting used to it. We never ignored the gunshots; they just didn't startle us as much. Wave some, take cover! No big deal. You got used to it.

The Naval complex at the base in My Tho consisted of three buildings leased by the Navy, fenced in, and secured. At our base (the smallest Naval base in Vietnam), we had our SEAL facilities, a restaurant with cafeteria services, and a three-story building serving as Administration Headquarters. The perimeters were fenced off with Cyclone and barbed wire fencing, extending from the river and around the buildings. Additionally, the fencing enclosed the one-hundred-square-foot courtyard in front of the complex. Close to the river stood butler buildings where we "built" our gear. "Building our gear" referred to the process of going to the storage area where our weapons and materiel were kept, then putting it all together for that night's operation. The butler buildings were large, hangarlike buildings with wooden floors.

Our living quarters were down the street and around the corner at a high-rise hotel. It was leased for us and other Naval personnel working in My Tho. The hotel had a French-inspired design, was probably built in the 1930s. It stood four stories tall and had eight rooms on each floor (four in the front and four in the back). All rooms were accessed through exterior doors, meaning external stairways and balconies were the only way to get to our SEAL Team rooms on the third floor. Antigrenade netting canopied out from the hotel walls, rising up to the second story, which took away from the elegance of the aging structure.

When we set up for an operation, or "op," we would go over our insertion point and extraction point, as well as our route and target. We discussed our itinerary using the term "klick." A klick is roughly one thousand meters, one kilometer—or about a half mile. For example, one op might be designed to go one klick north, three klicks east, and then four klicks back out. Then, we would figure out how long it took to walk the eight klicks—how long it took to get in, how fast we could move—all within the constraints of nighttime. It was critical that we were in and out while it was still dark. SEAL teams operated primarily under the principle of surprise. If we didn't have surprise, we lost. We didn't have the numbers or the firepower for a lengthy battle. SEALs would shoot up a large group and run like crazy. We were about to try it out, firsthand.

After a six-hour ride, the truck entered the compound. As I looked around, I thought back to a few months ago when we (my SEAL Team Two buddies and I) stalked through the local junkyard in the dead of night. Sneaking over mounds of refuse, I'd see a refrigerator or a stove and open up on it. A successful "kill"! It hit me again—now we would be shooting for real. This was not fun and games anymore. We'd sat at briefings during training and listened to some old chief tell us how serious these drills were. We would all smile to ourselves. *Yeah, right. Real serious.* But, when I got off the truck and began taking my gear to the butler building, I thought in earnest about shooting for real. Unlike the refrigerators, these targets shot back!

I shrugged, looked at my team, and smiled. *Can I kill?* Bring them on; we're ready to find out!

CHAPTER 2

IF IT'S LIKE THIS EVERY NIGHT . . . I MEAN, IT JUST CAN'T BE, CAN IT?

WE SPENT THE NEXT WEEK ATTEMPTING TO GET ACCLIMATED. Concurrently, the sounds and the populace—all were beginning to come into perspective for me.

"Gentlemen," our master chief said, "we'll be going out on an operation tonight so I want you all down at the huts at 1300 hours. Preliminary briefing."

Here we go. This is it. No more playing. Time to take the guns off safe.

We walked down to the ready shed. Standard protocol was for them to give you a warning order, and sure enough, there it was. A warning order was a directive telling us where we were going that night and what gear we needed. In addition, it gave the times needed to get it together, to be back for the muster, to get our gear, and to take off on the operation.

The two SEALs who led our team, Lieutenant "Pete" Peterson and Master Chief Gallagher, were taking us into a hostile area tonight. They wanted us to get into a "small" battle with five or six VC, matched against the six of us. Since we'd be ambushing them, the odds were in our favor. Lieutenant Peterson figured this was a fair way to get into a fight with minimal danger of our sustaining a casualty. It was an ideal way to get our feet "wet" (literally and figuratively), see what it was like, and probably not get anyone hurt.

So, we had this big, elaborate briefing and everybody was very serious. It alarmed me a little bit. They talked matter-of-factly about people killed, what to do should this or that occur, as well as what VC do to SEALs. The VC and NVA hated the "men with green faces." There had never been a POW (prisoner of war) SEAL. We paid close attention. Grim faces abounded.

All afternoon, my SEAL Team Two, Seventh Platoon teammates were quiet, contemplating the evening's activities. Finally, five P.M. arrived and we walked silently to where we kept our gear.

I got into my tiger-striped clothes. I painted my face with green and black face paint, double-checked all my bullets and triple-checked my gun. I checked my pistol and I checked my knife. This was it; no more games. The war in Vietnam was about to become real for SEAL Team Two.

Just after dark, we loaded into the boat and quietly cruised downriver. We used a team of two boats, one of which was a large, slow, and well-armored transport known as a Mike boat. Once we arrived at our insertion point, we moved into the second boat. It was a high-speed, eighteen-foot fiberglass SEAL Team Assault Boat (STAB). While traveling in the Mike, no lights were on. The pilot navigated only by using a fluorescent orange radar scope. All you could hear from the boat was a faint chugging of the twin diesel engines from below.

It was a moonless night, with a soft breeze blowing. Very tropical. Banana trees, coconut trees, and mangroves edged the riverbanks. It was roughly 85 degrees and 80 percent humidity. Mosquitoes flitted about.

At least we were in an area that didn't contain alligators.

There were several river areas in Vietnam that had alligators to contend with. Sharks were another hazard, although rare.

"Harry, stand by. Five minutes," instructed Master Chief Gallagher, the ranking Navy SEAL enlisted man. Gallagher had the sensitivity of a rock. With his square jaw and crew cut hair, he resembled a weathered, muscular bulldog.

"You ready for this, Constance?" he asked, referencing the fact I was the point man.

I could taste bile as we prepared to unload. We climbed from the river transport, into our SEAL Team Assault Boat. We were approximately 200 yards from shore. The driver quietly chugged toward a banana and coconut grove along the shoreline. As we approached, it became blacker and blacker as we came under the 150-foot-high jungle canopy. I felt the boat rise up on the dirt as we slowly ran into the embankment. *Nice landing. So far so good.*

I eased over the bow into the water and into the nipa palm along the shoreline. Nipa palm was tall jungle grass that grew eight to ten feet high. It was *only* five to six feet tall at this location, but I was quickly hidden amongst it. Above the nipa palm was the second canopy, consisting of banana tree leaves and coconut tree palm fronds. The murky darkness was palpable. I lifted my hand up to grasp the hand of the next guy. Even from such close range, it was so dark and obstructed that I literally could not see the guy next to me. He dropped silently into the water beside me. The others repeated the procedure. As the men dropped into the water, we formed a chain that became a small semicircle. The last man off was Master Chief Gallagher. We referred to Gallagher as "Eagle." While he was not the ranking officer (Lieutenant "Pete" Peterson was), he was the most experienced. They say he had a knack for the surroundings, as if he had a sixth sense of where the enemy was.

Where will we best be able to interdict them for the most advantageous ambush location? I hope he knows. I hope he's as good as they say he is. I may be point man, but right now I'm in drastic need of some direction.

He whispered in my ear, "Everything okay?"

"Yeah," I replied.

"Good. Signal the boat to leave. Give it five minutes. Come see me," he said in a barely audible voice.

I knew he would be in the center of the circle after I finished the task, as that was his designated position. I signaled silently to the sailor lying on the bow to back up. As the boat slowly eased away from the shoreline, I suddenly felt something wrapping around my leg.

What the . . . ? I wondered, panicked. It tightened firmly, gripping the calf of my right leg. I struggled frantically to free myself. *What is this!* I was being pulled forcibly into the river. I couldn't yell for the boat to stop without jeopardizing the team and our operation.

It must be the bow rope. It must be the bow rope! my mind screamed.

In the darkness, my frantic actions went unseen by the sailor on the bow. I was sliding haphazardly, sinking into the river. The nipa palm sliced into me, its razor-sharp edges not yielding without exacting a price. I could not extricate my leg! I was dragged farther and farther into the water.

A 180-pound man with 60 pounds of gear does not float well. I plunged to the 18-foot depths of the My Tho River. As I was pulled away from shore, I attempted desperately to unravel myself from the rope. I was fifty feet out into the river now and dragging along the river bottom. My lungs were screaming!

Come on, come on! I said to myself, in desperation.

With a start, I was suddenly free of the rope. I lay softly on the river bottom. Half jumping and half swimming, I scrambled to my feet. I turned and began jogging on the bottom of the river toward the embankment. Fighting the current and the burning in my lungs, I feverishly clawed my way up the bank. In what seemed like an eternity, I finally raised my head above the waterline.

Have you ever tried to drown quietly? As I came out, I could not let myself gasp and sputter as anyone would normally do in a situation like this. I was working to get as much air as possible—as quietly as I could—when I looked up into the face of Gallagher. He was kneeling on one knee looking at me, a serious look contorting his face. His nose was a scant three inches from mine.

"No swimming," he stated succinctly into my ear.

"What!" I exclaimed in as quiet a voice as I could, my chest heaving up and down.

"No swimming," he repeated, flatly.

I couldn't help but grin. This was like saying "Are you okay? That was close!"—except in "military-ese." No swimming. My respect for Gallagher was established, and would be validated time and time again.

Although Gallagher could not possibly have seen me, he realized from the sound not being quite right that something had happened. When I'd gone over the edge of the bow, I must have inadvertently knocked the bowline off the boat and into the water. I stepped right into the middle of the coiled rope without knowing it. The rest of the team didn't realize anything was amiss. Gallagher did. He came over to the water's edge and was waiting as I surfaced. As I came out, thoroughly soaked—my rifle and pistol included, Gallagher gave me his version of a pep talk. Instead of berating me for screwing up, he realized how close it had been and gave me a roundabout pat on the back. "No swimming" was all he said, but it spoke volumes. He allowed me to regather my wits about me, and then pulled me to his side.

"Take point. I want you to move a couple of hundred meters in that direction"—pointing to his right and giving me a compass bearing—"be real slow and keep everybody tight. Find me a trail."

So off I went, starting my very first operation, dripping wet, bleeding, already tired, and my adrenaline at the proverbial redline. Quietly, I began moving through the thatched nipa palm. The nipa palm was over our heads, and we were knee to hip deep in water. Occasionally, the man behind me, Eugene "Night Eyes" Fraley, tapped me on the butt. This let me know that he was still right behind me. Fraley was tall and skinny, yet deceptively strong and catlike. Ten minutes later, we broke through the thatch of nipa palm, into a banana grove. We were now only in ankle-deep water, making it considerably easier to move. The visibility improved. I could see perhaps thirty to forty yards into the distance. Breaks in the canopy above allowed me to see an occasional star or two overhead.

We ascended from the river bottom and climbed onto a dike that framed a large rice paddy. In Vietnam, there were a lot of dikes. To protect from the rising waters of the rivers or to control water levels for the rice paddies, dikes crisscrossed the countryside. As such, the dikes served as trails for the locals to travel on. They were flat, above the water, and continued for miles. They also served as ideal locations for booby traps. That lesson we learned the hard way.

I was now on an "official" dike trail. I began to see, picking up shadows of the men behind me. I could tell who was who. Behind Fraley was Eagle, then Roy Dean Matthews, followed closely by Keener and Ashton. It was a reassuring feeling, the sense that we were working together as a team with each man having his specific duties as we patrolled and set ambushes.

"Move down the trail until you find the first junction," said Gallagher. "Then stop."

"No problem," I replied.

I then went into what I call my ninja walk. It was a good characterization of how I, as point man, had to function in order to keep myself and my team from waking up dead and not able to play anymore. With this much visibility, I had to be as observant as possible. Who was to know if someone was waiting in the tree line or behind the dike? I had my gun pointed out in front of me. I took one silent step forward with my right foot, turning almost sideways, then stopped, and scanned to the left. I took another step with my left foot forward while turning to the right, stopped, scanned to the right, and repeated this over and over. I swiveled from side to side, hence the ninja reference. Couple this with the balance that must be maintained as I put my foot forward, to allow me, should there be a trip wire, to retract my foot without already committing my weight to the forward position, and you had a slow, tedious process. That is why it took hours to traverse short distances. Step and look, step and look, hour after hour.

My senses groped the darkness, a mixture of fear and adrenaline pounding in my ears. Eventually, we came to a perpendicular, well-worn trail. I signaled Gallagher up to evaluate.

"Here's your perpendicular trail. It looks like a fairly well used pathway," I reported.

"Perfect," Gallagher replied. "Let's set up an ambush here. Put two guys on the trail we've come up on; you and I will be at the T. Place the other two on the new trail, so that we're in an L formation." We were able to see anyone coming from the north, west, or south. On the east side was a ditch. We settled in and watched.

Every time I saw a shadow move, I was on edge—*Should I shoot? Well, no*—I was going through this anxiety, not knowing what I was supposed to do, just taking it from training. The adrenaline continued to pulse through my temples.

Gallagher knew I was worn out. He leaned over and said, "Calm down, relax. We're going to be here all night. It's a long war. You're not going to do everything tonight."

Yeah, right, I thought. *One momentary lapse and it's a short war for ol' Harry.*

"Look," he said, "I'm going to take a break and get some sleep. You keep an eye out."

"Yeah. Okay," I replied. He lay down and my eyes never flinched. I was looking for the enemy. I knew they were coming any minute. How in the world could he possibly sleep?

Nothing happened. Twenty minutes later, Gallagher rolled over and tapped me. Leaning over, he whispered, "I can't sleep."

"Yeah. Me either."

"Why don't you lay down and at least try to get some sleep," he suggested.

"Man, I can't sleep," I said.

"Well, lay down and close your eyes and try it," he interjected.

I couldn't believe it. The chief said to take a nap. Yeah, right! I lay down and looked up at the stars. I stretched out. There was a little bit of a breeze, and it had cooled down some. I peered at the foliage, the banana trees, the jungles of Vietnam.

Sleep! You have got to be kidding me. I can't possibly sleep!

I tried to identify each of the myriad sounds that made jungle operations so challenging. I was soaking wet from the river and uncomfortable, but figured I should do what he said. So I closed my eyes and started thinking about things. *How's the patrol going? What are we going to do next? What will it be like to shoot someone and see them die?*

Next thing I knew, Gallagher was punching my shoulder. I sat up— but I sat up slow. The enemy's coming. *The enemy's coming!* Otherwise, he would not be shaking me. *The enemy's coming!* I eased my gun up, ready to do battle. My senses were on full alert and my heart raced.

Gallagher leaned over and instructed, "Quit snoring."

"What!" I demanded.

"You've been asleep for forty-five minutes and you've been snoring. The rest of us have really been getting a little bit nervous, buddy," he said.

"I can't believe it. What do you mean I've been sleeping?" I looked at my watch, and sure enough, it had been almost an hour! I could not believe I'd fallen asleep.

"When you get that excited," he said to me, "and you get that much adrenaline running through your system, after a while your body just can't handle it anymore. Your body automatically starts to shut down. If you can't control it, your body will help you. It's a good thing you were able to fall asleep and rest. You'll find that you will be a lot sharper now and a lot less jumpy."

"Okay, okay. I've slept and I'm all better now," I said, trying to hide my embarrassment.

Gallagher decided to move because nobody had shown up, and it was getting closer to morning. No action whatsoever. So we moved farther along the trail. After about an hour, we came upon a hooch as the first light of dawn approached. A hooch was a small home made up of bamboo and jungle materials. Before us was a group of two or three small hooches. They were spread out in a grove of trees, cut starkly from the dense jungle forestation.

Gallagher pointed to one of the hooches and indicated that something was amiss at this early hour because a light was on. He and two other guys would go into the house. He directed me to move forward along the main trail, past the junction of the offshoot trail that led to the houses. He placed Ashton midway, with the remaining SEAL in the rearward position in case someone snuck up behind us.

I moved on up to the junction of the trail and set up. Just then, I heard voices emanating from the house. There was a ruckus. Someone screamed, and there was a gunshot. *Oh man, what's going on?* Nobody's telling me anything. I searched the murky darkness of night, trying to catch a glimpse of anything. Then, just as quickly as it started, it got quiet again.

My attention was riveted away from the houses. I caught movement coming up the trail in front of me. I stared intently ahead. Sure enough, there came an honest-to-God, "official" Viet Cong guerrilla! He was dressed like he was supposed to be dressed, wearing black pajamas and carrying a carbine rifle. An official, VC guerrilla just like in the training pictures! *Oh God! Here we go!*

I signaled Keener, who was about forty yards away. He did not respond. I signaled again. Nobody's watching. They're all concentrating on the hooch and any possible reprisals. *What do I do?* I asked myself. *Do I shoot him? Do I not shoot him? Do I tell him to put his hands up? I don't speak Vietnamese. What do I do? Come on—this is real!*

Just then, Gallagher walked up to within twenty yards of where Keener was standing—approximately sixty-five yards from me, and, thank God, saw me signaling in the faint light of the moon. I let him know someone was coming, and inquired as to what he wanted me to do. He gave me the finger over the lips—be quiet.

I signaled again, *What do I do!*

This time, he gave me the signal to stab him. His thumb and forefinger were in an L position, similar to a kid making a pretend gun with his hand. With his forefinger pointing upward, he moved his thumb to his throat. *Stab him.*

I peered yet again, but Gallagher was gone.

I'm supposed to do what! My meditation silently intensified. I was supposed to stab him. My heart rate quickened. "Oh, great. I can't stab him. I don't know how," I muttered to myself.

In training, we didn't spend much time on stabbing procedures. Oh, sure, we did practice, but it wasn't even close to the real thing. We used a rubber knife, and the person we stabbed was always cooperative. That was because if we didn't do it right, we had to do it over again. For the "victim," a rubber knife to the throat was uncomfortable. We submitted easily so we didn't have to do it over again.

Now the VC was within fifty feet of me. He couldn't see me crouching in the shadows. My mind raced and my hands trembled lightly.

Suddenly, other activity began taking place. People started moving behind me. I dared not look, for fear any movement might give me away. I sensed my team moving away from me. Something was going on at the other hooches. Unbeknownst to me, the rest of the team was silently setting up, attempting to pin down and grab several other people who had run from the hooch. Everything was happening within a matter of seconds! The Viet Cong soldier was now twenty feet from me.

I can't stab this guy—at least, not in a face-to-face confrontation. I quickly decided I would jump out and, since I was bigger than him, haul off and hit him really hard.

Twelve feet, then ten; now he was six feet in front of me! I jumped out into the middle of the trail. A look of astonishment swept across his face. It startled me that I jumped out. He looked at me and I looked at him. My feet felt like I was trying to run in neck-deep water—my two feet seemingly encased in lead.

You've got to do something! Come on, do something! It was the strangest sensation for me. Here was the moment of indecision, similar to the first time I jumped from an airplane. My legs seemed frozen. What would I do?

He took a few seconds, then decided to run. It seemed like it took an eternity for me to realize that he was running—running away from me. I sprang into motion, leaping toward him. I grabbed him. In the same motion, I pulled my knife from the scabbard. I couldn't stab him in the throat—there was just no possible way. I was just too scared. Maybe I would hit him with the blunt end. My knees weak, I felt like I would throw up. He pulled away from me. I lunged forward. For some reason, when he turned his back to me it became less personal. I hit him with everything I had, my knee, my knife, and my body. We both went down. My knife embedded just above the kidney and into his ribs. I pulled myself on top of him by forcibly grasping the hilt of the knife. I wrenched the knife from his body and thrust it deep inside of him several more times. That was it. There was an eerie hissing sound as he took his last breath. The blade of my knife looked dull and dark with his viscous, warm blood. I shoved the knife back into the sheath. His body was motionless after twitching a few moments. I assumed I killed him.

My world went still in a cacophony of silence.

Get a grip, man! Although I wasn't tired, my chest heaved up and down. *Calm down, calm down.* My ears were ringing.

Suddenly shaking me from my reverie came the crack of gunfire close by. Guns, more specifically, M16 guns, were going off at the hooch.

I realized my gun was six feet behind me. Wild-eyed, I scanned back and forth for anybody else coming in my direction. I was lying in the middle of a rather exposed trail. I quickly dragged him over the dike and into the ditch. I searched the early, predawn twilight, desperate to analyze the situation. All I knew was I had to get back to my gun, then back to my team.

I gave the signal (a series of clicks) for the team. Dead quiet. No more sounds. No more talking, nothing. It was like nobody had ever been there. I signaled again. I was alone.

I've got to get out of here. I quietly moved to where I'd last seen Gallagher. When I got there, I looked around, and nobody was "home."

Maybe there were bad guys nearby and the team had to leave quickly!

I started moving. I went back to where the hooches were. Lying in the dirt were a couple of dead Vietnamese, but no SEALs. *Three dead—unbelievable! Fractions of a second in time. What amazing violence can be meted out in the blink of an eye.*

"I have got to get out of here," I said, enjoying hearing my voice after hours of solitude.

I've lost my entire team, I thought. *Here I am, in Vietnam. It's later than we like to be out, six-thirty in the morning. I've just killed a guy—I think—and there's nobody around. Is the rest of my team dead? I only heard one or two shots. But why would they leave me?*

I didn't know what to think. All I could think about were all the stories I'd been told about E and E (escape and evasion) tactics. How not to be caught by the enemy.

Obviously, I must patrol myself to the river. As quietly as I could, I moved back down the trail. This time, the safety was off and I hoped desperately I didn't run into anyone. Lights were coming on, dogs were barking, and human voices added to the sounds of the normal jungle harmony. If I had to shoot, I could just imagine the hornet's nest I would stir up.

Unbelievable, I was thinking. *I cannot get through my first op without incident. How in the world did I screw up?*

I moved slowly along. I used every tree, every blade of grass, and every shadow to hide behind. At every turn, I had my rifle (a Stoner, my favorite, which was a large machine gun capable of shooting up to nine hundred rounds a minute) leveled with my finger on the trigger. I traveled several meters, then stopped and waited. Looking and listening for any detectable sign. Again, I did not know if there was a VC company pursuing my team—and me by extension—or what. But I continued to hear sounds that seemed to indicate I was being followed. There were gunshots and other activity in the vicinity. I wasn't sure, but it sounded like this was an enemy formation lurking around. I moved slowly forward. Every minute seemed an eternity.

By eight-thirty A.M., the sky was fully lit, and it started warming up. Several times, I saw VC patrolling along the trails. More noises started occurring, but I was within seventy-five meters of the river.

Come on! Just a little farther and I can signal a Naval patrol boat to pick me up, I hoped as I came within view of the river's edge. I descended into the river bottom area. Reaching hip-deep water, I climbed back into the nipa palm, which made me feel at least a little safer. Not much, but at least a little.

''Harry.''

Alarmed, I jerked my gun barrel toward the sound. ''Harry, it's me, Fraley,'' he hissed from behind a large coconut tree. It took every ounce of concentration I could muster to keep from pulling the trigger.

He walked out from behind the tree and smiled. Then, from the thatch, came the rest of the team.

Fortunately for me, Fraley knew what I would do. Having worked, played, studied, and partied together for two years with the same group of guys, an understanding had developed among us. Fraley was the only guy in my team with vision better than mine, and he spotted me before I was able to pick him up. He was our rear security, but when they realized that I was missing, Gallagher placed him at point.

To say that I was relieved was putting it mildly. Relief flooded over me! ''As knotted up as I was, I'm sure glad you saw me before I saw you guys moving in the bushes,'' I said. Then, as if to punctuate my feelings, I said, ''Boy, am I glad to see you guys.''

We quietly moved back to the extraction point, radioed to the boat, and climbed on board. Everyone started taking off their gear and stripping down to their swim trunks. As we washed the mud, slime, and typical jungle debris from our bodies, we discussed what we'd seen and done.

"I didn't see anything," said Keener.

"Neither did I," added Ashton. "Just heard a few shots and that was it."

"I was around back when Gallagher toasted those two VC," said Roy Dean. "You actually killed a VC?"

As it turned out, everyone else was out on perimeter while Master Chief Gallagher went into the house, shot two bad guys, dragged them out, and then left.

I started thinking over all that had taken place and my mind started to spin. I suddenly realized how tired I was.

Gallagher walked over to me and looked at me with a half smile, half inquisitive look on his face. "I saw you signaling to me. What happened?" he asked.

"Remember when I signaled you that a VC guerrilla was coming down the trail?" I reminded him.

"No."

"What?" Now it was my turn to be surprised. "Sure you do," I insisted. "Don't you remember telling me to knife him?" As I said this, I again repeated the hand signal where my right thumb and forefinger made an L.

"No. You're kidding me."

"You gave me the signal to knife him, or at least I thought that's what you did," I pressed, somewhat dumbfounded. "Look at the blood on me and my knife." I produced my knife for his inspection.

"I was simply telling you to be quiet. We had business to attend to, and I just wanted you to be quiet. I didn't realize someone was coming. Otherwise, I would've come over to help. So, what did happen?" he asked.

I sat down and began recounting what had taken place. The sun was starting to get hot. I smelled the mixture of sweat, salt air, and diesel fumes from the boat, and I started to stretch. As I finished, I looked over at Gallagher. "Do SEALs do this *all* the time? Man, if it's going to be like this every night, I don't think I can handle it. This is tough! If this is any indicator of what I'm going to see for the rest of the tour, this is going to be one bitch of a job!"

I just assumed it was going to be this frightening every time out— that I was going to be this scared to death every night.

Gallagher looked over at me and began to chuckle. "Harry," he said, "you've done more in one night than most of these guys will do in their entire tour."

I didn't know whether he was trying to make me feel better or what. All I knew was I got dragged into the river, I almost drowned, it was my first time in the jungle for real, I fell asleep, set up an ambush, killed a guy in hand-to-hand combat, lost my team, had to E and E, tried not to get captured by the enemy, tried not to get shot by my own team, not shoot my own team, tried to find another American unit, found my own unit largely by accident, then finally got on the boat—what a night!

Gallagher looked back over to me. "You know that the team moved in a crescent out toward where you were, going through the underbrush. Had you not been backtracking us—moving away from your position—we would have come right up to you. Don't worry. Tomorrow night'll be better."

"Oh good," I replied with some degree of sarcasm.

I stretched out on the bow of the boat and, for the second time in a matter of hours, fell asleep. The gentle morning breeze as the Mike boat rocked slowly on its trip back made sleep come easily.

As I faded off, an excited voice from across the boat exclaimed, "This Gallagher guy really knows how to find the enemy!"

Don't worry?

CHAPTER 3

FROM TEXAS TO COLORADO TO OKINAWA TO RHODE ISLAND TO . . .

ENSIGN WALTER E. CONSTANCE WAS A NAVY PILOT IN THE PAcific theater during World War II, stationed on the USS *Ticonderoga*. It was late September 1944 and the U.S. Navy was chasing the beleaguered Japanese back to Japan. Spirits were high, especially since VE Day some months back. Hopefully in a year or two, with the reassigned European divisions committed to the Pacific, the Japanese would be forced into surrender and the Second World War would be over.

"I just received a telegram that my son's been born!" said Ensign Constance to his fellow pilots. "A round of beers on me!"

It was September 23, and Ruth Constance proudly held her firstborn son. "We want to call him Walter, Walter Harry Constance, after his father. His daddy is off somewhere in the Pacific flying for the Navy," she said proudly to the nurse on duty. "I can't wait until he can see him. I tell you, he looks just like his father!"

I was soon called by my middle name Harry so the family could tell the two Walters apart. My mother, the former Ruth Johnson, was one of ten children born to Mr. and Mrs. Luther H. Johnson, ranchers in the Austin/San Antonio/Corpus Christi area. There was some relationship to the future President, Lyndon Baines Johnson, although I'm not sure exactly what it was. My grandpa was known as LHJ, and there are a lot of Johnsons in that part of Texas.

I spent my early years living at my grandfather's ranch. My father was away at sea with the Navy, and Mom preferred the close-knit family atmosphere in Texas to a Navy wife's solitary confinement in San Diego at Naval housing. It wasn't until I was about a year old that I finally met my father. My mother describes me as hiding behind her skirt, holding on to her leg when this Naval officer, in full dress uniform, came striding up to us at the airport where we'd gone to meet him. I was peering out from behind her at this person with brightly polished shoes and fancy doodads on his chest and shoulders. I was as shy as any young child would be. I was not going near this stranger. My mother still laughs when we talk about it.

One of my fondest memories came at about the age of six. My dad was then stationed out of Corpus Christi. It was 1950, and he was back from the war in the Pacific. He still was in the Navy, home for a while and gone for a while. When he was home, we'd go to Corpus Christi and stay there. But, when he was gone, we packed up and went back out to Granddad's ranch. Dad bought one of the early television sets available. We'd watch the Gillette fights and *Your Hit Parade*. My favorite show was *Hopalong Cassidy*. I would not miss it; it fueled my imagination out on the ranch. I played by the hour, pretending I was Hopalong or one of his sidekicks.

It was September and my birthday was coming up. Dad knew how much I liked Hopalong Cassidy, and bought me the "official Hopalong Cassidy" uniform and related paraphernalia—boots, chaps, vest, hat, and double gun set—for my birthday. Unfortunately, he wasn't going to be able to get home for my birthday. He had a number of operations he was to fly that night, so he couldn't get out from Corpus Christi to Austin. He was still getting to know me, and felt bad about not being able to be at my birthday party. The driving time from Corpus Christi to Austin is four to five hours today, but in those days it was a good eight- to ten-hour drive. Dad figured out a way to sort of be there.

"Tell Harry to go stand out in the back pasture Granddad just plowed and keep an eye out around noon," Lieutenant Walter Constance told my mom.

Dad asked his crew if they'd mind deviating from the training flight plan "just a little bit" in order to drop off something important to his family. Sure enough, about noon we were standing out in the pasture when a Navy attack plane came in low over the ranch. It was quite intimidating having a jet scream overhead, a scant two hundred feet above us. Suddenly, the cargo door opened. Out came a box attached to a parachute. It landed, and there was a Hopalong Cassidy set and a birthday card.

My memories of Texas and my early childhood are filled with warm remembrances of Grandpa and Grandma Johnson's ranch.

My father was career Navy. He was a pilot in the Pacific theater during World War II. He was shot down three times—and lived to tell about it. After the war, he rose through the ranks: lieutenant, then lieutenant commander. My dad, along with his small family (which now included my younger brother Charles, and our new baby sister Madjie), were stationed in San Diego, followed by a tour at Leonardtown, Maryland, as a Naval Test Pilot. Then, knowing he would be unable to advance any further without a college degree, he entered a Naval program and went to college as part of his official duties. So, off we went for two years to Boulder, Colorado. He finished his degree, graduating Phi Beta Kappa.

He was promoted to commander, where he changed from attack, dive-bomber-type Naval aircraft to ASW (antisubmarine warfare) aircraft. These were large planes that could stay up all day, hunting for enemy subs: P3's and P2V's, large four-prop-driven aircraft. Shortly thereafter, he was promoted and reassigned to Okinawa, Japan, as an ASW Squadron Commander. We lived there for two years.

Dad earned the right to go to the Naval War College, so off we went for yet another two-year stint in Rhode Island. Graduating from the War College got him the ranking of captain, and with it a transfer to the Pentagon. He had one tour at the Pentagon, and it was at that time I graduated from high school. His next tour was in Keflavic, Iceland, but my dad was able to cut it short since my brother Charles was a highly regarded football player and wrestler. Dad left the family in Virginia and traveled up to Iceland for the year. He was reassigned back to the Pentagon, where he stayed until retirement in 1969, after thirty years.

After attending high schools in Okinawa and Rhode Island, I graduated from Yorktown High School in Arlington, Virginia, in June 1963. We had moved to Alexandria, Virginia, where my brother Charles attended Mount Vernon High School. It was there that he was named all-Virginia middle linebacker, all-Virginia wrestler, along with lettering in track. He was heavily recruited out of high school, but went into the Marines, where he played football and wrestled at Quantico.

My father didn't push me to go in any particular direction. I was an average, B to C, student, and my parents left the decision up to me. My dad felt that at eighteen you had to take care of your own obligations and pay your own way.

"If you want to take the SATs, fine, but you pay for it. Whatever you do, young man, you do on your own. You're eighteen. I expect you to grow up, become a man, and figure out what you want to do," he stated.

I had no idea what I wanted to do with my life. So, I figured I would take a year off from school, go to Texas, earn some money working for my uncle's construction firm, and taste a little freedom before buckling down and hitting the books. I lived with my grandparents, drove a new pickup, and made $125 a week. As wages went in 1963, I did well, able to have fun while saving money, proposing to attend Texas Southern University in the fall.

My only problem, however, was that I had filled out, was immature, and had a girlfriend for the first time in my life. I was intoxicated by the freedom, the money, and the puppy love. Unfortunately, she lived in Virginia, and I was in Texas. So, with money in my pocket, I squandered it buying her things, then flying to Virginia for the weekend to be with her.

Debbie was much like me, a military kid who had moved from Naval base to Naval base. Most recently, her family had moved from Coronado, California, to our street in Virginia. We met by accident when her brother's baseball landed in our backyard and he was too scared to retrieve it.

"Hi. I'm Debbie and my brother lost his ball in your backyard."

"You're the new family down the block, aren't you?"

"Yeah. We just moved here from California. My dad's in the Navy."

"Really? Mine, too. We've been here for just two years now, ourselves."

Soon we were fast friends. My head filled with feelings and emotions I'd never known. Debbie was all I could think about.

"Texas! Why Texas? I thought you wanted to go to college. Why don't you stay and go to school here, Harry?"

I struggled for weeks with my decision. The Texas job with my uncle paid well, and it was a real opportunity for me to get out of the house.

Dad had made it abundantly clear that I needed to "grow up," and I was bound and determined to show him I was. *What do I do? Maybe I could fly home once a month to spend the weekend with Debbie.*

"You know I love you, but this is such a great opportunity for me to earn money and go to college. I can stay with my relatives, work part-time, and fly home to see you once a month. Maybe you could even fly out and see me. What do you think?"

"I . . . well, I don't think it will . . ."

I held out a small jewelry box. Caught by surprise, she stopped talking. She reached for the tiny box. "Oh, Harry."

Opening the box, she let out a squeal. "Harry, it's beautiful! Nobody's ever given me jewelry before." Debbie threw her arms around me and kissed me.

"Baby, I promise I'll visit a lot. I just need to do this," I said, the smell of perfume and the feel of her body pressed against me sending me into a dizzying, light-headed passion.

Before long, my dad was demanding to know what I was thinking, shelling out hundreds of dollars on airplane flights instead of saving my money.

"I can afford it; it's my life and my money," I responded anytime I was questioned. Unfortunately, when it came time for school, I didn't have money for tuition.

After a year of this, I decided to move home to Virginia. I believed I could get a local job that was equivalent to the Texas job—especially when you considered the cost of the commute. I got a job working with a D.C. construction company laying underground pipe. It started out well enough, but it gets cold in Washington about the end of September. Quickly, my immaturity manifested itself.

Soon after I moved home, Debbie began distancing herself from me. I felt as if I'd had the "stuffings knocked out of me," walking around in a blue funk.

"Harry, you're nice enough, but when we lived in Coronado, there were these special Navy men—I think Dad called them SEALs— that were secret agents or something like that. I met several of them. They were really cool. What are you doing with your life? My parents are concerned I'm getting too attached to you. My dad introduced me to a couple of cadets from Annapolis. You don't mind if we date other people, do you?"

I muttered something, or at least I remember my mouth saying something like, "Sure, I've been thinking about dating other people, too."

"Good. You're really sweet, Harry."

With that, she left me doing everything I could to fight back tears of grief.

Debbie is gone. I hate my job. . . . Life isn't fair!

"Harry, you're acting like a big baby. There are lots of girls out there. Find someone else," my brother said, with the sensitivity of stone.

One late November day, I came home from work and my father had a fire in the fireplace. We had a fully finished basement that served as a game room. My dad had a pool table, a rattan bar from Okinawa, rattan furniture (which my brother and I routinely broke), all making for a comfortable lifestyle. I came home, my hands frozen, cracked and bleeding. Charles was stretched out (at six feet four and 240 pounds, he readily consumed a piece of furniture) across the couch, and my sister was sitting next to my mom. It was about 30 degrees outside, and dark. I came home to the warm, pleasant aroma of dinner, a fire, and a standard of living a laborer's life could not support.

"Come over to the bar, son." My father motioned, as he poured himself a drink. "Can I get you anything?"

"Thanks. I'll have a beer," I replied.

As I stepped up to the bar, I saw, lined up across the counter—in order—recruiting pamphlets for the Army, Navy, Air Force, and Marines. All stacked up and neatly organized.

"You know, son, you ought to pick one of these."

I looked down at the pamphlets, I looked at my dad, and that was it. I stood there for a moment and replied, "Well, okay. I pick the Navy."

Dad swept all the other pamphlets away and handed me the Navy collection. "Look through it. You oughta sign up."

I went down to the Navy recruiting office and took the test.

"Mr. Constance, you're the sort of man the Navy is looking for. You scored extremely well. Let me be the first to welcome you into the Navy!"

It was a good thing. I was at one of those "critical junctions" in life that each of us faces. I was going downhill emotionally—just going with the flow, without any sense of goals or direction. Fortunately for me, I was pointed in the right direction in time to avoid some of the other influences that were starting to beckon to me.

I was sworn into the Navy by my father in December 1964, and reported to boot camp in San Diego on January 4, 1965.

CHAPTER 4

I'LL TAKE THE EASY ROAD (I.E., HOW I GOT TO THE SEAL TEAMS)

WHEN YOU LOOK BACK TO CERTAIN DEFINING MOMENTS IN your life, many of those will involve career choices. For me, the Navy was a turning point. I did well, adapting easily to the opportunity that came my way. For me, a military career during the Vietnam era got me focused on achieving my potential. I received the opportunity to be one of the best at what I did. This is a circumstance I am forever grateful for. Many people take jobs they do not enjoy, spend years there, and then languish because of family, mortgage payments, and lethargy until they retire. There is an excitement when you are fortunate enough to find an activity that allows you to be recognized as one of the best in the country at what you do. It may be work, but for me it was an energizing passion.

I wanted to be a frogman. I still can't say exactly why I wanted to be a frogman, but I did. I was forced to apply over and over before I succeeded in getting into the Underwater Demolition Teams (UDT) and SEAL (Sea, Air, and Land) Teams, only to come close to having it ripped away from me.

Boot camp was a busy affair. All I remember is learning how to stand at attention, how to make my bunk, how to wear my uniform, how to march, and how to shine my shoes. That's it. Oh, and I received the Official Blue Jacket's Manual for Navy Knot Tying. There was so much to learn, I hardly remembered any of it.

In the Navy, everyone is expected to have a trade. My father was an electrician prior to his becoming a pilot, so I figured this was what I would use as my avocation before becoming a frogman. Early on, when I was queried as to my trade, I put in for Electrician's Mate.

A few days later, a recruiting team came through asking for volunteers for UDT at boot camp.

"Anyone interested in UDT, muster out to the rec center offices at 1400 hours," came the call over the loudspeaker. Off I went. After a brief question-and-answer period, we were required to go through a regimen of push-ups, pull-ups, sit-ups, and extended swimming. I passed everything.

"Congratulations! Sign right here," the recruiter said. I signed my name to a special request chit that would go up the chain of command and release me to go into UDT training. There I was, barely three months into the Navy and I was moving ahead of the program—doing what I'd set out to do. I didn't really care to be a pilot like my father. What did excite me was working up into the highest level of finely trained Navy men. The demands, both mental and physical, appealed to me. This seemed to be an area where I could excel and "be the best."

UDT. Underwater Demolition Teams, the Navy frogmen. These groups of well-trained men traveled to far-flung regions of the world and snuck around gathering information and blowing up obstacles. In World War II, the Germans had what they thought was an impenetrable defense against Allied amphibious assault upon the French beaches at Normandy. Besides having the obligatory barbed wire and troop patrols on shore, the Germans had placed large numbers of mines in the water. They also positioned large metal devices to destroy landing craft foolhardy enough to try to launch an assault on the beach by impaling the underside of the boats. For weeks, UDT frogmen swam several miles underwater to the beaches at Normandy. The frogmen placed explosives on each of the mines and on the metal landing deterrents. As the assault date approached, they crawled out of the sea under cover of fog, rain, and darkness and cut the barbed wire and placed explosives on the fortifications on the beaches. At the flip of a switch, hundreds of explosions rent the night sky. The minefield was destroyed. The metallic landing deterrents were destroyed. All as a result of the dedication and courage of the frogmen. This sounded much more exciting to me than a career as an electrician buried deep inside a Naval frigate somewhere.

How about that—UDT, here I come!

Shortly after was graduation from boot camp. My parents didn't bother to come out, as my father didn't really feel that boot camp was any big deal. Soon, however, the chit would be approved and I'd be on my way to Coronado, California. I knew I wouldn't have to go to Electricians School because I would be a frogman instead.

"Constance," came the call from the dispatcher at graduation.

"Yo," I replied, with a smirk on my face. Give me those three little letters. Right here, in front of all my graduating class. I relished this.

"Electrician's Mate A School, San Diego, California. Report one week from Monday," came the order. I couldn't believe it. It had to be just a slow-processing foul-up.

Early the next morning, I flew home to Virginia. My father was proud of me, and congratulated me on getting through boot camp.

"Good job, son. Do good in A School," he told me.

"But, Dad, I want to be a frogman!"

"You have to go be an electrician. Work on being a frogman later," he replied.

I was in the twelfth week of a sixteen-week course, when the UDT recruiters came in. I decided to take the test again, rather than hope the request would resurface.

Push-ups, pull-ups, mental aptitude tests, sit-ups, swimming—all over again. Again I passed everything. When I showed up for my interview, the recruiting officer looked at me and got a puzzled look on his face.

"Didn't we evaluate you a couple of months ago?" he inquired.

"You sure did. I passed everything. I thought I was in, but I guess I didn't make it," I replied.

He thumbed through his records and looked at me with a quizzical look. "Your chit was processed forward. You were to have been over to our place for last class."

"Well, I didn't make it. My orders were to here."

"When do you graduate?" he asked.

"In about three weeks," I answered.

"Sign right here," he said, pointing to a new application chit. "I personally am going to sign you in. You're in, partner," he said as he shook my hand rather officially. "That's dedication, buddy! Way to hang in there."

"No sweat," I said as nonchalantly as I could.

As they left, I did my best not to let my excitement show. I was strutting. Three weeks!

The next three weeks flew by. Finally, we were in a big, long second-story hall set up for graduation. We were all to be given a manila envelope with our assigned destination, orders, plane tickets, instructions, and money. They started out alphabetically, name by name, with graduation papers, duty station, and the manila folder.

"Anderson. SBN-two-two-seven, Anchorage, Alaska," came the call. The guys cheered, patted him on the back as he went forward, and then the next name was called.

Several names later came my call. "Constance."

"Yo," I blurted out, with great anticipation, awaiting the justification of my bragging.

"*Wallace L. Lind,* DD-seven-oh-three, Norfolk, Virginia."

"What!" I exclaimed, trying to sort through the sudden onslaught of anger, emotion, and disbelief. "That sure doesn't sound like UDT!"

I took the manila folder and stared dumbfounded at the orders. This couldn't be. I read it again. There must be some mistake. I had to talk to somebody.

I went downstairs directly to the senior man at the school, the "chief," hoping he could straighten this out for me.

"Look, I don't know what is happening, but I have taken this test twice, I've passed it twice, and they keep telling me that I'm in. UDT. That's where I was assured I was going. Would you mind looking into it for me?" I pressed.

The chief picked up the phone on his desk and made several phone calls. "Oh, I see . . . uh-huh . . . no kidding . . . all right, I'll tell him," he said to the dispatcher on the other end of the line.

"Look, Constance, somehow your paperwork got all dicked up. The dispatcher tells me we really needed somebody to go onto this ship. You're it. Either you meet this muster time on that ship, or your ass is grass," he said sternly, looking for my response.

I exhaled slowly as I lifted my brow and rolled my eyes. I walked quietly out of the office. Later that afternoon, I boarded a plane headed for Norfolk, Virginia, via Washington, D.C. Before I boarded the plane, I put a call into my dad at the Pentagon.

"Well, Dad, I'm coming home. I finished A School, and I'll see you soon," I stated.

"So, when do you report to training?" he asked.

"I don't. They put me on a destroyer—the *Wallace L. Lind,* based out of Norfolk. It's in Guantánamo Bay, Cuba. I'll be home early tomorrow morning, and then I head to Norfolk."

There was a pause on the other end of the line. "What?" he finally questioned.

"Yeah. I'll show you my orders when I get home," I said, suddenly ready to get out of San Diego.

The moment I got home, I showed my dad my orders. Looking them over, he said, "This is unusual. You sure do have to go to the destroyer. Look, when you get there, see what you can do to find out about what happened to your request for UDT."

"Okay, Dad," I said, hoping maybe he could do something.

When I got to Guantánamo Bay and went on board ship for the first time, I was greeted by the Personnel Officer, who checked me on board. In walked the Chief Electrician, extending his hand with a smile. "Welcome aboard, sailor. Aren't you the guy who volunteered for UDT?" he asked.

How did he know this? I wondered. "Yeah," I replied.

"Well, buddy, you got two years on this ship. In order for you to get a chit off this ship, it has to be approved by me—and I'll never approve it. So, you can just kiss that good-bye. Get to work, learn your job, and stay out of trouble," he said matter-of-factly as he left the room.

I hate to admit it now, but that devastated me. I quit getting haircuts; I wouldn't talk to anybody. I just did my job, went to my bunk, and sulked. Several months later, the chief came to me and said, "Son, we're pulling into Mayport, Florida. Get a haircut and you can go on liberty."

"No thank you," I said curtly.

"Come here. I want to talk to you. I hear you aren't talking to anybody, and that you aren't friendly."

Before he could say anything more, I said in clipped cadence, "So."

I hadn't been saying a word to anybody. I was hurting inside and was quickly closing myself in. I detested being on this old World War II destroyer, doing a job I didn't enjoy.

The next day, we arrived in Mayport. The Chief Electrician came to me. "All right, Constance, you can leave the ship, but you can't leave the base."

"Thanks," I replied softly. I went off the ship and walked directly to a phone, where I called my dad at home.

"Hey! Good to hear from you, son. How're you getting along?"

"Well, Dad, the chief says I'm here for the next two years. The funny thing of it is that the chief knew all about my volunteering to UDT. He has assured me that there is no way, now that I am on the ship, of him approving a chit in order to go to training. I'm not sure what's going on. Somebody is screwing me over."

Evidently, there was a Navy detailer—a person who hands out assignments and destinations from the offices of Navy Administration in Washington, D.C.—who was a friend of the chief on the *Wallace L. Lind*. My chief called the detailer, asked for an Electrician's Mate, and was told there was no one available.

"You gotta have somebody available. Send me someone," he implored.

"Well, I've got this kid who is an Electrician's Mate, but he's slated to go to UDT," the Naval detailer said with a pause. "It looks as though I don't have anybody else."

"Look, I need someone now. Couldn't you just lose the request, and send me the kid?" asked the Chief Electrician of the *Wallace L. Lind*.

That was exactly what happened. My "approved" request chit for UDT was dropped into the garbage can. The detailer actually felt he was doing me a favor. "The kid's young, and most likely stupid— why else would he want to be a frogman? He doesn't know. We'll do him a favor and let him be the electrician he's trained to be," he said.

My mind tormented me as I thought about my proud and successful father, and how he'd advanced with pride throughout his career. I thought of Charles, my brother, and how he seemed to have this same gift of successfully maneuvering into being on top in athletics and academics. I, on the other hand, always seemed to be a "day late and a dollar short." Reckless emotions—anger, self-pity, disgust, guilt, blame—coursed for hours through my mind.

I didn't want to beg my father to intervene. I'd been brought up knowing he valued self-reliance. At twenty years of age, it seemed, at least to me, my life had ground to a halt.

I decided to swallow my pride and call my dad. "Dad, I know you can't pull any strings for me, but I would appreciate it if you could find out who I could write to or who I could volunteer to since you have access to a phone and I don't," I said, trying to make it seem that I really wasn't asking for help. I knew full well that when someone of my father's rank called, doors opened. While I hated to ask, it seemed that, after everything I had been through, swallowing my pride wasn't all that hard.

My dad realized what I was saying and said, "Stiff upper lip. Go do your job, quit acting like an ass, and let me check into it. When does your ship pull back in?"

"In two or three weeks," I answered.

"Good. Now you go do your job. Do good," my father stated.

"Yes, sir," I replied. So back to the ship I went. I went straight to the barbershop and got a haircut.

The chief approached, puzzled at my new disposition. "Why'd you get a haircut?" he asked.

"I'm going to square away, Chief," I answered.

A puzzled look momentarily crossed the chief's face. "Ahh, good. I knew you'd come around to your senses."

He was at a loss to explain my newfound cheerfulness. So, he continued to send me to mess cooking duty. I still don't know whether he distrusted me, or whether this was some sort of mind game to make me realize how wonderful a position as an Electrician's Mate on the *Wallace L. Lind* was compared with being a cook. He enjoyed lording it over me, while I in turn had made no effort to hide my exasperation and dislike of him. Regardless, I was determined to do whatever I could to fulfill my father's request. It was, after six months on the *Lind,* at least a sliver of hope.

"Chief, can I go ashore and make a phone call?" I inquired.

"No, you have duty tonight. Tomorrow," he told me.

"Okay," I replied, knowing we would be in port for the next four days. I figured it really didn't matter whether I called on Friday night or Saturday night.

It was at this time (approximately four P.M.) that the offgoing mail left the ship, while new provisions and oncoming mail were brought aboard ship. I finished my chores and was at my bunk, reading.

"EMFA Constance, lay to the Admin Office. EMFA Constance, lay to the Admin Office," came a call over the loudspeaker.

"Me?" I wondered. Admin was somewhere "up" in the upper reaches of the ship, somewhere I'd never been. That was where the officers stayed and you were not invited—unless you were in trouble.

I quickly put on my uniform and went up to the Admin Office. Before me stood the Personnel Officer, the Senior Personnel Chief, my friend the Chief Electrician, and the Executive Officer, whom I had only seen once in my entire tour.

The Senior Personnel Chief stood there tapping on an IBM printout card. I stood at attention, trying to look as respectful as possible. *I cannot believe it. Here I am in trouble again, and I don't know what for.*

"At ease. At ease," he said, pacing back and forth. "Who do you know?"

"I don't understand, Chief," I said, questioningly.

"What do you know about *this*?" He held out the IBM printout card. Across the top was my name, "CONSTANCE, WALTER H. 9145307"—all my numbers. Then I spied, farther down the card, the words "UDT-R, Little Creek, Va."

The realization hit me. "All right!" I blurted out. "My request was approved!"

"Your request never left the ship," he stated. Once someone received a new assignment, all requests from their last command had become null and void. The chief had told me he would never approve my new UDT request. The realization of what had occurred hit me. "You don't have a request that left the ship, so how did you get approval for UDT training?"

"I don't know. Maybe my dad did it. All right, Dad!"

"Who the hell is your father?" demanded the Executive Officer.

"Oh, he's a Naval captain assigned to the Joint Chiefs at the Pentagon," I replied innocently. "He is in charge of Antisubmarine Warfare Operations."

"Holy . . ." the chief said, wide-eyed, realization hitting him. He threw the card down on the table in disgust.

"Why didn't you tell anybody your dad is with Joint Chiefs?"

"Well, when I got here, this particular chief," I said, pointing at the Chief Electrician, "told me he would *never* approve my leaving. He let me know it wouldn't do any good for me to open my mouth and try to straighten things out. Come hell or high water, he wanted me in mess cook."

They all looked at him. The Chief Electrician just stared straight ahead, frozen. After a long pause, the XO (Executive Officer) said to me, "When we get back to Norfolk—and we're leaving tomorrow— you are to be discharged early and are to report immediately to Little Creek Amphibious Base, Virginia. They don't have another class starting for another month, but you're going to go early. We no longer want you on this ship."

The reason was that it was illegal to alter an already approved assignment. It would leave the Navy with a potentially dangerous legal liability, especially should the reason for alteration be discrimination. That could affect someone's career, and most assuredly would if "higher-ups" were pulled in. That was why there was so much alarm among the administrative officers on board ship.

"Tell your father we're sorry."

"That's fine. I will."

If I had been smart, I would have taken that time before reporting to Little Creek and started a vigorous workout program. I had a 38-inch waist, weighed 240 pounds, and was walking into a program that required miles of running, swimming, and endurance. But, like those professional athletes who cannot find it in themselves to report to training camp in shape, I would pay for each excess pound.

As I left the ship, the chief looked at me and shook his head. "Listen to me. I'm going to tell you something, fat boy. You're going to go over there and you are going to flunk. And they are going to put your ass on an oiler off the Aleutian Islands. I'm going to laugh my fool head off."

I looked at him with youthful contempt. Here he was telling me how fat, soft, and weak I was, and all I could do was seethe with the belief that *he* was greatly responsible for my condition. I would realize later that I held the responsibility for me. I couldn't always control circumstances that arose, but how I dealt with them fell under my control.

"Chief, if I ever see you again, you'll be speaking out the other side of that mouth of yours."

His mouth curled up into a half smile, half sneer. "Yeah, right— outta here!"

A few weeks later, I reported to UDT training at the Naval Amphibious Base in Little Creek, Virginia. I walked up to the desk to check in, and, as I was filling out the paperwork, Chief Blaise walked over. He looked down at my papers, then at me, then back to my papers yet again. His eyebrows lifted as an incredulous grin came over his face.

"Holy mackerel, would you look at this!" he almost yelled. "A butterball! Hey, everybody, come and look at this, this clown wants to go through training!"

My face got feverish, beads of sweat forming on my forehead.

"You two, come here," said Blaise to two other UDT recruits who'd gotten to Little Creek even earlier than I had. "Take him over to the obstacle course. If he can make any of the obstacles, bring him back and we'll keep him.''

I surveyed the obstacle course. Lucky for me, I made one. *Whew,* I thought.

So the two guys took me back to the chief, and reported that I did pass one obstacle. "Yeah, Chief, he passed the easiest one.''

There was a long pause. Slowly, Chief Blaise walked up to me and stood next to me.

"Son, are you sure you don't want to save yourself some pain and just go on back to your ship?'' he inquired. "Are you sure you want to stay? 'Cause, son, it's gonna hurt.''

Something inside me clenched my gut as hard as I had ever known. There was absolutely no conceivable way I could go back. My internal image of myself, my hopes, and my goals were based on my finally being successful at *something.* My something had come down to this moment, and my spine straightened. I looked directly into the chief's eyes.

"There is no way I am going back, sir.''

With a shrug, he turned and walked out of the room. I could tell he was certain I would not last. Maybe it was the rolling of his eyes, or perhaps it was his glance over to the Staff Instructor where he smiled and shook his head from side to side, scornfully. Funny, how adept I was at reading body language!

I set my resolve. I was absolutely, positively going to pass. This was as great a time of mental conditioning as of physical. We got to do this fun drill they called "sugar cookies." We all loved sugar cookies. Discipline and mental stability are critical to frogmen. This drill was designed to instill those qualities. Sometimes, the instructor would come up with a real or contrived shortcoming.

"Johnson! You and Smith were dogging it! I don't care if you finished first or not—you let up!'' the UDT instructor screamed, barely six inches from Johnson's ear. Johnson, a lithe young man with a sinewy physique, rolled his eyes, betraying for a moment his feelings. This is what the instructor was hoping to elicit.

The rest of us moaned.

"Swim trunks! Hit the beach! All of you—NOW!''

The entire team stripped down to swim trunks, ran out to the ocean, dove in, got out, rolled in the sand, and raced back into rank. Hence the term "sugar cookies." I started UDT in December 1965. We did sugar cookies in the winter. In Virginia. In our swim trunks.

If a trainee wanted to quit, the instructor would stop right there, pull him out of whatever he was doing, give him a towel and a blanket, and then see that he was taken back to base for a warm meal. Shortly thereafter, he was gone. There was never any harassment of anyone who quit. UDT training was voluntary, and trainees were not goaded into staying if it meant that later, under possible life-and-death circumstances, they might regret not having quit earlier, do something stupid, and endanger the team. The rest of us, on the other hand, were a little less forgiving. When eight guys were running over obstacles, carrying a six-hundred-pound raft-boat in a winter snowstorm and two guys quit, it then meant we had our own version of the children's song of "Eight little monkeys jumping on the bed, one fell off and broke his head . . . seven little monkeys jumping on the bed . . ." Several times we finished with just four guys after starting with eight. Once someone quit, that was it. There were a number of guys who were every bit as physically capable as I but, in a moment of weakness, threw in the towel.

Six months of UDT training later, I stood with 18 other guys at the graduation ceremony. We started with 125 "wanna-bes." In addition, I was now a lean 180 pounds with a 31-inch waist. It was approaching June, and I really felt good about things.

Following UDT training, we traveled from one school to another. We immediately went from Little Creek to Fort Benning for the Army's jump school. It was at Fort Benning that we began to show a mischievous streak. Before we were allowed to go up and jump from an airplane, we first had to master jumping from the towers they had there for that purpose. Fort Benning has four of these 250-foot-high towers with an arm that protrudes out like an upside-down L. The trainee is suspended from this arm, and he is to learn how to (1) master any fear of heights he may be experiencing and (2) gain experience with the parachute from a more manageable height.

Just the same, 250 feet up is not exactly akin to jumping from the high board at the high school pool.

One night, three of us took three bedsheets and drew a large "U" on one, a "D" on the second one, and a "T" on the third. We climbed over the barbed wire fence that surrounded the base of three of the towers, and started climbing. Up the towers we went, with the sheets stuffed inside our shirts. We then crawled upside down, looking like possums hanging from a tree branch, out on the arms of the towers. When we got to the midpoint of the arm, we tied the sheets to the three arms. The next morning, there they were, "UDT," hanging smartly from the towers, 250 feet up in the air.

On that bright, July morning, our team was in trouble. We were pretty shocked ourselves as to who would perpetrate such a ghastly thing as hanging "UDT" from the towers. We pleaded to no avail that someone was framing us unjustly.

"Sir, why in the world would we purposely place ourselves and the good name of UDT in jeopardy? We need to catch the dastardly cowards who would stoop so low," my teammate, Roy Dean Matthews intoned, stopping for melodramatic effect as we snickered. "Who would stoop so low as to sully the good name of such a proud Naval tradition as . . ."

"SHUT UP, sailor boy!"

"Nobody can jump until we get the sheets down!" came the orders.

UDT 22 comprised nineteen men out of the five hundred there preparing to jump. We were commanded to go to the end of the line and start doing push-ups.

"Get your sorry, your pompous, your, your . . . Na-val asses down and give me push-ups until I say you can stop!" he commanded, spitting out the word "Naval" with as much venom and disgust as he could possibly inject into a word.

As the line progressed across the field, there was our team, moving across doing a push-up "hop." We were in such good condition that we were carrying on conversations and laughing while continuing our push-ups. Ten minutes. Twenty minutes, then thirty. Still we carried on doing push-ups. The sergeants were trying to humiliate us in front of everybody, but we were spoiling things because of our tremendous level of physical conditioning.

Then an unfortunate event occurred. There was this Army kid, Private First Class Rodriguez, a somewhat slight five-foot-four-inch trainee, who was scared out of his wits. It was slightly windy, and little Rodriguez was released from the tower. He was told to take a rear slip. There were four parachute cables strapped to each jumper, and a rear slip meant that the jumper was to pull on the back two cables in order to realign the chute to compensate for the wind direction. Unfortunately, Private Rodriguez was frozen in fear, his body rigid, his arms crossed across his chest, and he didn't respond to any instructions given. He landed on his heels with no bend in his knees. He bounced up, almost as if he had been on a trampoline, and, as the wind propelled him backward, he did a back dive onto his neck. The force broke his neck and killed him. No one could believe it. Shortly thereafter, an ambulance came and took his body away, sirens wailing.

A solemn silence ensued, an awkward moment when no one knew how to react or how they were supposed to react. Everybody was shook, especially the Army guys who were next on the tower. In typical fashion, we came out quick with our own jokes, akin to those that seem to occur after every tragedy—jokes made up in an attempt to lighten the heaviness of the moment, not to make light of the incident. UDT was there with some great one-liners.

We started yelling as we did our push-ups, "Man, this is tough training."

"I'm glad I'm at the end of the line. So all you Army guys can get killed first."

"Any one of you guys want to start doing push-ups with us so you can save your neck?"

"Okay, let's do reverse push-ups. Now, regular push-ups. Now reverse . . ." we huffed.

Guys started murmuring.

"It's crazy to have two-hundred-fifty-foot towers. They're the perfect height to be high enough to kill you—what'd you think of poor Rodriguez?—but not high enough to allow you a few extra seconds to react," several guys said.

"Hey, get those Army guys outta there so we can go play on the towers," we started yelling.

The sergeant came back to where we were in line. His face twisted, white with anger at our insolent insincerity. His words came out clipped. "You guys think you're so big and bad?"

"Say hey, we're here for a jump."

"You guys willing to go up the tower now?" he hissed.

"In a heartbeat."

"Would you mind going in front of the Army guys to show them that it is okay?"

"Only if we get two turns," I said, in perfect deadpan.

"Jeez!" exclaimed the sergeant. "Get up there!"

We ran up to the tower, practically ripping the harnesses off the guys waiting their turn. "Take us up. Take us up!" we yelled.

"Drop us. Come on!" we would yell. Then, as we were falling, we would start screaming like we were on a roller coaster. "AAAHHHH!!"

We would hit, rip the harness off, and run to the front of the line.

"I want to do it again!" And the guys at the front of the line were only too willing to oblige us.

After about twenty minutes of screaming frogmen jumping from the four towers, the mood began to lighten. Now we were all jumping and screaming—Army, Marines, Air Force, all of us. It was quite a sight, but I think the instructors didn't mind as we were all jumping . . . and put the fear that killed Rodriguez behind us.

A week later, we were to graduate from jump school.

We were becoming the men necessary to carry out the assignments given out in Vietnam. The camaraderie and bravado were beginning to show in our team mentality and in our individual characters. We were being constructed to be capable of running through a brick wall.

Shortly after jump school, we were off to Key West for advanced scuba training. We worked out daily in the sun, running on the beach, turning in ten-mile runs at an average pace of six minutes per mile, and thinking life couldn't get any better. We began to hone an attitude as a bunch of "badasses"—tanned, strong, well trained, and we knew it.

Early one morning, we headed out to formation with our uniforms on. We were wearing our wings, scuba helmet insignia, jump wings, heavy felt (Marinelike) hats, all spit-shined and polished. We were ready to fall into formation when I looked out to the harbor and saw a Navy destroyer. *Wallace L. Lind.*

"Hey, guys," I blurted, excitedly. "Look! Seven oh three. Let's go!"

The whole team went with me running up to the ship. "We want to see the Chief Electrician."

It had been almost a year since I was last on the 703. Just then, out walked a familiar face, the Chief Electrician.

"Hey, Chief. Would you mind stepping off the ship? I want to show you something," I said.

"Holy shit!" he replied, his eyes widening as he realized who I was. "I'd like to congratulate you," he said as warmly as he could. Haltingly, he walked toward me.

"I wouldn't get that close if I were you."

"Hit him. Hit him," urged my UDT 22 team members. I'd told them how he had tried to undermine my efforts.

"Hey, look. I didn't think you had it in you," he said, apologizing. "I'm sorry."

I reached out and shook hands with him without saying a word, turned, and walked away with as well-concealed a grin as I could contain. I breathed deeply. For me, just walking away proved to myself I had started to grow up.

We were sent from one training school to another, learning skill after skill that were starting to make us valuable participants in Naval operations.

Several months earlier, there had been an international incident when one of our nuclear bombs had been lost off the coast of Spain. The Navy had searched frantically to find it in order to save political face in front of the world as well as to keep the top-secret components away from Russian salvagers combing the area. Unfortunately, we lost another bomb off the coast of Puerto Rico. As quietly as possible, the Navy assembled a complete Naval Amphibious Unit (eight ships), a prototype of the exploratory sub *Alvin,* and two other mini-submarines.

UDT 22 was called upon to help look for the remnants of the bomb. I still think we were being dragged around the ocean floor as shark bait, but our official purpose was as divers in search of the lost bomb. There was a big LST mother ship (a huge ship whose front ramp drops down) and several "Mike" boats, which fit inside the LST mother ships. It was to one of these Mike boats that we were assigned. The LST ships mapped out huge grids of suboceanic topography for underwater exploration. From the Mike boats, 10-foot-long sections of 3-inch steel pipe were suspended that were drilled at either end with eye-bolts attached to them. Two-inch-thick nylon rope was tied to the two ends, and the pipe was dropped to a 120-foot depth. The ship would then begin to slowly traverse over the grid section it was assigned to, and the bar would rise to approximately 90 feet. Two divers were then sent down to hold on to the lines and visually inspect the ocean floor. At "dead slow" speed of approximately one and one-half knots, we had to hang on firmly. Should we turn our head to the side, our masks would be forcibly ripped from our faces.

We dropped down the lines using open-circuit, twin 90 (cubic centimeters) scuba tanks. Hanging on to the lines caused our bodies to drape out behind the line. We concentrated on looking for wreckage. Back and forth we went, looking for any recent scrap and trying to differentiate it from other man-made clutter.

Several days later, one of *Alvin's* magnetometers located the wreckage. The bomb had propelled into the ocean floor, furrowed out a channel along the bottom until finally stopping at a depth of 135 feet. Along the pathway were strewn parts that we were told to salvage. We were sent down with sacks to retrieve as much of the electronic circuitry as we could. We came up with about eight bags of sophisticated materiel. My partner signaled me, holding three waferlike gold bars, *Should we put these into our wet suits?* They were approximately one-pound conducting wafers of gold. I told him no, as I did not want to do anything that could jeopardize our careers. They were 24-karat solid gold.

Each day, after we finished working, we got into our UDT boat and let the lieutenant know that we were going out on "an official UDT training dive." We then went out around the point and went swimming. Several times we went diving for lobster, and then, along with beer we had brought, we headed for the shore to relax, barbecue the lobster, and relish the thought of the other sailors confined to the ship for days and weeks on end.

CHAPTER 5

WHAT GOES AROUND COMES AROUND

THREE MONTHS AFTER OUR PUERTO RICAN MISSILE SEARCH, President Johnson and the Pentagon brass realized the Vietnam conflict was heating up. Decisions were quickly being made about how best to deploy the fighting forces of the United States of America.

In 1962, President Kennedy had wanted an elite force of men who were well trained and well conditioned to carry out special warfare objectives. Those men were to be sent to unstable "hot spots" all over the world. The Navy was chosen to provide the manpower. Fifty men were selected from the West Coast UDT base at Coronado, California, and another fifty from the East Coast, at Little Creek Amphibious Base in Virginia Beach, for a total of one hundred men. They got involved in some very interesting training and some even more interesting operations. They became the "secret agent men" that Johnny Horton sang about and were popularized by the TV shows of the time. These one hundred men were taken to all the elite training centers of all the branches of the services. One month they would train with the Marines, the next with the Army Special Forces and Rangers, the next month somewhere else.

After training these one hundred SEALs, the Navy wasn't exactly sure what to do with them. So, right or wrong, many SEALs were sent to troubled countries around the world. Greece and Turkey have had long-simmering feuds concerning territorial waters and who should control Cypress. We had SEALs on both sides of that particular conflict and a number of others.

But, it wasn't until the Vietnam War that a clear understanding of SEAL capabilities came into focus. The West Coast SEAL team was originally the only SEAL team assigned to Vietnam. As the realization set in that Vietnam was a jungle warfare arena, so did the understanding of how effective SEALs could potentially be. The one hundred SEALs (who were known as plankholders, since they were a part of the originally commissioned group) had not been increased in number since their formation in 1962. Now, in 1966, it was apparent that more SEALs were definitely needed. SEAL Team Two was added for Vietnam deployment, and the decision to bring more men into SEAL training was initiated.

When we returned from Puerto Rico to UDT headquarters at Little Creek, the announcement was made that fifty additional SEALs (twenty-five West Coast and twenty-five East Coast) were to be chosen.

SEALs. They were admired, almost revered—at least by sailors. Frogmen were able to dive, blow up obstacles, and provide cartographically detailed maps of the terrain of shoreline waters. They were not allowed to go on shore. SEALs, on the other hand, traveled all over the world. They weren't confined to ships as UDT frogmen were. They were provided with civilian clothing allowances, had three times the training of UDT, and traveled by air, sub, and ship to their objectives.

My mind wandered back to conversations I had had with my girlfriend Debbie. ''There were these really cute guys where we lived in San Diego. They were called seals or dolphins or something. Anyway, they are really important and special Navy men. My dad said that they are secret agents the Navy has.''

''Yeah, but why would you want to go out with a sailor who's gone all the time?''

''Oh, that's okay. They look so handsome in their uniforms and everything.''

It didn't take much for me to make up my mind to apply. Immediately, I was told why I couldn't possibly be selected. First of all, I was only three months into UDT operations. Protocol stated that you must stay with UDT for a year of operational service before applying for anything further. There were several directions I could go, such as minisub operations or explosive ordnance demolition (EOD), or even saturation diving (deep-water diving), that were opportunities—but I was supposed to wait a year before applying. Second, I had only attained the ranking of EMFA, which meant I had only two Naval stripes. This was referred to as being nonrated. The next level was EMFN (known as a fireman by classification). This was followed by the "V" insignia known as a chevron. The SEALs had never chosen anyone with less than a single chevron (an "E-4"). There were three prerequisites in order to volunteer: (1) one year as a UDT operator, (2) rank of E-4 or above, and (3) approval by a board composed of SEALs.

I had had such poor luck getting into UDT that I figured it was at least worth the effort. Maybe my luck would be better and, as a fluke, I would somehow sneak by the selection board and be chosen. So I applied.

I began talking to a number of people—SEALs, officers, and others—and while they suggested I apply, they weren't overly optimistic regarding my chances.

A week later, they called us out of quarters on a Friday afternoon. All three hundred men from UDT 21 and UDT 22 were present. "Gentlemen, I have the list here that has been approved by SEAL Team Two. The following twenty-five personnel have volunteered to transfer to SEAL Team Two and have been approved," came the announcement.

"Adams."

"Ashton."

I stood there with a feeling of ambivalence. Life had been good to me since being sworn into UDT, and I enjoyed the camaraderie and respect that was drummed into UDT members. It would be nice if, because of Vietnam, there would be further commissions into SEAL Teams. Maybe in another year I would be a legitimate candidate.

"Constance."

My eyes practically popped out of my head! Did I hear that right? In a fraction of a moment, a dozen thoughts raced through me, and then, that sweet feel of exhilaration! It was one of those indescribable moments when you don't expect anything—and walk away with a life-altering new direction.

Instantly, guys were clapping me on the back. "I can't, for the life of me, figure how in the hell you got in," I heard over and over from my UDT team members. I was beaming from ear to ear!

"I'm in SEAL Teams! I am going to be a SEAL!" I blurted out.

"You lucky son of a bitch!" said Johnson, one of my UDT buddies, who'd told me all the reasons I shouldn't set myself up for disappointment by applying.

"Monday morning report with bag and baggage to SEAL Team Two HQ," came the instructions. Out of three hundred frogmen, more than half had volunteered to go to SEAL Teams. I was going!

We met in a small briefing room. "Put your bags in here, get in the briefing room, and shut up," came the order. The tone was arrogant—similar to the disdain drill sergeants expressed in boot camp. We looked at each other. We hadn't been talked to like that *since* boot camp.

Master Chief Rudy Boesch (who would spend forty-two years in SEAL Teams) strode to the podium. "Welcome to SEAL Team, gentlemen. A whole new ball game. One screwup and you will find yourself back in UDT."

We realized quickly that, whereas in UDT they were flexible, here in SEAL Team it was another round of strict regimentation.

"Get a locker," Master Chief Boesch continued. He then proceeded to tell us what was expected and what our individual assignments would be. We were broken down into platoons and told what we could expect. "One screwup and you're gone. We only want the best, and the demands upon you will be substantial. We anticipate losing many of you."

I was assigned to parachute detail. All of us had subspecialties. Mine was to be parachute operations.

The chief scanned the room approvingly, and, with a wave of his hand, dismissed us. As we were filing out of the room, I heard him say, "Constance, just a minute."

Oh man, great. I'm at the back of the room—maybe they've changed their mind about me. Crap! I'd only been in UDT for six months, certainly not long enough to garner any unfavorable attention. *What does he want,* I wondered. Everyone else left the room.

He met me in the doorway, and stood there chest to chest with his face inches away from mine. "You are now an EMFA. You have one week to make fireman or I'm dropping you from the team," he stated flatly.

Meeting his gaze with mock assuredness, I replied, "Sure, no problem."

This was maddening. I'd had numerous opportunities to study and take the test for fireman. In the Navy, you took the tests when you were eligible, adding stripes, responsibilities, and increased pay scales as you passed them. When I graduated from A School, I was eligible to take the test. When I didn't get UDT, I pouted. While I was on the *Wallace L. Lind,* my immaturity had mixed with my increasing despondency, and I had turned down every chance.

Who cares about more money—I can't spend it anywhere in the bowels of this stinking ship, I had moped.

Then, when I decided that it would definitely be to my advantage to start upping my rank, I was traveling about in UDT training. When I finally got back from the various classes at different bases, I was immediately shipped to Puerto Rico. I went through all this training and didn't have time to take the test. Now I had one week to take the EMFN test—in addition to my heavy SEAL training.

So, in between carrying parachutes around in air operations, PT (physical training), and classes, I studied like I'd never studied before. I was fortunate, because the guy in charge of air operations kept asking me questions from the book while we worked. Every spare moment I was at it.

When Friday came, I went down and took the test. We were to be given the results on Monday. Friday afternoon, Rudy called me into his office. I was fairly confident I had passed, but stood there apprehensively, nonetheless.

Master Chief Boesch broke into a grin. "Congratulations! You are now a fireman, and I expect you to have the stripe applied to your sleeve by Monday morning."

"No problem," I exulted. "That's the easiest assignment I've had in a long time!"

That afternoon, I found my wallet a little lighter as I provided the obligatory keg of beer for the "party" that was expected when one of the team received any type of promotion. Guys were again congratulating me, more on my staying on the team than obtaining the EMFN rank.

"Damn, Harry, we were certain you were going back to UDT. We all lost big money bets because of you. You owe us a lot more than these beers!" said Eugene Fraley, himself newly selected to SEAL Team Two.

Monday morning came, and I mustered out in the "uniform" SEALs wore on the base. It consisted of our blue and gold UDT/ SEAL T-shirt, swim trunks, sweat socks, and sneakers. We ran (usually a six- to fifteen-mile run), then did an hour of PT, after which we showered and changed—back into fresh sets of blue and gold T-shirts, swim trunks, and sneakers. We stayed in multiples of this "uniform" all day long.

On Monday afternoon, I was working in parachute detail preparing and moving about one hundred parachutes, when Master Chief Rudy Boesch walked in. "How're you doing?"

"Just fine, Master Chief," I replied.

Rudy looked over at my boss, SEAL Bob Stamey, and asked, "How's Harry working out?"

"Oh, he's doing pretty good," Bob said, as he reached for another parachute.

"Good. The CO's pleased you made fireman. However, there's never been a man assigned to SEAL Teams that was less than third class. You are a tryout. You're a test. In fact, there's never been a Navy man who has come to SEAL Teams nonrated," Master Chief Boesch stated flatly.

"Man, they must've really gambled on me," I said, realizing this wasn't a "Hi, how's it going" visit.

"You've got thirty days to get your first chevron," he said, turning to go. He paused, glanced over at me with a smile that said, *You've got your work cut out for you, kid,* and left.

I inhaled slowly, pursed my lips, and sighed. I now had to accomplish in thirty days what was usually done in six to twelve months. My schedule had intensified with a significant increase in course load. I was in great shape, but this schedule was tiring.

"You did it once; you can do it again," Stamey offered, pulling me away from my frustration. "I'll help you with it," he said with a laugh. And he did.

The thirty days flew by, and on another Friday morning, I went in and took the test for third class. On Monday morning, we were out for "muster of corps" where everyone was at attention in formation. Rudy Boesch looked over our platoon, and barked, "Attention to orders."

This was formal stuff. "Constance, front and center."

Oh crap. I hope I passed. So, out I went, standing at attention.

"Congratulations. You have advanced to third class." The Commanding Officer walked up and handed me an eagle with the electrician's ball with the chevron "V" underneath.

A cheer broke out as the guys surrounded me. Before I knew it, I was hoisted up into the air, carried around back, and dropped into the dip tank. That was where we tested our scuba gear for leaks. It was a six- by four-foot tank. I was drenched in full dress regalia.

Still dripping, I made my way to the barracks to retrieve money enough for my second keg purchase in less than sixty days.

Fraley was the first to toast me. "Harry, maybe it's a good thing they selected you. You keep buying kegs of beer every few weeks and you'll hear no complaints from me, you punk kid."

It was now March 1966. Over the next six months, we went through counterguerrilla warfare training with the Marines in Camp Lejeune, jungle warfare school in Panama in the Canal Zone, gunfire support school, and foreign language school at Old Dominion University, where I became fluent in Spanish. We returned yet again to Camp Lejeune for medical training and more guerrilla warfare tactics, and, later, advanced training with the Rangers. Finally, at Fort Bragg, we went through much of the Special Forces training, such as weapons training, both of the U.S. issue as well as Chinese, German, and Soviet varieties. (After my first tour in Vietnam, we received our Raider certification.) In other words, we were schooled in every aspect of warfare the U.S. military could devise.

By June 1967, we shipped back to Little Creek, Virginia, for final preparation before heading to Vietnam. We were precision-trained killers—only we hadn't done any of the killing part, yet. Psychologically, we were just about ready. We were comfortable with jungle stealth, swamp maneuvers, and Vietnamese weaponry.

Shortly before shipping out, we were granted leave for four days. My parents decided they wanted to come down to see me in order to spend time before I left for Vietnam. It was now late August 1967, and we were weeks away from combat. On Friday afternoon, my folks arrived in their new, white Buick Wildcat convertible. My father was delightfully happy and proud of me. He knew that few Navy men attained SEAL certification. Eighteen months earlier, he was not sure I would make it past cook. Now there I was, considerably changed from the naive young man he had known as a resident of his household.

"Get in, son. I want to show you my new car. It has a four-forty-cubic-inch V-eight, red leather interior, and man, does it fly!" he exclaimed.

We traveled along the ocean boulevards and talked, laughed, and had a fun afternoon. I was in the best physical and mental shape of my life, and, like any parents would be, mine were proud of their son's accomplishments. In light of the predicaments they had seen me in literally just months before, they were generous in their praise. I could not help but grin, effectively breaking the ''mad dog'' serious scowl that was a staple of the military persona.

We went to the Duck Inn, a small seafood restaurant, and swapped stories over dinner. Dad was sure the Vietnam conflict would be a short affair once the military establishment committed its considerable resources to pushing back the front line of communism.

''You seem to have excellent timing, son. If you had had to wait another year or two in order to get into SEALs, you might have missed the entire engagement.''

I smiled, knowing I would soon have the opportunity to be the noble, battle-educated veteran like my father. Vietnam would surely not be of the same scale of warfare that World War II had been, but in his mind it was an important war effort nonetheless.

We spent a relaxed, enjoyable weekend together. I appreciated my father and the stability and calm under pressure he always exhibited. One thing that always irritated him and, by extension, me, was abuse of authority. It was a common occurrence in bureaucracy, whether in business, government, law enforcement, or the military. For some reason, there seemed to be more intolerance in the military than was warranted. No sense of humor and people taking themselves far too seriously. It was a trait that would endear me to my fellow SEALs and, later, the men under my command, yet undermine my very career.

Back at Little Creek, our orders arrived detailing us to leave for Vietnam the last week in September. Three weeks to go!

We wondered aloud about who, among our friends in other military units, would not be coming home. But, of course, it wouldn't be any of us. We were SEALs. We were invincible. I mean, I really hoped we were.

CHAPTER 6

LEARNING THE ROPES

ALLAGHER LAUGHED. "SORRY, HARRY, IT WASN'T SUPPOSED to happen that way; it was a fluke. We wanted to take you guys out into an area close by and relatively quiet so you could get a feel for things. I never dreamed we'd run into anybody. Those hooches—and for that matter, the entire area—has been vacant for months!" He paused, smiled, and shook his head while sticking out his lower lip like someone contemplating a good idea. "I'll try to keep it a little less rough for the next few ops so you guys can learn the ropes."

"Doesn't matter to me, Chief," I lied. "I didn't come all this way to sit around the pool."

Over the next two weeks, we went out every other night. True to course, we didn't see any bad guys.

As I mentioned previously, operations started at noon, with the issuance of a warning order. We went down after lunch to the Quonset hut to review our gear, polish our bullets to keep them free of rust, make sure our guns were "super clean," and repair our clothes. We went through our flares and grenades, checked the retainer bands used to keep our grenades on, checked our knives to make sure they were sharp, and generally freshened everything up so we were "good to go." The operation was detailed, so that we could determine when to depart.

51

If, for example, we were to travel to a destination coordinate six "klicks" in, and the drop-off point was twenty miles upriver, we knew we needed to leave around nine in the evening. So, were we to leave at seven P.M., we would go to dinner at five and arrive around six at the Quonset hut in order to prepare for the operation. We arrived in civilian attire—cutoffs and T-shirts—and began to get dressed. On went the cammies, jungle boots, "Pancho Villa"-style bandoleers, vest, grenades, flares, sidearm, and knife. The mood in the room changed quickly. Even after numerous ops, we continued to take our "game day psyche" very seriously. Next came the rubbing on of the green and black face paint. Once the face paint was on, we had faces only our mothers could love!

The briefing was typically scheduled for six-thirty, when a group of interesting-looking soldiers came walking in, loaded for bear with all our ordnance.

The team leader walked over to the situational map board and said, "Gentlemen, this is where we are going. We are here at point A, and our destination is over here at point B. We have information that there is a Viet Cong battalion crossing the river tonight at this locus. They have come down from such and such area. We're going to set up an ambush here."

He then pointed out the directions we needed to travel and where we would set up. As the point man, I paid particular attention to this segment of the briefing. I needed to know the exact compass bearings and commit them to memory. Often, there was more than one platoon in the area. It was not healthy to accidentally stray into another team's locale. Our guns were off safe, and we weren't taking names and asking permission to shoot. We were told of other "friendly forces" in the area, other enemy forces in the area, and what their objectives were. The radiomen were given the frequencies to communicate on, where to contact the helicopter gunships should we become pinned down. It was a complete "patrol order" brief.

"Our job is to set up and interdict the VC at this point. Good luck, gentlemen."

We grabbed something to drink and snack on and boarded the Mike boat. It, too, was loaded with guns, howitzers, rockets, and weaponry. The rivers we traveled were typically several hundred meters wide, and the Mike was reliable transportation. The only drawback was that maximum cruising speed was five miles per hour, traveling upriver or down.

Upon completion of the op, we got back on the boat for the return four-hour ride, which allowed time to clean everything up. We were always filthy. We'd been through the mud, dragging our guns through rice paddies, dikes, swamps, and frequently, mangrove trees. We were a slime-covered mess. Almost always, at some time each night, we were neck deep in water. The water was not exactly "mountain pure and sparkling." Another reality of jungle life was the bugs, especially mosquitoes. They were everywhere. We could not risk wearing commercial insect repellent as the distinctive odor would give us away. The "natural" approach was to take swamp mud and cake it on our neck, arms, and other exposed areas. Somehow, we blocked out the stench.

As soon as we got back to the boat, we laid all our guns, grenades, rockets, and weaponry on the deck. Then we went to the back of the boat and climbed down the stern. We grabbed a rope and tied it to the ballard (small marine eyebolt), and then jumped into the water to be towed behind the boat. There was really no danger of being sucked into the prop, as it powerfully propelled water outward. We rotated around doing 360-degree loops in the eddy churning behind the boat like we were in a giant washing machine! It was a great way to get clean. We got the twigs, leaves, slime, swamp goo, mud, and everything off. We played back there in the water, particularly after more harrowing operations. It was a great letting-off-steam cleansing time. The water was generally freshwater, although certainly not clean enough to drink. There were often dead things—people included—that floated by. But it sure got us a good deal cleaner than we'd been moments earlier.

We laid our clothes out on the deck to dry in the sun, burned off leeches that had attached themselves to us, and went down below to get a beer. We relaxed for the ride home.

Once home, we hung up our clothes in our cubicle (if they were fully dry), and then attended to our weaponry. We each took a fifty-five-gallon drum that was cut in half and filled with gasoline. All of our bullets and magazines soaked in the gas. I pulled a couple of quick-release pins on my Stoner machine gun, and it fell apart. Everything except for the plastic stock went into the barrel of gas. I grabbed my flip-flops, a towel, and a bar of soap to take a shower while everything was soaking.

We soaped up and scrubbed off the black and green face paint, got all the remaining scum off, and started to unwind. By then, we'd been up for twenty-four hours straight.

I went back to where my gun and bullets were, pulled them out, and began to wire-brush the "pieces parts" before reassembling the gun. I then wiped it down clean, spraying it with WD lubricant. "Mr. Stoner" was ready to return to the jungle once again. SEALs were the only military group to utilize the Stoner. It had been offered to other branches, but had been deemed unreliable because it had to be kept cleaned and serviced to be consistent. We cleaned our weaponry after every operation anyway, so that was a nonfactor to us. The Stoner was an ideal weapon for me, especially when running point.

Lunch was next on the agenda, consisting of a mixture of standard American fare and local Vietnamese dishes. By two P.M., we were stretched out asleep on our bunks. We got up around eight, had dinner, played some cards, then went back to bed around two in the morning. Come ten A.M., we would wake up, get dressed, and go to lunch, at which time we were informed of the next warning order. Down to double-check our gear again, and out we went. Thus this rotation lent itself well to an every-other-night schedule. For the most part, we were "on" one night and "off" the next.

On my first tour of duty, I was in-country 180 days and went out on 116 operations. There were some times when we were going out every night, and on several occasions we would be out for as long as three nights running. At other times, we completed two and three short operations in one night.

The first six weeks were spent learning about the community. The initial contact with the local farmers was critical. The master chief watched us as we went into and about the local village. We were monitored closely to see how well we related to the local citizenry.

There was a Rand Corporation study that found that approximately 40 percent of the American servicemen in Vietnam had a racial dislike of the Vietnamese people. This was not good from any standpoint—moral, political, or tactical. We had two choices: One was to be the "ugly American" who ate the food, screwed the women, drank the beer, and displayed an open contempt for the local people. The other alternative was to acknowledge that we were in someone else's country and show respect for the people and their culture. With SEALs, it was critical that we adapt and show respect to the people as we lived in and around their villages—in small numbers.

Gallagher walked us into the hamlet to see how we handled the villagers, how we questioned them, how our field interrogation was, how well we picked up the language, and whether we paid attention to our flanks—how our security was. Were we getting correct information, or were they feeding us bogus details? Were we buying it? Should we be buying it? Were we walking in the correct direction or were we walking in circles?

After we left the village, we watched to see what occurred. Did people run out to tell the bad guys? Did we discern any codes being sounded?

There were all sorts of codes the Viet Cong and VC sympathizers used to warn of American presence in the area. For example, they'd place a guy on the perimeter and call him a woodcutter. He was busy getting wood together for the fire. Depending on how he chopped determined whether he was sending a signal to the VC or not.

"Hey, there are Americans in the area! I just heard Nguyen send the code."

It was really rather comical. *Whack whack whack whackwhack, whack whack whack whackwhack...* Like we couldn't figure it out. Just moments before, he was chopping without any particular rhythmic pattern. *Whack whack... whack whack... whack... whack...*

I walked up behind him and said, *"Ciao, ong muy khong?"* (Hello, how are things?)

Immediately, he smiled brightly. *Whackwhackwhack... whack... whack... whackwhackwhack... whack whack...* breaking into the signal.

I smiled back at him. "I'm glad you are not a Viet Cong sympathizer," I said, without letting go of the smile—in English. He smiled and shook his head vigorously up and down, figuring he should agree.

"Bao nhieu viet cong dau?" (How many Viet Cong in the area?)

"Noo, no!" he replied, by then sweating profusely at the increased tempo of the signal beat. "Oh, no. No VC!"

"Lai Day," I said. (Come here.) I extended my hand out with the palm down and my fingers moving in a raking motion. With my interpreter at my side, we chatted quietly while I was still ordering the woodcutter to come forward. The poor man had most likely been pressed into service by a demanding VC official, likely wanted to be left alone, and here he was under questioning from an American wearing sinister-looking green and black face paint. He walked slowly and looked more guilty with each step. It usually wasn't difficult to gain the information we desired.

Many times, we came through the village, or through the bush to a hooch, and I said, *"Lai Day.* [Come here.] *Khong co chay!* [Don't run!]"

Then I said, *"Can couc"* (which was the demand for identification).

Every person in South Vietnam was issued an identification card.

They were to have it in their possession at all times. Unfortunately, no one told the farmer. If they had happened to give one to the farmer we were interrogating, it was likely he had already used it for kindling.

"Can couc," I repeated. The farmer smiled and, through his body language and hand motioning, in effect said, *Yeah. I know all about it,* nodding his head up and down.

"Can couc," I said, a little more demandingly.

Beats the crap out of me where it is. Yeah! Smile and nod. Nod and smile.

"If you want to fight the VC, go right ahead. Just go around us, knock yourself silly, shoot it out to your heart's content, but leave me alone." This was the people's feeling throughout the Vietnamese countryside.

Walking into small villages with my field interpreter, I enjoyed asking the locals about their views.

"Who is the president?" I asked.

"President of what?" came the reply.

"The president of your country."

"Beats me."

"What kind of government do you have set up?"

"Pretty lousy."

I got these same basic answers all the time. They had no apparent link to the Saigon government at all. They knew the regional chief and the regional police officer(s), because of limited contact with them, but that was about it.

They really didn't want to have anything to do with us, and, conversely, they didn't want anything to do with the Viet Cong. The Viet Cong, however, came into the village and said, "We're taking him, him, and him. We're going to kill you, you, and you. The rest of you, stay in line." And that's what they did.

We came in and said, "We're going to take him and him—and we just shot him because we thought he was VC—and please tell us who the Viet Cong sympathizers are so we can keep the town in line."

So what was the difference? To the people in the village, who was the bad guy? Often, it was whoever was there—VC or us—because the villagers' day-to-day life was disrupted.

As part of the cultural demeanor, we had to learn to deal with each group of Vietnamese people—city residents, villagers, students, politicians, "cowboys," farmers, VC, and NVA. One interesting fact of rural life was the standing rule that we never shot a water buffalo. They were the farmers' only livelihood. We paid for it if we did. We could shoot the farmer and have virtually no repercussions. But, if we shot his water buffalo, we'd better explain how we made this obviously stupid mistake. Then we had to ante up to the farmer. If we shot the farmer, we could claim he had a gun or was making hostile actions with something that resembled a weapon. Funny how war turned things upside down. Traditional values of life and death went out the window.

In Saigon, there were people who just wanted to work, and they worked either for the government or for private industry without any politics or acting out of their beliefs. The masses wanted stability, in the home, the workplace, and with whatever social order (i.e., government) that was in place. There were some smart-ass college kids who thought they were pretty smart, but not that smart. They knew they couldn't pull practical jokes that made too great a political statement because this ended in someone getting tossed in prison and/or shot.

The other group of people we saw frequently on the streets of the larger cities were those I referred to as "cowboys." Cowboys were young kids who were not smart enough or mature enough to notice they needed to stay in school and make something of themselves. They had decided being gang members and ripping off the government, Americans, and other Vietnamese was the easiest way to get thrills and money. They lived this way day-to-day by joining with three or four others and beating up and intimidating first one poor, old Vietnamese man and then another.

While there, a dozen times I saw three or four guys, all riding on the same moped, pull alongside a parked U.S. Army truck loaded with, say, rations, or boots, or other materiel. Two of the cowboys jumped off the bike and grabbed a couple of cases. Often, a Vietnamese man nearby blurted out, *Hey! Don't do that!* One of the cowboys would vault toward him, and hit him full in the face. The passerby would fall to the ground as the cowboys got back onto the moped. Just about then, the American driver came around the rear corner of the truck, saw what was happening, pulled his M16, and shot all three of them. Solved the problem. Then, the guy who tried to help and had gotten hit, walked over—laughing—and assisted the American in returning his cargo to its position in the truck.

So the cowboys learned that if they were going to play, they were going to pay. In Vietnam, there were consequences to be paid, and brazen criminal activity was held to a minimum.

We had quite a few VC who, when ambushed, dropped their gun,

raised their hands, and surrendered. I was obligated to take them prisoner. I captured close to sixty VC during my first tour. Many times, I
let them carry their AK-47 as we went out of enemy territory. With all
my gear, was I going to carry it? Did we want to leave it for another
bad guy? No. It all revolved around a few tenuous seconds when there
was a mental understanding forged between capturer and captive. I
looked in their eyes, and spoke with hand signals. Regardless of language barriers between us, we all spoke the same ''Smith and Wesson''
language. Watching how a man in a desperate situation responded came
down to few possibilities. Closely observing the body language of
enough men yielded predictable patterns. If he became agitated and his
eyes darted quickly back and forth, he was likely either to start to shoot
or to run. If he made slow, wide-eyed movements, locked onto my eyes
while lowering his gun, and then bowed his head, it didn't take a doc-
torate in psychology to read the body language. All of this was a learning process.

An important lesson to learn was how to interrogate women in the
village. We were told of a VC sympathizer who lived in a certain
hooch. We silently snuck in but found he wasn't there. His wife was
in a panic, as anyone would be, petrified that we were there to hurt
her, barbecue her son, rape her daughter, and kidnap the baby. How
could she know? How would you react to heavily armed men, replete
with awful green and black face paint on, who just awoke you at two
in the morning?

Many times, I'd pat mama san to try to calm her down. The field
interpreter let her know all we were after were main force VC, and we
were told that her husband was somehow involved. She realized that if
she confessed that her husband was VC, then she had just signed his
death warrant. But, if she told us that it was Fred, two rice paddies to
the north, who pressed her husband into service, then these Americans
could help make her and her husband's life much easier. Many times,
we received tremendous information about who were important VC
leaders and NVA contacts in the village from wives who were angry
at the treatment their husbands had been subjected to. We were only
too happy to weed out the higher-ups, and then build a relationship
with the grateful family. They were always reluctant to be involved any
further in providing us intelligence about the community. They were
fearful that aligning with the Americans was even more dangerous than
being harassed by the VC. That is, until we showed them a year's worth
of earnings. A little money went a long way. Learning the language as

best we could, making friends, and buying influence were effective ways to gather important information and help keep ourselves alive. Referencing information that came from dubious sources with what our tried-and-true sources heard kept *us* out of ambushes on a number of occasions. Setting up an ambush on Viet Cong attempting to ambush us was even more fun.

I enjoyed going to town with my Vietnamese field interpreters. We went to their side of town, away from areas frequented by American servicemen. Authentic Vietnamese food was wonderful; it was a combination of Chinese and French cuisine, with local seafood elements, all mingled together. We ate the rice, using chopsticks, and talked. It was a lot of fun learning their culture and traditions. There was a ritual we went through when we ate together. I had to maintain a certain protocol to keep them from losing face. When I was not paying for dinner outright, I let them pay for dinner. Except for one small detail. They bought dinner, as long as I paid for the shrimp, fish, mushrooms, and other costly items. But they "paid" for dinner. Those dinners were filled with memorable moments.

Part of developing trust and camaraderie with the Vietnamese meant putting up with some strange behavior. The Vietnamese were extremely fascinated with blond-haired people; I was blond. They walked right up to me and began touching my hair. They liked to rub the hair on my forearms and chest, as well as running their fingers through my hair. It just fascinated them. We'd be out on the boat, coming back in from an operation, relaxed in our swim trunks, and they were running their hands through our hair. It was not a sexual thing. It was akin to small kids being fascinated with something so much that, try as they might, they couldn't keep their hands off it.

That was a part of the development of a rapport and a level of trust with people who knew a lot more about the environment, people, customs, and tendencies than we did. It also offered us more opportunities to learn to gauge whether someone was being honest or not. Many Vietnamese did not expect me to know what they were saying, or what they were doing—only to find I'd already been briefed by a friend of theirs. It was amazing what buying a beer (Ba Muoi Ba, which translated as "thirty-three," was the common Vietnamese beer) could do for community relations.

"I no were in town last night. I home mama san."

"Papa san! I think you out with beaucoup VC!" I would press. "Shooting at Americans!"

His eyes widened and his arms flailed animatedly. "Oh, no. Me no VC. Me no VC!"

I laid my Colt .45 on the table, changing my demeanor from friendly to menacing. "I *know* you VC. You either tell me who big boss is, or I *Sat mau* you," I said, gesturing at the gun. *"Sat mau!"* (Kill you.)

Once the realization hit and he knew that I knew—it was all over. A couple of beers for the right people, treat them with decency, and what a treasure of information came our way.

Through our first ten operations, we had only one gun battle. We heard movement, saw this or that, but we didn't make contact. In ops eleven through fifteen, things started to pick up. Not real dangerous, but we were getting into gun battles almost every night out. We shot at them, they shot at us, and then we hightailed it out of there. Several times, there were two or three VC coming up the trail into our ambush and we all unloaded on them. By operation fifteen, we began expecting contact every time out. We learned how to sneak into the jungle, in enemy territory, in the dead of night, and still keep the odds in our favor. We had been to roughly thirty dinners, bought countless beers, were gathering (and more important, learning how to utilize) useful intelligence, and were developing a rapport with people and the environment. Things were starting to click. I was able to talk to mama san downtown, learned words from mama san, from the girl san, from the shoeshine boy, and generally interacted with people in a human fashion and not from a business-only approach. We learned from other teams. Contacts they had made, booby traps encountered, and enemy tendencies became topics of conversation among the teams. The morale and psyche of our team was rapidly being positively transformed from when we arrived just forty days earlier.

Then, my most painful experience as point man occurred. In early November 1967, I was gaining confidence nightly. I was pleased with my aptitude as point man. Developing night vision, I was picking up trails, the enemy, booby traps, and punji pits with regularity, and developed a little bit of a swagger. As point man, I got to see things the others behind me only wondered about.

It was operation seventeen, and we were in a heavily contested area. Punji pits were all along the trail. These were hidden pits in the trail that contained sharpened bamboo stakes placed at all different angles. They were designed to trap a leg in it, as well as being covered in excrement to cause infection. I had found trip wires attached to grenades and punji pits on the last two ops in this one area. So, Lieutenant

Pete Peterson decided we needed to investigate further, as the VC did not go to all that effort to place these traps in areas devoid of troop strength.

There were fourteen guys in our platoon who'd come over from Little Creek—two officers, two chiefs, and the rest of us enlisted men. Any combination of "us" constituted a team. We were a platoon, and we worked mostly as three teams. Officers Pete Peterson and Charlie Watson and master chief Gallagher went out with each team as the leaders. The three teams were called Alpha, Bravo, and Charley— Alpha being Pete Peterson's, Bravo being Gallagher's, and Charley being Charlie's team. On this operation, we had me, Pete, Erasmo Riojas (the corpsman/radioman who had served in the Korean War), Keener, Eugene Thomas Fraley, and two Vietnamese. On Gallagher's team were Roy Dean, Hooker, Mikey Boynton, and several others. Charlie had Curtis Ashton, Jack Rowell, and it broke on down from there. Some nights, we needed more than four or five, so we borrowed guys. Depending on the operation, we went from a five-man team to a ten-man team routinely.

I thought that, by operation seventeen, I was *pretty* good at spotting booby traps. Wasn't it funny that just when you thought you were pretty good at something, God had a way of showing you you weren't? It was a warm evening; the moon was out. We were in a jungle area where it wasn't overly dense, so the team spread out to avoid detection. I was doing my "ninja" walk; everything was looking good. I carefully checked the trail as we moved stealthily along. *Whoosh.* Down I went, into a punji pit. The hole was so deep I dropped fully up to my crotch. Pain exploded inside my gut. Immediately, Pete was beside me.

"Don't move," he said with quiet urgency. He assumed I had stakes stuck in me, and thought it remarkable I hadn't screamed. He didn't want me to move, in fear of worsening the injury. "Get Riojas up here!"

As soon as Riojas saw me, he quickly shucked his gear and began digging. Pete retrieved the medical gear. They both worked feverishly in an effort to extract my leg without causing additional damage. I tried to tell them I was okay, but they figured I was just masking the pain.

"I'm okay, Pete."

"Look man, you're gonna be all right. We'll have you out in just a couple of minutes. Rios, you got plenty of hydrogen peroxide?"

"Guys," I hissed, a little louder.

"Plenty of hydrogen perox—" Finally, I grabbed them both by the hair and pulled their heads down to mine.

"I'm okay, guys." They looked at me without really knowing what to do. Was I serious, or was this just an increased pain threshold that sometimes occurred when someone was in shock? "I'm okay. There's nothing in the hole."

I slowly pulled my leg out. Riojas shined his light into the hole, switching from the red lens to the white lens, confirming what I told him. Sitting less than three feet from the hole was a brand-new bundle of punji stakes ready to be installed.

Pete looked at me ruefully. "Man, are you lucky."

"No kidding," I replied, still feeling a bit nauseated from the slam to my groin. They quickly checked me over and found I was indeed intact.

"Let's get our gear on and go," Pete ordered. Immediately, when I went down, the team took on different roles. The man behind Pete, in this case Keener, and the last guy, Fraley, fanned out in order to provide security as we were afraid of someone walking in on us. At that point, we needed to get moving, so we teamed up once again.

"Okay, settle down, get tight, and let's go," hissed Pete. Off we went.

No sooner did we go forty yards than *Wham!* I stepped in another one!

Aaahh! Oh man, not again!

Pete ran up to me, leaned down, and said, "Well?"

"It's got something in it, but it didn't stick me," I replied, gingerly moving my leg and foot ever so slowly. As I was doing this, there came Erasmo Riojas, panting as he ran quickly up to me. He had to carry, in addition to his normal supplies and weaponry, the radio and medical gear. I motioned to him not to shuck his gear. Again, I slowly extricated my leg from the hole. Riojas shined his light into the hole only to find that the hole had filled with water and the bamboo punji stakes had turned to mush, similar to spaghetti softening when placed in water. I didn't know what hurt worse, my groin or my ego. Two quick missteps.

Pete shook his head slowly from side to side. "Damn!" He shrugged, and looked at me with an "I think I just saw lightning strike twice" look.

I again redoubled my efforts *not* to miss another one of those stinking holes. In a period of just ninety minutes, I fell prey to *five* more traps. Seven punji pits in just one operation! Even more remarkable was the fact that *every single one* was either brand-new and without stakes installed, or so old the stakes had disintegrated. I was extremely lucky, but right then it would have been hard to convince me of it. The holes were extremely well concealed, and I could not, for the life of me, find them. By the fourth one, Pete came up to me and, with my face contorted in silent rage, whispered to me, "You're my point man?"

I couldn't answer. All I could do was gasp and heave silently.

"Do you think this is the way to handle these traps?"

Riojas appeared, leaned over, and said, "You know, you really look stupid!"

The next time, he remarked, "Gee, I suppose you are trying to break your leg so I get to be point, huh?"

The ribbing got worse and worse—and more painfully funny with each drop. It really hurt. It happened in just a three-hundred-meter-long corridor. To make matters worse, the other guys were silently laughing so hard tears rolled down their faces.

"Why don't you just go around them?" Pete asked with mock sincerity.

"Because I want to show you where they're at, so you won't step in them. If I saw them, I'd go around them, smart-ass!"

"Well, you're supposed to be my hotshot, find 'em, tough guy point man," Pete countered scornfully.

"I'm working on it. Haven't I been doing good? I've found every one of them!"

"No kidding! You sure have. I hope you don't do the same thing with trip wires," Pete said, barely able to contain his laughter from reaching an audible level.

"Oh, no. No. I can't wait to run into those."

That proved to be an invaluable lesson on punji pits and the importance of really watching the trail. I'd been too focused on looking ahead without watching each and every individual step.

Just two ops later, we were back in a similar area, searching for a VC battalion. It turned out to be trip wire time. Through the nipa palm, across the rice paddies, we came upon a coconut grove and a well-worn dike trail roughly eighteen inches wide. Just as it had days earlier, the moon lit up the night, casting images upon the water. Shadows, or at least murky light and dark areas cast by the moon as it reached through the branches of the tropical jungle foliage, peppered the landscape. At one time, we were able to view expansive distances within the arc of the moonlight, while simultaneously being unable to detect even limited sights or movement just a few feet away in the murky darkness. After the episode of the "frequent faller" operation just nights earlier, I moved a little slower. Still feeling the bruised soreness, I was considerably more cautious—continually focusing from the horizon and then to my next footfall. Scan, move my left foot silently forward. Scan, silently move my right foot forward. Over and over and over, visually scouring 180 degrees in front of me. Our entire, heavily armed team moving in silent rhythm through the shadows. Moving from one shadow to the next. Many times, I couldn't see the next guy in the squad, but I knew he was there. When I saw someone moving, it was almost ethereal. There was absolutely no sound, and in the moonlight the images seemed like surrealistic apparitions.

As I moved along with my Stoner positioned in my hands, I led with my left hand. A thin, reedlike four-foot branch was held in place by the fourth and fifth fingers on my left hand, against my gun barrel. The branch hung down, lightly brushing against the ground. In the darkness, we weren't going to see thin monofilament line stretched across the path. Should the thin branch (the upper half of a fishing rod was ideal) come in contact with a trip wire, it would gently bow, letting me know something was there. I could readily feel it. It worked much better than my leg—much less traumatic! There was very little pressure in my fingers as the twig bent back, and I stopped immediately. I ran my hand down and found very fine fishing line running across the trail. It was nice and taut. *Whoa! Trip wire.* My heart skipped a beat as I thanked God I was paying attention.

"Pete," I hissed. "Trip wire. Booby trap."

"Very good."

I checked in front of it with the thin branch. Stepping over it, I reached in my pack for toilet paper and tore off a two-piece segment. Gently, I laid the perforated border between the white sheets over the line. In the moonlight, we couldn't miss it.

I walked thirty yards and found another one. "Pete, trip wire." Mark it and go.

Fifty yards more, and I felt light pressure as the branch bowed yet again. I quickly marked another trip wire—the toilet paper was not buried as deeply in my pack as it was prior to tonight. "Pete, another one!" Mark it and go.

On this night, I uncovered a dozen trip wires! I went weeks and weeks without finding even one, and on this night—my first to find them—I was initiated by twelve of them! I didn't know if this area was designated "booby trap training grounds" or what. I do know we had a lot of them. Where there were new traps, there were bound to be VC. This proved to be true, resulting in some great firefights.

I was on the tenth trip wire, busy checking it out. Enemy gunfire was not too far behind us. Pete came up to me, equally amazed we were getting so many. "How does it look?" he asked worriedly, wary of having to increase our speed in order to escape.

"There is a grenade right over there," I responded, pointing to the right side of the trail, looking at a grenade attached to the branch of a tree. "Probably instantaneous. I'll mark it and step over it."

I marked it, and just as I was stepping over I heard a sharp *ping!*

Oh no! I froze (instead of hitting the deck). My mind was racing. That *ping* was the unmistakable sound of a grenade being detonated. I couldn't figure what was going on. It wasn't the grenade attached to the trip wire—I didn't think—as the sound came from behind me and not from my immediate right. *What was it? Nothing happened. What was it?*

I knew I'd heard the unmistakable *ping* after a retaining pin comes out of a grenade and the spoon flies. When the spoon has flown off, having been ejected by the detonation spring, it allows the striker to impale the percussion cap. An explosion was imminent. But it didn't come.

Every one of us froze. We were fairly close together, and all of us were at full battle alert, our senses groping outward into the jungle surrounding us. A cold sweat layered our already soaked jungle perspiration cover. I looked back at Pete, and he shrugged his shoulders. He couldn't figure it out, either. Just then, there was a little movement and talk from behind. Fraley walked up from the rear, moving past the other guys.

Coming up alongside, he shrugged. "Here."

I looked down; six grenades were in his hands, trip wires wound tightly around each of them. I was aghast.

"What the . . . What do you think you're doing!" I demanded, horrified.

He turned to Pete. "Oh, after you guys stepped over them I've been trying to safe 'em. In case we had to run back out, I don't want any of us to trip over them," he said matter-of-factly. "I'm sorry I didn't tell anyone."

"What was that *ping*?" I asked, already knowing the answer.

"That was the third one. You didn't hear the other two?" he asked.

Pete was visibly upset. "You mean to tell me you accidentally detonated three of these grenades?"

"Yeah, but they were all duds," came his reply. "Most of these aren't any good."

"Mother!" I blurted out. "What the hell are you doing, Fraley?"

"Here, put these in your back pocket so we can take them back and check 'em out later."

"Put them in your own damn pocket."

"I got too much stuff," Fraley implored.

"I'm not carrying them!" I insisted.

He looked to Pete. Pete quickly said, in a singsong voice, "I'm not carrying them."

He looked at Riojas. Riojas looked at him and said, "I've got the radio."

He looked at Keener. Keener said, in his best caveman imitation, "Machine gun!"

He looked back to me, pleadingly.

"Point man. Gotta stay light."

Fraley shrugged in annoyance, opened his shirt, and dropped the remaining grenades in.

"Man, if those things go off . . ." I said, starting to suggest he leave them behind.

"Hey. I'll never know!" Fraley carried them in his shirt the rest of the night for the rest of the operation. That was Fraley.

There we were, large beads of sweat pouring off us. Our hands soaking wet, afraid of detonating anything. Then there's Fraley, screwing around as if it were a carburetor he's trying to adjust. Typical SEAL. The front half of the team scared half to death, and the back taking a break and playing around!

Three days later, Pete came in and told us we were going to the beach. He was alluding to the South China Sea, which took us a minimum of a day and a half to travel to. We loaded our gear onto the ship, heading east to the northeastern side where the river met the ocean. We had our full team, all fourteen of us, along with four Vietnamese translators.

The area we were to assault was considered a VC stronghold. The ARVN, as well as our Army, had found it difficult to assault, as it was on an isthmus that made it dangerous to get close to the beachfront village. We disembarked from the boat into the surf to make our assault. In front of us lay the beach, a big open field of approximately two hundred meters, beyond which was the village. There were a couple of dozen houses. It was not a confined area, although it was rimmed to the east and south by swamp. The beach extends fifteen hundred meters down the coast.

"Load and lock!"

We prepared to assault.

"Let's go!"

We ran, haphazardly, through the surf, right at the houses before us. Shots rang out, bullets whizzed around us. All of us dove onto our stomachs in the surf. In short order, perhaps thirty to forty enemy were shooting at us. Bullets and tracers flew like missiles. We started to leapfrog forward. Leapfrogging was the maneuver in which some of us shot while others moved ahead. While two guys were sneaking closer, we delivered heavy fire. Then we stopped, and they sent a crossfire while we traversed forward. Thus, when we got into position, one group was firing into the front door, while the other was shooting into the side door. The houses were largely made of palm fronds and nipa palm. As bullets ripped through, bits and pieces splintered off. If we were able to get close enough, we would toss one of our HE grenades into a house. Use of a grenade would completely demolish an entire house.

They were ready for us. Machine-gun fire pelted our position. We were winning, although, with hilly terrain and trees, it was not a simple, textbook assault. We had more firepower than they did, with our Stoners, grenades, and M79, a 40-mike-mike (millimeter) projectile called a golden bullet, a highly explosive round. When the golden bullet hit, it exploded like a grenade. I carried three thousand rounds, and shot my Stoner with reckless abandon.

This was one of the few times Charlie Watson showed true bravery. I watched as Gallagher's and Charlie's teams moved, about a hundred meters away. Keener and I were on the extreme left perimeter. All of a sudden, a grenade came flying out of a house and Gallagher hit the deck.

Charlie Watson stood up and led a charge! "Let's assault the house," Charlie yelled, extending his arm and giving the vintage forward-charge arm movement. As he ran toward the house, two guys came running out the back. I watched as Gallagher and Company hosed the two down. They were hit with such extensive firepower by six or seven SEALs that their bodies just exploded into small pieces. At least one thousand rounds were expended.

Watson could not possibly see that the men had left the house, and no one remained. He was busy pouring heavy M16 gunfire into the house. He got up to the doorway and stopped. Reaching down, he grabbed a grenade, pulled the pin, and tossed it in through the door. Much to our horror, he turned his back and backed up against the wall of the house. For some inexplicable reason, Charlie forgot the walls were paper thin.

"Charlie, get away from there!" I screamed. "It's nipa palm. Thatch. Get down!" Keener and many of the others yelled, as well.

The grenade went off. Grass, thatch, twigs, and dust exploded skyward—up as high as sixty feet. At first, we could not see because of the dust. Then, miraculously, there stood Charlie Watson, his hands and arms extended over his head. The debris rained down all over him, but he was still standing! He didn't take any frag from the grenade! The roof of the house was gone, as were all the walls. There was a gaping hole in the floor, but Charlie stood unhurt.

The war stopped. Everyone stared at Charlie. Guys were dropping their guns and laughing. A highly explosive grenade had gone off barely six feet away. Nothing was left standing except Charlie. Even his hat was blown off. Amazing. He started yelling, "Yo! Get 'em!"

Hooker ran over to Charlie, grabbed him, and ran him back to the safe side of a dike. He checked him over for holes and wounds. Charlie had a concussion.

He was dazed. "Go. Let's go get 'em!"

"No more war for you today, Charlie." Hooker had to pull him into the surf, placing him on board one of the STABs.

"Did you see me?" he inquired.

"Yeah, Charlie, we saw you. You did good. You were one lucky SOB!" we told him. "The only bad thing is that there isn't anybody in there. They had all run out the back."

"No they didn't. I was taking heavy fire!" Charlie insisted, adamantly.

"Get in the boat, Charlie."

We began the assault at dawn. We wanted to see how effective we could be in a full daylight attack. By one P.M., it was all over. We finished the body count and destroyed four houses. I came out with 300 or 400 rounds remaining. Running, shooting, weaving, shooting some more. Guys ran out and we hosed them down. Grenades were thrown, and we continued forward. We ran up over the dike. We ducked down into the canal, next to bodies that were presumably dead, "tapped" them—a short burst of bullets into the bodies—and kept going. I knew it was heartless, but we were in a killing business. It was extremely bad form to run past someone only to have them sit up and shoot us in the back.

It was a sweet feeling, traveling back to My Tho, feeling at once both totally spent and totally exhilarated. Charlie, Gallagher, and Pete were in good spirits, and we were building ties among us that would last a lifetime. Roy Dean and I were developing a good-natured competition between the two of us. We were the top point men, and a natural rivalry emerged over successful operations, number of kills, and especially the degree of difficulty and importance of the operations we conducted, which were fiercely argued over.

We'd been involved in a significant head-to-head battle, nighttime surprise attacks, and intelligence gathering among the townspeople. We were no longer scared of the unknown. Apprehensive, maybe even somewhat afraid, but only of a reality we were starting to understand. Besides, the adrenaline was getting to be addictive. Things had started to heat up.

CHAPTER 7

INTO THE FRAY

IT WAS THE FIRST OF DECEMBER 1967. I WAS HALFWAY THROUGH my first tour, having been in Vietnam three months. On this particular morning, the decision had been made to sweep through another "free-fire zone" to the east of us, trying to find a VC company reported to be there. We had sketchy intelligence data, but the information came from fairly reliable sources.

I was learning VC routines. It was a typical operation; the sun was setting, and the weather was clear. We traveled downriver as nightfall descended. As we got close, the radar was scrutinized to help find our insertion point. There was a quarter moon on the horizon as we went ashore. I was the first one off—as always—and the nipa palm and jungle vines were especially thick at this point along the river.

I held my gun up as I submerged myself in the river. I found it more advantageous to get wet because I was always crossing little canals. Those who tried to jump across the canal or tried to walk across the little footbridges ran the risk of slipping and falling, possibly breaking the bridges, and making a lot of noise. It was very easy, when wet, to slide down one embankment, take two steps, climb up the other bank— nice and quiet. It was easy, when I was dry, to decide that staying dry was better than getting wet. So I got wet immediately, so I wouldn't be tempted. While climbing out of the river, I scooped a handful of mud and started wiping it on all exposed areas—the back of my neck, the V at my collar, behind my ears, on my forearms, and on the backs of my hands. The mosquitoes and other insects wouldn't eat through the caked-on, hardened mud. Especially if we had to sit all night without moving. Being unable to slap at insects that were crawling on us— or worse yet, biting—was an awful mental challenge.

The traverse that night through the dense jungle was especially difficult because it was pitch-black and difficult to walk in. After an hour, we ascended from the floodplain into a heavily wooded jungle area overshadowed by a double canopy of banana, palm, and coconut trees. As we gingerly groped our way through the foliage, we came upon a trail. Soon, we ran into a junction of two larger trails.

"This looks like it meets the descriptions from the maps and intelligence reports. They are supposed to come right along here, so let's set the ambush up here," said Pete.

We deployed into our ambush positions. As we had done in previous operations, we formed an L along the junction of the two trails in order to adequately cover all four directions. Then the mental games began. *Did I hear something? Is somebody coming?* All night long. It's like waiting for that first strike when you're fishing, only with much deadlier consequences. You sit there. You don't move. Things eat on you. Nothing happens. *What was that? No, that's just wildlife. Was that a light moving over there?* I watched for a moment. *I guess not.*

Every so often, I reached over and touched Keener, or Ashton, or Pete—whoever was next to me—if for no other reason than to break up the monotony. I squeezed his arm, he squeezed mine, as if to say, *Everything's okay.* We used several hand and arm signals as we passed the night away.

Lieutenant Peterson stood up after we'd been sitting there all night fidgeting and said, "Let's pick it up and start patrolling."

We were approximately fifteen hundred meters inland from the river, and we patrolled parallel to the river. We went one klick farther and the jungle began thinning out. A little farther yet and we hit a main trail that was running perpendicular (north-south) to the trail we were on (running east-west). This trail was six to eight feet wide and obviously well traveled. At the junction of the two trails, the thicket we were in ended. The visibility increased dramatically, and now there were only scattered trees dotting the edges of this main trail. Pete looked it over and decided it was open enough to allow for a sweep patrol northward to the river.

"I want to put everyone on line, spaced out at about thirty to forty meters apart, then sweep toward the river," Pete declared. "Okay, Constance. I need you to be the farthest man to the west. Since we will straddle this north-south trail, I need for you to run up ahead approximately one hundred twenty meters."

We spaced out along the east-west trail, and looked at Pete. He signaled us to go on his order, stay on line, head north toward the river, and stop at the next clearing.

The signal to begin was given and we all stepped off the trail and into the jungle. I took a dozen steps or less and noticed a house at a 45-degree angle immediately to my left. The house was approximately thirty to forty meters away, and I decided I should check it out. I was now at least seventy to eighty yards from Keener. As I peered into the clearing, I saw four guys, all about twenty years old, cooking breakfast in the courtyard. I decided to go into the courtyard and ask them for their identification cards.

I had seen and done a lot, but I hadn't been in this particular situation before. It just didn't dawn on me that four males—four *young* males—fit the criteria of VC to a T. I assumed they were farmers. But, deciding I didn't want to get too separated from my team (visions of my first operation), I went back, got Keener's attention, and attempted to let the team know what I was doing.

Moving into position where I could see Keener, I got his attention.

My hands signaled him, *I have found a home with four residents and would appreciate assistance.*

Keener signaled back, *Pete, Riojas, and I have found possible VC to our right. We will assist you as quickly as we can check it out and get to you.*

I headed back to the house to watch the four guys.

In front of the dirt courtyard was a ditch. At the edge of the ditch stood a big coconut tree. At the ridge on top of the ditch were grasses and weeds that were a good eighteen inches high. I positioned myself behind the coconut tree where I could look through the brush in order to see what the men were doing. I watched them drink their tea and eat their rice. I planned to stay there until Pete arrived to determine how to handle things.

Abruptly, the situation changed. Standing at the doorway was a fifth guy. He was wearing black pajamas and carried a German Mauser in one hand and a bunch of flowers in the other. I was a genius at assessing the situation now. *This guy, a VC, was going to see his girlfriend.*

The man with the Mauser was holding his gun by the barrel, the wooden stock resting on his right shoulder, and holding the flowers in his left hand. He said something to his buddies and started walking out of the courtyard in my direction.

Man, now what do I do? I wondered. *He's coming my way. If I let him go by, he might spot some of the team on their way to help me. Oh, great. I can't shoot him without alerting the guys in the courtyard and anyone else in the house.*

Hhhhh . . . I sighed, in frustration. Here I was again, wondering what I should do. If he continued south and, for some reason, came back because he forgot something, he could shoot me in the back. If he turned left, he turns right into me and I would have to shoot him, arousing the others. It didn't dawn on me that the easiest way was to knife him. I wasn't that cold and calculating, yet. I glanced back to the southeast of me, hoping to catch a glimpse of the rest of the team. *Well, what do I do?*

I stood up, trying to stay within the shadow of the coconut tree. He walked to the trail and turned north. When he did so, he took two steps and was even with the coconut tree I was hidden behind, barely five feet away. I turned sideways with my shoulder up against the tree. He took another step. I made a pivot turn and was now face-to-face with him. I shoved my gun barrel into his stomach. My finger was on the trigger. I reached out and grabbed his right arm—the one holding the gun—and pulled him up to me. My eyes bore into him like those of a venomous snake. He released the Mauser; it slid off the back of his shoulder and hit the ground. Because it was dirt, it didn't make much noise.

"Khong co chay!" I ordered, through clenched teeth. (Don't run!)

I watched his facial expressions. In my peripheral vision, I saw him begin to drop the flowers, one by one. Just like in the movies, the flowers fell, *plink, plink, plink, plink, plink, plink, plink,* until they were all on the ground.

Time almost stood still. Everything seemed like it was happening in slow motion. It probably lasted a matter of a few seconds, but to me it felt like hours.

Up to this point of my tour, I had captured more than thirty VC. I was definitely better versed in tying up and taking prisoners than in cold-blooded killing. I figured I might as well take this man prisoner, too. I increased my grip on his arm and began pulling him to the ground. He looked at me, and his expression changed markedly. His eyes were wide in a mix of fear, terror, and hatred. I figured if I laid him down I could tie him up.

He must have thought that I was *not* going to take him prisoner. I pulled a little more and he dropped to one knee. Suddenly, he lunged backward away from me. I caught his black pajama shirt but it ripped free of his body. As his arms were flailing, he twisted back toward the courtyard. His mouth opened and he began to say something as I pulled the trigger. Twenty or so rounds, from a distance of just three feet, exploded through his body, blood and lead peppering the foliage behind him. The force of the impact picked him up, threw him across the trail, over the dike and into the ditch. *Badadáda-dap!* The staccato burst destroyed the stillness of the morning.

Instantly, I ran into the courtyard. I didn't have time to check whether he was dead or not. I had four guys that needed to be arrested! With five steps I was directly in front of the four men cooking breakfast. *"Ngung Lai! Ngung Lai! Khong co chay! Khong co chay!"* I screamed.

I still, naively, felt it was my duty to arrest them. The four men were in the mid-position of getting up. I had them! They were looking at me and I was looking at them. Everything froze. I'm not moving, and they were posed in mid-motion like mannequins in a department store. I thought I won for a second. Then it began to unravel.

Coming to the front door of the house was another man. He too was wearing black pajamas. Unlike the guy I just shot, he was carrying an AK-47, holding it at the ready.

I looked up at him. "Oh, shiiiii—" I said as I jerked my Stoner around, firing at the man in the house. The other men in the courtyard instantly sprung to action. Fear and adrenaline mixed to squeeze my guts with an intensity I hadn't experienced before. I didn't have to be told I was in a life-or-death situation, and that I was on the short end of the stick. I tried to shoot and blast my way out of this dire threat. So I shot with my forefinger spasmed and my knuckle white on the trigger.

I watched as the men in the courtyard surrealistically moved through the air in the herky-jerky dance of death. I poured every round I had at this threat before me. Suddenly, the ground about me was exploding. Clouds of dust enveloped me. I tried aiming the Stoner at the house, where the man with the AK-47 had disappeared.

This all happened in a matter of seconds. Peace, calm, routine order, and solitude all swallowed in yet an instant within the gates of hell.

Bap! Click... My gun was empty. I needed to put a new belt of ammo in. In my mind, I swear, I did a backflip that landed me in the ditch eighteen feet behind me. A new Olympic record! I was on the side of the ditch closest to the house. The first man I shot lay nearby in the ditch. I tried to get my hands to work to open up the feed tray cover, break open a belt of ammo, slap it on there, close it down, charge the gun, and come up ready to do more battle.

I can't get it open! What's wrong with my hands? Don't cramp on me now!

The guy with the AK-47 continued shooting at me, dirt kicking up about me. I was scared to death he was going to walk over and shoot me if I couldn't get my gun reloaded quickly. I couldn't get my hands to work! They shook violently and my mind raced. Finally, the feed tray opened. I breathed again. I struggled to get the belt broken and slid it in there. Slamming the cover back down, I lifted the gun up with the belt of ammo draped over my arm and extended, reaching the ground. I needed as many shells as I could possibly get!

Jumping up, I looked wildly back and forth. Everything was deathly quiet except the ringing in my ears and the pounding of my chest. I started opening up on the house, figuring maybe the shooting stopped because the guy with the AK-47 was out of ammo just like I had been. I ran toward the hooch. Glancing furtively throughout the courtyard as I ran, I quickly spotted the four guys lying dead. I leapt up onto the porch, my gun screaming as I bolted through the door. There was one guy lying dead in a pool of blood right inside the door where my bullets had gone undeterred through the thin thatch-made walls.

''Hot damn! Stop shooting! Stop shooting!'' I heard coming from behind the house. I held up on my firing, crouching as I came to the rear of the house.

''Back here. Back here!'' It was Keener calling out.

Yes! A surge of relief rushed in. Keener! The team had to be here! I ran out the back door, and there was Keener standing in the ditch behind the house. He was ashen-faced.

''Two of them. That way!'' he said, pointing to his left. ''Help. Get me out of here!''

He was hip deep in mud in the middle of the ditch. I stopped and, while looking carefully south in the direction he was pointing, reached down and pulled him out of the muck.

"I hit one and he's wounded. He's over there," Keener said, excitedly.

I couldn't see anyone moving in the southeastern direction Keener was pointing. I turned quickly, hearing sounds of movement coming from the opposite direction. "There's Pete and the team!"

I signaled by hand to Pete, *We've got bodies in the front. Circle around and form a 360-degree around the house. Keener and I—over here—one guy wounded, we're going to look for him.*

Okay, you've got five minutes, came Pete's reply.

We headed off down the trail, following a blood trail indicating whoever was hit was wounded pretty bad. We both panted heavily. Try as we might, it was difficult to slow our breathing down to where we were undetectable. Fear, adrenaline, and excitement all cascading together over a period of minutes could send your system through physical gyrations! I was not physically exhausted, and yet I was panting and my heart beat wildly. Helping keep the spigot of adrenaline wide open was the fact that looking for an armed, wounded man in all this underbrush was like searching for a wounded tiger. It's not a particularly healthy thing to do, especially when the tiger had a gun. We crawled, keeping low as we tracked the blood trail. The trail wound first to the right, and then along to an elbow to our left.

As we rounded the corner, we saw two kids. By now, we were 150 to 200 meters away from the rest of the team. As we peered around a tree, we saw another clearing and another house. We'd just left the forested area and were entering an area of rice paddies, one of which buttressed up against the house. We watched the kids, as they took palm fronds and brushed down the dirt trail in order to obliterate the readily evident blood marker that could lead us directly to possibly even more VC.

We looked at each other and shrugged. We watched the two brush the trail for a few moments. We stood up and, in unison, yelled, "Hey!!"

Those kids jumped into the air! They barely even glanced at us as they fled as fast as their little legs could carry them.

We analyzed the situation, figuring they had brushed enough of the trail that "Charlie" could easily have gone in a dozen different directions. However, there was a haystack at the edge of the clearing, adjacent to the rice paddies.

"I bet he's in the haystack," said Keener.

"Do you want to fire it up?" I asked.

"What the heck," Keener replied, quickly. With that, we both raised our guns and sent straw showering into the breeze. Between the two of us, we touched off approximately 225 rounds. We quickly reloaded our guns to full capacity, turned, and "beat feet" back to the house where our Bravo team was mopping up.

When we arrived, everybody was all pumped up, ready for combat because of all the shooting they had heard.

"No, no. It was a wounded guy. We think we know where he was, but he had a gun and we didn't want to get any closer. So we fired it up and backed off," I reported.

"There were some innocents over there [meaning the family and the kids] so we decided it was better to back off," added Keener.

While we were gone, Riojas had gone around to all of the bodies to make sure they were dead and to collect the necessary documents that were part of intelligence gathering procedures. This, along with watches, wallets, and rings. That was standard protocol. Many of the Viet Cong carried pictures of themselves or of their squad in their wallets. Often we would circle a number of guys in the picture we had shot in that particular firefight. It was a way of gathering information. A SEAL tradition was that the guy who shot him got the watch. We were talking about watches worth all of about two dollars—not Rolexes.

Riojas handed me five watches. I placed them on my left forearm in keeping with "tradition." I had five confirmed "kills" and one "partial": the guy with the Mauser and the four guys in the courtyard I had killed; the guy in the doorway with the AK-47 I had wounded.

The fascinating thing about what happened was that Keener had just gotten into position at the rear of the house when I started shooting. Bullets were flying everywhere, flipping above his head, and he scrambled into the ditch. He was carrying an M16 with an M203 grenade launcher that attached underneath it. He leaned his shoulder up against a footbridge that crossed the ditch immediately outside of the back door of the house. The M16 was trained on the back door, waiting for anybody to come out. The VC with the AK-47 and two others inside the house decided, evidently, after I had quit shooting, that it was a good time to flee out the back. The first one out was the VC with the AK-

47. Keener hit him full in his chest. The second shell to go into Keener's M16 expanded in the chamber and would not extract. The gun jammed! One round and the gun quit. The guy Keener shot was thrown back into the house. The other two VC coming out were carrying AK-47s, as well.

"All I know was that I was looking down, trying like hell to release the shell from the chamber, I look up and here came two VC across the bridge. My arm was laying across the bridge in a bent L, and they both had to jump over it! I couldn't believe it!" Keener marveled. "As they fled, I brought up the .two-oh-three forty-mike-mike and shot one of them in the back as he stepped off the log bridge. I guess I was too close or something, because the high-explosive shell did not detonate."

Keener decided quickly that another .203 40-mike-mike might not be the safest alternative, so he fished inside his pack and pulled out a canister fleschette round. This was akin to an ultra high-powered shotgun blast. At that point, I was assaulting through the house. Keener started yelling and I ceased firing as I came to the back. When I arrived and saw Keener, he had his gun apart and had just freed the shell from the chamber. He cleaned off the bolt face and put the M16 back together, good to go! I helped him out of the ditch and away we went after them.

The dawn was breaking into early morning, and we needed to extract as soon as we could. Things like Americans, the shooting of loud automatic weaponry, and the killing of VC in their own neighborhood did not go over well with the locals. We rechecked our compass, Riojas signaled via the radio that we were returning, and I assumed my point position. As we were leaving, I noticed the Mauser lying on the dike. I picked it up and, for some reason, decided to keep it. We'd captured many weapons, and most all were turned over to materiel stockpiles.

As we headed back through the jungle to the extraction point, it dawned on me that we—I—confronted eight VC in that one house. Eight. That was a full platoon. A wry smile pursed my lips. *Arrest them. Yeah, right!*

Roy Dean, the point man in Gallagher's Alpha team, and I were good friends. But, as point men, we took personal responsibility for our respective teams. If we had a successful operation, the point man took credit. Conversely, if an operation failed to draw contact with the enemy, it was the point man who took the ribbing over "pussyfooting around the VC or NVA" in order to avoid a firefight. It was the point man's responsibility, or at least we saw it that way.

We started, buoyed by a good deal of egging on by our teams, to compete over who was the better point man and, by association, which was the better team. We were betting that whoever got the most kills received the honor of making the other eat crow while drinking the loser's beer. In fact, the bet evolved to the point that the loser was going to have to buy the other guy a beer at each and every stop on the way back to the States at the end of the tour. With these five kills, I moved from being behind Roy Dean by one to being ahead by four.

The Mike boat came to extract us. Roy Dean was up there, on the boat. He'd heard over the radio that we'd been in a hellacious firefight, and this had been further substantiated by the crewmen on the boat and SEALs who had been picked up earlier who reported seeing the tracers flying.

As the STAB pulled up alongside, Roy Dean was there tossing down the safety ropes for us to pull ourselves up with.

"How'd you guys do?" he asked.

I didn't say a word. I just held up my left forearm. My sleeve fell back to reveal the watches. My watch and five others.

His eyes grew wide. "No way! NO WAY! Son of a bitch!" Roy Dean then launched into a tirade over how I must have cheated, how I must have been given credit for other team members' kills solely to embarrass him. . . . He was pissed!

"Come tell me about it!" he insisted.

This was how my reputation as a killer got started. Everyone kept saying that a man in his right mind would not have assaulted eight people by himself. I never saw it as eight people. I saw it as one guy I had to handle and then four others that I could probably get the drop on. That's all I ever saw it as. I just got caught up in it to where there were more and more guys and I had to keep shooting. I knew Pete and the team would arrive to bail me out.

Keener and I surveyed the damage, talked it over, and then took the most logical course of action. To others, it was reported, "Harry was still shooting at them—by himself—chasing them out across the paddies!" That's how the story was told.

As we got on the boat and I told Roy Dean the story, Riojas said, "Damn, Harry!" Then he started hitting my pant leg. "Did you say you were getting shot at and the guy was kicking up dirt all around you?"

"Yeah."

"Look at your pant leg!" he said, pointing at my right ankle.

I looked at my pant leg and there were two bullet holes. Two clean holes, right through the material. Nothing hit me!

We got back to My Tho later that morning, and, as was protocol, we got everything cleaned up. After finishing, I returned to my room in the hotel. Later, Gallagher walked into my room.

"I want you to write a statement for the after-action report," he said. This was a memorandum detailing what took place. "But I want you to change a couple of parts in it."

I look at him, puzzled. "What do you mean?" I asked.

"Here's what I want you to do. I want you to put down that you shot that first guy coming out. Then, when you went walking back in there, the rest of the VC platoon started shooting at you, forcing you to dive for cover in the ditch. You were pinned down. And then, Pete Peterson arrived in time to provide suppressing fire from the flank. You were then able to escape, and Lieutenant Peterson proceeded to kill the rest of the enemy."

Why? I wondered. My puzzlement was apparent to Gallagher, so he continued.

"Look, Harry. It's important for you to do this so Peterson gets his Silver Star. I know you. You'll earn more than one Silver Star on this particular tour alone," he stated confidently. "I know how you are. As an officer, Pete needs a Silver Star for advancement opportunities. Since he has to be the team leader, you will have far more opportunities to obtain Silver Stars than Pete will. What do ya say, can I count on you?"

"I have no problem with that, Eagle. After all, Pete, Keener, and Riojas did show up to bail my ass out. And besides, if anyone deserves recognition it's Pete," I confirmed. "I do get to keep the watches, right?"

Gallagher grinned, shaking his head. "You and I have a lot more combat ahead of us."

I wrote the report as if I was pinned down and Lieutenant Peterson came to my rescue. Sure enough, Pete received the Silver Star.

Shortly thereafter, the intensity of the competition between Gallagher's team and Pete's team increased. It's to be expected from a group of highly trained young military men in this situation. Harry versus Roy Dean. Alpha versus Bravo. Our team, your team. We

cared about each other, but this was a friendly form of intense competition.

After that first operation, when I had killed a guy by knifing him,
the word went around, *Harry, he's not squeamish about killing.* Many
of the new guys, when sitting around, said things like, ''I'm not sure
I can do this. I don't know if I could deliberately slit somebody's
throat.'' War forged our personalities. We now were able to kill—and
kill brutally—then return to base and shake it off. As if nothing had
happened. We didn't—couldn't—let it bother us.

After a couple of beers, trying to relax at the club in My Tho, it was
more a matter of, ''I wonder how I will do.'' I think we all agreed we
were going to do it. Then someone would say, ''I don't know, man.
Constance knifed a man last night and you wouldn't even know it!''
As if it was supposed to change me.

By now we'd had quite a few skirmishes. But what we'd been doing
had been a lot of us shooting at a couple of them. We would walk over
to the bushes, look in, and see a couple of dead bodies. There's nothing
really personal, just some bullet holes and pieces of body missing. We
personally wouldn't really say, *I toasted this guy* or *I really kicked that
guy's ass.* It was more, *We all shot them and it was a fair fight because
bullets were flying.*

As time passed, the competition started getting serious, to the point
it was more than just losing face. It was more than embarrassment. It
was more of a referendum on who was the best in SEAL Team Two.
The best of the best.

Obviously, all of us were SEALs—an elite group that needed no
justification. However, we had a group of ''the best'' who were com-
petitive. I wanted to be known as the best overall operator in SEAL
Team Two.

So when I got back up on that boat after getting those five kills, and
I showed Roy Dean all those watches, it was like I was saying, *Now
you know who is the best damn operator around here, slick. I don't
want to hear any more words from you.* This did nothing but burn up
Roy Dean. He wouldn't talk to me for a while.

After my first tour in Vietnam was over and I was back at the SEAL
facilities, I was pulled aside. I was told, ''Oh, by the way, they are
writing out the evaluations. And you are tied for first place.''

At that point, I was tied with another guy in another platoon, followed closely by Roy Dean Matthews. The evaluation was based on
overall operational performance. So, there I was, this kid who should

not have gone to SEAL Team when he did, being told that he was one of the best SEAL Team operators going. I barely passed the entrance requirement of UDT, let alone SEALs. There I was, having gone over to Vietnam on my first tour, finding myself moving from obscurity as a new kid to about the best operator in SEAL Team Two.

I relished the beer on our way home to My Tho.

CHAPTER 8

"ALL YOU GUYS! PUT YOUR HANDS UP!"

OUR OPERATIONS WERE NOW BECOMING MORE AND MORE sophisticated and dangerous. We were developing quite a network of intelligence within the community around us.

Time after time, people came to us and said, "The VC killed my sister [or my mother or my father]. I will do anything I can to get even." And they would.

"Keep an eye out and let us know what you see and hear," was our reply. By mid-December 1967, we had many of these clandestine surveillance channels working for us.

We had tremendous respect for the North Vietnamese Army (NVA), because they were a well-disciplined, tactically correct, well-supplied, and well-led fighting force. They were motivated and aggressive in their approach to warfare, and they fought that way. Their talent level and ability to fight was akin to the difference between the Special Forces and the regular Army.

The VC just weren't trained as well. The majority of VC were reservists and clandestine groups of operatives allied in a loose confederation. They were either idealists, idiots, or ex-jailbirds who wanted to fight against the South Vietnamese government. They rallied to the cause of the Communists, and were given guns, which allowed them to be big fish in their little pond. They could run around and terrorize the rest of the villagers with impunity. There were some main force VC units who were full-time, soldiered fighting units, but the vast majority were not. Their ability to move with stealth tactics, camouflaged, in formation with coordinated troop movement, was minimal. I am not suggesting that we didn't have problems with the VC, because we did, but their talent level was less. Obviously, they had an immediate advantage from the perspective that this was their "backyard" and they knew the countryside very well.

The VC, however, were light-years ahead of the ARVN—the South Vietnamese Army. ARVN was mostly a joke. It was generally accepted that if the ARVN was around, you knew the VC and NVA were not anywhere near the area. One of the funniest things I ever saw first occurred after I had been in-country just a few weeks. We were driving down the road just outside of Can Tho, and there were twenty or more ARVN soldiers in formation across the road in front of us. They were shooting round after round into the paddies and tree line ahead. We pulled up behind them.

I picked up my gun and took it off "safe." Pete reached over and pushed my gun back down with a smile.

The leader of the ARVN signaled to us with great animation, *Don't come any closer! Viet Cong! Viet Cong! Firefight! Big firefight!*

They were all standing there shooting. *Badadada-dap! Badadada-dap! Badadada-dap!* came the continual onslaught of firepower.

Over the din, Pete yelled, "There aren't any VC around here." He proceeded to honk the horn. *Beep beep!* Then he drove right through the ARVN line of soldiers. They were still blazing away at the "enemy" ahead of us as we eased past them.

I was not so sure. I thought it just might be a good idea to at least have my Stoner at the ready, so I started to raise it once again. Pete started chuckling and again pushed my gun back down. I looked at him with a look of *Shouldn't we take more of a better-safe-than-sorry approach?*

"There are no VC around here. Because if there was anyone—anybody at all—shooting at them, they would all be laying on the ground. Wait till you see these guys in real combat. They disappear as quickly as they can. The ones who can't escape immediately lay on the ground like scared puppies. The only way they stand up is if there is nobody shooting at them. I guarantee it!"

Sure enough. We drove on without incident. They'd been shooting at nothing at all. An understanding was established as to what our SEAL capabilities were. The ARVN were useless, and our fear of the "deadly Viet Cong" had passed.

There we were, six, seven, maybe ten guys (depending on the op), assaulting VC forces numbering anywhere from ten to fifty—and even with these numbers the odds were stacked in our favor. After a while, there wasn't a lot of fear in us even when we discovered instead of two or three guys coming down the trail, there were forty or fifty. We would shrug, glance over at one another, and, while cracking a wry grin, remark that now the odds were a little more to our liking.

Camaraderie, many soldiers will tell you, develops with the guys in your unit, creating a powerful emotional tie. It's a kinship that bridges racial, economic, and cultural differences and arises when teamwork is the only way any of you will survive. It's almost a brotherly rapport.

My closest friend was Eugene Fraley. Fraley was superstitiously lucky. Before coming into SEAL Teams, he was in the aviation branch of the Navy, serving as an "Airdale." He flew in the plane's jumpseat, nicknamed the "death seat." He was involved in two crashes—sitting in the death seat—where he was the only one who survived. Not once, but twice. There was an uncanny, almost mystical air about him.

Several times, we were set up in an ambush, with Pete closest to me. All of a sudden, we heard people whispering as they passed along a message. Then Pete would touch me on the arm.

"Be careful," came the message in a hushed tone. "Fraley's out moving around."

I'd shake my head. What this meant was he had taken off and left us to go out exploring all by himself.

Returning, he reported, "There are a bunch of VC cooking about a mile over there. Over that way is a village with three houses, two dogs, and a woman in a red skirt already up preparing something."

I was amazed the first few times this occurred. He moved like a shadow. He knew how to step, where to step, and how to blend in. He had an uncanny sense of when *not* to move—he did those things naturally.

Fraley had an interesting thing that he liked to do. Fraley liked to leave his "calling card"—which was one of several cleverly disguised explosives that an unsuspecting VC would think nothing of until it was too late. These were Fraley's little "presents" for someone to find.

His favorite ploy was to take an AK-47 magazine and remove the first bullet (which was the one at the top). He emptied out the lead, gunpowder, and primer and in its place put a compression detonating cap, which he packed with C4 plastic explosive. When an enemy soldier found this "lost" magazine, he might possibly take out a bullet or two, quickly reassuring himself that someone had carelessly lost it. However, the first time he decided to use Fraley's little "present," the weapon would explode when he pulled the trigger, driving the bolt into the face of the unlucky soldier.

We had also been working with radios and canteens. Turn on the radio and it powered up just fine. The only problem was that should you try to change the channel, the nylon line that moved the channel indicator would move two foil strips together. Maybe you realized it or maybe you didn't, but you just turned to the wrong station—and now you're dead.

The C4 by itself was like Play-Doh or Silly Putty, and was quite stable. The hazards came when an electrical charge was attached to it.

On this particular day in early December, we were working on canteens. I'd just finished placing C4 into several different canteens, and Fraley was carefully rigging the detonator. It was rather clever. When a VC would pick up the canteen, he could shake it and hear the water inside. As he was unscrewing the lid from the canteen, he was unwittingly lifting the foil strip (which was attached to the chain that kept the lid attached to the canteen) upward where it came in contact with the charged strip, thus completing the circuit.

I was busy putting in the C4 and wire, while Fraley rigged the canteen cap. We did not "play" with explosives haphazardly. We had a miniature bunker assembled alongside one of the huts for protection. It consisted of sandbags covered with flak jackets. During the critical assembly time when Fraley would set the "hot" detonator in place, the booby traps were placed in the bunker. Fraley could reach under the flak jackets and connect the charge. Should it accidentally detonate, you might lose a hand, but not your life.

Fraley, Ashton, Keener, and I had finished up on three canteens and were working on a fourth. It was two P.M., and we were getting hungry.

"You guys—go ahead and take off. I'll cap this, clean up, and meet you at lunch," said Fraley.

"All right," we replied. So we jumped in the jeep and drove on up to the mess hall.

Shortly after we arrived at lunch, sirens started going off. We jumped to our feet. The sirens indicated a possible enemy attack on the base. The room was deathly still as everybody strained to extend their senses—hearing and vision—to pick up what type and where the possible attack was coming from. We obviously had been too far away to have heard the explosion or explosions.

"Explosion in Sector Two. Explosion in Sector Two," came the cackle from the radio. "What is the status, Sector Two?" came the call from command center.

I looked at Keener as our eyes widened. We had just come from Sector 2 twenty minutes earlier. "Let's go check it out," said Keener, as we half walked, half ran out the door.

Just then, a couple of sailors driving another jeep came to a halt alongside the two of us. "There's been an explosion! One of your SEALs has been killed."

"What?" we both said, simultaneously. We looked at each other, our eyes wide.

Fraley.

I started running to see what had happened, when a rescue jeep came driving up, headed to sick bay. Sick bay was located next door to the mess hall. There was a tarp over what I presumed was Fraley's body, lying on a stretcher.

The reality of seeing a friend and valued member of our team all torn up felt like a percussion cap detonating. I swallowed hard and turned around. All I could do was shake my head slowly back and forth, a distant stare on my face.

Fraley had been bending over the canteen, and the blast propelled him up twenty-five feet into the air, onto the roof of our Quonset hut. His body slid down into the space between the Quonset hut and the sandbag bunkers surrounding all of the buildings as a defense against rocket attacks. The sailors had to pull the sandbag walls down in order to retrieve the body. At least it was an instantaneous death.

Fraley's death disturbed us deeply. It was the first casualty of an East Coast SEAL in Vietnam. Our first taste of death among our own. It was not the result of an enemy bullet, but it might as well have been. The most troubling factor was that we'd bought into the belief that we were above being killed because we were better trained, more courageous, smarter, and tougher. Our youthful see-the-world-have-an-adventure machismo was shaken. The reality of our own mortality set in.

The second-in-command in our platoon was a warrant officer by the name of Charlie Watson. He was one of the older guys, and reacted as if the air had completely gone out of his sails. Each operation brought out an adrenaline high. As we "improved" our operating tactics, the rush came only with more daring and harrowing events. We were going out on operations, returning, resting, and then going out again. We had trouble coming down. Depression did not set in, as the need to get back out in the bush constantly pulled at us. We needed the "fix" that only combat could give.

Fraley's death broke the adrenaline-induced delusion of invincibility. Especially for Charlie Watson.

Two days later, we received word from reliable sources that the VC were going to be moving several captured Americans from a jungle location south of us. They were allegedly going to travel westward along a particular trail onto the Ho Chi Minh Trail in Cambodia. From there, they were to be taken to Hanoi. We had been getting reports for several days of the movement of this group, and we had been trying to plot their coordinates on our topographical map. Now, on this Tuesday afternoon, an informant appeared, literally breathless from exertion, to tell us the captors had just moved into an area controlled by the VC.

"They've just shown up. Their intent is to stay four or five days. They need rest," he said through our interpreter. Apparently, the guards were tired from being on the move and wanted to rest for a few days.

Gallagher furrowed his brow and scanned the room. "Let's plan to go the night after next." He then looked to the interpreter. "How many guards and VC were there?"

"Six to ten Viet Cong," came the reply.

"No sweat," I blurted out. "Two of us should be all that's required."

Gallagher smiled. "No. There could be more of them. There could be twenty, possibly more, or perhaps they were waiting to join up with another group. Let's take a team of twelve."

In our arrogant opinion, twelve SEALs were equivalent to two hundred Viet Cong. We looked at each other.

"Okay," said Roy Dean, "let's take twelve of us and go kick some ass."

In a hostage situation, we had to be extremely covert. The VC absolutely could not know we were there until the shooting started. Then, we must be the first ones to get on top of the POWs. Our preparation had to be thorough. If we started shooting without administering a lethal first strike, the VC would run in, shoot the American prisoners, and melt away into the jungle. We might kill many of the enemy, but the entire mission had failed if our fellow Americans were killed.

The next day, we assembled to pore over intelligence reports we had received. Gallagher gave one of the most detailed briefings I could remember.

"We will get off the boat here. Then we will head to here. Twelve klicks northwest will place us here," he said while thumping the map with his pointer. "We know there are VC platoons here, here, and here," he stated, pointing to a four-square grid on the map. "There is a company of VC housed here. There is another company of VC housed here. And, although the details are suspect, there may be some NVA activity in this region two klicks to the northeast."

This would be interesting. Twelve klicks was approximately six miles. Six miles at night, through banana groves, coconut groves, jungle, rice paddies, and the like. With all the other enemy locations, we would be traversing like a pinball, back and forth in order to avoid booby traps and premature enemy contact. Obviously, if we made contact, they would know we were coming. Then, it's not a surprise anymore.

Normally, I took twelve hundred rounds of Stoner ammo on an operation. For this night, I took twenty-two hundred rounds. I had my flares, grenades, and all my other military paraphernalia with me. We were going such a long way, I figured, should we get in a gun battle, I'd better have extra bullets.

We left midafternoon the next day, headed downriver, southeast on the Mekong River, to a point about halfway to the ocean. At that point, we disembarked and headed due south. We arrived at the drop-off site right at dusk. This allowed us to get into position to undertake the operation by midnight, hopefully allowing us to still be able to get out under cover of darkness.

"It's a shame Fraley isn't here," said Ashton to no one in particular. No one replied. The drone of the engines churning along the river complemented the hypnotic lapping of the water against the bow.

When we arrived, I moved quickly to pick up a trail. It was the dry time of the year, and most of the rice paddies were barren. This was to our benefit for several reasons. First, when we were waist deep in water, we obviously didn't move as fast. Second, when we moved in water, our feet kicked up a muddy trail. The muddy trail amidst the rather clear rice paddy water stood out like a sore thumb. When we crossed over a dike, the water was a dead giveaway to our presence, revealing our whereabouts and where we might pass on our trip back to home base.

It was almost midnight and we were nearing the objective location. It was a typically tropical evening, with warm, gentle trade winds softly blowing. The palm trees rustled in the breeze, the mosquitoes were out in force, and, all in all, it was a perfect Hawaiilike evening.

"Hold up," came the command. We stopped to allow Pete and Gallagher to review the map.

I moved back from my position at the point in order to consult with the two team leaders. "Can you see that tree line up ahead? They've got to be in there," I stated.

We whispered quietly for several minutes as we attempted to make last-minute plans. The adjustments to the terrain, countryside, light levels, and so on were made. "All right, Harry, take us on in."

"Okay. Fine." I gently slipped my gun off safe and moved across the last half mile of dry rice paddy toward the tree line. Within two hundred yards of the tree line, I stopped. I slowly raised my left fist up, signaling everyone to freeze. At a 45-degree angle to my left, setting out from the tree line by a distance of about a hundred yards, was a house.

Suddenly, two guys emerged from the house, one wearing a white shirt, the other black pajamas. We were little more than one hundred yards apart, and they could see us as well as we could see them. We absolutely had no way of melting away into the shadows. The guy in the white shirt stared straight at me. He waved his hand in a slow arc over his head. I didn't know what to do. *Well, hey, how are you doing?* I was thinking, so I waved my arm back at him.

This must have appeased him, as he flicked his wrist into the "hi" symbol, turned, and the two of them went back inside. Quickly, Pete was beside me.

"What was that about?" he demanded.

"I don't know. The guy came out, he waves at me, I wave back, and he goes back inside."

"Man, let's get the hell out of this field! We can't let ourselves be exposed this close to the target," Pete hissed, urgently.

Our fear was that the sentries might think about our encounter, realize it wasn't quite normal—maybe we were too tall, or improperly dressed—anything, and then sound the alarm. We kept our eye on the house and moved as quickly as we could into the tree line.

I stopped, dumbfounded, about fifty yards into the jungle. I suspected the VC encampment would be in the tree line, based upon past experiences. I was more "right" than I wanted to be. There was an entire developed city built up under the thick jungle canopy. Buildings, houses, crosshatched roads, and all the necessities of a town appeared.

We were looking for ten or so bad guys and a couple of Americans. Great. We expected to find a hooch or a campfire. Now, what were we to do? How were we to find them? Suppose we did. Suppose we shot the bad guys, grabbed the Americans, and ran; could we really expect to escape in this large, openly VC-controlled area?

"Look. It's a large area, so let's divide up into two teams and see if we can find them," said Pete, quickly assessing the changing situation.

I went with Pete and four others, and the six of us moved down a trail heading due east. Overhead was a jungle canopy of one-hundred-foot-tall trees, moonlight filtering downward like light diffracting through a thousand prisms.

After going for perhaps fifteen minutes, I spotted two men walking directly toward us. Reflexively, I glanced at Pete and stepped off the trail into the shadows to the right. This was standard operating procedure. I always stepped off to the right. Everybody was supposed to step off the trail to the right. The textbook approach was that I, as the point man, was supposed to wait until they were close to me, let the first guy go by, then take out the second guy when he was right in front of me. While I literally blew him off the trail, the guy behind me was to take out the first guy. I reached down and unstrapped my knife.

Glancing back to look at Pete, I saw that he, for some reason, was standing on the left side, perfectly parallel across the trail from me. I was stupefied. If I shot my guy, I hit Pete. *Why did he do this?* I wondered. Now, when I took the second man, that meant the first guy would have passed me, would be behind me, and there would be confusion among my teammates as to who would take the first guy—and more specifically, how he was to be taken. A pause of even a few seconds could prove fatal. Pete was the one who was designated to have the "honors." He had abdicated his duty by mistake. Now what were we supposed to do?

A moment later, they were upon us. I couldn't take out the first guy, as the second man would turn and run away. I prepared to take out the second man, and the entire team assumed Pete would take out the first man. I tensed up as if I were a weight lifter preparing to bench-press a heavy weight. My hand squeezed tightly around my knife.

The second man was directly in front of me. I stepped out in front of him. I hit him hard in the solar plexus, burying my knife. *Ummph,* came the sound of the air forcibly being expressed from his lungs. The knife impaled up to the hilt, and I lifted him up and to me. Our faces touched. His eyes were wild with disbelief. With my other hand, I grabbed his shoulder and dropped to the ground.

The first man kept walking. The corpsman, realizing Pete was not going to apprehend him, watched as the guy started to turn around, since he heard the noise of my hitting the other guy. He didn't think to grab his knife, but instead, hit him with his fist. *Thwack!* The force of the blow knocked him into the water-filled irrigation ditch on the other side of the trail.

Pete sprang from his position. "Get him, get him, get him!"

No one moved to dive into the water after him, as he was carrying a rifle. Pete wanted someone to keep him quiet, but his excited staccato of "Get him, get him, get him" was interpreted as "finish him off." Had they gone in immediately after the corpsman hit him, they could have gotten him. Unfortunately, he came up from under the water, clutching his gun and turning toward the outer bank away from us. He started to yell.

KaBooom, Boom! resounded the Ithaca pump shotgun, driving the VC against the bank. Slowly, he slid down into his watery grave.

We started running. This had to have awoken people, as a shotgun blast in the middle of the night wasn't hard to miss. We made a turn, then another. Our hearts pounding in our ears, we sprinted over into another bank of shadows.

We looked at one another. We already knew we were in the wrong place, we had alerted attention to us, and we had no idea where Gallagher and the other "split squad" was. We had bad intelligence, not fully detailed data, and we were deep in enemy country.

"Eagle. Come in, Eagle," said Riojas as he attempted to reach the other team.

"Eagle here, over," said Gallagher over the radio.

After discussing coordinates and locations, we asked what he had heard.

"We heard a muffled shotgun blast, but it was minimal."

We were fortunate. Anyone could readily hear the difference and recognize an American M16 or Stoner compared with an AK-47, but since it was a shotgun, it did not elicit attention.

We linked up with Gallagher. Moving forward, we came to what looked like one long house. It looked, literally, like a barracks. We stood outside, hoping against hope we would find the house that contained the Americans. Looking at me, Gallagher motioned to the long house.

"Check it out," he whispered.

I nodded, crept up the stairs to the door. I stepped inside the doorway (being cautious to stay out of the light surrounding the door opening) and clicked on my red lens flashlight. In the middle of the room, running the length of the building, was a gun rack, loaded with gleaming SKSs and AK-47s. *Oh, boy.* I shined my red light across the room, only to find two rows of bunk beds. *We are in the WRONG place. I can't believe this.* I counted nine guys sleeping on either side of the aisle. I quickly stepped back outside.

As I backed out of the building, Gallagher walked up to my shoulder. "What's in there?"

"You won't believe it! There are two rows of nine guys sleeping on either side. In the middle of the room is a gun rack with SKSs and AK-forty-sevens."

"Good," came Gallagher's measured reply. "Let's take 'em out."

I turned my head, gazing out of the corner of my eye at Gallagher. I was at the same time perplexed and stymied. "Aren't we looking for POWs?"

"Things are dicked up," he replied calmly. "We've got to take what we've got."

And with that, I slowly turned my head from side to side. "Okay." I could not get switched from the *let's save the POWs* to *let's go into a hornet's nest and see if we can run through the hive without getting stung.* What the hell. I figured we'd want to keep as quiet as possible. Translation: Kill them with knives.

The alarm at the prospect of having to knife one person after another must have registered on my face. Gallagher, I think, read my mind. He cracked a wry smile as he caught my eye.

"Harry, get your gun ready," he said, watching for my expression. Then his face got serious. "Roy Dean, Ashton, Hooker."

Immediately, they came forward. Gallagher motioned for me to go to the right, with Curtis Ashton as my backup. Roy Dean moved left, and Richard J. Turrey was poised behind him.

"Just shoot 'em while they're laying in their bunks," came Gallagher's order.

"Okay. But what happens after you shoot the first guy and everybody else jumps up?" I asked.

Gallagher said, "You might be surprised. Do it."

We figured this to be a VC company. We paused for a moment to allow time for the guys who had gone around back to get in position. We walked up the steps and, in tandem, stepped through the doorway. I took a step to the right, Roy Dean took a step to the left. He nodded his head at me, and I nodded my head at him. *Let's do it,* I said, mouthing the words.

I took my Stoner and went to the first guy. The VC were lying on their bunks in their black pajamas without sheets. Their beds were canopied with lightweight mosquito netting. *Badda da da dap!* I unleashed a quick ten to fifteen rounds through the body. Then I walked to the next bunk. *Badda da dow!* Walk. *Badda da dow!* Walk to the next one. *Badda da dow!* Again, I walked to the next one. The flash of violence pouring from our guns mixed with the smoke and cordite to erase our dark-adapted night vision. I strained to see the next man in the next bunk. I didn't dare look ahead to see if anyone had jumped up and might be grabbing a gun, as it would have hindered my concentration. *Badda da dow!*

Ashton carried the Ithaca pump shotgun. Staying right behind me, he unloaded a second blast into each man in order to make sure they were dead. *Chit. Chit. Kaboom!* Pump and shoot, pump and shoot, then reload.

Methodically, we moved through the dormitory with deadly precision. I shot exactly nine guys. Roy Dean, on his side, shot nine guys. We went all the way through the house, then out the back door. Sweat poured off of us.

All hell broke loose. Whistles pierced the night stillness. People were yelling and screaming. Pete and Gallagher immediately decided to split up, again. I went with Pete to the right; Gallagher and Roy Dean headed left.

Gallagher got into another firefight at another hooch a half mile away. A grenade was thrown. Gallagher and Ron Yeaw were seriously wounded. The Vietnamese guide with them was killed. Only Hooker, Roy Dean, and one other guy were unscathed. They were in trouble. Lieutenant Yeaw was "peppered out," meaning he had taken heavy frag from the grenade and was bleeding profusely.

"What is it, Rios?" asked Pete.

"Eagle's team's been hit. Eagle and Yeaw are down."

"Oh chit."

Pete looked at each one of us. Mean, animal intensity gripped us. Like trapped wolves, an angry determination to survive welled up inside.

We began running in the opposite direction, headed south. We were on the edge of the rice paddies, moving as quickly as we could on a well-worn dike. Guns were going off; people and shadows moved around about us.

Suddenly, a reinforced squad came our way. They were heading north on the closest dike in proximity to ours—some twenty yards away. They hollered, *"Ai Do?"* (Who's there?)

We obviously couldn't answer.

They opened up on us. We kept moving. The first few rounds were high. We kept running. The aim was lowered. Now the bullets were approximately five feet over our heads. I brought my gun into line with their column. If the rounds came any closer, I would open up on them.

They quit shooting.

Whew! That was close.

We kept running. Another ''bullet'' dodged! They obviously didn't see us well enough in the moonlit jungle shadows to positively identify us. When we did not return fire, they must have surmised we were a ''friendly'' VC squad running to join up with our company. On the dike beyond them was another company of at least fifty more men. They all yelled back and forth, trying to determine what was going on, who was who, and what their response should be.

We broke out of the jungle. Right in front of us was another hooch, and beyond that loomed a good two thousand meters of rice paddies. This time, the paddies were all out in the open without benefit of a jungle canopy overhead. Unfortunately, there was so much activity throughout the jungle that we were compelled to travel even farther south, away from the river where we'd inserted. It seemed the entire jungle was teeming with Viet Cong. *Unbelievable! Where'd they all come from?*

Before running into the rice paddy, we stopped in the darkness surrounding the lone hooch. We'd been on a dead sprint for a good eight hundred meters. We'd stopped once at approximately four hundred meters to see if Riojas could radio for assistance. Adding to our misfortune, the radio was not working. Now, approaching the jungle clearing, Riojas could not run any farther. He immediately was on his knees, trying to get the radio to work. Still, it refused to function.

''Harry, look in the house,'' Pete said quietly.

I snuck up to the doorway and peered in. Amazing! More bunks and a gun rack. Half of the bunks, however, were turned on their side. As I was about to turn and leave, I noticed some movement. Straining to focus, I saw what appeared to be the tops of at least ten heads, all huddled down. I backed out silently and moved to Pete.

"It's loaded!"

Pete pantomimed the act of pulling a pin and throwing a grenade. I nodded acknowledgment, and slipped two grenades off my belt. I slung my Stoner by its strap behind my back, and proceeded to pull the pins on the grenades. Pete and the team then took off running. I gave them time to get sixty to seventy-five yards away before attacking the house. As point man, I carried the least amount of weight, so I was the natural one to toss the grenades and run. Also, by allowing the rest of the team to move away, I was guarding against possible counterattack. Should someone not get hit or if a grenade was a dud, it would be very easy for them to step out and shoot us in the back as we fled. From thirty yards, we were an easy target.

After they were sufficiently downrange, I lobbed the two grenades into the house and started to run. *BOOOM! BOOOM!* The earth shook. Immediately, more people were screaming and shouting. I don't know if I killed anyone—I probably did—but it sure livened things up. I sprinted away, abandoning any pretense of stealth.

Guns started going off. Then more guns, and then still more. Guns to the right, to the left, in front of and behind us—all over! There were people coming out of the woodwork, all with guns. The tree line was abuzz with activity. Tracers flew in multiple directions—literally from all over. A healthy sense of fear began welling up in the pit of my stomach. All I could think was *This is it, man. This is the end. In less than a week, first Fraley, now us. Damn it all!*

I rejoined the team, and still we ran, farther and farther into this dry, barren rice paddy. We got approximately five hundred yards from the tree line and the house/dormitory. Have you ever tried to run five hundred yards when you were scared to death? It seemed but a moment.

Unexpectedly, we came upon a bomb crater. We all piled in, grateful for the momentary respite. Even more pleasing was the fact there was water at the bottom. While we didn't dare drink it, it was so refreshing to splash all over us. It helped get our temperatures down. Our chests heaving, we attempted to regroup and assess our predicament. When we were running as fast as we could with our back to the enemy, all we could do was hope we weren't going to be the recipient of a bullet in the back.

I started taking stuff off, my jacket, my shirt, all my military hard-

ware. My breathing became somewhat less labored. I lined up my
bullets so they could be readily fed into my Stoner with as little dis-
ruption as possible. An assault on our position was imminent. The
stark reality was that, come morning, they would see us and overrun
us easily.

We were five SEALs and one Vietnamese guide, for a total of six.
Riojas worked feverishly to get the radio to work. It was our only hope.
I didn't know how far it was to the river where we were dropped off,
but we had been going the wrong way for the last two hours. The next
major waterway was the ocean, and it was quite a ways away, perhaps
ten or more miles. Helicopter extraction was the only way out, unless
we could break back through the enemy lines in the direction from
which we'd just come.

The Vietnamese guide's eyes were wide with fear. All he could tell
us, once we had gotten him to calm down, was that we had just attacked
a main force VC battalion. Estimated strength, three hundred people.
They were full-time soldiers, trained by the NVA. We had just hit three
hundred of them, and they were obviously upset.

We hunkered down in a crater six to seven feet deep and ten feet in
diameter. All of a sudden, Ashton gasped in disbelief.

"Look at that. You guys, look at this!" he said. He was no longer
whispering.

I stood up and my jaw dropped. "Holy crap! There must be two
hundred of them! These are bad odds!"

In the eerie, predawn hours, it was almost surrealistic to watch your
enemy silently moving in your direction, about to unleash a lethal
amount of violence at you.

Good thing we have that element of surprise! I thought wryly.

"If you ever have five of you fixing to take on two hundred, important safety tip—have an awful lot of bullets!" we all whined. But,
rather than an emotional "woe is me, we're not going to make it"
sobbing, everyone whined in a funny, dry sense of humor, sort of way.

"They had better start lining up. I don't have enough bullets!"

Pete looked at us with as stern a look as he could muster. "Let's
ambush 'em!"

"Yeah, right. Like they don't know we're here!" came the reply.

Very quickly, a glimmer of good fortune emerged. We were positioned in a 360-degree circle so as to best be able to fend off a mul-
tipronged attack. Fortunately, they bunched together, with the majority
of soldiers standing within no more than a 30- to 40-degree arc.

"Harry, get your stuff and come over here," commanded Pete, as I was on the other side of the crater.

The Vietnamese guide came with me. He was unable to remove an expanded round from the chamber of his M16, so he was instructed to assist me. I laid my shirt down and placed my bullets on it. Deftly, I put a bipod onto the front of my Stoner and flipped up the sights. I had time. Next, I began connecting the bullets together into five-hundred-round belts. Then, the two of us began connecting the remaining bullets into a four-hundred-round belt. When one belt was empty, he would assist me by feeding the next belt. We laid the grenades up, flares up, and looked at one another. It was, in a rather macabre sort of way, reminding me of the biblical account of the loaves and fishes. I hoped we could got a lot of mileage out of this amount of ammo.

To my immediate right was the M79 man, Jack Rowell, getting his gun set and ready to fire. To his right were Ashton and Pete. We were as set as we were going to be.

To our astonishment, we could not script their onslaught to be any more of a tactical blunder than it was! We were almost laughing. Not quite, but almost.

Okay, bunch up you guys! Good. Now, stand shoulder to shoulder. Good. Hum. We need to make you stand out so that we can aim better. Yeah, that's it. Yes. Have every other man wear a white shirt. Good. See how much better that is? You reflect so much better that way! Let's see, it sure would be nice if the full moon would break through. Hey! Good! Now you all are casting a serious shadow. Way to go! Now, walk real slow so we SEALs will have time to prepare.

And that was what they did. Rather than breaking into groups of forty or fifty and attacking from all sides, in a hammer-and-anvil tactic, they bunched together.

Soon, they were two hundred yards away. "Let's open up," I suggested to Pete.

"You got extra bullets? Hang on. We're gonna let 'em get close enough so we can try for a few two-for-one specials!"

Pete looked at the M79 man. "Jack, d'you have any Willie Pete in there?"

"Well, no. I have one Willie Pete, but mostly HE."

"One will do. I want you to set up to fire the Willie Pete as our first round. Shoot it for the back of the group."

"Can do, sir."

"Okay. On my mark." Pete was counting down as the VC were

now at little more than one hundred yards away. At this distance, even if they panicked, should they run at us we'd be overrun.

"All right, you sonsabitches, you're SEALs. Let's see what badasses you are! Open up."

With that, we unleashed a torrent of violence upon the enemy. The Willie Pete was placed perfectly behind the approaching Viet Cong. Landing, it made a lot of noise, exploding like a Roman candle, almost giving the appearance of a mortar round. By shooting behind them, Pete was attempting to create tactical confusion by establishing an illusion as to where we were and the enormity of our firepower. *Dounk!* The sound of the Willie Pete even sounded like a mortar. Sure enough! They paused and stopped for a second. The white phosphorus of the Willie Pete was really pretty to watch as it went off in the middle of the night. *Boooom!*

I opened up. My sights were fixed on one, then another, then another and another. I was almost surgically exacting with my sights and close proximity. The battle raged. After what seemed like just moments, the VC turned and ran. They couldn't run 300 to 400 yards very quickly. We picked them apart. They zigzagged back and forth in their attempts to get away. Some hit the deck.

Round one was over. We couldn't get too excited, though. At the most, it bought us time. We started to play games with them. It had started at one A.M. We continued to play cat and mouse for the next three hours. They sent out one group after another, and we shot them up. By now, the M16s were out of ammo, the M79 grenade launcher was out of ammo, the shotguns were out of ammo, and Pete's M16-203 was out of ammo. Our Vietnamese scout was out of bullets, as well. The only ones with bullets left were myself and Fred Keener.

"Fred, how many rounds do you have left?" I asked.

"I've got fifty rounds left. How many've you got left?"

"Let me count them," I replied, sliding down from the perch where I had my Stoner positioned. "I have seventy-five rounds left."

With a gun that fires up to nine hundred rounds a minute, it was hard to get excited about an approximate five- to ten-second burst of ammunition. It was about the amount I normally used to shoot two guys.

The hardest decision a commander has to make was what Pete Peterson now faced. Not a word was spoken, but there was a clear understanding of what was at stake. He made his decision.

"Gentlemen, we are not going to be taken alive. We are not going to be captured, and you know what happens at daylight. There are a lot of pissed-off people in the tree line. Before daylight, we're leaving!''

Riojas had the radio working weakly, but unfortunately, it didn't have much range. We were able to call Gallagher's team, but when we asked for help, we realized they were in worse shape than we were. Having taken a grenade that had wounded everybody but Roy Dean and Hooker, they were in dire need of assistance themselves.

''Look,'' Riojas told Roy Dean, ''when you guys get picked up, tell 'em where we are—tonight. Roger?''

''We can hope. Over,'' came his reply.

Pete intoned, ''Here's what we're going to do, gentlemen. In roughly forty-five minutes, the moon will set and it will be the darkest time we'll have before daybreak. I want all of us to strip down to our T-shirt and swim trunks. We are going to belly-crawl to the tree line to the west there.'' He pointed in a sweeping motion to the tree line on our left flank. ''According to my map, inside that tree line one hundred meters is a really nice canal. The tide's running out. If you hit the canal, turn right. The water is heading out to the main river. Just take that canal to the main river and wait for one of our patrol boats to pick you up. What we'll do is spread out, so by the time we're at the tree line, we are approximately fifty yards apart. It is imperative, gentlemen, that we travel slowly. We should all arrive at the tree line at the same time. Then, at my mark, we will all stand up and run like hell. Any questions?''

We knew there were guys lying in the tree line with guns pointed in our direction. Hopefully, some of us would break through and escape. Unfortunately, what were the odds we could crawl three hundred meters without being seen, jump up, and not have someone right in front of us?

I thought for a moment. ''Lieutenant, you know, I've always wondered why, when I was watching the old cowboy and Indian movies, when the Indians attacked the wagon train, were repulsed, regrouped, and then attacked again, why the cowboys didn't go pick up the guns that were lying around the Indians they killed. Why don't Keener and I crawl out with our knives and police up as many guns and ammunition as we can find? We could drag it back in here before we have to hit the tree line.''

''Good idea. Since we are leaving soon anyway, I don't think that will be a problem. We can afford ten minutes, tops.''

They'd been trying to hit us for several hours with a mortar. We would hear a *BaDouff*. Then, out in the field, the round would hit, *KaBlam!* They had what we figured was an 80-millimeter mortar. Whoever was working it was inexperienced. When they started, they were way off—perhaps 500 meters or so away. By now, the range had lessened to bctwccn 100 and 150 meters from us.

"All right, gentlemen, strip down. Leave your empty guns here."

I looked at Keener. "What happens if they assault when we're crawling out there? How do we play that?"

Keener looked at me and gave me a momentary grin. Matter-of-factly, he laid an M26 grenade down between us. "This grenade's for you and me, buddy. One holds it and the other one pulls the pin."

"Man. The only thing that pisses me off is that some dumb-ass farmer is gonna get to kill me," I said, exhaling slowly. Somehow, it was all right to die at the hands of a "specialist," but not all right to be killed by a reservist or main force VC. "Here some dirt farmer is going to get credit for toasting a SEAL."

Keener nodded, ruefully acknowledging the inevitable.

I chattered on. "I don't know if I could just pull the pin. Maybe it would be better if I pulled the pin and you threw it at them—but up high. We could run at them and at least try to take one more with us when it detonates."

"You can hear me? You can hear me?" Riojas erupted. "Hot damn!"

"Rios, d'you get somebody on the radio?" Keener blurted out.

Riojas looked up at us and nearly shouted, "Helo's inbound! Helo's inbound!"

We started laughing and clapping each other on the back. We were hugging and shouting and enjoying an unbelievable euphoric rush.

Sure enough, three minutes later came the unmistakable *Pwop Pwop Pwop Pwop* from rotors of incoming helos.

"YES!" I cheered, clenching my fist and bringing my arm downward in the universal physical expression of triumph.

"Do you want a cigarette?" asked Keener.

"Damn right I do." I took the cigarette and lit it.

"What are you guys doing?" Pete asked.

I looked at Pete and grinned. "They know we are here. We just won!"

I grabbed Keener and the two of us started jumping up and down and dancing a jig. "We win! We win!"

We must have been quite a sight. A faint glow of two lit cigarettes and two heads bobbing up and down. I guess we were lucky someone didn't shoot us in our childlike, silly exuberance.

"How do you guys know the helos have guns? What if they can't slick us out?" asked Pete.

"It doesn't matter," I retorted. "The VC don't know, either."

We looked up and saw two Navy Sea Wolf gunships. They began to unleash a torrent of rocket and large-caliber ammunition into the tree line, giving us cover. Unfortunately, Sea Wolf gunships were unable to pick us up.

They called for Army "slicks" to fly in and pick us up.

"Is it a hot LZ?" asked the inbound Army helo pilot.

"Yes. They're under fire. Over," replied one of the Sea Wolf pilots.

"Well, we can't land. Over," said the Army slick pilot.

Our hearts sank.

Another voice came over the radio, interrupting, "Outlaw two three, this is Sea Wolf one zero. Be advised that either you set down and slick those guys out, or we'll shoot you down. Over."

We started smiling again. The Navy pilot just told the Army slick pilot to set down or he was dead. He was "dead" serious. "All right," he replied, disgust evident even over the radio. "I'll go in, but I'll need cover."

"Look. If I have to, I'll drop my gun pods and go in and pick up the wounded myself. But we aren't leaving here, folks, without them. Over."

We listened to the argument on the radio. At this point, we were ecstatic and relieved at our sudden reversal of fortune. It was decided that they needed to evacuate Gallagher and his men first. The fragmentation wounds they sustained were certainly more pressing.

The helo landed in a dry paddy near Gallagher and his team. Roy Dean and Hooker provided cover fire while Gallagher painfully climbed into the helicopter. As he balanced in the doorway helping others get on, he was hit by an AK-47 round in the back, blowing him out the other side of the helo. The pilot was getting nervous. Gallagher picked himself up, and, with every ounce of strength he possessed, climbed back into the helo. His blood was everywhere. Taking his flashlight, he signaled for Hooker and the others to come on.

Immediately, the pilot started pushing the power lever forward, giving it more juice. Simultaneously, Hooker was grabbing and assisting men into the helicopter. The chopper started to lift off. Realizing Roy

Dean was not on board, Gallagher yelled to the pilot to set it down. "We got a man over to our right. We gotta wait for . . ." Gallagher was saying. There he was, multiple frag wounds and an AK-47 shell in his back, still directing the evacuation.

"Can't stay. We're leaving." The chopper lifted off the deck.

With all his strength, Gallagher pulled himself up the back of the pilot's chair. He screwed his .45 pistol into the ear of the pilot. "Set it down. NOW!"

The pilot complied. Funny the things you had to do in a war zone. Roy Dean dove on board. Immediately, the helo leapt into the sky. Navy Sea Wolf gunships buzzed around like hornets, while Hooker poured as much firepower out the door as he could.

The slick left with Gallagher's team. The primary gunship called us. "We have another slick arriving. However, we have only one gunship left—us, but we are out of rockets, and all we have left is one M-sixty machine gun. Over."

Pete grabbed the radio microphone. "Look. We're not taking serious fire. None of us are wounded. You slick it in and we'll jump on real quick."

The Huey pilot responded, "All right. I'm gonna have to come in hot, and it's touch and go."

"You touch. We're on," said Riojas. "Don't worry whether we're in or not. We'll get in."

He came over the tree line at approximately one hundred miles per hour. He pulled the nose of the chopper up in order to slow down and land. Right behind him came the Sea Wolf. The M60 unloaded into the tree line, until out of ammunition.

We piled into the helo. Keener had given me his remaining Stoner bullets, and I was the last one on. All I saw were bodies and boots. I jumped onto the skid and leaned my back against the doorway. A hand reached out and grabbed ahold of my shirt. As we lifted off, I saw tracers coming at us from the tree line. I opened up and propelled my remaining rounds at the muzzle flashes I picked up. Within seconds, I was out of bullets. We were now eighty feet off the deck.

I realized I was still not in the helo, and that it might be a good idea to get in. As I fell in, I positioned myself against the interior wall. In what seemed like a moment, total mental exhaustion enveloped me. It was five A.M., and we had been at it all night long. A flood of relief and fatigue swallowed me into darkness.

The helicopter joined the other slick and headed for the 29th Evac in Dong Tiem, which was the medical evacuation hospital for My Tho. We landed and were greeted by a senior SEAL advisor, who had heard what we had been through. He held a bottle of Jim Beam, extending it to each of us as we came off the helo. It seemed like the right thing to do at the time. This was one of the few times we drank hard liquor. It was almost medicinal after all we had just been through.

After taking a big swig, I went walking into the hospital.

"Where's Gallagher and where's Yeaw?" I demanded.

"They went into the sterile operating room there," came the reply, motioning to the right. "You can't go in there."

"Out of my way, slick."

He went to bar the door. Someone behind me hollered, "You better get out of his way."

I was in no mood for being hassled. I burst through the operating room doors. The doctors had masks and surgical gloves on, and were just about to put Gallagher under.

"Hold it!" I strolled over to Gallagher. "How're you doing, Eagle?"

He looked at me and asked, "Did you all get out?"

"We all got out. We're all okay."

"Good. I'll be okay, too."

I reached down and affectionately patted him on the shoulder. "We'll go have a drink for you!"

I walked over to Ron Yeaw. He was unconscious, lying there on the gurney. He had more holes in him than a pin cushion. He looked like a sieve.

I looked at the doctor. "Is he going to live?"

"I don't know," he replied.

"Do your best. Thanks. I'm outta here."

With that, I walked out. I went over to the SEAL Advisors building, and we all proceeded to get drunk. We passed out, and came to later that night. This particular operation just took so much out of us that we all slept through that day and well into the next morning. We got up, expecting to eat dinner, only to find it was breakfast time.

That next morning, Pete was smart enough to call back to our agents who worked in the area, and they went out and assessed the results. They returned and reported confirmed kills of 125 Viet Cong. This was, by far, the most deadly operation carried out by SEALs in terms of the number of enemy killed by so few.

Gallagher and Yeaw were medevacked out to Okinawa. We settled in to fill out our after-action reports that were to be sent up through the chain of command, to SEAL Team headquarters in Virginia, and to the Naval Unconventional Warfare offices in Washington, D.C.

After we were done, Roy Dean and I walked out onto the pier. I relished the cool river breeze ruffling through my hair, bringing with it a relaxing effect. It was a pleasant afternoon. I looked over at Roy Dean.

"Hey, Harry, what were you thinking when we went into the barracks and saw all those VC the other night? Could you believe all this started out as a simple op looking for two prisoners and six guards?" He laughed for a moment. "I still can't believe we marched in and announced, 'Hey! Listen up! All you guys! Put your hands up!' '' He laughed some more.

"All you guys! Put your hands up." Everything seemed different, somehow.

CHAPTER 9

LIFE'S LITTLE BURDENS

SEVERAL DAYS HAD ELAPSED SINCE WE RETURNED FROM THE medevac unit where Gallagher was first treated. The word going around was Gallagher would receive the Navy Cross for his heroism, and would likely accompany Ron Yeaw back to the States. It was mid-December 1967.

There were two events occurring simultaneously. First, we were performing well. Concurrent with that, however, was the fact we were going through personnel. We had just gotten two new replacement guys wounded, and there was no telling whether they or Gallagher would make it back.

The environment was changing. As our operations had intensified, SEAL teams were sustaining casualties. On the one hand, our familiarity with the jungle and our nighttime surroundings boosted our confidence, causing our operations to take on a more fatalistic "Screw it, let's push the limits and see how far we can go" mentality. Our skill levels were significantly higher. On the other hand, people—good people—were being killed. Dealing with death for the first time—up close and intensely personal—was never easy.

Some of the older guys had quite the opposite reaction. This was most apparent with Warrant Officer Charlie Watson. Alpha and Bravo teams continually made contact night after night. Sometimes we had to search for it, sometimes it found us. Contact with the enemy really was not hard to achieve. Conversely, Charlie's team rarely made enemy contact.

We couldn't understand this. Our mental attitudes were intensely aggressive, a cool-under-fire assurance that we could own the jungle. Sure, we were blown off the beach a few times and had to run to escape against enemy forces that we could not effectively engage, but we had contingency plans we deployed that worked well.

"Poor Charlie's team. I can't believe their bad luck at not finding any Viet Cong," I said casually to Keener over lunch.

Keener looked up at me, a pained expression clouding his face. "I'm not sure why, but on some of the ops I've been on with him, all Charlie's doing is getting off the boat, moving in fifty yards, and setting up. It's like he's not sure where he should go—like he's having a difficult time making up his mind."

As fate would have it, several nights later Charlie's team was in need of another guy as one of their guys was sick. I volunteered.

After lunch, I mustered with Charlie's team to the briefing room. "Harry will be your point man tonight."

We moved inland after getting off the boat. Sure enough, after I had gone fifty yards, Charlie gave the order to set up.

"All right," I replied, nodding approval.

After no more than what seemed half an hour, Charlie stepped up next to me. "Let's move back toward the river," he whispered.

"No problem." I turned the team around and took six or seven steps back along the trail from where we came. Suddenly, I stopped. I leaned forward and craned my head forward. I motioned frantically for Charlie to come up alongside of me.

"I hear something. Straight ahead," I said, motioning worriedly in front of us. "Can you hear them? I can't tell how many, but they're coming straight toward us. We better move or we'll get in contact. What do you want to do?" I asked.

He indicated he wanted to move. We turned around and moved back the other way. I had the team almost running. We came to a fork in the road, where the decision was to either move inland or back toward the river. I held up.

"Look! Over in the tree line I think I saw some movement. Which way?"

Charlie pointed farther inland, away from contact with the imaginary enemy. So inland we went. For two hours, I played this game with Charlie. Down the trail. Stop. Into the canal, out of the canal. Run some more. We were all sweating profusely and breathing hard when Charlie gave the order to stop.

"Exactly where are we?" asked Charlie.

As point man, it was my responsibility to keep track of our location as closely as possible. I was an excellent cartographer (map reader), and had gotten very good at mentally keeping a running tab of where we were.

"We are approximately two thousand meters from the river," I reported in an innocent tone.

Charlie's eyes went wide with a mixture of fear and anger. His chest, already heaving, seemed to stop moving as his shoulders slumped forward. He leaned his head back, looked upward, and shook his head back and forth in disgust.

"Well, there's only one way out. I'll lead you back to the river. It's about time to go."

With that, we headed back in the direction of the river. It was now three in the morning. As we were about to move out of the tree line, I saw someone coming up the trail. He was carrying a gun and walking straight toward us. I gave the signal to hold up. We all stepped off the trail. I decided to do my knife routine. I slid my gun around my back and unsheathed my knife.

Charlie was standing right next to me, staring at the silent figure thirty yards away. He leaned his head toward me and whispered, "Prisoner."

That figures. That really figures. It was now my turn to be disgusted. In Pete's team—my team—we had captured more than thirty prisoners. It was early December 1967, and late the past week I was operating with Pete in a zone northeast of My Tho. We were set up for an ambush along a trail that was reported to have heavy VC traffic within the last month. Sure enough, we were not disappointed. Unfortunately, armed VC came by at a rate of one every ten minutes. Pete would look at me and instruct me to take them prisoner. The first guy came along. I grabbed him, put him in a choke hold, threw him in the ditch, and told him to sit still. Through a variety of Vietnamese phrases, English, and hand gestures, he got the point. If he ran, he died.

Minutes later, another gun-toting VC came along. I stood up, grabbed him, and deftly subdued him. In the next hour, I captured a total of ten VC. I was sitting in the ditch surrounded by ten VC—none of whom were tied up—when I looked over at Pete.

"Hey, Pete! It's getting real crowded down here. What are we going to do with these guys?"

Pete thought for a moment. "Why don't you take them to the river and put them on the boat. We'll wait for you."

After tying them together with some string, I walked ten Viet Cong prisoners all the way to the river by myself. The STAB pulled in, and I directed all ten Viet Cong to climb aboard. "These guys are all Viet Cong. Take them back to the main boat and keep an eye on them."

The two guys on the boat were not too sure about this. "Jeez, Constance, we don't even have a gun. Why don't you come with us?"

"I got to get back. Don't worry, it's not a big deal. They'll do whatever you tell them to."

"No, man. We'll get killed! They'll see that we don't have a gun and then they'll jump us and kill us."

"Okay. Here. You can guard them with this," I said, handing them my 9-millimeter pistol, "Just don't let them get away!"

"Oh, thank you, man!"

Now, I glanced over at Charlie, shrugged my shoulders, and knelt in the shadows. *You want him taken prisoner? No problem, Charlie.*

I put my knife away and waited. *If he wants a prisoner, I'll give him a prisoner.* When the VC was right in front of me, I reached out and grabbed him. I held him by his throat, administering a textbook choke hold. When he went limp, I dragged him over to Charlie and sat him next to him. Charlie tied his hands behind his back. "Let's get going," he said.

I started moving us to the river, for which Charlie was relieved. No sooner had we gone another hundred meters or so than we heard people talking. I moved forward and looked through the bushes to survey the scene. There were two hooches off the trail to the immediate right. There were several men with guns, as well as a number of civilians. To the left of the courtyard was a mama san cooking breakfast over an open flame.

I signaled Charlie that there were enemy VC here and we should assault. (This was done by taking my index and middle finger, making a V, and pointing to my two eyes—I saw something. Then, I mimicked pulling the trigger of a gun, which indicated *bad guys* as they were the only ones who had guns in a free-fire zone.) Charlie vigorously shook his head from side to side, panicking. I walked back to him.

"Let's assault," I said, in a hushed tone.

"No, man! Don't make contact. Don't make contact!"

I looked at Riojas, the corpsman, standing behind him, who was rolling his eyes. "Hey, Riojas, you want to assault?"

"Yeah."

I turned to Charlie and said, "Rios and I will assault. You watch the prisoner. We'll be right back."

Charlie bit his lower lip, giving the appearance of pensive assessment and evaluation. He nodded his head to concur.

Riojas trained as a Marine before becoming a corpsman. If ever there were unsung heroes, it would have to be corpsmen in SEAL teams. They didn't go through the training SEALs did, yet had to perform flawlessly with their team. They were indispensible.

"You ready, Rios?"

He nodded. We moved into position and assaulted. Our guns blazed as we fanned the houses and perimeter with heavy fire. The civilians hit the deck. We brought our aim upon those with guns. Our eyes searched the shadows for unseen enemies. Riojas, in a classic Marine assault, had his M14 spewing forth a steady torrent of bullets. Our tracers eerily lit up the grounds, adding to the flickering flames cast about by the cooking fire. Riojas shot with his M14 positioned so his right hand was on the trigger and his left hand was free. His left hand deftly jerked a grenade from his web harness belt. Pulling the pin with his mouth, without missing a step or slowing his fire, he lobbed the grenade into the hooch where two VC stood moments before.

KA-BOOOM! Screams pierced the air. Just as quickly as it began, it was over. We killed two, while several others escaped out the back.

One of the escapees ran out behind the hooches and into the jungle. He curved to the left and, without realizing it, headed directly toward our team. Charlie saw him and started shooting. The VC dove into the ditch. While Charlie was reaching to release and reinsert a new magazine into his M16, the prisoner under his foot sensed an opportunity to escape. In a flash, he was on his feet. With his hands tied behind his back, he ran off into the jungle. Charlie turned and watched helplessly as our ex-prisoner descended into the darkness.

Two minutes later, I was in Charlie's face. "What happened?" I demanded.

"What's it look like happened? He escaped." Charlie paused, then looked at me. "Watch it, Constance. I'm the team leader and I will not be spoken to like that by you or anybody else!"

I was puzzled. We were all here to fight. Most of us were hitting the enemy hard and with vicious ferocity. To my way of thinking, anything less opened up a greater probability of being killed. Slowly, over the past weeks and months, Charlie Watson seemed to change.

"Dammit, Constance. When you operate with my team you will operate as I see fit. Smart-aleck stunts like you pulled tonight can get people killed."

When we returned to the boat, Charlie went to Pete and complained. "There's no way I want Harry on my team. He's going to get us all killed."

Pete smiled. "Aw come on, Charlie. You look fine to me. I'll talk to him for you."

I didn't know if it was animosity or an ornery streak in me. All I knew was that I kept volunteering to go out with Charlie's team. Charlie openly despised me. I began to find it humorous.

It wasn't long before, in mid-December, things came to a head. I was with Pete. Charlie and his team were to work in concert with us. We were to insert from the My Tho River into a hotly contested area. Charlie's team was to insert fifteen hundred meters farther east. In tandem, both teams were to travel north one thousand meters, turn right, traverse another one thousand meters, then turn and make our way south, back to the river. Sort of an upside-down U, parallel pattern operation.

We traveled northward. After heading east (turning right), we made contact with the enemy. Bump and run, bump and run. Several hours later, we started our movement back to the river. It was three A.M., and we were approximately two hundred meters from the river when we received a call from Charlie's team. They'd moved very slowly, and were just then making their first right turn.

Pete thought for a moment, then decided we'd better head back and rendezvous with Charlie. "Let's go see if we can't hook up with them and get them outta there."

I had a choice. I could turn and backtrack up the north-south trail we had been on before heading west, or I could take a westward trail and then go north. I decided to go west.

Suddenly, someone in back screamed, "Grenade—get down!"

We hit the deck as a grenade went off thirty yards to our right. *KA-BOOOM!*

Obviously, we were being stalked by Viet Cong, in an attempt to ambush us. They were on the trail we'd just left.

Whew! Good thing we didn't head back up the northward trail we were on!

I looked at Pete and he signaled, *Get us out of here!*

I broke into a quick jaunt. The trail we were on ran almost parallel to the other trail before turning west, meaning we were very close to the VC—and moving closer. Fortunately, not one of us had fired a shot. The grenade they threw was a best-guess attempt at figuring out where we were at. They knew we were close. Should it not hit us, the Viet Cong hoped, we would fire indiscriminately in the direction of the explosion. This undisciplined, gut-level reaction was understandable, but deadly. Our tracers would have given our location away, and they would have surrounded us. Keeping low and silent, we reached the westward turn. I increased our pace, racing the team farther westward. After about twenty minutes, we broke into a clearing. The jungle just stopped, leaving us exposed. We were on the edge of a big, two-thousand-meter, rectangular rice paddy. Worse yet, the sun was just beginning to cascade its rays throughout the morning skies. Pretty, but no friend at this particular moment.

Sixty meters ahead was a creek, running north-south. On the other side of the creek was an eight-foot-high dike. In what seemed like just a moment, we all slid down into the creek. Quickly, we scanned the rear flank. Pete glassed the tree line behind us for VC pursuit. Not seeing any, we scampered up and over the dike, back into the rice paddy. This time, Pete glassed the horizon ahead of us. He fixated on a point diagonally to our right, near the northeast corner of the rice paddy.

"There's Charlie's team. They're moving south through the paddy."

All of a sudden, the tree line nearest them erupted in flames. There must have been fifty to sixty guys pouring a fusillade of bullets at Charlie and his team. We watched the ambush unfold, tracers streaking straight for them like angry hornets. The team hit the deck. Roy Dean had his hat shot off his head and Mikey Boynton got his heel shot off his boot. The dirt kicked up around them, creating a dust cloud. They were lying behind a berm that was, at most, twelve to eighteen inches high. At once, from out of the dust came Charlie, running as hard as he could go, away from the tree line, toward the river. It was a wonder he was not hit, as bullets splattered up dirt all around him.

"Dammit!" exclaimed Pete. "He's got the radio! He's got the damn radio!"

This was serious. When your team was pinned down under heavy enemy fire—as Charlie's team was—it was the radioman's job to call for helo support. It was imperative he stayed there in order to vector in helos to the correct location. In the misty early light of dawn, misinformation could not only imperil the beleaguered company, but could also lead to the helos' being blindsided.

Pete got on the radio and started hollering. He was yelling into the mike. "Charlie! STOP! Stop running! Rejoin your team! You have got to save your team! You have got to call in support!"

Charlie, without stopping, pulled his mike and screamed back, "Enemy fire is too intense! I'll get to the boat and direct helos from there!"

Pete kept yelling for Charlie to stop, but with no luck.

I knelt on one knee and watched the whole thing unfold. Seething, Pete slammed his fist down. "I can't believe it! We've got to go save them."

Pete pointed to the northeastern perimeter of the rice paddy. "I need you guys to assault from the right—let's defuse their ambush."

Curtis Ashton and I took off running along the backside (western side) of the dike, allowing the eight-foot dike to keep us from being seen by the ambushers. Unfortunately, we also had to be wary of enemy movement in the tree line to our right (where we had just emerged). Keeping low against the dike, we crested the northernmost dike without detection. Ten minutes later, five hundred meters farther west, we were in position at the junction of the northern edge of the east-west dike and the western edge of the north-south dike. I linked several bandoleers of bullets together in order to give the appearance of significant firepower to convince the VC we were a large force arriving on the scene. Ashton carried his M60, a more powerful, louder, and more destructive shell than my Stoner.

We opened up into the tree line. Quickly, some of the enemy fire was diverted and redirected at us. We then really poured it on. Several banana trees fell over, cut down by the scythelike delivery of bullets.

Sensing a lessening of enemy fire, Roy Dean and the rest of the team got up, crouched as low as possible, and ran in a southwest direction until they were able to crest a dike and get their bearings. We provided cover fire until they were safe. Hastily, we backed away from our position in case the Viet Cong made a pincer movement to attack us from a parallel location in the tree line adjacent to where we were hiding. We ran back to the east.

Badadadadadap! Badadadadadap! Bullets fell harmlessly ten yards to our left. VC in the trees to the left; VC in the trees to our right! Take your pick. We hopped back and forth over the central dike that split the rice paddy depending upon whose bullets were closer. Fortunately, we soon were beyond their range.

An hour later, we met back at the boat. The mood was subdued, a mix of fatigue and appreciation for narrowly averting disaster. Charlie was in an "admin" mode, sitting in the galley belowdecks with all his gear off.

Pete was livid. As we climbed aboard our Mike boat, Pete instructed all of us to go to the bow of the boat. He walked over to the stairs leading to the room belowdecks. His voice shaking angrily, Pete seethed, "Charlie, get out here now."

He went to the stern of the boat, behind the coxswain's mast. From the back of the boat we couldn't see them. We all wondered what Pete would do to Charlie. You just didn't desert your men. Especially SEALs. Pete unleashed a tongue-lashing I didn't think he was capable of. Ever the diplomatic one, Pete rarely went off on anyone. But he let Charlie have it. Pete was absolutely irate Charlie had left his men, that he had the radio, and that he disregarded orders to stop. Poor Charlie. He was thoroughly disgraced in front of his men.

I leaned over to Mikey Boynton. "How are you guys going to operate with Charlie now?"

"I don't know. I really don't know."

At the next warning order, Pete reported that, after slightly more than a month, Gallagher was coming back. All twelve of us lit up.

"All right! Eagle's back in town!"

"Hooyah!"

We were thrilled. If anyone had the right to, with dignity, head back home, he did. Fortunately, he rejoined us.

"All right, all right. Stop all this mush crap. Do you think I'm going to lay around letting you derelicts take an extended Christmas vacation? I couldn't stand the thought of you assholes operating without me."

It was early January 1968, and everything was hitting on all eight cylinders. Our intelligence was excellent. As a result, we were starting to make strategic "hits" on targeted individuals. We carried out a number of assassinations of high-ranking Viet Cong officers in their beds without alerting sentries posted out in front of the hooch. Besides that, we were able to supply other military units (Navy, Army, and Marines) with details and information that were extremely valuable to them. We started getting requests from other Naval units in the area. For example, several big ships anchored offshore were being harassed by VC sampans attempting to ambush boats leaving the mother ship. The request was to have a team of SEALs assigned to them. PBR units informed us of other hot spots around the delta where patrol boats were being shot at while attempting to transit the rivers. Rapidly, we were getting a tremendous amount of message traffic requesting assistance. *We need SEALs here, we need SEALs there*—all of a sudden, everybody needed SEALs. Word of our success was getting around. When we came off an operation, we had to generate the requisite reports about what we had done. Everyone up the chain of command had the opportunity to read them. The requests for assistance indicated to us our efforts weren't going unnoticed.

We had a chain of command within the TO (theater of operation). Lieutenant Pete Peterson was required to report to the senior Naval officer in the region. The senior Naval officer with jurisdiction over our SEAL team was a Navy captain, Captain Gray.

Shortly after arriving in-country, Captain Gray let Lieutenant Peterson know that no SEAL team had ever captured a ''crew-serve'' weapon in Vietnam. ''I have a standing offer that any unit that captures one of these weapons will receive a case of Scotch that I will personally deliver.''

Shortly after our resupply, we received word of an enemy weapons cache approximately thirty miles from My Tho. We hit it hard one night and captured a huge volume of weaponry. Among the items captured were two Communist Chinese machine guns classified as crew-serve. Pete was elated.

He sent a short message to Captain Gray.

FROM: Platoon Commander, 7th Platoon, SEAL Team Two, My Tho
TO: Captain Gray, Commander, Naval Forces, South Vietnam

Dear Sir,

Weapon is ours. . . . Scotch is yours. . . . Let's trade!

Regards,
Seventh Platoon

Unfortunately, Captain Gray got upset. I don't know if it was because we had the audacity to suggest that he owed us, or what. It was common knowledge he had placed the offer on the table. Why he got upset, no one knew. We could care less about the weapon . . . the loss of the Scotch had us all pissed off.

Two weeks later, we were required to attend a "top-secret" meeting, called by Captain Gray, to be held in Can Tho. As he was the commander, attendance was mandatory.

By now, our SEAL Team platoon had been in-country four months, the longest time of any in the region. We carried ourselves with a swagger and confidence that came from the thorough success of our mandate as a SEAL platoon. There was a brand-new SEAL platoon there at the meeting as well. While they all had proper military attire and haircuts, we came in jeans, ragged hair, and a devil-may-care attitude.

Captain Gray's assistant stood and walked over to the map. With a pointer in his right hand, he began. "Gentlemen, we've been getting some serious intelligence lately about a Viet Cong battalion operating with impunity in this area here." He struck the map with the pointer and made a swirling motion surrounding a rather large, densely forested region on the map. "Captain Gray has looked it over and has an operational plan that we are going to implement starting tomorrow morning. Captain Gray is now going to describe the facets of the operation and what you are going to do."

Captain Gray rose and walked to the podium. He smiled and said, "We need you SEALs to parachute into this area here, locate the VC battalion, radio their position, and then get out of the way of a B-fifty-two air strike I will personally call in."

Pete's face fell, a look of serious calculation rippling across his brow. Already knowing the answer, he leaned over to Gallagher. "What do you think? Can we make it work?"

The VC battalion was operating in an area known as the Nam Can forest. Similar to the VC battalion operation we were involved in two months earlier, there was no way they could be detected from the air because of the densely forested, triple canopy of trees. The top-layer trees were between 250 and 300 feet tall. The second, middle-layer trees were between 150 and 200 feet tall, while the third layer was up to 100 feet tall. Somehow, we were to find a way to parachute into and through the trees to the ground below. We were to do this without support, without being detected, and without means of being extracted. This was scary. We looked back and forth at one another, realizing the dangers inherent in such an operation. We were expert parachutists. To land in the treetops safely, cut yourself free of your chute, manage to climb down to the ground, then start scouting an area we knew very little about, this really had our full attention.

As Captain Gray continued to detail his plan, Gallagher stood up. Captain Gray stopped. He paused and stared disdainfully at Gallagher. "Excuse me, Chief, I am not finished with my brief. Sit down."

Gallagher looked at him. "Captain, you gotta be shittin' me. This is the dumbest thing I've ever heard. I am not going out on an op like this."

With that, Gallagher walked slowly toward the door.

Captain Gray retorted, "You will do what I damn well tell you to do! I am a Naval captain. You are only an enlisted man. SIT YOUR ASS DOWN!"

The room got real quiet. Gallagher stopped. With deliberate motion, he swiveled his head to look at Captain Gray. "Volunteer in, volunteer out. Color my ass gone." And out he went.

I regarded Gallagher as my "sea daddy." I jumped to my feet. With an aw-shucks expression, I looked at Captain Gray and shrugged. "I'm with him."

One right after another, each one of us got up and left.

Poor Pete Peterson. He was suddenly in a position of trying to save his career. He was on his feet trying to explain to Captain Gray there must be some sort of misunderstanding, that he was sorry for our behavior, and that the last time we were involved with a battalion, Gallagher had nearly been killed and that maybe that was why . . .

All the while, Captain Gray was ranting and raving over how we all would be brought up on court-martial charges, and how dare we defy him, the ranking Naval officer in charge of the entire South Vietnam theater of operation. . . .

Like I said, poor Pete.

There had been very few times that I had seen Gallagher so visibly upset. That afternoon was one of those times. He was furious that we were to be sacrificed for the sake of an officer's attempt to become the next George S. Patton or Dwight D. Eisenhower.

Pete came in an hour later. "Captain Gray is pissed. But, I have figured out a way to smooth out his feathers."

When Naval officers came into a war zone, such as Vietnam, they needed to earn a combat medal in order to further their careers. When they returned home, they wanted to show themselves deserving of being promoted. They couldn't do this with their feet sitting on top of a desk. Chair riders got plenty of splinters in their butts, but very few promotions.

"Captain Gray wants to know if we would like to go with him on a Silver Star operation. I told him we would lead the way. C'mon, you guys," Pete said, with a "help me out here, guys" look at Gallagher. "This is a good way for us to get out of trouble."

When Pete asked us for help, we could not turn him down.

Two nights later, we were instructed to go downriver. At about nine-thirty P.M., we got into the STAB and took off. The driver dropped us off, and we began patrolling, looking for VC.

About an hour later, we ambushed three guys walking along a trail at the river's edge. Two of them carried guns. The My Tho River was about thirty meters to our immediate right. Since we were in its flood-plain, the vegetation on either side of the trail was extremely dense. I could stand two meters off the trail and go totally undetected by those passing by. The three VC walked right into our ambush. We stepped out onto the trail and shot them at almost point-blank range. Two seconds of frenetic chaos and three men were dead. *Too bad, guys. Wrong place, wrong time; you lose.*

We radioed Pete that we'd made contact. "What? No, it wasn't any problem. We shot and killed three Viet Cong. We have two guns and a knapsack containing various and assorted documents. Any further instructions?"

"Could you find a sampan?"

"Well, I suppose. Why?" I inquired.

"Look, see if you can find a sampan. Call us back when you do."

I walked quietly along the riverbank, hoping to find a sampan. *What in the world did we need a sampan for?*

Another 150 yards downriver, I came across a small hooch setting back off the riverbank by 15 to 20 yards. Adjacent to the hooch was a small inlet canal, with a sampan just sitting there. *There's my sampan.* So I "procured" it. I quietly floated it into the river, then dragged it back upstream to where Keener, Ashton, and three dead VC were waiting. Once again, we called back on the radio for instructions. Little did I know that I was about to become involved in one of the more stupid charades I saw while in Vietnam.

After going through the routine of giving all the required call signs yet again, Keener said, "Be advised, we have three dead guys and a sampan. Now what do you want us to do?"

"Put the VC aboard the sampan. Stand by until you hear the engines of our river boat. When you hear us, let us know so we can tell exactly where you're at."

We waited. Minutes later, we heard the rumble of diesel engines. We contacted them once again. "We hear you."

Pete came on the radio and said, "Be advised, Captain Gray is manning the forward twin .fifty-caliber machine guns. Over."

What had happened was that Naval intelligence believed there was a main force VC battalion crossing the river tonight. Supposedly, they were heavily armed, carried weapons and supplies, and were using numerous sampans. Captain Gray was personally leading the assault in attacking this large Viet Cong force by shooting the twin machine guns mounted at the front of the boat. Captain Gray would lead his men into battle with the enemy!

Captain Gray looked over at Lieutenant Peterson. "All right, Lieutenant, I am ready to engage the enemy."

Pete called on the radio once again. "Take the sampan with the three dead guys on it. Push it into the middle of the river. Then, when you do, get the hell out of there because we are going to start shooting."

"What?"

"Push it out and get out of the way."

The three of us pushed the sampan out into the middle of the river. We scurried out of the water, up and over the bank, and into a ditch on the other side. Moments later, Captain Gray opened up on the sampan. It was riddled unmercifully. Tracers skipped across the water. Other gunners on board opened up on the left and right flanks. Bullets went everywhere.

After five minutes of shooting, flares were launched, illuminating the night sky. Captain Gray called for a cease-fire. He then ordered a PBR forward to check the sampan. They radioed back to Captain Gray's big boat. "Captain Gray, there are three dead in the sampan. All other enemy activity has ceased. Congratulations!"

"Right," came his reply. "Let's return to home base. We have disrupted the enemy crossing."

Upon returning, Captain Gray's aides created this write-up of the operation.

Be advised that Captain Gray intercepted three hundred main force VC crossing the river. He engaged the enemy without regard for life, confirmed three killed, and disrupted the enemy crossing.

The aides, along with Lieutenant Peterson, signed that this was indeed what occurred. Captain Gray received a Navy Silver Star.

It was a difficult thing to swallow. When a high-ranking officer would initiate an operation primarily designed to make himself look good, with the potential for men being killed as a result, then I called it a travesty. This grated on me more than most.

After Charlie had deserted his team, we began giving him a lot of grief. Guys came in after an operation and told Charlie about it. They purposely made it out to be more gory, violent, and obscene than it was—then pretended to revel in the macabre. "We killed ten tonight. Stabbed most of them. You should have seen them bleed. . . ." The more we exaggerated, the more flustered Charlie became.

One night, it was my turn. We'd been involved in a bump-and-run gun battle with the Viet Cong. We realized we were in a contested area, and had made repeated contact. The VC were all over, so we mostly attempted to make our way back to the river. We may have been brave, but we weren't stupid. We kept as quiet as we could, almost in sight of the river, when we came upon a hooch. The Vietnamese scout working with us firmly grabbed my arm. He pulled at my arm in an attempt to tell me something.

"VC. VC," he whispered excitedly, pointing at the hooch. "VC."

I passed it on to Pete. "The house is loaded. Possible VC leader."

Pete thought for a moment, then whispered back, "Sneak around back. Let's take them out with knives as quickly as we can and keep moving. We want to keep the noise to a minimum."

We had VC shooting 200 to 300 yards away in attempts to locate us. We knew they were on our trail, but weren't real close.

I moved alongside the hooch. Leaning my Stoner up against the wall, I cut an opening through the thatch into the room. It was almost pitch-black. I could barely see what looked like a bunker or mound of some sort on the other side of the room. Next to this was probably a table, as I caught a slight gleam from a lamp base seated on it. Silently, I moved toward the bunker. Unexpectedly, I bumped into something. I reached my hand down and felt what appeared to be a bed. Suddenly, the bed squeaked, and it was painfully clear that it was occupied. My right hand reached out to steady myself, landing on a web belt containing ammo clips.

Oh, crap. I cannot see to save my neck and this is serious!

Whoever was on the bed rolled over to where his shoulder touched the back of my hand. He jumped at the sensation of touching me, letting out a startled yelp in the process. I grabbed onto his arm and plunged my knife into his chest—or at least where I perceived his chest to be. The blade struck a rib.

"UUUmmph!" he gasped. All hell broke loose as my intended victim started swinging wildly for his life. Screaming desperately, he valiantly struck blindly in my direction.

I pulled back the knife and viciously stabbed at him again. This time, I sunk the blade deep into his stomach cavity. He contorted his body, his arms flailing wildly to strike me. His fists struck my sides. I retracted the knife once again, and he half jumped, half flung himself at me. We collapsed onto the floor. He was desperately trying to grab for my eyes and face, while I was groping—stabbing blindly for his chest. His chest was heaving, and I stabbed yet again, this time into his throat. Immediately, the gurgling sound of air and fluid being drawn into his chest as he gasped for breath indicated I had finally hit the mark. Blood spewed all over me. I was sweating, my heart pounding, and my head and upper body were soaked in sticky, warm blood. His screaming caused a commotion outside, with people shouting. One of our M16s issued a protective blast at enemy outside. *I've got to get out of here!*

Without warning, someone jumped on my back, their knees slamming into my shoulder blades. Their face was against my back and their hands around my throat.

OOOWWWW! How many are there? How many are there? I can't see!

The person bit into my neck and shoulder. My right hand was grasping the handle of the knife. My left hand went flailing up and down, attempting to stave off falling to the floor. I let go with my left hand and reached for the person on my back. I grabbed a handful of hair and, with all my might, pulled the person off me, over my back and onto the floor in front of me. Deftly, I plunged the knife quickly and deeply into my assailant. Three quick piercing blows, and he was still.

Shaken, I gingerly felt for a pulse on either of the two Viet Cong.

The first man was dead. I reached for the second one. Suddenly, I realized that the second Viet Cong was a woman. I struggled to my feet. I was covered in warm, sticky, and nauseatingly sweet-smelling blood. It was all over my head, face, arms, and shirt. I felt the bite mark and scratches.

I have got to get out of here! I hope I haven't taken anything greater than surface wounds.

An oppressive stifling heat compressed in upon my lungs. I sheathed my knife, grabbed my gun, and raced to where the team was to rendezvous.

Everything happened so fast. I battled with my mind. *Deal with it, Constance. You have to stay cool. But I just killed, in as barbaric a fashion as possible, two people. Most likely a man and a wife. What was it that unnerved me? Was it the heat and the blood, or the darkness and being jumped from behind....* A sudden flurry of gunfire shook me out of my reverie. I fled out of the hooch, my thoughts racing as I moved along the trail and into the nipa palm at the river's edge.

We called for the boat and an emergency extraction as we were hearing voices all around us in the reeds and fog hovering alongside the river. We were all breathing hard, trying to gauge the shadows and breeze-induced movements all around us. While we waited, Riojas looked at me with a quizzical look.

"Man, you look awful. Are you okay?"

"Yes. I think so," I said, gently rubbing the tender area where I'd been bitten.

Pete was staring at me now. I quietly recounted what happened.

Curtis Ashton looked at me and smiled. "You know, Chicken Charlie is on the boat tonight."

Suddenly, my spirits heightened as the idea of a new challenge formed in my mind.

"You're kidding."

"No. He went out tonight, but he was mostly just operating the radio. If I were you, I'd make a big deal of what just happened. See if you can't get Chicken Charlie sick."

This was the new game recently. We boarded the boat and quickly went down below to the well deck.

I hollered to the corpsman. "Corpsman. Corpsman, I think I've been hurt. I think I've been stabbed. Hurry."

Everyone came into the area where I was situated. They were all curious as to the extent of my injuries. The corpsman came over and turned on several positional lights similar to the lights used in a doctor's office to observe an injury or illness. He shined them on me. I was caked in drying blood.

I looked at Charlie. His mouth was agape.

My light blond hair was thoroughly doused in blood. I knew I looked scary. I acted the part. My breathing intensified. Roy Dean, as if on cue, leaned over and put his arm around me. In a melodramatic fashion, he frowned with concern and said, "Harry, tell me, how bad was it."

This was my moment. In the stark light of the ship's first aid station, my face took on a ghoulish appearance, like someone with a flashlight shining on their face while telling ghost stories around a campfire.

"Oh. It was . . . it was bad. I mean, really terrible. I don't know that I should tell anybody what happened. But, oh, it was terrible."

With a little coaxing from the guys, I continued, becoming more fiendish with each word. "I snuck into this house. There was this man and woman there. I killed the man and grabbed the woman by the hair and dragged her outside. I began to cut her up . . ."

The rest of the guys were starting to snicker. I stopped. I stared at Charlie intently so that I didn't break my concentration and start to laugh. With sinister delight, I described in detail how I went in and got another girl and began to cut her up. My face was now less than two feet away from Charlie's, and he was getting whiter and whiter. The guys were proffering other details, as if they were there. Charlie was starting to look ill.

I pressed my advantage. "I think I have her liver here in my pocket." I fumbled in my pocket as if in macabre glee. "It has got to be here somewhere."

"I can't find it. Hey, would one of you guys check my pack? It's got to be in my pack."

With that, Charlie had had it. He grabbed his stomach and walked quickly from the room. Immediately, guys started clapping. They all knew it was a ruse—everyone, that is, except Charlie.

We'd all been telling Charlie stories of our escapades in the jungle for several weeks now. Whether because of the visual sight that I made or a combination of my appearance and my storytelling, Charlie bought it hook, line, and sinker. He was convinced we were deranged.

Pete looked at me, a smirk on his face as he shook his head from side to side. ''That was bad. I can't believe you said that.''

Charlie spoke with Pete and told him that he could no longer go out. He ''simply could not operate with such uncouth animals''—such as me.

Yeah, right. What a weak excuse not to operate. We might have been animals, but at least we didn't stink of fear.

CHAPTER 10

FLIP OF THE COIN

SHORTLY AFTER CAPTAIN GRAY LED US INTO BATTLE AND WON his medal for killing a sampan, his attitude toward the SEALs improved markedly. Our dubious good fortune at being back in Captain Gray's good graces resulted in more and more orders from headquarters for SEAL involvement in Naval maneuvers. We were none too happy about it. As TDY (temporary duty), we were assigned to that specific theater of operation of which Captain Gray was the commander. He had control of all of the toys in his jurisdiction. Since it was his sandbox, he could play with the toys any way he wanted. He told the boats where to go, the helicopters where to go, personnel where to go—and all we wanted was to tell *him* where to go.

The guerrilla and psychological warfare that we had been inflicting upon the Viet Cong was bearing fruit. We'd become so effective at these operations that we were taking cards—business cards—with the caption COMPLIMENTS OF THE MEN WITH THE GREEN FACES written in Vietnamese on them. We left them in the bedrooms and on the bodies of Viet Cong officials we were sent to assassinate. In the morning, the wife or bodyguard would find the VC official dead, find our card, and realize they had not heard a thing. I captured a handwritten sign saying, in Vietnamese, BEWARE OF THE MEN WITH GREEN

129

FACES. From every indication, we were exacting a heavy psychological toll upon the VC.

So, there we were, the pride of the Navy, and Captain Gray wanted to play with us. This one particular op called for us to travel all the way down the Mekong River to the ocean. We were to insert onto the beach and go find the enemy. And I quote, "go find the enemy."

We were given no intelligence other than "reported enemy activity in the region." We were basically going out in the middle of nowhere, being dropped off, and left to walk around calling, "Yoo-hoo, enemy. Where are you?"

"We are to go look for any VC we can find," Pete told us, straight-faced and matter-of-factly, at our warning order conference.

"Why?" I retorted. "Are they lost?"

It had gotten so bad that when Pete got up to discuss the newest warning order, someone from the back of the room responded with "Who's the jerk who thought up this one?"

Then someone else would respond, "This sounds like a Gray op!"

Pete, ever the politician, invariably took the focus away from anger at being asked to do these crazy maneuvers and placed it on fulfilling our duty. "Gentlemen, pay attention. We could run into contact. We gotta be ready."

This was why Pete was such a good officer. He always upheld what the front office desired. Because of our respect for him, we did whatever he asked.

We disembarked and inserted into the surf zone. Furtively, we moved onto the beach. Directly inland and behind the sandbar was a mangrove swamp similar to those found in the Caribbean. Interspersed in and among the mangrove swamp was a nipa palm thicket. It was extremely slow going.

"Man, where's Humphrey Bogart? Where's the *African Queen*?" asked Keener as we bivouacked through the inhospitable terrain.

There were leeches and mosquitoes. Reeds so sharp that when we pushed them aside we got razorlike cuts. And, there was enough swamp ooze—putrid, stagnant swamp slime—that in as little as five minutes, we could be mistaken for a distant relative of the Creature from the Black Lagoon.

We hit the beach at eight P.M. By three A.M., we had barely covered two thousand meters. The mud was above our calves, and the water was up to our diaphragms. Our guns were balanced on our shoulders, as we couldn't afford to leave them in the water all night. Then there was the scum. Every now and again, we would sink into the mud and the brackish scum would get on our faces. Boy, did it smell terrible! Besides the smell, even worse was the fact we couldn't be quiet. Slosh slosh slosh . . . twigs and mangrove branches breaking; we had no problem making plenty of noise. As we moved through the bands of reeds and nipa palm, our hands repeatedly parting the stalks before us (most were an average of ten to fifteen feet tall), it sounded like someone traversing through dense shrubbery. We were tired, we stunk, and we were in the middle of a futile operation. . . .

After hours of struggling through the underbrush, we suddenly came upon a man-made dike. As we climbed out of the water, the reeds and nipa palm still were densely overgrown above our heads. The land rose until we climbed a small, mounded earthen berm. To our amazement, above the dike the nipa palm was tied together with fishing line and formed a canopy. It extended as far as we could see, providing cover from airborne surveillance for anyone traveling on the trail. We'd just stumbled upon a man-made tunnel of leaves and vines in the middle of a swamp.

We dropped to one knee and began picking twigs, scum, and leeches off of us. We needed a moment to catch our breath. We realized we would likely "find the enemy" soon. Unfortunately for us, we were at a tremendous strategic disadvantage. Suppose we found another VC battalion? That was not unreasonable given the extensive work that went into developing this dike-and-canopy system in the middle of a mangrove swamp. Should we ambush them? Not likely, as we could hit them only so hard with six guys. Then, supposing we did ambush them, what route would we use to escape? There was a labyrinth of crisscrossed, canopied trails. If we stayed on the trail, there was a high probability of our crossing paths with Viet Cong. Jump back into the swamp? We would make a significant amount of noise so, even if they couldn't see us, their bullets would.

"I am amazed we made it this far without alerting anyone," I said, surveying the intricate, time-consuming handiwork all about us.

"Yeah, no kidding."

The moon cast its patchwork shadow through the vines, there was a mild breeze, and clouds of huge mosquitoes buzzed around us.

Pete signaled it was time to go. Through hand signals, he directed that we were to head north down the trail.

We need to keep our ears and eyes open wide, he motioned.

A minute later, we hit a trail junction where we could either continue to travel north or turn and travel east or west. I looked at Pete and he indicated we should turn right, heading east. That should head us back to the ocean.

No sooner had we walked a dozen steps than we heard, coming from somewhere back along the western leg of the trail no more than fifty yards away, *"Ai Do?"* (Who's there?) We all dropped to one knee and froze. All our guns came off of safe, we positioned our bullets and grenades, and prepared for battle.

What we recognized was that, when someone challenges you in the middle of the night, it told you something. The NVA, Viet Cong, and VC main force all share one thing in common. If they were in a small unit, at night they would hunker down and be as quiet as field mice. By the same token, *we* were very quiet when traveling in a small group.

At a military installation, however, you had a sentry whose job it was to control entrance and exit to the outpost. To be challenged like this meant we had been detected. Having been in this type of situation before, we all went deathly quiet, waiting to see what they were going to do. We did not have to wait long.

In perfect English, the Vietnamese guard hollered, "Tomatoes."

That's a code word. This was exactly like our U.S. military guards calling out a code word to a unit that just returned from being out beyond the perimeter. Their reply to his *"Halt! Who goes there? Advance to be recognized"* would determine whether the sentry recognized them as a friendly force and opened the gate or not. The ramification was that the only time people talked like this was when there were a *lot* of people. I figured we had stumbled upon either an NVA or main force VC battalion rest area or first aid station. It was not uncommon for them to build a small, nondescript trail into the jungle, leading to a major outpost.

So there we were, realizing immediately that we were dead if we fired a shot. Pete gave us the signal of walking on our tiptoes and *Let's get the heck out of here.*

Fortunately, as we moved silently away, no one detected us. Nearing the ocean, we stepped off into the reeds. We moved a few feet at a time and then stopped. This was to ensure we didn't alert some perimeter guard so close to being picked up. It would have been a bad deal to go to all that work only to get shot in the back attempting to leave!

Unbelievably, our departure was uneventful. I had no idea exactly what we had found. All I knew was that it was sizable. Sure enough, we had "found the enemy." Had we gone a little more to the north or the west, we might have been in the middle of a VC hornet's nest.

After reporting what we had found, headquarters questioned why we left prior to establishing exact enemy position coordinates! We were asked to substantiate why we did not thrash around along the perimeter of the enemy encampment, mapping the boundaries.

"Listen! Next time, get us exact coordinates when it's hidden in the jungle like that. How in the world are we supposed to know whether we are shooting in the dark or not? The captain is going to be rather upset if we find out we missed due to insufficient information," one of the junior officers told Pete.

"We'll keep that in mind," Pete replied in an even tone. When he turned away, his eyes were smoldering. They bombed the hell out of the area.

Fortunately, as our irritation and anger increased over these senseless operations, relief was on its way. Our after-action reports were also sent to SEAL Team Two in Virginia, as we had an open, daily communication channel. SEAL Team Two then condensed the information and issued reports to the Pentagon, Naval Special Warfare, Unconventional Unit. The captain in charge was a man by the name of Captain Phil Bucklew.

It just so happened Bucklew's office was right across the hall from ASW, which was my dad's office. As fate would have it, my dad and Bucklew had become friends and took coffee breaks together. When my dad discovered Bucklew was in charge of SEALs, he wasted little time letting him know I was in SEAL Team Two, Seventh Platoon. When classified secret messages came in from SEAL Team Two, Seventh Platoon, My Tho, Bucklew would, out of courtesy, make a copy of the report for my dad. Whenever I was injured, my dad was among the first to know. Before anyone had the opportunity to notify family, my dad knew.

Bucklew had been reading the message traffic. He wasn't happy with how SEAL objectives were being subverted through incessant orders issued by HQ.

Suddenly, everything stopped. After several months of *We want you to go here. . . . We want you to do this. . . . We want you to go there. . . . We need you to do that* . . . all of a sudden, nothing. Headquarters acted like we didn't exist. It was like Captain Gray had kicked us out of his sandbox. There was no doubt in my mind that Bucklew wrote a short note, something to the effect:

Dear Captain Gray,

Would you care for your career to go any further? Please leave my SEALs alone.

Sincerely,
Captain Bucklew

We all assembled in the SEAL Team hut for our warning orders.

"So what are we doing tonight?" asked Keener from the back of the room, more bored than curious.

Pete looked at Fred with a faint smile. "No traffic."

It got quiet in the room. "No traffic" meant there were no messages from HQ. This was fantastic. After receiving scores of requests and messages, to receive not even one in two days was remarkable.

There was general agreement that we were puppets on a string for Captain Gray to play with. Big Buck reached out with his scissors and cut the string. What a relief.

Several days later, we were to go after a Viet Cong sector chief. In Vietnam, rather than call areas of the country "states" or "provinces," they were instead referred to as "sectors." There were legitimate, South Vietnamese governors within each sector. The strength of the American or ARVN control of the area determined the political clout and muscle of the governor. Often, the VC sector chief was just as powerful, if not more powerful than the recognized governor. The only difference being that the VC guerrilla sector chief moved around within the sector to avoid being captured or killed.

The military and psychological impact of assassinating such a high-ranking official was immense. Questions came up immediately regarding who had tipped us off and compromised the VC intelligence. In addition to the loss of a leader, the compelling question of who, if anyone, was a mole was such a disrupting factor as to be almost paralyzing to the leadership hierarchy of the local VC.

Our intelligence report on one particular individual indicated he was a powerful leader, knowledgeable concerning enemy strategy within the region. Our goal was to take him alive if at all possible. Allegedly, he had a bodyguard, slept with a pistol, and had escape routes specially designed within each of the safe houses. Supposedly, he had an escape door right next to his bed. Should he hear anything, all he needed to do was grab his .45 pistol and escape into the jungle darkness.

We quietly traversed all night through the jungle and into the small village he was supposed to be staying in. We followed the directions to the safe house. The night was darker than normal, with just a sliver of a moon adding definition to the outline of the hooch. We were hidden behind banana and coconut trees that were everywhere in that certain region. Even in daylight, we were indistinguishable due to the lush jungle flora. The courtyard in front of the house was a thirty- by thirty-foot square of dirt. Alongside the house, there was ten feet of clearing separating the side walls from the jungle. There was approximately a twenty- by twenty-foot dirt square in the back.

"Harry, I need you to position yourself at the rear of the house in order to prevent escape. Keener, Riojas, and I will assault through the front door. Don't let him get away. Listen carefully. If he eludes us and is able to get outside, forget the capture. Shoot anyone that comes out the back. I don't care if it is eight or eighty, blind, crippled, or crazy. If it comes out, you shoot," said Lieutenant Peterson.

"Just give me some time to move around back. Give me ten minutes."

Because I couldn't walk in the open area adjacent to the house, I needed the extra time. I had to invisibly traverse through the banana trees, low-lying shrubbery, and nipa palm.

As I was halfway to the back of the house, I heard Pete making his entry. I wasn't anywhere near where I needed to be!

I heard a fistfight going on inside the house. *Oh great!* Losing all pretense of stealth, I raced to the back of the house. *I have to get in position! I have to get in position!*

My gun was at the ready when I came flying around the corner. My eyes darted to and fro, seeking any movement. Suddenly, I went sprawling. My Stoner flew free, out of my hands. Pandemonium and stench burst on every side. I had tripped over an eight-inch bamboo fence surrounding a duck pen. I went flying, spread-eagle, onto the top of squawking, terrified ducklings. Ducks went everywhere. A cacophony of indignant, angry, quacking ducks erupted. I was sliding and scrambling in the muck, trying to get up. Giving up, I rolled onto my back and reached for my 9-millimeter pistol.

The window opened above me. I brought my pistol up in line with the window. There, standing in the window with his arms crossed was Riojas. He had a Cheshire cat grin. Despite all the camouflage face paint, his stupid smile radiated from ear to ear. I must have looked like one of the Three Stooges. A mixture of fear, anger, desperation, stupidity, and embarrassment washed over me.

"Way to go, Harry. Shhh," he said, bringing his index finger to his mouth and speaking in a loud voice. His lips puckered and his head swept slowly from side to side like an indignant professor in school. "SHHHH!"

"It's a little late for that," I said, ticked off.

In what seemed like an eternity, slipping and sliding like a person trying to stand on a slick ice-covered lake, I finally rose, grabbed my Stoner, and walked off. There was one man inside who was a VC official, but not the sector chief. We took the prisoner back with us to My Tho.

All the way back, I mused over how lucky I was. *SEAL Team luck! It was with me tonight.* What would have happened if this really had been where the sector chief was holed up—along with his bodyguard and the cadre of VC soldiers who normally traveled with him? Sure, I stunk, but I was alive to laugh about it. Had the guards been there while I was sprawled outside the rear porch, I would have been an easy target.

Time after time, when we screwed up, SEAL Team luck prevailed. I reflected on the punji pits and trip wires I had fallen victim to without incident. Just two weeks earlier, we had made contact with the VC and been involved in an ongoing firefight. They had better tactical position and manpower superiority, so we fought fiercely, then broke contact and ran. We made repeated contact, all the while working our way back to the river for extraction. We'd gotten approximately 300 meters away from the river when we came to a big open paddy. There was a sparse tree line along the riverbank. We began crossing the dry rice paddy, reaching within 80 to 90 meters from the tree line, when Pete decided we should turn left and move 300 to 400 meters east before moving to the river. We did so, and were picked up an hour and a half later, without incident. The truly amazing thing was that, as we found out two days later, from our agents who worked the area, there was a VC platoon in the tree line. They saw us coming in the light of a full moon and had set up to ambush the eight of us. Twenty VC with AK-47s, all good to go. Just before we were in their shooting range, we happened to turn. No reason, no rhyme; we just did. SEAL Team luck. The real kicker for me had come just a week prior. I'd been on point, and was leading the team back to the river. All of a sudden, I heard a click. Barely four to six feet to my immediate left came the unmistakable sound of an AK-47 coming off safe! My finger spasmed on the trigger as I assaulted.

Less than two strides in the dense jungle undergrowth to my left were four Viet Cong—just five, maybe six feet away! In a blinding flash of cordite and death, I lived and they died. All because one man took his AK off safe a moment too late. I stuck my tongue in my cheek as I wrinkled my forehead. I stared into the distance for a moment, considering how lucky I'd been. With a shrug, I got on the boat for the return trip to My Tho.

Shortly thereafter, we went out to dinner at a restaurant in My Tho. It was always interesting, trying to tell mama san with her pidgin English and our halting Vietnamese what we wanted for dinner. An interesting event occurred. A PBR sailor came over. "Are you guys having a hard time with the menu?"

"No, not really. We just point to these Chinese characters here, and whatever it is, she brings it and we eat it," came our smart-aleck reply.

"No. Let me translate it for you."

"Sure," we replied, not knowing what to make of this.

So he sat down with us, we bought him a beer, and he fluently translated for us. To our amazement, he spoke fluent Vietnamese. He was a petty officer, first class, signalman, by the name of West. His command of Vietnamese was so convincing that people in the restaurant treated him like a local. It was hilarious! Here was this six-foot-four, blond-headed, blue-eyed kid from Alabama who spoke English with a distinct southern twang—yet he spoke perfect Vietnamese.

I didn't know who it dawned on first, us or him. This could be an ideal situation for us to improve upon our intelligence.

"How would you like to add a little more adventure to your life, sort of spice things up a little," asked Curtis.

West lit up. "I think it'd be neat to work with you guys. Questioning valuable prisoners will save lives."

"You bet it will."

He agreed to use his knowledge of Vietnamese to help us interrogate prisoners.

We didn't have to wait long to put him to use. Our operation the very next night resulted in four prisoners.

Getting back to the Mike, we called West's boat. "Hello. Is West available?"

"Petty Officer West is in his barracks. Can I help you?"

"Yeah. Please tell him to meet us at the SEAL hooch. We have some people we want him to talk to."

Shortly after we arrived back at the compound, West showed up.

"Hey, thanks for coming. Talk to these guys, will you?" we asked.

He garnered all kinds of information from them. We were delighted. There were NILO (Naval Intelligence Liaison Officers) available whose job it was to interrogate prisoners within the district, but often that took weeks to get details back. With many of the details, a few days made the difference between extremely valuable information and "old news." West was valuable.

Two days later, we again called for him. West began interrogating another two VC we'd just brought back.

"They're telling me that there are a number of documents and money in one of the walls of the house where you captured them. They're saying that since you never asked them about it, they didn't want to say or do anything that might be misinterpreted and get them killed," West reported.

We decided to go back to the same area that night. So, after a quick nap, we reassembled and headed back to the same house where we captured the two VC. Unfortunately, the documents and money had been removed.

"What would you think if we ask West if he'd be interested in going out with us when we suspect there's a good chance we'd be taking prisoners?" I asked Pete.

"I don't know. I don't really like the idea of risking getting him killed."

"We could keep him right behind you."

"I don't like it, but perhaps we could try it once."

We asked him. Incredibly, he agreed to come with us. PBR sailors had seen firsthand how crazy SEALs were, and what kind of battles we got ourselves mixed up in. I had to hand it to him, he had guts.

"Yeah, I think it'd be a lot of fun," was all West said.

On our next op, West came along to have some fun. Going in, we covered at least three klicks. I was impressed with him. He was not panicky, he didn't appear to spook, he was quiet, and he blended in well. He did not jump at any little noise. He appeared smooth and relaxed.

The intelligence report stated that in this one particular village hooch resided the local VC captain and his wife. From what we were told, he was newly installed, so we decided to go pay him a visit.

We snuck up to the rear of the hooch and entered. Sure enough, laying there sleeping were the captain and his wife. We woke them up. Interrogation was so effective when we woke someone from a peaceful night's sleep, immediately plunging them into a "reality nightmare." The look of terror gripped their faces.

"West, start questioning them."

He began by telling them what a terrible predicament they were in. But if they were truthful and cooperative, we would not kill them— and possibly would not turn them over to the dreaded South Vietnamese. The two chose to cooperate.

"There are two homes down the path from here that house twenty-six main force VC that arrived recently from the north. There also is a courier with documents from the north."

Pete and Riojas stayed with West, while Keener and I stood guard at the front door. The two other SEALs were positioned outside in the jungle alongside the path leading to the hooch. The early rays of dawn filtered through the trees. It was a gray, flat light of early morning.

The construction of the nipa palm walls of the hooch left an eight-inch gap between the top of the wall and the plate of the roof. This allowed Keener and I to survey outside activity.

"Harry, look over at that next hooch."

The next hooch was about one hundred meters away. Emerging from the hooch came two men, both of whom were armed. They were walking on the trail in our direction.

"Pete, don't look now, but here come two guys. They're going to be walking right in front of this house," I said. "Do you want us to shoot them?"

"I don't know. Once you shoot them, everyone knows we're here. I'm not done getting all the information and details on where all the secret stuff is at."

West stood up and walked over to where we were standing. He peered out at the approaching figures. "You want those two guys?"

"Well of course, West," I replied, my voice laden with sarcasm.

"Okay, watch this. Constance, you stand there," instructed West, motioning to the right side of the doorway. "Keener, stand to the left side of the door. Lieutenant Peterson, stand back."

Pete and I looked at each other, each of us with a silly grin on our face. West, our PBR petty officer, had just taken charge.

"This could be interesting," I said, taking my gun off safe, along with Keener.

West reached over and touched my arm. "No, just grab them."

It was five o'clock in the morning, and the VC were about one hundred feet from the front of the house. West opened the front door wide enough to talk, but not wide enough to be seen. In perfect Asian intonation, he invited them in for morning tea. They answered him. The two VC paused for a moment—turned and walked to the hooch. They climbed up the steps and in the front door.

"*Ciao,*" said West.

The look on the face of these two! They could not reconcile the voice they were hearing with the body it was coming out of. They were shocked.

Keener and I quickly laid them on the floor and tied them up. The interrogation of these two yielded even better information. They were part of a six-man team ferrying documents and diaries northward from the south.

"Gentlemen, this is too good an opportunity to pass up. Let's have the other guys take these four prisoners back while we go after the couriers," Pete decided.

Amazingly, West filled an important slot within the team, as we had to leave the other SEALs behind with the prisoners. He quickly loaded his M16, and away we went.

We arrived at the other hooch. Pete and Keener went around back, while Riojas, West, and I positioned ourselves in front. Using hand signals, I told West to post himself next to a tree as I couldn't afford to get him killed. I instructed him to shoot if someone came out only if they were to his immediate left where we would not be in danger of him shooting in our direction. Riojas agreed to stand at the door while I assaulted. With seasoned confidence, I prepared to assault the house.

West motioned me to move over to his side. "Why don't you let me try to talk them out?"

In a barely audible whisper, I replied, "There are at least four guys in there with guns. I cannot take the chance. We can't be sure what will happen if you start hollering."

I signaled to Riojas—*Open the door.* He did.

I walked in. Four guys having breakfast. I put on my best Jerry Lewis smile as I made visual contact with each one. "Hi, guys!" I said in English.

They all froze. Their guns were over against the wall. One by one they all looked over at their AK-47s, then back to me.

"Uh-uh-uh . . ." I said, shaking my left index finger at them.

"Okay, everyone outside. *Di di.*" (Let's go.)

The four VC got up and walked out the door. Immediately, West was all over them. In perfect Vietnamese, he was yelling at them. "*Get*

*down. Hands behind your back. Do this. Do that. What's your name—
no monkey business—we want straight, honest answers to all questions
or you, your family, and your family's family will die!"*

All four guys were on their stomach. West was tying them up while
simultaneously interrogating them. Riojas and I were laughing heartily.
He was bouncing from one to the next. I didn't have them raise their
hands or do anything other than go outside. Now West had them all
doing circus gyrations.

I glanced up as Pete and Keener came running through the house,
bursting out the front door, ready to save us. All they heard was Vietnamese shouting going on. Pete looked puzzled as he saw Riojas and
I laughing. He start smiling when he spied West bent over two of the
Viet Cong, kicking their legs, barking out orders and tying them all
together.

West took seriously his responsibility of guarding the prisoners. He
didn't realize that without guns they weren't going anywhere. He did
the absolute best job he could.

The bad thing about this whole incident was that not only did we
have eight prisoners, but we had five haversacks full of documents and
an additional eight guns to carry. What a nice problem to deal with.

After we distributed the load among the prisoners and ourselves, we
radioed the other members of the team. We agreed to join up in the
middle of a large field we'd passed on the way in, then return to the
boat.

When we returned to our base in My Tho, Pete took inventory on
our haul. We had captured five AK-47s, three SKSs, fifty pounds of
documents, and eight Viet Cong. Two of the prisoners were couriers
from Hanoi, part of the intelnet. Two of the captured VC were locals,
while the remaining four were bodyguards. They were part of a security
detail dispatched to do the bidding of the couriers within the local
communities. It was a very productive evening.

True to form, West had a ball. "Thanks for letting me come with
you guys. That was fun!"

Two weeks later, West's unit was transferred, and he had to leave.
What a shame! He had been a terrific contributor to our Team.

We had an amazing assortment of weaponry and electronic devices
at our disposal, some of which helped, and some of which did not. One
part of the SEAL Team arsenal was a dog. Each platoon had one. The
dogs were extremely valuable in some operations, while in others they
were a hindrance. We had a valuable black and silver German shepherd

we called Rinny. Rinny was short for his American Kennel Club-registered pedigree name of Baron Himleich von Kaufman. A good German name for a German shepherd. Rinny was a bit unusual in that he weighed 110 pounds. His head was larger than normal, and we referred to him as having four meters of teeth and the heart of a lion. He was very intimidating to the local Vietnamese. The average Vietnamese man weighed between 95 and 105 pounds. Rinny, obviously, was larger than most Vietnamese adult men.

Rinny, as he grew up, was sent to school. He learned attack commands, bomb detection procedures, and obedience about as well as a dog could be taught. Rinny could be a lot of fun to be with. He had a mischievous side to him as well, reminding me of the cartoon character Mutley the dog. We could almost hear him snickering after some of the surprising pranks he pulled. He loved sneaking up behind an unsuspecting person, then barking fiercely. His bark was enough to make most people jump out of their skin!

Rinny was primarily an attack dog. Most team members couldn't get near him. He had one handler, Eugene Thomas Fraley. Fraley and Rinny were a pair. I don't know what precipitated this, but shortly before Fraley died, he came to me and said, "You know, you'd make a good alternate dog handler. Rinny really likes you. Just in case something ever happens to me."

I agreed, and started learning from Fraley how to work with a dog. I learned how Rinny worked, how to get him to obey, what he was capable of, and, mostly, how to get him to respond to me.

One simple benefit in working with Rinny that I really appreciated involved our taking him to dinner. Whenever we went somewhere to eat, we were continually on guard for the threat of a VC coming by and tossing in a grenade while we were sitting there eating. Rinny solved this problem quite nicely.

There were several restaurants we frequented in My Tho. Typically, we went in and asked if we could take over the entire restaurant for a party of ten or twelve. As we paid well, the mama san quickly closed the restaurant to any further business and prepared tables for us. I then unhooked Rinny and told him to go over and guard the door. Understanding what I told him, Rinny walked quickly to the front door and sat up, his back straight and head alert to any movement around him. Little kids followed Americans all over, offering to shine their shoes, sell peanuts, candy, or fruit—or perhaps even a grenade. They would come to the restaurant door and start to open it.

Rinny would growl, *I wouldn't open that door if I were you. Because if you do, you're dead meat in three seconds.* The kids would slam the door real fast!

Sometimes, I went out into the street and selected one kid.

Come here, I motioned to a young boy.

Rinny would look at the kid. If he had explosives on him, Rinny would tell me. Rinny understood what I was doing, and would allow just this one kid to come in and out, bringing us peanuts or fruit or whatever. He would also allow the mama san to bring us our food or pour us more beer. If anyone else even started to come near us, Rinny was in front of them with teeth bared.

Rinny was great to operate with. We'd move down a trail with Rinny out in front. At least a dozen times, Rinny had come to a taut mono-filament trip wire and stopped in his tracks. I walked up to him, ran my hand up his neck, between his ears, down his nose, and, right at the end of his nose: *Twang*—a trip wire.

Now that it was the dry season, Rinny operated more frequently with us. We were walking along and Rinny would stop and look down. The first time it happened, I couldn't figure it out.

"What's going on, Rinny?" I would ask.

Finally, after the third time Rinny did this, I figured it out. The VC had what was known as a "tangle-foot wire." The VC would take vines and run a fishing line around several of them, tie the line to a grenade, and lay the vine on the ground. They did this in hopes that our foot would become entangled in the vines. Should we jerk our foot loose, *Ping,* we had just set off the grenade.

Rinny would say, *Don't look now. This is the old loose-trip-wire trick.*

He was amazing. If it was a loose trip wire, he would tell us. If it was a taut trip wire, he told us. If we came across a punji pit, Rinny told us. Several times we came across a bunker with a little door. They were designed so we had to make a right and then a left in order to enter into the room. If anyone was waiting for us, we were dead. We'd open the door, Rinny would stick his head inside, sniff, and then tell us whether or not anyone was in there.

No one in there, guys.

"Thank you, Rinny." And we kept going.

We'd be about to cross a paddy when Rinny would stop. His ears stood at attention and the hair on the back of his neck bristled.

I walked up next to him. "How many are there?" I asked.

Oh, there's a few.

"Where are they?"

About six hundred meters, over there in the other tree line.

We began to pick up the nuances of his manner and what he was communicating. Sure enough, when we got into position to reconnoiter the tree line, there the VC were.

The only thing Rinny could not do was go through swamps. We couldn't use him during the rainy season. No matter how much he tried to be quiet, Rinny thrashed through water. During the rainy season, when everything was underwater, Rinny was pretty helpless. On the other hand, he was a delight to work with when things were dry. He'd run out ahead, meaning that I and the team could go into a half trot and cover a lot more area. I didn't have to worry about booby traps or ambushes, as Rinny's nose and senses were incredibly acute. I just had to be certain that when he stopped, we all stopped!

Rinny stayed in an area set off by chain-link fence within the SEAL Team complex in My Tho. Inside the fenced area was an aluminum air shipping cargo box we adapted to serve as Rinny's doghouse. I cleaned it out, cut out some holes for windows (mostly ventilation), and put carpeting down for him to lay on.

We had just been on an extended operation that took us a day and a half to complete. We killed several VC, and captured three prisoners. When we arrived back in My Tho that afternoon, we were all tired. We weren't making enemy contact nearly as frequently as we had weeks earlier. The last few weeks had seen a steady decline in enemy contact. As a result, we had to travel longer and farther to make contact with VC or NVA. This op was a "success," as we had trekked down near the ocean to find these Viet Cong. Guys in the team started joking about trying to call to see if we could rent some VC to play with.

"Hello? Ho Chi? Look, if you guys are serious about this Commie Democratic Republic crap, then you'd better send some more of your troops after us. You serious? You want us to march into Hanoi to play with you boys?" mimicked Keener, pretending to have a phone conversation with the Communist leader Ho Chi Minh.

We got off the boat and everyone headed to the showers to get the muck and slime off. I wanted a beer and I wanted to eat.

Gallagher looked over at me and said, "You're the dog handler. Take care of the prisoners, too."

"Oh man!" I complained. "That's not fair. This damn war is getting less and less enjoyable by the day."

This meant I had to sit with those three bozos while the other guys got cleaned up. Then, eventually, one of them would be assigned to take over while I got cleaned up. I just had to sit there.

Maybe I can clean my gun. No, I guess not. How can I guard them with it torn apart and walk from the gasoline barrel to the WD-40 and all? I looked around, and then it hit me.

I mused further. *Doesn't it make sense that Rinny ought to be able to guard these guys? Makes sense to me.* I looked around some more. *Where can I put them so Rinny can guard them?*

I smiled. Turning to the captured VC, I said, "You three. *Khong co chay,*" motioning with my hands. "Get inside this shipping container."

I ushered the three prisoners into Rinny's cage. Rinny's shipping container was six feet long by four feet tall by five feet wide. None of the three was any taller than five feet, so there was ample room for them to stay for an hour or so. I pushed the door closed. There was a latch on the door, but I didn't bother latching it since they could easily reach out through the hole in the door and undo it. In the center of the fenced-in area was an augur stake anchoring Rinny's leash. After shoving the three VC into Rinny's cage, I took Rinny off his leash.

"Rinny, watch these guys."

No sweat, came his reply, as he moved closer to the shipping container.

"I'm going to take a shower," I said out loud, smugly, to no one in particular.

Everyone had been gone for about ten minutes when I came walking into the showers. I walked in fully dressed with my gun and all my gear. I was filthy and everything needed to be washed off. I turned on the water.

Moments later: "Constance!"

"Yeah," I said, looking up innocently as the water washed over me.

"Where are the prisoners?" inquired Gallagher.

"Rinny's watching them."

By now, I was working on my green and black face paint. Out of the corner of my eye, I could see him thinking about this. Finished, I grabbed my towel, picked up my gear, and walked to the room adjacent to the showers. Here, there were pegs on the walls designed for us to hang our things on while we dried off. I hung my gear up, put on my flip-flops, and proceeded to dry off. Gallagher was doing the same.

"Where'd you put them?"

"Rinny's watching them."

"Constance, that's making me nervous."

"Well, come on." I was looking forward to showing off my ingenuity.

We walked around the corner of the team hut wearing nothing but towels and flip-flops. Neither one of us was carrying a gun. Approaching Rinny's fenced-in area, Gallagher noticed the chain-link gate was open.

"Damn it, Harry!" he blurted out. "They escaped!"

"No they haven't," I said, calmly. Rinny was still lying in front of the shipping container.

"Where are they? You son of a bitch. After all the work we went to in order to get those three—"

"Look." I smiled, pointing at the door of the container. All you could see were four fingers coming out through the window. One of the prisoners was gripping the door in an attempt to keep it *closed.* Rinny's nose was twelve inches from this guy's fingers. I just imagine what happened. I could see the first guy saying something to the effect, *Hey! There's nobody out there. Let's go! We run for forty or fifty meters and we're outta here!* So they pushed open the door. I had no doubt about what occurred next. Rinny began snarling and bared his teeth as he came closer to the container. *I'm not going first. You go.* Then another. *I'm not going. You go!* Then, wham! He slammed the container shut as Rinny came even closer. From then until the moment we arrived, I doubt seriously he released his grip for even a moment.

I opened the door. *"Cum Co De,"* I commanded. None of them wanted to come out. I looked at Gallagher.

Chuckling, Gallagher said, "Damn, Harry. You have a pretty good prisoner detention center here!"

"It ain't San Quentin, but it'll do."

Gallagher smiled and walked off.

"Come on. Come on," I said to the VC, motioning with a wide circling arc movement of my arm. "Come on, Rinny."

Hastily, the VC lined up next to me with one of those, *I'm with him! Me, too! Yeah, me too!* There was no mistaking the fear on their faces as they stared at Rinny. I got them some water, then took them over to where my bullets were soaking.

I told them where to stand and placed Rinny next to them. I went inside the SEAL Team hooch and got dressed.

I decided that having them help me clean my bullets would really save me time. To one of the VC, I gave a wire brush and had him clean all the mud, dirt, and debris off the metal links. Another one was swooshing them in and out of the solvent, while the third guy dried them off, sprayed them with WD-40, and hung them on my rack. They did great!

My bullets were there, my guns were there, my grenades were there—and Rinny was there. They were as polite as noble gentry.

"You guys want to get something to eat?"

Knowing they were probably as starved as I was, the four of us went down to the mess hall. These three Viet Cong and I had dinner—and Rinny.

One of the admin guys looked over at me as he finished eating. "These your new agents?"

"Who knows?"

A puzzled look came over his face. No one in the chow hall knew they were prisoners because of Rinny. We finished eating and it was over. I turned them over to NILO.

The next day we received another warning order directing us to capture the sector chief we had recently missed. This time they assured us the intelligence was accurate.

Rinny was our point. We quick-stepped our way along the trail. The mid-January, 1968, weather was perfect. There was a full moon out, which made navigation in the dark even easier. Our "doggie shuffle" was great. We didn't have to worry about mines, trip wires, or ambushes.

As we neared the village where the sector chief was supposed to be staying, I instructed Rinny to stay directly at my side. We patrolled farther into the jungle shadows away from the trails, moving slowly toward the VC hooch. This time, it was not going to be so easy. In the front courtyard was an armed sentry.

Pete walked up next to me as we surveyed the area. "We need to take out that sentry," he said, stating the obvious.

"I know." The problem was that the sentry was right in the middle of a well-illuminated courtyard. Compounding this dilemma was that the vegetation on either side of the hooch was very thin. We had to figure out a way to take him out.

The guard was sitting on a box. As part of his routine, he got up, walked ten feet to either side, returned, and sat down again. I calculated the distance from the shadows to the edge of his sentry patrol.

"I could attempt to get to the side and then try to cut him, but he's not coming over far enough for me to catch him off guard."

"I know," replied Pete. He paused a moment, trying to decide what strategy to use. "You, Ashton, and Hooker take Rinny and flank to the left. Watch for my signal."

The next twenty minutes were spent crawling slowly in the shadows to the left of the sentry. Pete and I were at a right angle to each other. He gave the signal to knife the sentry.

This was going to be close. I would have to try to sprint into the yard without him detecting my movement for as long as possible. If he picked up my movement, we would have to shoot him and the mission would likely be aborted. *Maybe I should try Rinny. Hmmm. He can certainly run faster than I can.*

I looked over at Pete. Then I pointed to Rinny.

Pete replied with the fifty-fifty handshake, meaning, *I don't know.*

I shrugged my shoulders and put my hands palms up, in effect, saying, *What have we got to lose?*

Pete nodded, All right.

I reached down and began to tap Rinny on his ear. "Watch him. Watch him, Rinny," I whispered.

The hackles on the back of Rinny's neck stood straight up. I felt him pulling his legs underneath him as he started bunching his muscles. I tapped him a little bit harder alongside his jaw. He began quivering with excitement. "Watch him, Rinny."

I tapped him harder. Every muscle in his body went taut. The sentry stood and began his perimeter march. He walked several feet in our direction, stopped, and turned back, walking in the opposite direction away from us.

"Get him!" I hissed, urgently.

At once, Rinny exploded toward the sentry. Rinny leapt through the air. The sentry, alerted to something behind him, turned. Here was a 95-pound man facing a 110-pound dog, sprinting at full bore with four meters of teeth. Before he could recognize and react to what was happening, Rinny buried his teeth into the sentry's thigh, at the uppermost part of his buttocks. Rinny's canine eyeteeth closed through the leg. His teeth raked around the thigh bone, shredding the leg and coming together as Rinny's head jerked violently from side to side. Rinny pulled all this gouged "meat" out of the sentry's leg. The sentry hit the ground. He writhed valiantly, trying to fend off Rinny, while, at the same time Rinny was already coming out from the initial bite. Rinny discarded the mouthful of flesh, quickly clamping his teeth down upon the left shoulder bone, collarbone, and the neck. Crunch. His neck snapped. The sentry died instantly. Two bites, that was it.

I walked out of the shadows and snapped my fingers. At once, Rinny stopped the violence, ran over to me, and sat down. Just like us, Rinny was able to turn it on and off. I looked at Pete and gave him the *tahdah!* hand gesture, meaning, *Well? What do you think of that? Was that amazing, or what?*

Pete just stood there. We were all stunned at the instantaneous, raw, aggressive brutality. Everyone there was thinking the same thing. *Did you see what that dog just did?* We stormed the hooch, capturing the sector chief.

I reflected on how pleased I was at how things were developing. SEALs were new to the strategic scheme within the Naval hierarchy. We were finding our niche in Vietnam, and what a niche we were carving out! We were utilizing every available asset. Vietnamese field interpreters, superior firepower, Rinny, PBRs and Sea Wolf gunships—all proved deadly effective. It was as if someone flipped a coin, and we came up the winners!

I thought back to about a month ago, prior to the Christmas, 1967, stand-down. Rules were handed out, dictating how we were not supposed to operate, where we could and could not go. How could there be rules in war? The winning side makes the rules. The rules set forth by the 1948 Geneva Convention covered treatment of prisoners, how to surrender, and other human rights matters, and this was necessary. But, how could there be rules for when and when not to engage the enemy? The North Vietnamese certainly did not abide by them. Our intelligence reports that came in during Christmas week indicated a massive troop and materiel movement. Solely because we were off on holiday observance. Now, they were talking about some truce accords that had been signed for a cease-fire in early February to allow the Vietnamese to celebrate a holiday referred to as Tet. During Christmas, we went out and took a look for ourselves. No, we didn't shoot anyone, but we did at least scout the VC and NVA. I wondered what we would do during this Tet holiday.

The strange thing about it was that right after Christmas, we had some major victories, as had the Army and Marines. I didn't think we had beaten them as badly as the lack of enemy contact was suggesting. Who knows, maybe it was an intimidation sort of thing.

When we went out on five operations in a row, covering 5,000 and 6,000 meters (or more) at a time, and did not find anyone, what did that tell us? There's nobody there. If there was no one there, could it be we killed them all? Hardly. Or, that they fled the area because of pressure the U.S. military was putting on them? Sounded reasonable to me.

We began staying out well into the morning hours. Where we used to make certain we were back at the boat by six to six-thirty A.M., now it was common to get back between nine and eleven A.M. Where we normally went *around* big, exposed, dry rice paddies, now when we walked out we weren't afraid to travel right through them. Yes, Rinny was with us on many of these ops, but even Rinny couldn't tell what we would find in the tree line at the other end of a 3,000-meter paddy. We started thinking we had won. We had the helos to blow them up, so the enemy might as well give up! It wasn't worth their time. Throughout Vietnam, the military press trumpeted victory after victory. There was widespread speculation that the war was being won!

Two days later, we were scheduled to go out again. This time, Pete was back with us. We were to try to disrupt the VC in a known "VC stronghold." Once again, we patrolled hour after hour without enemy contact. Finally, we turned back toward the river. Lately, the guys were starting to straggle, to spread out, and to relax. I was going nuts.

"Hey, Pete. Don't let these guys relax. I'm telling you, I know what happens!"

Pete smiled. He tried to make us focus. But guys were getting lazy and even starting to chew and spit tobacco. This was admin crap we couldn't afford when out on patrol. The spit and the smell could give us away should a situation turn desperate.

We'd had another night of futility, and were headed back to the boat. We were one hundred meters from the river. There was a lush, dense row of trees and foliage running parallel to the river. As we came up to it, I asked Pete to hold up.

"Let me go and check things out."

Pete gave his okay, and I crept around and up to the edge of the undergrowth. The dike trail we were on T'd and ran alongside the accumulation of tropical trees, reeds, overhang, and dense shrubbery. There was a six-foot drop off from the dike into the tree line, and then, thirty feet beyond was the river. Quietly, I moved farther, looking for booby traps and anything that might tip me off to enemy activity. I signaled for the team to come forward to the edge, as everything was clear. Ten feet farther, I caught a glimpse of a slight movement in the reeds below. Positioning myself so that I could not be seen, I moved nearer.

Gotcha this time! I said to myself. There, squatting in the reeds, looking out into the river were two Viet Cong. They had on black pajamas, web gear, an SKS, and a loaded B 40 rocket launcher. They were setting the sights onto the boat coming in to pick us up. The funny thing was, the boat, with its crewmen surveying the shoreline, could see me but not the VC. I was up on the dike, clearly visible from the river. Unfortunately for the two below me, they saw the boat and not me. I smiled at the irony.

I signaled to Pete to keep the team quiet. I pantomimed, *Two VC down below me.*

Pete signaled back a wide-eyed *What!* He then relayed the information to the others, *Freeze, we have something going on.* Everyone did just that.

The two Viet Cong chattered softly about aiming the rocket, clearly excited at the opportunity to take out an American boat. I signaled Pete to move quietly to where I was.

When he arrived and surveyed the details, he turned and signaled the rest of the team. Shortly thereafter, our entire team was standing there, overlooking the two, still-unsuspecting Viet Cong. This promised to be fun.

Seven of us now watched them get the rocket launcher ready. It had been three minutes since Pete arrived. One guy had the rocket on his shoulder, standing perpendicular to the river, while the other stood at his side, sighting in the rocket. Neither one had glanced around—too intent on shooting the boat.

The boat was nearing two hundred meters from shore so we couldn't let this go on much longer. All seven of us had our guns trained on the VC. Pete and I nudged each other. I mouthed the words, *Watch this!*

"Uh-huh, uh-hum," I let out, making the sound of someone clearing his throat.

As if straight out of the movies, the two, in perfect unison, slowly turned their heads and gasped at seven men with green faces standing twelve feet above them. The rocket wilted on the one VC's shoulder.

"*Ciao,*" said Pete to the two below. "Shall we take them prisoner, gent—"

Suddenly, the one with the rocket tried to swing it in our direction. We tore them both to pieces, a seven-man firing line, pummeling their bodies into the water.

Pete finished. ''I guess not. Not a smart move on his part.''

The one VC must have thought he could fire the rocket into the bank, killing us along with them. The rule was, when we had them ''dead to rights,'' they weren't to do anything or they'd be killed. We knew the rule and they knew the rule.

There we were, searching all night to find VC, and we ran into them at the river's edge as we prepared to depart. The very last moment. Maybe this was their new strategy.

Flip a coin. Shift the circumstances just slightly. And things could have turned out much differently. I think it was Kipling who remarked that there are no atheists in war. I have to say I really believe the Man Upstairs had to be watching out for us. How else could I explain all the times SEAL Team luck manifested itself?

I smiled as I recalled these brushes with death. What a deal! How could you explain these against-all-odds occurrences? I might make it through my Vietnam tour after all!

CHAPTER 11

TET

CHIEF CHUCK JESSE PACED ANIMATEDLY BACK AND FORTH across the SEAL Team hooch floor. "I don't know what to make of this cease-fire thing. I think we ought to go ahead and take a few days off and enjoy ourselves." He turned, shaking his hands in the air for emphasis, and continued, "Guys, I want you to honor the three-day stand-down. Me, I'm thinking about going to Saigon. Here it's February and we haven't been out for, what, since Christmas? If anyone cares to join me, I will be leaving at 0800 hours."

"I will," chimed in Charlie Watson.

"Is this Tet thing anything like Chinese New Year?" asked Roy Dean.

"I'm not sure, but I think so," said Gallagher.

"Let's go up on the roof and party and watch the fireworks ourselves tonight," continued Roy Dean, referring to the rooftop area of our Naval living quarters there in My Tho.

A murmur of concurrence rippled through the room.

"Good idea," blurted Mikey Boynton. "Let's get our CARE Packages from home together and go up top."

We didn't get much American food while in Vietnam. When guys got "CARE Packages" with cookies, cakes, candies, canned fruit, and other foods from home, there was an understanding that we shared it with one another.

"Hooker, you and Constance get the drinks from your refrigerator," instructed Pete.

"Aye, aye, Lieutenant," Hooker said with a smile.

"Let's go party!"

We grabbed our guns, bullets, and gear and headed through the gate to the hotel that served as our Naval housing quarters. It was built by the French in the 1930s in typical French provincial architecture common in Vietnam. We were roughly a half mile from the My Tho River, and three quarters of a mile from the fenced-in Naval compound where the SEAL Team hooch and assorted buildings were. The hotel was a four-story building the Navy had contracted to house Naval personnel located in My Tho. Constructed of mostly concrete and highlighted with decorative tile, it had been outfitted to serve Naval personnel needs. The first, second, and fourth floors housed the Navy sailors, while SEALs occupied the entire third floor.

All the rooms in our hotel/living quarters had doors facing outside. Each room was ten feet by twenty feet. Most rooms had two bunk beds, with footlockers at either end. In the middle of each room was a table and four chairs. Gray metal lockers stood at the end of each room, serving as the "closet." Next to each door was a three- by four-foot window. Each room had a standard, Casablanca-style ceiling fan that served as our only form of heating and air-conditioning. Also, at the back of each room was a bathroom, connected to the hotel's plumbing, which was placed in the center of the hotel behind the innermost walls.

To get to my room on the third floor, I went up two external flights of stairs, turned right, and walked on a five-foot-wide balcony to a room I shared with Hooker, Ashton, and Fraley until he died. There were two "sides" of the hotel, a north side and a south side, with four rooms on each side. The end rooms, farthest from the stairway, were for storage, with the other six housing us. Concrete stairs zigzagged upward on the east end, while on the west end there was only a cinder block wall. The top step of the stairwell on each floor was at the back (the north side) of the hotel. My third-floor room was immediately to the right, on the back side. The first room on the opposite side of our wall, at the front of the hotel, housed Riojas and Gallagher. (Only two in their room, since Gallagher was a chief.) In the room next to Gallagher were Pete and Charlie Watson, while in the next room beyond that were Jack Rowell and Chief Chuck Jesse. In the room next to mine lived Keener, Roy Dean, and Mikey Boynton. Two doors down from me were three new guys who had just arrived.

Outside the rooms was a three-foot balcony railing, consisting of a decorative wrought-iron piece that ran horizontally across the top. Along the base of the banister was a row of one-foot concrete blocks. Connecting the top to the bottom were wrought-iron rods spaced eighteen inches apart. Positioned every five feet was a square, concrete block pillar, which added support.

The Navy had built a screen mesh that came outward from the hotel walls at a 45-degree angle to its anchor point on the ground, protecting the first two floors. It was to keep people from driving by and tossing a grenade into our rooms. The grenade would hit the screen and bounce off. Should it detonate, the screen would protect us from the shrapnel; we would feel only the concussive force.

The roof, where our party was to occur, was flat. In the middle was a large rectangular water cistern, five feet tall, ten feet wide, by twenty feet long. The water in the cistern came from both precipitation and an external pump. It served three functions: sink and shower water, toilet water, and a "swimming pool" for us SEALs. We didn't drink it, as each room had a bottled water dispenser. The cistern allowed for gravity flow. Everybody had to be careful not to use too much water or we'd be forced to wait until we got back from work or, possibly, until the next morning for it to refill.

Hooker was elected to the honorable post of platoon treasurer, in charge of the platoon fund. One of the truly critical—if not downright essential—duties of the platoon treasurer was to maintain the soda and beer inventory for all of us. As a result, our room had the refrigerator. Riojas wanted one, ostensibly for medical supplies, and Gallagher wanted one because, well, he was the master chief. Priorities obviously dictated that the platoon treasurer had to be the one to keep the refrigerator. It worked well, provided we had electricity. Since we had the refrigerator, we also had cases and cases of soft drinks, beer, and, a Navy staple, rum, in our room.

Also in our rooms were cases of ordnance for our varied weaponry. For example, I had Stoner rounds while Hooker had M16 and M79 fleschette rounds. We used to leave all our weaponry at the Team hut and only carry our 9-millimeter pistols with us back and forth to the hotel. Several weeks earlier, however, Gallagher told us all to start bringing our weaponry back to the hotel after every op. He'd become uncomfortable, and wanted us to hang our weapons off our bunks rather than leave them at the SEAL compound. He also suggested we each keep a case or two of shells under our beds, as well. Several days earlier, we even brought up a couple of extra cases of odds and ends— grenades, Stoner rounds, M60 and rocket rounds. Gallagher had us scatter it throughout our third-floor rooms.

Pete stood to propose a toast. "Gentlemen, a truce has been signed between the North and South Vietnamese. No hostile actions are to occur. So, guys, please do not initiate any activities that might be construed as hostile by the rest of the Navy guys here at the hotel," Pete said, pausing. He looked around the room, then broke into a smile. "Are you ready to party? Here's to us, and the fact we will be going home soon!"

A chorus of "Hear! Hear!" reciprocated across the roof. Let the party begin!

It was a hot, balmy evening. Everyone had brought something. We had peanuts, cookies, hors d'oeuvres, and all sorts of food. We ran around in T-shirts, swim trunks, and flip-flops. Drinking a little, jumping into the water tank, talking, and carrying on as we were prone to do. Just generally having a good time horsing around.

It was just about midnight, and the air finally was beginning to cool a bit. We started seeing tracers going up at the edge of town, two miles away.

"See! I told you they have fireworks for this Tet thing," said Roy Dean proudly. Some tracers were single, and some were clustered, which meant that it was from automatic fire (machine guns).

"Look, guys," I called out. "Vietnamese Fourth of July fireworks!"

Everyone quickly brought up more food and drink so we had something to eat during the "show." A number of us brought up lawn chairs.

"Let's watch the show!" said Ashton, feeling good after an evening of rum and Coke, swimming, and more rum and Coke.

I was enjoying this. "Hey, this resembles fun."

There were red tracers, green tracers, what appeared to be white tracers—it was pretty neat.

Then, instead of being two miles away, they were about a mile away. "Hey, this is better. I like being right underneath the fireworks when they shoot them off at home," said Boynton.

"Listen," insisted Rowell. "They're getting closer."

Faintly in the distance, we started hearing the staccato of machine gun fire. *Tick tick tick tick. Tick tick tick tick. Tick tick tick tick.* Then, instead of tracers shooting in random fashion as was done at a fireworks display, the tracers were more focused in their direction of fire.

"This is getting a little more interesting," remarked Pete.

An hour later, the "festivities" were now a half mile away. The tracers were fired at a 45- to 50-degree angle. This was getting to be more serious! All the fireworks displays I had seen propelled fireworks almost straight up. At 45 degrees, you could hit stuff, like buildings and people.

Clomp clomp clomp. Someone was running up the stairs. At two A.M., sound carried. Appearing at the roof's edge was somebody from the radio room. (There was a radio room at the hotel that was used to rouse guys out if they were needed at the Naval outpost down at the river.)

"Have you guys been watching what's going on?" he asked, gesturing at the skyward illumination over My Tho.

"Yeah. What about it?"

"We have been monitoring radio traffic, like we always do. You won't believe what we're hearing. The frequencies are jammed, with installation after installation reporting they are under fire. In fact, we no longer have radio communication with Dong Tiem. Before we lost them, they were reporting heavy fire." (Dong Tiem was the Army base nearest to My Tho, twelve miles west of us.)

We all looked at each other.

"I guess we'd better start sobering up, guys," interjected Pete.

"Ah man, does this mean our party's over?" someone complained.

"Screw the party. How am I supposed to get to Saigon?" Jesse was saying, half serious and yet half eager at the likelihood of an impending World War II-style battle.

This was something new! The Vietnam War had been more like the Revolutionary War with its bump-and-run, hide-and-shoot sort of battles. World War II had clearly defined battle lines. You knew where the enemy territory was and what cities the enemy controlled and which cities you controlled. If what we were hearing was true, then the North Vietnamese and Viet Cong were taking the battle to the cities, highways, and byways.

Nobody was in a panic as we returned coolers, food, tables, and chairs to our rooms. But gunshots were getting closer, and an air of emergency was beginning to pervade the hotel. It was approaching three A.M.

I returned all my stuff to my room, then rejoined Gallagher on the roof. We watched the goings-on with interest. If anything, the gunfire was intensifying. Then, from off to our right, near the eastern edge of the My Tho city limits came sounds of mortars being lobbed.

PaDooomp! Then, several seconds later and to our left, *Kaboom!*

"Looks like we have a raging battle to contend with," observed Gallagher.

"Should we stay here or go to the base?" I asked.

Just then, Pete came running up the stairs. "Everyone, come over here." Pete paused a moment. "We're facing a major offensive—probably the biggest push the North has mounted so far. Radio reports are declaring numerous provincial cities in the delta are under assault. Many have probably been overrun, based on their desperate calls for help right before radio contact was lost. Even Saigon and Tan Son Nhut are under attack. I think it's only a matter of time before we'll be under fire."

We were stunned. A major North Vietnamese offensive! To simultaneously occur across Vietnam required a lot of manpower and an awful lot of planning. Entire towns overrun!

"Sorry, Chuck, we need you here, so leave for you to go to Saigon is canceled," Pete said, with mock harshness. "Guys, you all know your post here at the hotel. We will need to set up soon."

When we first arrived in My Tho, we were briefed on defensive positions at the hotel and at the base. Especially after the last month of inactivity, I would have never thought we'd be deploying in a defensive posture. War definitely has no rules.

When Pete finished, he turned and headed back downstairs. Gallagher looked at each one of us. "That's it. Everybody off the roof. Get your stuff downstairs. It's time for a brief. Start breaking out the hardware. There's a war going on."

We all started down off the roof. Right at the corner of the building where the stairway enters onto the roof was a small, rectangular, pill-boxlike guard shack. A sailor was always on duty, performing binocular observation ("glassing the perimeter") of the surrounding area as part of the Navy security detail. As we headed downstairs, Gallagher leaned in. "Get on downstairs with us."

"No, sir," replied the guard. "I'm on duty. I haven't been relieved."

Gallagher shrugged, and we walked down the steps. We turned left, heading toward the front of the building, in step to Gallagher's room for the briefing.

KAABOOM! The entire hotel shook! Concrete chips, dust, and debris cascaded down from above. A mortar had just hit the building! From behind us, Mikey Boynton, still coming down the stairs, screamed, "The guard shack. They just demolished the guard shack!"

Sure enough, barely ten to fifteen seconds after we'd passed by, the poor kid was blown to pieces. Suddenly, small arms fire was hitting the hotel. *Bidididip! Tick tick tick tick. Bidididap!*

It was pounding the walls and concrete pillars. Guys were hitting the deck. From somewhere below us, someone yelled, "Hey! What's going on?"

"We're under attack, you idiot!" screamed a reply from off to my right.

It all happened so quickly. Just a moment before, we were partying. We blinked and *bam!* we were taking fire!

"Everyone get to your rooms, get your guns, and get to your post," snarled Gallagher.

I crawled on my stomach, trying to stay below the one-foot-high cinder block that was the lower railing support. Bullets seemed to be striking the hotel all over the place. I got to my room, crawled in, and cracked open a case of Stoner rounds. With a deftness borne of months of practice, I began connecting two-hundred-round belt after two-hundred-round belt together so I could sustain a continual, withering fire, if necessary. Nine hundred rounds per minute could make you "shell poor" in very little time. Quickly, I got into my cammies and boots.

BDDDAAAP! BDDDAAAP! BDDDAAAP! Tick Tick Tick Tick. Tick Tick Tick Tick Tick. BDDDAAAP! BDDDAAAP! Tick Tick Tick Tick.

"Damn! They're really bringing it to us," I lamented to myself. I rechecked my gear. Grenades, check. Stoner and two cases of Stoner rounds, good to go. Then, from what I figured was the first floor, I heard American M16s going off. In the darkness, I found it ironic that brightly colored tracers were hitting our hotel. Mikey had his wish. The fireworks were right here.

Someone screamed, "We're being assaulted. We're being assaulted!"

I looked at Curtis. "Can you believe this?"

Curtis smiled coyly. "I think it's great. All of our trips into the jungle without finding anybody to shoot. . . . Now they are coming to us! We better hurry."

The assault was coming against the front of the hotel—Gallagher's side. I belly-crawled out of our south-side-rear, corner-end room and slid into the front corner. At the corner were two cement pillars that formed an L—a right angle—a natural shield. I peeked out over the edge at the street and area in front of the hotel. *Oh, baby! There are an awful lot of people out there! Let's see what happens to your little party now.* Sticking my gun barrel out through the railing, I pointed at the throng of soldiers in front of our hotel. I unleashed an ungodly amount of terror upon the crowded courtyard. Setting up next to me were Hooker and Ashton. As though a switch were turned on, all the SEALs opened up almost simultaneously. I don't think the NVA were counting on ordnance being brought against them like that. God bless Gallagher! If this attack had come when we were still leaving our gear on base, we would really have been in trouble. As it was, we couldn't sustain this for long—but at least we weren't returning fire with 9-millimeter pistols.

The frightened mood from below us was improving—if only momentarily. "The SEALs are getting into it! The SEALs are getting into it!" came a cry from the second floor below. "All right! Give them hell, guys!"

And boy, did we give it! Gallagher and Riojas pulled one pin after another, tossing grenades over the balcony. Ashton and Keener had M60s, but we didn't have any M60 ammo, so they were forced to use M14s and M16s. We also didn't have any LAAW rockets, which would have been real nice about then. From our perch, up above on the third floor, we easily canopied our fire up and down the street. *Let's see what they have.* If this was all they brought to the party, then we should win easily. If they had heavier fire, well, we could be wiped out. It was amazing how quickly my head cleared when my life was on the line.

They kept coming. And coming and coming. All night long, till six, seven A.M., they were still attacking.

Ashton looked over at Hooker and me. "Can you guys see all the bodies out there? There must be several hundred or more."

I had gone through approximately four thousand rounds, so far. I'd gone back for more rounds three times already. Each time, I came back, looked at the numerous targets, and let it fly. Shoot and get more, shoot and get more. My hands blistered from the red-hot barrel of my Stoner. When I went back into the room to get more shells around five A.M., I grabbed three sodas for us out of the fridge. I had to pause and smile. I never had the opportunity to operate like this before! It was nice not to get dirty for a change!

The shooting died down around seven-fifteen A.M. By seven-forty-five, the street in front of our hotel was deserted. Cautiously, I stood up and peered out around the concrete pillar. To my right and down below us were our "borrowed" jeeps. From here, it looked like they were untouched! I didn't know why they hadn't been shot up. This was good news.

There was general confusion throughout town. Civilians were, for the most part, staying hidden. The NVA, VC, and local VC were all doing coordinated attacks, but primarily against larger military targets. Dong Tiem, located to the west of us, was taking a beating. The ROK (Republic of Korea) Marines were to the east, Saigon was to the north, while a large ARVN complex was northeast of us. The major enemy forces were attacking these other large installations, while their "Zapper Units" apparently had filtered into town to overrun small bases such as ours. Our thinking was that these Zapper Units had not foreseen the level of resistance we would put up. They probably pulled back, waiting for assistance from one or more of the major units advancing forward after finishing with their initial objective.

Gallagher, Roy Dean, and I climbed back up onto the roof to scout things out. We glassed the entire town. As best we could tell, they had sent 200 to 300 men to wipe out us and the small 10- and 15-man communication stations (Com Stations), along with other small detachments. What we saw was fighting going on around us, with forces traveling streets around town rather than through. These "forces" were sobering. From the roof we saw tanks and half-tracks, lots of them.

Gallagher, being the brilliant tactician that he was, realized we had a window of opportunity right then. The Zappers had pulled back, with remaining fire being a minimal, ineffective, random sniperlike shooting. All the activity was elsewhere. I could see tank against tank battling just outside of town. This was just like in Europe! Big World War II-type stuff.

"There's nobody harassing us right now. We need to get down to the Navy compound and get the rest of our gear," Gallagher stated. "I need four volunteers—Curtis, Keener, Constance, and Matthews. Go get it."

We looked at each other. "Welcome to a firsthand glimpse of the 'military volunteer system'!" I muttered under my breath. "He thinks it . . . we do it!"

We couldn't take much with us *to* the base, as it would take up space for supplies we would carry back. Driving the three quarters of a mile with two to a jeep, the four of us drove as quickly as we could to the gates of the compound. The sailors at the base had set up machine-gun nests behind bunkers, and were dug in fairly well. When they saw us, they quickly opened the gates. They thought they'd saved us.

"No, we're just loading up to go out," remarked Curtis Ashton. "We're having a big party at the hotel today. What's with all this machine-gun nest stuff here, anyway?"

The guard smiled. He lightened up. "You guys are really going to go back out there?"

After we nodded with as much macho bravado as we could—giving them the "that's what I said, wasn't it?" look—he smiled again.

He uttered an increasingly common statement. "You SEALs are crazy!"

He gave us an update of what they knew. Can Tho, Vinh Long, and all other Navy bases they were able to make contact with, were under attack. Again, fortunately for us, because My Tho was the smallest Naval base in the country, it was, at that moment, not under fire. Like us, the base had seen heavy fire the night before.

"Are we lucky, or what? We'd better hurry before our luck wears out," I noted.

We pulled over to the SEAL Team bunker. We loaded cases and cases of ordnance into the jeeps. A half hour later, we were seriously highly explosive and heavy-laden.

"Whoa, baby," said Roy Dean. "If we get hit we'll never know it! We'd be part of the largest Roman candle ever seen!"

We had cases and cases of LAAW rockets. Cases of M60 ammo, cases of grenades, cases of Willie Pete, cases of Stoner rounds, and cases of M26 grenades. Roy Dean grabbed four new M60 machine guns and just threw them in the front seat of his jeep.

"Hey, guys, we can't load anymore. Let's get back," worried Keener.

"Gallagher. Gallagher, be advised. We are returning. Please have the entrance clear, over."

"Will do," came the reply.

We had several guys deployed on the hotel roof in order to immediately return fire in the event we were attacked. They were to provide cover as we came up the street.

We arrived back at the hotel having taken only a couple of odd rounds, and they weren't real close. Before we could turn off the motor, guys were streaming out, forming a human chain to pass ordnance on up to the hotel. *Pass it on up. Pass it on up.*

Gallagher had enlisted the help of about half the sailors in the building. He'd gone through the entire building and, with the support of the other officers, made strategic adjustments. All sailors on the first floor relocated to the second floor. He teamed them up, and made sure they had the necessary equipment for their assigned firing positions. Gallagher found out who was senior and who was junior, then made teams out of them. The team leader reported to us. In the two hours we were gone, the sailors had completely sandbagged the openings in the second-floor banister railings, effectively expanding the firing positions we could utilize.

Morale went up exponentially. Most of these sailors hadn't fired a gun in-country. Their pistols were ineffective against the onslaught that came at us last night. Knowing this, they were excited about getting hardware and ammunition to effectively fight. They appreciated us, realizing we weren't going to abandon them. Guys were acting cocky, yelling, and putting that little extra bravado into their voices. It was not a bring-'em-on sort of thing, but neither was it the paralyzing fear evident the night before. Having our shelter blasted at with close-range mortar and machine-gun fire, and the radioman reporting many other bases under heavy fire, it was natural to feel panicky, trapped, and claustrophobic.

Moving first-floor residents up to the second floor gave us several little advantages. The first floor took an awful lot of fire the night before, largely because it permitted level shooting. When they had to shoot upward, they would be shooting at an angle. If we were lying down on the second floor, this angle allowed us a zone of safety.

I personally had twelve thousand rounds of Stoner, my sniper rifle, sniper ammo, and half a case of thermite grenades. I was good to go. The "assembly line" outfitted everyone very well.

"Case of M-sixty," someone yelled out.

"Pass it up and left. I'll take it," someone else replied.

"Case of Stoner."

"Pass it up and straight to the back."

On and on it went. Everyone knew their deployment positions and what they needed before we got back. So, when we arrived and started passing things in, everyone knew what was needed where. It was slick.

Our hotel and the My Tho Naval base were on the north shoreline of the My Tho River. Our observers/snipers installed in sandbag bunkers on the roof called down to tell us an armored column was headed toward My Tho on the road descending out of the north. This road wound right past the ARVN base. From what we could figure, the ARVN base gave the NVA forces very little resistance.

Radio reports from the ROK Marine base indicated they were under fire, but were withstanding the enemy pretty well. The Republic of Korea was one of six nations in addition to the United States who sent troops to Vietnam. I had a lot of admiration for the Korean Marines. They were all "kick ass, take names, and don't bring a pencil" men. They were rough, tough, and mean. The fact they had repulsed the NVA did not surprise me.

I looked at my watch. It was a few minutes past six. All day long, civilians had been running around with white flags, working frantically to pick up the bodies littering the streets. Hundreds of "friendly" casualty bodies, killed by the VC and NVA, were stacked in the courtyard between our hotel and the Vietnamese hotel next door. Suddenly, the locals were gone. *Here we go.*

Bddddaaappp! Bddddaaappp! Biddoumph!

Months of combat still had not deadened the gripping sense of dread that intertwined amidst the volume of earth-shaking artillery. We waited as, like a hurricane approaching a battened-down eastern seaboard, the ground-shaking fury came ever nearer.

Minutes later, main force NVA attacked. We received a full, World War II-type assault attack. The hiss of rockets in flight wreaked the evening air. Rockets exploded into brick walls of nearby buildings. Rubble was strewn into the street, leaving behind gaping holes. Fifty-caliber machine guns rattled furiously. M60 machine guns were going off. The main push came at us.

Our large-caliber guns started pouring out lethal doses of lead into the streets in front of our compound. Strategically, it was difficult for the NVA to direct their fire at us as they had to turn the corner on either side of the street in order to enter the street we were on. This bottlenecked their entry. Obviously, we focused our fire upon these junctions. Unfortunately, if tanks and half-tracks rounded the corner, the battle would be more difficult to sustain at arm's length. So far, the armaments were confined to rockets and heavy-caliber machine guns—crew-serve weaponry. Time dragged on.

As the sun set, things went quiet. We waited. No one was certain why, but it appeared the offensive might be stalling with the eve of night.

Pete and Gallagher ordered half the team up on the roof in search of targets. Tactically, our thinking was they were scouting us before continuing. It figured that, if we killed as many of their reconnaissance team as possible, it would make them think twice about our capabilities and firepower. We wanted to give the impression we were "loaded for bear," and good to go. In war (as in so many things), the more time we had, the better our strategic viability. If we could stay alive, it bought time for reinforcements and relief. We lugged as much ordnance onto the roof as possible. At each corner of the roof were the M60s. We taped sticks to the wall to anchor ponchos shading us from the sun. Since nothing was happening, we grabbed our sniper rifles and shot at anything that moved.

As morning arrived on day two of the attack, our problem was not weaponry or ammunition, but food and water. The bottled water went fast in the warm weather, and we didn't dare drink any of the water from the tank on the roof.

"Well then, as I see it," Gallagher began, "the admin offices should still have sizable supplies of food and water. Let's run over there and get as much food as we can."

Keener, Roy Dean, and I averted our eyes downward, careful not to make eye contact with Gallagher.

"Good. Ashton, why don't you take Keener, Constance, and Matthews with you, seeing as how excited they are to go. Get your rucksacks on and get over to the admin chow hall without getting killed—or too shot up. I just hate blood-tainted food."

We were not smiling. The tension mounted as we once again prepared to venture out from the hotel. I forced myself not to let my mind wander—to thoughts like *Could the NVA clandestinely be sealing the perimeter around us? Are we stumbling right into their reinforced positions? The streets have been deserted for hours . . .*

We belly-crawled along the sandbagged pathway to the doorway on the first floor of the hotel. As the fourth-floor gunners began shooting to divert attention, we ran out the front door and raced to the abandoned cars along the street. We "ping-ponged" from car to car to telephone pole and then to an occasional tree. Quickly, we were down the street and around the corner. After turning right, we were one half block away from the Naval Administration building where most of the sailors at the hotel worked. Whereas our SEAL Team headquarters was at the base along the river, this was the Naval Administration center communications room, chow hall, and Red Dog Saloon. It was set up so sailors could go there in the evening, have a beer, and watch a movie or some form of entertainment provided to the local troops.

Sporadic gunfire was not close—at best, within one hundred feet. We opened the compound door locks with keys issued to us. Unfortunately, the chow hall refrigerators were not so easily opened. We had to scrounge around for bolt cutters to cut the locks. Seconds and minutes ticked by. Frantically, we threw food that would not spoil too quickly into our rucksacks. Large cans of soup, rolls of bologna, cheese, and crackers. I had roughly sixty pounds of food, in addition to the bullets I carried with me.

The trip back to the hotel seemed like it took forever. Amid cheers from the others at seeing their next meal arrive, we bounded upstairs. Gallagher instructed us to deposit the food in his room for distribution.

"Nice job, guys. But we've got one little problem. Do you think you could go back over to the Red Dog and get me a beer?" Gallagher inquired, in as meek a voice as he was capable of.

We shot our way back to the saloon, with Roy Dean leading the way. This time, we took fire as we darted between obstacles. Arriving back at the compound, Roy Dean was smiling, obviously enjoying the running-gun-battle tactics we'd never had the opportunity to engage in before. We made our way to the back room behind the bar. With a look of fiendish pleasure, Roy Dean gleamed. "Gentlemen, stand back." He proceeded to shoot the lock off the door of the Red Dog Saloon. There was more booze than we could drink in a year.

"Look at all this. Maybe we should make two trips," Roy Dean said, excitedly. We started loading all we could carry.

"We gotta get it before they do," Hooker growled, deadpanning in a solemn voice. "I mean, they take our booze and, that's it, man. It means WAR!"

"Yeah. No more just playing with them if they take our sauce," added Ashton, playing along. "Maybe we should set up an outpost here. If we get overrun, we might not even know it!"

Sure enough, we got back, dropped off cases of beer, then turned right around and headed back over. I think we had more liquor than we had bologna and cheese!

Talk about a morale boost. There we were, passing around cold beers to everyone. A lot of bullets and mortar rounds were being shot off around about us. Those Navy guys were wide-eyed with fear. They didn't have the firepower to withstand a full onslaught from the NVA. Then, during the night before last, radio reports came in that city after city and installation after military installation were being overrun. Most of our city had been overrun—and we were next. There we were without clear communication, without food, and without ammunition. The noose tightened. Then, all of a sudden, they saw us carrying first ammunition, then food, and then drinks.

"Get over here and start making bologna sandwiches," demanded Gallagher.

Keener grabbed the bread and unsheathed his knife. "I'll slice the bread." He stabbed the several-day-old French bread and started ripping off chunks.

"Keener, what's wrong with you? You stab VC and *slice* the bread."

"I volunteered for SEALs so I could get out of KP. You want me to call out for a delivery of Rainbo bread, or what?"

We carried sacks of bologna sandwiches and a sack with beer in it. We walked up to each of the rooms, put down the sacks, and took out several sandwiches and beer.

Chomp. Chomp. "Any of you guys want a sandwich and a cold beer?"

With a look bordering on bewilderment, almost to a sailor, they started laughing.

"Damn straight, we do!"

"Nothing like a good gun battle to make a man hungry," I pronounced as I handed them the food. "It's more fun when we do these battles out in the jungle 'cause of the snakes and leeches, but this is almost as fun."

Quickly, glum faces showed signs of registering a glimmer of hope. The combination of food and levity was a tonic to their souls. They started realizing we had a fighting chance to survive—provided we all hung tough together.

Our SEAL audacity became infectious. Guys started to laugh, and several guys down the hall were hooting and hollering. Someone leaned his head out the door—exposed to possible sniper attack—and yelled, "Hey, what's for dinner. I want to know what my choices are going to be."

"Yeah. What time is dinner?"

Riojas leaned his head out the door. "Dinner will be served at nine P.M., sharp, with cocktails at eight. In case of attack, we will dispense with the enemy and begin promptly at nine-thirty."

I looked at Riojas and smiled. "Hey, pretty good British accent there, Rios."

Then the city warfare began. They knew where we were, and we knew where they were. No more sneaking around in the dark, ambushing the enemy, then disappearing into the night. The battle was fierce. Hour after hour the standoff continued. We readily heard the concurrent battling going on at our Naval base and throughout town. My ears were ringing from the continuous staccato of machine-guns bursts. *Tick tick tick tick. Tick tick tick tick. Tick tick tick tick.* It went on and on and on.

Pete and Gallagher decided we needed to take the battle to the enemy. The concern was twofold. First, we needed to attempt to reconnoiter adjacent Naval and other military positions in the area to see if we could rescue any possible survivors. Second, by going out and taking the battle to the NVA, we issued a strong message that we were not in battle just to hunker down in a siege mentality. Rather, we were ready, willing, and able to bring it to them.

Our first excursion was a disappointment. We had, for the past several months, been training with an extremely talented karate instructor who was a member of the ROK Marines. He was about five feet ten inches tall, and solid muscle. He could probably beat most of the SEALs in hand-to-hand competition. We had all grown to like him. His English was quite good, and he frequently joined us for a beer on weekends. He lived nearby, so we started off in his direction.

Rounding the corner, we saw stark manifestation of the reality of urban warfare. Within two blocks of us were three burning car wrecks. The streets were littered with rubble and garbage—strewn up one side and down the other. Window after window was shattered, having been either shot out or exploding in the concussive force of the many rockets that had rearranged the architecture. Gaping holes gnarled most of the stately, French-inspired buildings that overlooked the streets of My Tho. *What a shame,* I thought.

Coming out of one of the buildings approximately forty feet away were six or seven NVA soldiers. *Here we go.*

Simultaneously, we blasted the men into oblivion. We had announced our presence. It didn't take long. We took position behind a burned-out Army truck and an adjacent pile of rubble. *Whhooosh!* A rocket streaked past, barely missing the hulking mass of the truck. For the next five minutes, we exchanged gunfire. As a team, we moved in leapfrog fashion to another rubble pile, splaying firepower in a wide arc for protective cover. It really was exhilarating. The clatter of gunfire, the hiss of rockets, followed by earth-shaking explosions as they found their unfortunate targets—all made for a better-than-Fourth-of-July pandemonium.

We delivered a deluge of fire as we moved in the direction of the enemy. Snipers were shooting at us, while concurrently we were pulsing bullets into windows and roosts they were hiding in. Whether we actually hit them or caused them to move to another location was unknown. We just moved when they quit shooting. Running as fast as we could, we turned right, then left, and were soon six blocks from our hotel.

The ground about us erupted. We all dove for cover. Fortunately, no one was hit. Gallagher, lying on his back, quickly began setting up and extending his LAAW rocket launcher. The strongest fire was coming from either the second- or third-story windows of the building across the street.

''Where are they?'' screamed Gallagher, above the roar of gunfire.

''Third story is what I guess,'' surmised Riojas.

''All right. Give me some cover so I can get the rocket in position.''

Lying on our backs, we held our guns up and pointed them in the direction of the building. It was hard to hold the gun, pull the trigger, and brace to offset the recoil. Gallagher rolled over, lifted the LAAW up, and propelled the rocket into the middle of the building across the street.

KABOOOOM! The building shuddered, absorbing a gaping hole to its midsection. Dust and debris rained down on the sidewalk and street below, sounding oddly like a hailstorm.

The shooting stopped. Scrambling, we raced down the street and around the corner. Darting back and forth from entryway to entryway, we arrived at ROK Marine Lieutenant Soon's home. Cautiously, we set up a perimeter watch and moved closer.

With rising alarm, we found his front door smashed in, fully torn from the hinges. We peered through the open doorway.

''What a shame,'' said Ashton.

There, in a pool of congealing blood, lay our friend. It was a gruesome sight. From what I could tell, the NVA, in their haste, went into his house one at a time. In obvious hand-to-hand combat, Lieutenant Soon killed six NVA soldiers before being overcome and summarily executed with two close-range bullets to his head. Lying strewn about the entryway were the bodies of uniformed NVA soldiers. Their broken necks were disfiguring and grotesquely eerie.

''I wonder if we could've gotten here in time to save him if we came yesterday,'' I mused.

"I bet you we could have. The push last night came from this area, I think," Gallagher said with a sigh. "Damn shame."

Gallagher continued, "Let's get going. The CIA safe house is about six blocks west of here. I want to see how they fared before heading to the Naval Intelligence Center."

Quietly, we moved in the shadows until we were at a large four-way intersection. Crossing streets was the biggest challenge because of the moments of outright exposure. Gazing to our left, we saw the Vietnamese equivalent of a military jeep driving slowly in our direction. We shrunk into the shadows in the doorway of a corner building. Gallagher signaled to me to take them out with my Stoner.

I waited. It was a little easier to ambush someone while ensconced in jungle foliage. I just hoped they didn't see us before I could open fire. The jeep had three soldiers in it, a driver and two men carrying AK-47s.

A little bit more. Just a little farther.... I stepped out as the jeep came right in front of me, barely fifteen feet away. Just as the NVA soldier closest to me glanced over in response to my movement, I sent a deadly burst into the car. *BDDD-DAP!* Then, as if in a surreal impression of a Hollywood war movie, the driver slumped over onto the wheel, one soldier fell out, and the other was laid out over the seat. The jeep just kept rolling on down the street, finally crashing to a stop as it hit a tree.

Crossing the street was an adventure itself in tactical design. Our eyes darted to and fro in search of snipers. My nerves were on edge as I saw people sneaking to glance out of windows around us. The key was to find the one with the rifle barrel. As we moved forward, Keener let out a burst from his Stoner northward, up the street. *TTCCHH TTCCHH TTCCHH TTCCHH!* Simultaneously, Ashton did the same down the street in a southern direction. We left the cover of the rubble-strewn sidewalk. We crossed, hoping the firepower created diversion as we dashed into the open. Racing down a side street, we reached the door of the CIA safe house. As discreetly as possible, we knocked, hoping not to encounter a repeat of the scene we'd just come from at Lieutenant Soon's home.

The door was locked. There was no sign of entry, forced or otherwise. Fanning out, we checked the doors on either side and then in back. Nothing. We "opened" one of the side doors.

"Anybody here? We're a group of American Navy SEALs on a rescue mission. If anyone's here, come out." Gallagher frowned.

The CIA safe house was normally a beehive of activity. For it to be abandoned and empty could only mean one thing.

The CIA knew.

We walked around the office complex. Nothing had been disturbed, other than key electronics and documents. They were all gone. Not the "ransacked" kind of gone, just disconnected and gone.

"Don't look now, but we just happened to take a vacation during Tet. Great idea, huh guys? Funny how we were gone when all hell broke loose. Can you believe our luck?" I mimicked, impersonating the officer normally seated at the desk before me.

Keener smiled, wryly. "They had to have known. They had to know."

"Damn right they did," Gallagher stated with disgust. "They just didn't bother to tell any of the rest of us."

"You know, Chief, they sure left in a hurry. Look. They left their booze, food, a stereo, their generators, refrigerators. Would you look at this," he said, admiringly.

Roy Dean opened a cabinet in the next room. "Hey, look at this. Sardines, chocolate, candy, all kinds of stuff!"

Keener walked in with a case of grenades from another room down the hall. We didn't see this as stealing, but rather, more as a "salvage" of American materiel that would possibly fall into the hands of the enemy, or of looters. All of us were talking and laughing and rifling through amply filled cupboards.

"Gentlemen," Gallagher said, slowly. The room quieted as we glanced over.

"Yeah, Eagle," I replied.

Gallagher was standing next to a great, big, brand-new Frigidaire refrigerator/freezer. He looked longingly at it. It was not one of those dinky old ones that curved at the top. Rather, it was a new, rectangular, twenty-nine-million cubic-foot refrigerator. Gallagher reached in and pulled out a cold beer. Popping the top, he leaned against the giant refrigerator.

In a subdued tone, he stated, "I want this."

Just the way he said it, I knew we were in trouble. I looked at Keener. We both sensed a "volunteer" mission in the offing. "Eagle, what do you mean, you want this? You want the beer that's in your hand? Or, do you want all the beer in the refrigerator?"

Gallagher turned around and hugged the refrigerator. "Mine," he grunted. For effect, he repeated it, "Mine! I need four volunteers to carry this back to the hotel.'' Without missing a beat: ''Keener, Ashton, Constance, and Roy Dean come here!''

''You aren't kidding, are you?'' asked Ashton, the realization hitting all of us at once. The realization that we could not shoot while running and carrying a fridge.

Grinning broadly, Gallagher raised his eyebrows as high as he could and smirked. ''Carry this home!''

''What!'' we all exclaimed in unison.

Hooker and Riojas joined Gallagher in running point as we hoisted the giant Frigidaire onto our shoulders. I was sweating by the time we were out the front door.

When we reached the corner, people were shooting at us. We stopped, just as a rocket flew by. *KA-BOOM!* Gallagher and Riojas touched off a lengthy round of shooting as we made a mad dash across the street. We hoped for two things—to beat the guy with the rocket launcher across the street before he could reload, and that there wasn't more than one!

We made it! Huffing and puffing, we rounded the corner diagonally from where we started.

''Stop!'' Gallagher commanded. He jumped over a downed tree, and blasted away at the corner building ahead. He dropped to his stomach as yet another rocket screamed by.

Instantly, he was on his feet. ''C'mon! Let's go!''

GO! Push! Get those guys over there! We bounced like a pinball back and forth from obstacle to obstacle. Then we were three blocks away.

''Good work, guys. Just a little further,'' Gallagher said, exhorting us onward.

After an eternity, we rounded the corner. Just one block from the hotel. Suddenly, we heard cheering. Bullets were coming from all over the place, many of them right around us. *Tick tick tick tick. Tick tick tick tick. Tick tick tick tick!*

They want to put a hole in the refrigerator and piss off Gallagher, I just know it!

DOOOP DOOP DOOOP DOOP! DOOOP DOOP! The M60s on the roof of our hotel deluged the area behind us with instant potholes. Concrete and asphalt residue mushroomed into the air in miniature clouds.

The rooms in the front of the hotel opened and guys were clapping, hooting, and hollering. *Way to go SEALs! You guys are crazy!*

"Up the stairs! Get it up the stairs!" Gallagher shouted, above the din. He was anxious to get it out of harm's way after coming this far. "Upstairs!"

We trudged up the stairs, finally arriving at Gallagher's room. "Way to go, guys. You knew if you screwed up and got it hurt I would've had you go back and get the other one."

In between the panting breaths brought on by his heaving chest, Roy Dean sighed. "We knew. . . . We were more afraid . . . of you shooting the fridge the closer we got. . . . We just knew you had so much fun and that you . . . that you would want to find an excuse to go back again."

"Hey! Not a bad idea. Anybody else want a refrigerator? Free delivery!"

"Yeah. Very funny."

After we had put it where he wanted it, he proudly walked over, picked up the cord, and plugged it into the wall. The compressor hummed. "Get that beer back in there. We should also put in the cheese and meats that are sitting out as well."

It was then late in the third day of this "Tet Invasion," and we were feeling better about our odds of survival. We improved our communication abilities by placing our antennas onto the roof. We were able to communicate with more people, and more people were able to communicate with us. This gave us the freedom of knowing we were not "the last bastion of Americans" locked into a modern-day version of the Alamo.

We'd been able to sleep in two- to three-hour shifts, depending on enemy activity. So far, we'd gotten one break during the first twenty-four-hour period, and three during day two. If we hadn't had the tremendous firepower we did, we most likely would have been overrun, and sleep would have been out of the question. By having M60s and LAAW rockets on the roof, we were able to keep the enemy at bay. The NVA were not stopping their shooting at us at any particular time of the day or night. There had been lulls when we received light fire, which allowed the groups of us there at the hotel time for sleeping— and suicide refrigerator missions.

Not everybody in the hotel had mentally adjusted to the harsh realities of siege warfare. When the rocket disintegrated the guard shack on the roof in the early hours of Tet, Charlie Watson realized we were under mortar attack. He immediately took the mattress off of his bed, went into his bathroom, sat down on the toilet, and placed the mattress over him. This was designed to act as a bunker in order to provide him with protection should the next rocket be targeted for his door or window. So far, he hadn't moved farther than the bathroom door, whether we were taking fire or not. He only came to the bathroom door in order to ask for food and water. Pete, as his roommate, took care of him.

Pete should have received the Silver Star for his performance in organizing and coordinating our defense of the hotel. Gallagher was the one who rallied the troops, but Pete was the master tactician. He ran meetings and instructed who was to report to the roof with their sniper rifles, who was to man the M60s, who was to man the LAAWs, what this group of sailors was to do, what that group was to do—all of this was coordinated by Pete. There was no doubt in my mind that, by being armed sufficiently, coupled with Pete's military intelligence aided by Gallagher, we kept My Tho from being overrun.

The battle raged on. As evening descended on the third day of the siege, our windows were being shot out by snipers set up in buildings around us. Hooker took some frag, as did two sailors on the second floor. Fortunately, no one was seriously wounded.

"Constance, you and Jesse go up to the roof. Take your sniper rifles and some LAAWs. Let's cut this sniper crap out," insisted Pete angrily.

We crawled up onto the roof and posted ourselves in the sandbagged lookout stations. Each of us had two avenues to shoot, provided we obtained targets. I didn't wait long before spotting two VC ducking from room to room in the hotel next door. They went to a window and shot a burst at us, then moved to another room. I picked up a LAAW and set it up. I waited patiently for them to move into my rocket sites. *There they are. Three, two, one . . .*

WHOOOSSH! The rocket propelled into the room where the two men were shooting. The explosion rocked our hotel.

"Good shot, Harry," joked Jesse. It was hard to miss with a rocket. "Watch this. Can you see that guy behind the car shooting at us down the street there?"

I looked down the street, and, sure enough, behind a burned-out car was a sniper shooting rounds into our west side. Jesse sent a LAAW into the side of the car.

"Perfectly positioned!" I applauded. Chief Jesse laughed.

We shot LAAWs at everybody! They were definitely more destructive than M16 fire!

Beyond three hundred yards, our LAAWs were inaccurate. This was when we utilized our sniper rifles. Chief Jesse and I were the best snipers, so we found ourselves up on the roof quite often. Most of the town's buildings were single-story, with a few two-story buildings. Three- and four-story buildings were scattered here and there, such as the hospital, several other hotels, and government buildings. Other than the hotel two doors down and the hospital at the end of the block, all of the buildings nearby were single-story. From our roof, we could see a long way with our scopes. We could see targets—bad guys running around, others lurking in the shadows—that couldn't possibly see us because we were 500 and 600 yards away.

I ran my scope up on twelve power and scanned the outlying streets. Approximately six hundred yards to the north of us was a group of seven NVA soldiers discussing something. I placed my crosshairs on them. At this distance, they had no idea I was there. I put a round in the chamber. Next, I laid the rifle onto the sandbags and took a deep breath. Sigh. Squeeze.

BAM! One of the NVA soldiers did a backwards cartwheel. Animatedly, the remaining soldiers looked around in alarm. They searched the surrounding buildings and touched off a few rounds for good measure. There was so much shooting going on all around us that they couldn't figure out where my one solitary shot came from. *BAM!* Another soldier hit. They went crazy. They couldn't think to look six hundred yards away. Fifty to one hundred yards away, but not any farther. Jesse and I had a ball.

An hour later, they launched a major assault. First, a contingent of about one hundred soldiers came to attack us. They were coming with guns blazing, following an armored personnel carrier. We sounded an alarm, while, at the same time, sent rockets descending upon them in droves. Long minutes turned into several hours. Fortunately, yet again we beat them back.

The three-story hospital was several doors down to the east of us at the end of the block. They'd been inundated with casualties, and worked feverishly to save as many lives as possible. Unfortunately, hundreds of people had died. The hospital had nowhere to put the bodies, so they stacked them in the alley outside. It was a gruesome, macabre sight. By this time, the smell of decaying bodies started to hang on every breeze.

Tick tick tick tick. Tick tick tick tick. Tick tick tick tick. Shells pounded our hotel. Heavy fire peppered indiscriminately. Any windows not already shot out were shattered.

"Where are they coming from?" asked Pete.

"I'm not sure," responded the roof sentry. "It looked like it's from the hospital."

The hospital had a slanted, tile roof that covered horseshoe shaped gables, giving it almost a Mediterranean appearance. The windows were within the gables, accented with wooden shutters serving as shade screens. The hospital presented a problem since it was overflowing with patients. We could not blast away at it with LAAWs, obviously.

"Take them out with the snipers," retorted Pete, almost nonchalantly.

"Lieutenant!" one of the sailors screamed as he hurried toward Pete and Gallagher. "Two men have been shot. One other took frag."

"Harry, you and Jesse get up there and stop the sniper attack."

After getting into position, we trained our scopes on the hospital, a scant three hundred yards away.

"Third floor, second window in!" shouted Jesse.

I moved my scope into position, just in time to see the shutters closing. I scanned the facade of the hospital until I picked out another shutter opening partially. Quickly, a gun barrel poked its way out, a dozen rounds touched off, the gun retracted, and the shutters closed. I watched, trying to pick up a pattern. If I shot too late, I might hit a patient. I waited. Slowly, a pattern seemed to emerge.

"See how he always seems to go from left to right, then to the center. Left one room, right three, and then to the center," I observed. "You shoot back, but I'll keep my sites on the left windows."

"Yeah, I think you're right."

I trained my gunsights onto the last window to the left. Sure enough, the shutters began to open. I squeezed the trigger. *BAM!*

"Yes! Got that sucker!" I exulted as the sniper pitched from the window and onto the street below.

Over the next twenty minutes, we took out four more snipers.

Jesse looked over, smiling. "Miller time!"

Both of us were sweating in the early afternoon heat. "Not a bad idea," I agreed.

I went to our room and came back with two beers, some rum, and Coke. "It's fair," I rationalized, "since our ops are here and we're not going out."

Jesse readily concurred.

We never drank before (or during) an operation. This time, however, it just made the heat more bearable. I guess the strain of being cut off from the outside world, fighting for your life four continuous days, along with fatigue was getting to all of us.

We both were wearing swim trunks, T-shirts, and flip-flops—"partying" on the rooftop while looking for targets. Jesse was also wearing a stupid-looking visor, like those worn by some of the pretty-boy professional tennis players. I had to laugh. There was little Chuck Jesse, all five feet six inches and 140 pounds, alternately applying suntan lotion, adjusting his hat, getting a drink, telling jokes, and then killing somebody. It just didn't mesh! Over the course of the next two days, Chuck and I practically lived on the roof.

Toward the end of the fourth day, we'd taken out close to fifty snipers from surrounding buildings. It had gotten to be a game.

In his best clipped, English accent, Chief Jesse would raise one eyebrow, look at me, then lift his glass in a toast. "I do say, 'ol chap, is that an enemy soldier o'er yonder there?"

"I do declare, I think you are correct, sir," I replied, mimicking the accent. "Shall I shoot, or would you care to take him?"

"After you, my good sir."

I took aim and shot.

"Bloody good!" said Jesse. We touched glasses together in a toast.

"Sir, does that bloke over there appear to be a civilian or an enemy agent? I believe he is acting in a hostile manner. It appears he is shooting at us. Blimey!" I reported. "After you, sir."

Jesse calmly placed the crosshairs on yet another NVA, exhaled, and pulled the trigger. "I believe I missed!"

Quickly, he chambered another round, took aim, and shot. This time it found its mark, another enemy casualty claimed.

"Jolly good shot. I believe you got him."

It was difficult to keep from laughing. We both looked like we were surfer dudes, dressed as we were. Talking like high-bred country gentlemen, shooting NVA in the Southeast Asian heat and humidity, it was a classic "what's wrong with this picture" non sequitur.

On the morning of the fifth day of Tet, we were summoned to Pete's room for a meeting. Pete quickly reported the recent message traffic coming over the radio.

"The tide seems to be turning. We've reestablished communication with HQ. A number of bases have been overrun, but friendly reinforcements are pouring into hostile regions. The enemy action has come to be known as the Tet Offensive. According to intelligence reports, the NVA have taken heavy casualties."

To cheers, he announced, "The worst is behind us. NVA troop activity appears to be receding back to the north. We'll soon be receiving help in cleaning up the area."

Gallagher stepped forward. "We need to get over to the ROK compound in order to see how they are doing, as well as to coordinate regional efforts."

Amazingly, our jeep still ran. A group of us (Curtis, Keener, Jesse, Roy Dean, Hooker, and myself) piled in and made our way to the ROK compound three miles away. A collage of bodies, burned wreckage, and rubble imparted a Van Gogh-like landscape. The shooting was light to moderate. I had my Stoner, Jesse had his sniper rifle, and the rest had their normal assortment of M16s and M60s.

The ROK compound was situated on the other side of a tributary of the My Tho River. We slowed and stopped as we came to the bridge leading to their compound. All of us except the driver piled out in order to check the bridge for booby traps. Jesse started across, followed by the rest of the guys and me. The jeep, driven by Hooker, would come across after we crossed. Halfway across, Jesse stopped. He was peering through the angle iron, gazing upriver. "Look!"

We all hit the deck. There, about four hundred meters away, was a sampan with four NVA soldiers. They were paddling northward, crossing the river parallel to us, two other sampans in tow. I pulled my Stoner into position.

"No! Let me take them with my sniper rifle," insisted Jesse.

He braced his rifle in position against the angle iron, sighted in, and squeezed. *PA-CHOO!* The soldier in the front of the sampan was shot out of the boat. The other three soldiers started paddling faster. They were only about one third of the way across the river. Why they didn't dive out of the sampan or turn around, I didn't know.

Chief Jesse took aim again. *PA-CHOO!* The second NVA soldier pitched into the water. Oddly enough, the remaining two started rowing even faster. We could not help but laugh. The crack of Jesse's rifle sent the third soldier to his riverbed grave. The last soldier paddled frantically. It was almost melodramatic. Pausing a few seconds, Jesse grinned. "I can't believe they're staying in the boat." He shot the last NVA soldier, propelling him into the water. Silently, the sampan drifted across and to the other side. We got up and moved across the bridge.

The jeep drove across. We moved to where the three sampans were lying, kept from the current by nipa palm alongside the river's edge.

"Can you believe this?" I blurted out, excitedly.

Preparing to don my equipment for that night's operation, I review my gear at the SEAL Team ready shed.
COURTESY HARRY CONSTANCE

Eugene Thomas Fraley, my friend and bunkmate. Gene was the first member of SEAL Team Two to be killed in combat.
COURTESY U.S. NAVY

Roy Dean Matthews with bullhorn and *(clockwise from bottom)* Richard "Hooker" Turrey, me *(standing)*, Curtis Ashton, and Fred Keener relax after capturing a huge weapons cache.
COURTESY CURTIS ASHTON

This was taken just after I received my third bronze star and fifth presidential Unit Citation. COURTESY U.S. NAVY

Richard Marcinko and I, each one trying to tell a bigger story than the other, at the annual SEAL Team reunion in Little Creek, Virginia, in 1995.
COURTESY RANDALL FUERST

Barbara and me in Escondido, where we live.
COURTESY RANDALL FUERST

I waded into the water to retrieve the sampans. The two "cargo" sampans were laden with all types of ordnance! Grenades, rockets, guns. What a find! Quickly, we loaded it all into the jeep.

We headed to the ROK compound. Arriving, we immediately saw they'd held up well. Other than some damage to the exterior walls of their complex, the two hundred ROKs hadn't sustained many casualties. In fact, they'd been more active than we had in going out into the community harassing and interdicting the NVA.

The return trip home to our hotel was uneventful. An early semblance of order was resuming. At no other time in the Vietnamese war had there been such a widespread, all-out assault as there had been that week. Questions arose regarding when the next wave of assault might come, whether this signaled an escalation in NVA activity, or whether this was simply a regrouping before attacking again; discussions were extensive.

The next day, day number six, found HQ bringing in helicopter gunships and a van with communications hardware. The battle was essentially over. The gunships harassed whatever fragmented VC units were moving in open areas, and control of the areas was reestablished.

Cleanup was horrible. We needed to pick up all of those dead bodies that had been laying there in 90- to 100-degree weather for about a week. The bodies were rank, bloated, and horribly disfigured. Many soldiers' skin looked like well-cooked hot dogs, swollen and splitting. One man's chest, arms, and legs were bloated, the web belt around his waist being the only object still of normal proportion. I reached down and grabbed his arm in order to put his body onto the back of a flatbed truck. His arm came off. It reminded me of overcooked chicken—the bone came out so easily. Worse yet, several of the bloated bodies ruptured, spewing a horrendous gas that was overpowering if we were too close.

We drove another deuce-and-a-half around town picking up body after body. Guard duty became a desirable assignment compared with cleanup! After picking up approximately three dozen bodies, we took them to the river and dumped them in. For the better part of two days, we spent our time picking up bodies of hundreds and hundreds of Vietnamese.

SEALs in Vinh Long piled hundreds of bodies on a funeral pyre in the center of town and burned them. Many, many Viet Cong and NVA were slaughtered in the Tet Offensive. For a while, it appeared it might succeed for them. Fortunately for us—and unfortunately for them—

they just had the Vietnamese version of Pickett's Charge, the infamous death charge of the Confederacy at Gettysburg. Perhaps with just a few more men, a little more strategic direction, or just a little more luck, they might have overrun us all. As it was, they gambled and lost.

Interestingly enough, my dad had flown in from Washington. When his plane touched down at Tan Son Nhut base in Saigon, he was quickly told to leave. The brass did not want high-ranking officials accidentally captured, as no one truly knew the extent of the NVA offensive, only that it had been effective. Before he left, he was told My Tho was overrun. He was further told that my brother Charlie, a Marine, was in a town north of Saigon that was overrun, as well. Thus, we were all in Vietnam during Tet. Before he left, he wrote a short note to each one of us, and mailed it to our APO address, hoping against hope we'd live to read them.

Also of interest was the fact that the *only* three provincial cities in the delta not overrun were the three bases of operation for SEALs— My Tho, Can Tho, and Vinh Long. Hue, Da Nang, and many other cities were overcome by the enemy. Not one person from our team received a medal. I guess we should have been happy we were not arrested for stealing booze and refrigerators. Probably fair!

Tet lasted about seven days. It took us another four days to clean up and police the area. A week later, several disaster crews came in to remove all the burned cars and rubble. Some of the villagers had come out of hiding, but the town was still largely deserted.

We had contacts in the community. Friends and agents, cooks, cleaning people, and an entire intelnet were in hiding, fearing for their lives should the NVA overtake the town. They had no way to get out to obtain food and water. We had been taking out C-rats to our contacts and friends while out on patrol. It was kind of a grisly sight to behold: food in the front, in the cab, with ghoulish bodies in the back.

Anyhow, we went and took cases of C-rats to mama san, and to our other friends in the community who were starving. They were so very grateful that we cared, and that we were not just using them.

"You come over after this all over with. I fix you very good meal. You never forget how good my cooking!" We were told this numerous times by grateful villagers unfortunately drawn into the web of war.

Ted Rischer, another East Coast SEAL, was in Chow Duc during Tet. He was in a similar position as myself, providing cover fire from the rooftop of their hotel. Unfortunately for Ted, he took a round right between the eyes, becoming the only SEAL casualty of Tet.

Now that what was being referred to as the Tet Offensive was over, there were investigations into everything. After the town was cleaned up, relatively safe and presentable, the Administrative guys came in to work fastidiously upon their voluminous queries and detailed analyses.

Everyone—most notably the CIA—had returned. They filed a report that the NVA had ransacked their station and taken all their materials. They filed for cameras, tape recorders, food, booze (and a refrigerator) with the government as "loss of property." To the best of our knowledge—and our inspection—they had ample time to take all of it with them. We didn't find any cameras or tape recorders, so we were sure they had taken it all with them. They filed claims as if they hadn't.

One of their informants must have told them about seeing some Americans "visit" their safe house. An agent arrived, wishing to speak with Gallagher. He was directed up to Gallagher's room on the third floor. I was seated on the edge of Gallagher's bunk when he arrived.

"Hello. I'm with the Agency, and we are under the impression that you may have visited our facility two weeks ago. Specifically, we're missing a refrigerator."

Gallagher, leaning up against the gleaming Frigidaire refrigerator, paused, screwed his face into a look of serious contemplation, then replied, "Ain't got it."

The agent smiled. "Well, that's good, because we would probably have to charge whoever took it with theft of government property."

"We'll keep an eye out for it. Anything else?"

"No. That's about it."

The agent turned and walked off.

After he had left, I looked at Gallagher. I was concerned, as he obviously had to have seen the new Frigidaire refrigerator Gallagher was so nonchalantly leaning against. I have seen guys' careers derailed for significantly lesser violations. "Chief, do you think they'll do anything?"

"Hell no! Those bastards leave town when the war gets here. They're too afraid to fight, and then they come back, throw their weight around and start whining about stuff—half of which I'm sure never was taken—that disappeared when they were gone. Sorry you missed the battle, gentlemen. I hope you can excuse us but we just happen to have a war going on," Gallagher charged, with a huff. "I still cannot believe they didn't have the decency to make a few phone calls to let people know what was happening."

Both Pete and Gallagher deserved medals for their valiant efforts in brilliantly keeping My Tho from being overrun. They never received so much as a commendation.

Oh well, I thought, *we'll be heading home soon.* With a degree of satisfaction, I reflected upon the past seven months. Sure, I could have done things differently a time or two. But, the fact that I handled things—I did not panic or develop "stage fright"—gave me a great deal of inner strength. Poor Chicken Charlie. He took off right after Tet as a medical evacuation. He just cracked.

Tet was war, in the classic definition. It was "Line them up and move forward. Give them your best and see if you can overrun the enemy." Fortunately for us, only one tank came at us, which was neutralized by three LAAWs. They brought the battle to us, and we were victorious.

CHAPTER 12

MO CAY

INTELLIGENCE REPORTS CONTINUED TO CLARIFY THE MAGNITUDE of the victory American and allied forces achieved during the Tet Offensive. *Tens of thousands* of casualties were confirmed. Viet Cong forces had been decimated. We truly believed we may well have broken the back of the North, and winning the war was only a matter of time. The VC and NVA had failed to obtain their military objectives, and their losses in personnel and hardware had been substantial.

Their extensive onslaught of personnel was designed to overrun American positions, take over our significant stockpiles of military hardware and assets, and hand the Americans a stunning defeat. Regardless of cost. Thousands of Vietnamese were sacrificed during Tet, all for naught.

By our estimation, the only way for the North to continue to survive would be in utilizing guerrilla warfare tactics. The only way guerrilla warfare could be effective was with a strong intelligence and supply network. We referred to this as Viet Cong Infrastructure—the VCI.

In order for them to be effective terrorists, they had to be able to have the people in the neighborhoods not tell on them when the cops came by, whether due to fear, respect, payoffs, or relationships. The terrorists needed to obtain weapons and intelligence so they could attack the Americans. The VC had clandestine networks, with cells of sector chiefs controlling small villages, large neighborhoods, and rural areas. Over them were area chiefs, with controlling leadership from the North overseeing the entire network.

Thus, when guns were transported from the North, they were first delivered to the province leadership. They kept some, disseminating the rest to each area sector chief. He, in turn, kept some, and distributed the remaining weaponry to cell leaders, who provided them down their chain of command.

The VCI was the pipeline used to bring these weapons and documents to the South, while, at the same time, moving other materiel and documents to the North. The VCI was a perfect target for SEALs. If we could work our way "up the line," we could take out entire provincial VC webs. There were a number of distribution centers where materiel had been transported along the Ho Chi Minh Trail. Our feeling was that if we could hit those centers, the impact would be substantial.

We understood the VC were in a very weakened, vulnerable position within their communities in late February 1968. We needed to strike as quickly as we could. We targeted local sector chiefs, their chain of command, and those places where they would be receiving supplies. We knew what they did, where they went, when they ate, and when they slept. For as many of the higher-ranking officials as we could, we paid them midnight visits without alerting the guards, without leaving discernible tracks or evidence as to our presence. Several times, I was able to cut a slit in the thatch wall of the hooch, cut the official's throat, and leave without awakening his wife or alerting the sentries posted outside. On a number of ops, we were barefoot. Had we worn American-issue boots, it would have alerted them that Americans were in the area. Our footprints in the mud were a bit bigger, while their footprints were wider—but few, if any, could tell because of how heavily traveled the trails were.

Our operations following Tet were hot and furious. Local communities that had not offered information to us concerning VC activities out of fear of reprisal were doing so now. They, too, recognized the weakened state of the local VC cells. The results were devastating, with VC bases and provincial VC headquarters being wiped out. If you had been able to read *Stars and Stripes,* you would have thought the war was on the verge of being won!

We received a call from the West Coast SEAL platoon located farther down in the delta at Vinh Long, a village along the Co Chien

River, requesting we all work together on a large-scale operation in their AO. They were a newer platoon in-country, and the area in question was in very difficult terrain that would be hard to hit without them knowing we were coming. The town was supposedly a major distribution center, openly Communist, with numerous Communist flags and pictures of Ho Chi Minh brazenly displayed.

The West Coast SEAL platoon asked if we would be interested in participating with them in an assault on this city known as Mo Cay. They called us because we had been in-country the longest.

"I told them that absolutely we were interested," reported Pete at our briefing. "This war could be over before we are able to get our next assignments into country."

We were flown by helicopter to rendezvous at their base at Vinh Long. Upon arriving, we watched as a seagoing LST arrived to support us, four more helicopters, several Mikes and STABs, and a whole lot of ordnance.

Mo Cay was known by the locals as a main force VC stronghold. It was a moderately sized town that boasted several restaurants, some stores, a bicycle shop, a rice mill, and a city hall. It had never been visited by ARVN or U.S. forces. Roughly half the population were said to be soldiers. The plan we devised was to overrun this town of between 300 to 500 people. We implemented a two-pronged attack. From the staging area on the beach, we would travel by foot in a southeasterly direction. Vinh Long was located on the Co Chien River, one of the three major waterways that constitute the Mekong Delta. The Mo Cay River traverses from the Co Chien River in a southeast to northwest direction, dumping eventually into the Pacific Ocean. The "armada" of ships would run up Co Chien to the mouth of the Mo Cay, and then go as hard as they could, coinciding their arrival at dawn with ours.

"We had better take at least twenty SEALs, 'cause this could be tough," said Keener.

The truth was, we could do well to take more men. Fortunately, when and if the firefight got hot and heavy, one quick call and several helicopter gunships would markedly shift the balance in our favor in a hurry.

We left Can Tho about one P.M., bound for the coast. We were let off late in the afternoon, and began our inland trek. Leaving from the staging area at dusk, we walked all evening and all night, arriving just after dawn. Mo Cay sat on the wide Mo Cay Canal, with the town center facing the water's edge. We circled around in order to come in from the eastern, rear flank of the city.

They did not suspect a thing! No one had detected our movement.

Mo Cay had one main street running parallel to the Mo Cay River. It was wide enough to drive a jeep through, but not much more. Midway down the street, another street shot off perpendicular to the main street. Both streets were lined with hooches, their lawns neatly manicured. At the junction of the two streets was a large wooden rice depository with two concrete pillars. Across the top of the pillars was a slab of concrete. On top of this was a four- by eight-foot, four-inch-thick concrete slate brightly painted with the Viet Cong flag. Written on the pillars were slogans such as WELCOME HO CHI MINH! and VIET NAM, ONE COUNTRY OUR COUNTRY. Every home had a picture of their son in uniform, along with the requisite picture of Ho Chi Minh. Almost every house had a Viet Cong flag, Buddha altar and candles adorning the entryway. The VC used Mo Cay as a center of operations to resupply and meet others without incident.

The citizens there had built up a series of dikes. The top of the dikes were packed hard enough for people to ride bicycles across them. With the level of humidity and annual rainfall here, this was a rare sight. There were numerous water buffalo in town, many tethered to Asian carts serving as utility trailers for the families.

I was on point for this op. After scoping out the perimeter of the town and everything else I could see, I signaled, *All clear.* Pete called up the other six-man team and instructed them to flank to the right, positioned to provide rear guard and a blocking force against fleeing townspeople. Like the goalie in soccer, those six SEALs were to take care of anyone who came out—preferably taking them prisoner.

We headed left for a northerly position near the river. The twelve of us would assault the town, leapfrogging from house to house as we systematically invaded each hooch and business.

The first two hooches had only civilians in them. We motioned to them to move quietly outside and they would not be shot. They were aghast with fear, as we presented quite a sight with our green and black faces. The mama san, busy fixing breakfast, dropped her stirring "spatula" as we walked in. Our height and weight were significantly more massive than that of any of the local men, and most of the civilians had never come in contact with Americans before.

Once outside, they were instructed to move to the cement rice building. "Go to the flag," Riojas instructed.

The people were made to stand in the hip-deep water of the Mo Cay Canal where they would not be harmed. We had high-speed boats coming upriver and helos landing to take possession of those captured. Some would be taken back to detention centers and interrogated, while most of the civilians would be allowed to return to their homes after we left.

I made my way to the third home and approached the front door. It was just after six A.M. and no one was out. As I reached for the door handle, the door opened and there before me were two VC. They were in full uniform with web belts, magazine clips, and SKSs slung over their shoulders. Startled at my standing a mere three feet away, the two stopped short. The ramifications of my being there quickly dawned on them.

BDDDD-DAP! I shot both of them before they could react; the impact slinging their riddled bodies back through the doorway and into the front hallway. I bounded through the open doorway. Searching, I looked intently for any other men in black pajamas. Fortunately, there were none, so Keener and Riojas herded mama san and her two kids out into the backyard.

Tick tick tick tick! Guns erupted all over town. Once I pulled the trigger, it woke everybody up. The seasoned VC soldiers suddenly realized something was amiss. They grabbed their guns and sprang into action. Amazing how our element of surprise was compromised when I let loose a short burst of machine-gun fire!

We stormed through house after house, having split into two four-man teams. My team consisted of Riojas, Keener, Curtis, and myself. The other team included Gallagher, Roy Dean, Hooker, and Jesse. The remaining four comprised the "prisoner handling detail"—Mikey Boynton, Jack Rowell, and two others. They instructed civilians to go immediately to the "big flag" on the concrete pillar over the entrance to the town. Two boats pulled in on either side of the large rice building, and four men were there to herd people into the water where they could guard them.

We leapfrogged from building to building. Keener, Curtis, and I raced in shooting, with Riojas coming in more slowly as the mop-up detail. The other team would then run past us and blow through the next house. As they were going through that house, we'd run past them and into yet another.

Every time people heard noises coming from the house next door, their adrenaline surged and they jumped to varying states of readiness.

All of a sudden, we came blowing through the door so fast that, even though they thought they were ready with their guns in hand, they weren't. It was essential that we kept running. Funny how such a slim margin in time was so often the difference between success and staying alive versus being shot and killed. I'd hear bullets hitting right behind me.

This was an incredibly wild shooting experience. Bullets sprayed all over. Helicopter gunships were screaming overhead. The wind and dust and bullets created an instant havoc of fear throughout the village. With panic etched across their faces, the civilians readily hurried to the river with their hands up. The hard part was shooting around the stream of villagers at the bad guys who were shooting at us. We desperately didn't want to hit any women or children, and wanted to capture as many soldiers alive as possible.

Several hooches were returning strong fire. Concussion grenades were tossed in, and the shooting ceased. Running, yelling, and screaming, we blew through Mo Cay. A number of VC walked out with their hands up, while most chose to fight it out.

The operation was carried out with brutal efficiency! Two hundred eighty-five civilians were captured, fifty-seven Viet Cong captured, a dozen killed, and another thirty-something escaped. No children were injured, and only one woman had been hurt. Fortunately, almost all of them instinctively knew to get down when the shooting started.

The violence of the action we'd instituted was swift, deadly, and sure. It took us just five minutes to go through forty to fifty homes and round up more than three hundred people. People were confused as to what had just occurred.

As we prepared to make a second sweep to thoroughly search each hooch, the wailing started. Suddenly, I noticed fifteen or so VC coming into town from the north, their guns ablaze.

"A platoon of VC is coming in from the north. Please engage them," I screamed over the radio to the helicopters aloft.

"Roger that," came the reply.

He banked the gunship around. His machine guns opened up and his rockets were launching.

"I got them in the open," the pilot said, in an understatement.

"Nice job!" I said, congratulating him. He decimated the entire platoon of VC.

Several times, surrounding detachments of VC attempted to attack us but were repulsed by the helos. They sustained heavy casualties.

It was now six-twenty in the morning. The early morning air was thick with smoke from all the shooting. Dust was in the air, the smell of cordite wafting throughout town as a result of grenades that had been used. The then-unattended cooking fires that had been started in order to cook the morning's breakfasts also contributed their own distinctive smell.

Pete gathered the team. "Go back and start your search."

We searched for people hiding, documents, and for other things that were part of the war effort. We found numerous diaries, letters from the North, letters to the North—all sorts of major military information that later would have significant impact upon VC efforts in the delta. The intelligence was incredible.

"Pete, you'd better come look at this!" yelled Roy Dean.

From the next building: "Lieutenant, you gotta see this! It's unbelievable!"

There were photo albums of companies, platoons, and battalions. Military directives and supply lists. We found numerous backpacks containing letters, documents, money, and personal belongings.

We'd been told to try not to trash the town. So far, so good. After two hours, our second sweep was almost through. The only building we had not searched was the huge rice depository.

I had to smile. Coming through the white, billowing smoke lingering over the village came Archie Grayson, his gun slung over his back, riding a bicycle and ringing the little bell. Jack Rowell came walking out of one of the buildings without his gun. He was carrying two twenty-pound bags of intricately carved artifacts. They were beautiful—water buffaloes, Buddha, and other oriental items.

"Look at these, would you!" he exclaimed. "I am taking very seriously the directive that any item of benefit to the enemy is to be eliminated and/or removed. What do you think?"

Walking into the rice building, I began investigating. I started hoisting out bags of rice. The floor of the building was made of wood. This was unheard of in Vietnam—unless something was underneath.

I think something's under here! This should be fun, I thought as I pried up one of the boards. Suddenly, an explosion rocked the building. It was not a TNT-type explosion, but more of a gasoline detonation. Instantly, I was engulfed in flames. Searing heat pervaded every pore of my body. I jumped up, turned, and started running toward the door. I squinched my eyes closed, running blindly. I missed the door by a good four feet and banged through the side of the wall. My whole body was on fire. I had my sleeves rolled up on my jacket to my biceps, thus exposing my forearms. I was wearing a beret, no scarf, no gloves, and long pants.

Hit the deck! Get in the dirt to extinguish the flames! Roll!

I flung myself onto the ground and started rolling. The stinging, burning sensation and smell of all my hair being burned was overwhelming. My brain screamed, awash in pain, shock, and the sickening stench of burning flesh. Guys were flapping on me, helping extinguish the flames.

I opened my eyes. Smoke was coming off my body. I knew I was hurt. I just hoped the pain was not an indication how bad it was. It hurt.

Riojas came over and knelt down next to me. My entire face was burnt, my lips, cheeks, ears, everything. My mind flashed to images of the Phantom of the Opera. "How bad is my face, Rios? How bad am I hurt?"

Ever the sympathetic corpsman, Riojas gazed intently at my face. "Man, you're screwed."

"Course, you were always ugly anyway, Harry, so it's no big deal," he continued. "You know, when you came through that wall, you had flames coming off you six to eight feet into the air. Pretty neat, Harry! You make one hell of a human torch!"

Riojas shot me up with morphine. He took me on board ship and began cleaning me up as best he could. Even with the drugs, the pain was almost unbearable.

Unfortunately, the wind kicked up. The explosion caused the rice depository building to burn out of control. The wind rapidly spread the blaze to every building in the row. The entire village was lost to fire. There was no stopping it. We couldn't stop brittle, dry nipa palm thatch from burning in the wind.

Two elderly men worked feverishly with buckets of water, attempting to save one of their homes. They'd left the detention area when the fire erupted, and were desperately trying to squelch the flames.

Two West Coast SEALs grabbed an interpreter and walked over to the two men. "Why are you doing this? It's hopeless."

The taller of the two paused for just a moment. "This is the mayor's home. He has more than twenty thousand dollars hidden in the roof. It's American money that's been collected on the black market."

At once, the SEALs dropped their weapons and joined in. Unfortunately, the house incinerated quickly. All of the cash was lost.

On the boat, I was approached by yet another corpsman. He didn't know I had received a shot of morphine. In a somewhat delirious state due to the intermingling of the morphine and the pain, I was complaining, "Man I hurt! I'm tingling and I'm burning."

He grabbed several codeine pills and gave me two. The pain went right away!

"Great! I am feeling good!" I told him. "I must have been burnt just a little bit!"

I went and grabbed my stuff. I clicked my Stoner off safe, and, in my drug-induced delirium, arrived at the conclusion that the only way to save the "battle" was to shoot all the "assaulting" VC coming at us in the river right next to the boat.

A quick-thinking officer on board ship realized what had happened and yelled at me. "Not those people. The assault is much worse over there in the tree line." He pointed away from the civilians in the river to the adjacent treeline, 180 degrees in the opposite direction.

You did not tell a SEAL with a loaded gun not to shoot. *Where to shoot* was a much wiser decision.

"Hey! Could I borrow your gun to shoot at the enemy?"

"Sure!" I replied, happy at the world and this nice sailor. I was in La-La land.

He quickly used up all my bullets. "Thanks!" he said, handing me back my Stoner.

Meanwhile, the town was burning, smoke all over the place, and helos flying overhead telling us there were a lot of people coming our way and that we needed to get out of town.

I was medevacked out to a hospital ship with Riojas. The doctor looked me over. "Take him in the shower and scrub him."

Not only was I burnt, but all the green and black face paint was mingled in with burnt flesh. Riojas grabbed some Phisohex and a nylon brush and commenced to clean me up. By the time he was done, my skin was pink—or, rather, mostly red and bleeding. Morphine and codeine combined were extremely helpful, however. I hardly felt a thing.

I lost my eyebrows, eyelashes, and much of my hair. Several days later, my mouth was distended, chapped, and swollen with edema. Golf ball-sized water blisters dotted my body with painful areas of sloughed-off skin. The left side of my face took direct exposure in the blast, and was more badly burned. I listened as the doctor told Riojas I would probably lose vision in my left eye and there would probably be permanent scarring.

Oh man, am I ruined! I thought, feeling exasperated and irritated at the same time.

They recommended I stay in the hospital for two to four weeks. After several days, I'd had enough of the hospital. Riojas and I convinced the doctors that I could convalesce just as well in My Tho. Fortunately, the severity of my injuries was not as bad as predicted. I didn't lose vision, and there were very few disfiguring scars. *Whew! Back to my old lovable self!* A week later, I was ready to go out again.

The Mo Cay op was a very large and important one. A journalist came along on one of the ships, recording details of the invasion. It made U.S. military papers across South Vietnam.

The data collected from Mo Cay prisoner interrogation unearthed an incredibly valuable piece of information. Halfway between Mo Cay and Vinh Long was a major weapons storage and manufacturing plant. The person offering all the information stated they had lathes and molds for bullet, grenade, and mine manufacturing. He agreed to help us find the facility in exchange for favors to him and his family.

There was considerable enemy activity in the area surrounding this weapons plant. Again, we traveled all night with our twelve SEALs, six West Coast SEALs, and two guides. There was a VC battalion reported in the area. I definitely did not want to run into one of those again. I'd already done that, thank you.

In the early hours of the morning, we came within 130 yards of a hooch with a light. "That's it," said the VC, who'd agreed to lead us.

I signaled Pete up to me and pointed out the purported weapons facility. Pete called the other officer from the West Coast SEALs, and showed him. He then laid out his strategy.

"We'll travel down these two different, parallel dikes. When we get to here, you guys are to provide the rear blocking. We'll sweep around to do the hammer-and-anvil attack. You block here and we will assault towards your position."

I grabbed my point man counterpart, a guy by the name of Dagle. Dagle was a SEAL Team poster child. Six feet three, 240 pounds, and not an ounce of fat on him. He was a handsome, dark-haired man, in contrast to my still char-broiled complexion. Dagle kept his hair perfectly groomed, while the rest of us looked like slobs.

I grabbed his collar and brought him close to me. "Listen. Here are the hand signals we will use. Also, I can see down the front of your trail further than you can, so watch me. I will tell you who is coming and what to do. Let's really watch for each other. You can see further down my trail than I can. Don't be surprised if we run into guards. Just use your knife to take them out.''

We walked down the trail. Dagle gestured excitedly that someone was coming down my trail. He and his team blended into the shadows. I motioned to Pete that someone was coming. Pete nodded his head. I stepped behind a tree. No more than fifteen seconds later, the guard walked by. I stepped out, drove the hilt of my knife in at his solar plexus, lifted him off the ground to me and into the ditch. He died instantly.

I resheathed my knife. It was just after dawn, with weak rays of light filtering through the jungle canopy. Scanning the horizon, I saw another guard coming down Dagle's trail. I motioned that someone was coming and that he should take him out with his knife.

Dagle was in a quandary. Like me on my first patrol, he'd never stabbed anyone, having arrived in Vietnam just weeks earlier. He also was concerned about taking orders from me instead of his lieutenant. He had not learned that in these situations where an enemy soldier, deep behind enemy lines, presented him with a serious threat, he had ample latitude to develop his own ''rules.'' He gestured back and forth to the lieutenant, *What do I do?* It so happened the lieutenant was watching me, as well.

The guard walked right past Dagle. Unsure what he should do, he instead did nothing.

Immediately, the lieutenant grabbed the VC around the throat and started choking him. He had the VC draped across his left leg, as he was standing in a wishbone-type stance. The VC's back arched across his thigh. The diminutive VC's arms and legs flailed in the air. Here was this small, 100-pound, five-foot-two-inch man having his lights squeezed out of him by a 200-pound, six-foot-one-inch, well-conditioned SEAL. What a sight.

''Dagle! Stab him. Hurry!''

''Okay, all right!'' Dagle replied, urgently.

Dagle only then unsheathed his knife. Everyone in our team had exchanged our nine inch Ka-bar knives for aircraft crewman's survival knives with a five-inch blade. They just worked better and were easier to wield with their shorter blade.

Dagle took his knife and, in a mixture of adrenaline and fear, thrust it viciously into the VC's midsection, at his belly button. Remember, the VC was a very small man. He couldn't be more than six inches thick. Dagle had a nine-inch blade. The blade ran completely through the VC, into the lieutenant's thigh and embedded into his thighbone.

The lieutenant wanted to scream, but knew he couldn't. "Yee-awww," was all he allowed himself to hiss. "Pull it out. Pull it out!"

The VC looked at Dagle. A stomach wound was not lethal.

Dagle yanked the knife out, and the lieutenant fell to the ground. The VC had been balanced on his leg, so that, when the lieutenant fell, he was left standing there, looking at Dagle's back and the fallen lieutenant.

Dagle was looking into the ditch at the lieutenant he'd just stabbed. The VC was in shock, and he, too, looked into the ditch at the lieutenant. I frantically tried to get Dagle's attention.

"Would someone please finish the job!" I implored. "Come on! Kill the SOB!"

If the VC yelled, we were compromised.

The VC realized he had a chance to escape. He started to lumber off, blood oozing from both his stomach and his back. Fortunately, one of the other team members jumped forward and finished off the VC—just as he began to yell.

Everything went quiet again. Fortunately, his attempt to yell was more of a weak yelp and nothing too alarming. The focus then shifted back to the lieutenant. The corpsman quickly began bandaging his wounds.

I stepped across the trail and into the paddy in an attempt to be better seen by Dagle. Seeing that the VC was neutralized, I stepped back onto the dike.

"Watch out," I heard someone behind me hiss.

I froze. I was next to a small tree. I tried to blend into the shadows. I heard the jingling sound of someone running with things hanging off of him. He was probably one of the security guards running late and hurrying to his post. Why else would someone be running? If he had spotted us, alarms would have already sounded.

Out of position, having crossed over the trail during the ruckus, I could faintly see him jogging toward us. He had an AK-47 slung over his shoulder, the barrel pointed forward and parallel to the ground.

I hope he can't see me. One tap on that AK and I'm dead. Nervously, I caught Riojas's eye. *You gotta take him,* I mouthed. He nodded, acknowledging the obvious. I could attempt to jet up the dike, but should he notice me, he would have ample time to shoot, hitting me, the team, or both.

I slowly turned my head back from Riojas to the oncoming soldier. He noticed the movement of my head!

Riojas, as a corpsman, was charged with keeping us alive. He had never knifed anyone before—it wasn't his job. He, having trained with the Marines and having seen duty in Korea, was very capable of killing. Riojas carried an M14, a heavy gun with a wooden stock favored by Marines. It was a well-built gun, not a little plastic Mattel gun like the M16. It made a formidable club.

In an instant, the VC slowed, bringing his gun around to his left in my direction. Simultaneously, Riojas swung his gun by the barrel for all he was worth. *Wham!* The wooden stock smashed into his head, dropping the VC like a sack of potatoes. He was laid out cold.

"Nice," I whispered, relieved.

"Sorry," said Riojas, apologetic at not stabbing the soldier.

"Hey. It worked." I shrugged.

We moved in closer. Unfortunately, cover was sparse. We moved very slowly, hoping not to be detected.

"AHHHH!" a shout reverberated across the field. Someone had seen us.

We assaulted. It was almost big enough to be called a village, consisting of three hooches under a canopy of trees. There were eighteen VC there, and we ruthlessly overran them. One of the hooches had an overhang attached to it, similar to a carport back home. Under the overhang were six ancient pieces of machinery. Walking into the house, I noticed a lot of molds, chunks of explosives, and cords and canisters necessary for grenade and mine production.

"The man from Mo Cay was right! This *is* a major manufacturing plant for VC explosives," I exulted, pleased at the accuracy of the information.

Several men were sent to the perimeter to provide cover and warning while the rest of us searched the hooches. All three buildings were laden with explosives. I worked with another West Coast SEAL in the building with the carport.

"Hey, Harry. Look, there's a wooden floor here. Remember what you told us about wooden floors? Do you think we should pry one of the boards up and check?"

I licked my burnt, chapped, and swollen lips. "Yeah. Go ahead. But pry it up slowly."

He stuck his knife in between two planks and worked one board loose. I took a step backwards. The one next to it was loosely lying there. "Got something."

There were boxes and boxes and crates of guns, bullets, explosives, everything. What a cache of weaponry!

"Guys, come over here!" I yelled. Soon, we had two guys passing up box after box of gleaming new ordnance. We piled it up outside, next to the hooch.

It was eight A.M. We called for help. "We need boats in here to pick up all this ordnance."

The procession of weapons continued. The fake floor was ten by twenty feet, five feet deep, and completely packed with weapons.

Enemy troops were spotted outside the perimeter. "Be advised," came a call from one of the perimeter SEALs over the radio, "I have movement in the tree line north of you eight hundred meters. I've picked up movement of approximately thirty individuals. Over."

VC units had deployed and were cautiously moving toward us, having heard gunshots. Our plan was to carry as much ordnance as we could to the boats. One SEAL was to stay behind, set a charge on what we weren't able to remove, light the fuse, and run.

The boats could come no closer than 150 yards. We enlisted the help of as many sailors as we could from the boat, to form a human chain to move as much of the ordnance as possible. First, we passed down "turtle" mines. These mines were the size of a bread box and weighed twenty pounds. Next came metal tins, about the size of four cigar boxes wrapped together. They contained brand-new AK-47 ammo. Then came two bundles of AK-47s. Having came down on a human transport, they were wrapped in cloth and tied together with twine. Dozens were sent down the line. Even Russian PPSH machine guns were there along with other crew-serve weapons!

"Constance, come here!" yelled the guy who'd noticed the plank flooring. "What do you think of this?" I was in charge of security, and was not working in the chain, so I trotted over.

I glanced down. All ordnance had been removed from under the floor. Instead of a dirt floor, there was yet another wooden floor.

"You know, I've never seen that," I commented.

"You think I should pry it up, too?"

"Yeah. I think it'd be a good idea."

He bent over to pry the wood up. After several minutes, a board came loose.

"Unbelievable," was all I could say, shocked at the magnitude of still another crypt of weapons.

I jogged out to Pete and Gallagher. Quickly, I filled them in on the second five-foot-deep, twenty- by ten-foot cache of ordnance.

"This is amazing," said Pete. "We have a problem, though. The boats are almost completely filled with all this crap. As it is, we'll have to sit on top of it going out of here. What an incredible find."

The VC were getting closer. A third boat was called in to retrieve us. Helicopter gunships were inbound, intending to keep the VC at bay. Rounds were hitting closer to us. It was almost ten A.M.

"Constance, we're going to have to blow this up. I want you, you, and you," ordered Pete, "to make up a real heavy-duty demolitions charge. Set it with a two-minute fuse. Blow everything that's left in there."

I nodded and grabbed several claymore mines. Taking them apart, I removed the C4 plastic explosive "ball bearings" from them. We wrapped the C4 together and placed it down into the second layer of ordnance. *It sure is a shame we can't take them with us.*

"Everybody to the boat! Everybody to the boat!"

The "bomb" was approximately equivalent to ten thousand pounds of TNT. We raced out of there. The West Coast SEAL designated as their demolitions expert pulled the fuse and yelled, "Fire in the hole! Two minutes!"

The helicopters overhead flew off as we raced to the ditch closest to the canal. We waited, staring at our watches. Two minutes passed and nothing happened.

What a dilemma! Who wants to go over to the cache and look down at the charge to see what went wrong? Not me. Was it smoldering, or was it a true dud, so that we needed to go back, reset, and reprime the charge? How long should we wait to find out? More and more shots were being fired at us.

We discussed how we might remedy this. Coming over to us was George Hudak, a West Coast SEAL who appeared to be a good operator, but who sometimes lacked common sense. His nickname was "Pigpen" because he was always dirty.

Hudak walked up and asked, "What's the problem? Won't blow?"

"Nope. At least not yet."

"Why don't you just go over there and toss in a second charge and beat it back over here?"

"That'd be great," I replied, "but we don't have any more time fuse."

"Watch this," said Hudak, taking off all his gear. He grabbed two concussion grenades, which were half-pound blocks of explosives in a pasteboard cylinder that looked like a beer can. He tied the two together. "Watch this," he said again as he jogged back to the hooches.

"George, where're you going?" I yelled, realizing the foolhardiness of his plan.

"Don't worry!"

Looking like a running back, he sprinted over to the hole. "It's a dud," he yelled. He lifted the two concussion grenades, flipped both spoons, and tossed them into the hole, on top of the charges we had just set—which were atop a ton of ordnance. He turned and looked at us with an expression of *See there, no sweat.*

It was then I believe Hudak realized what he'd just done. He couldn't possibly run fast enough to escape the force of the impending explosion. His smug facial expression suddenly went blank. He leapt out of there as fast and as hard as he could go. He sprinted for all he was worth.

KKAAABBOOOOM! Hudak was about halfway back when the mammoth explosion erupted. The concussive force alone picked Hudak up, throwing him a conservative *thirty* yards forward. His arms flailed like a windmill as he flew through the air. It was as if he had jumped on a giant trampoline and rocketed forward. He hit and continued to roll right up to us.

Dazed, yet reaffirming the worthiness of his "Pigpen" moniker, Hudak shook his head and looked at us. "There you go!"

Dust, dirt, and debris pelted the earth around us. That was one nice explosion. "Hudak, you have to be one of the luckiest guys I know. Anybody else, it would have killed them. You were in the air for close to one hundred feet! We thought you were toast."

"That was an incredible rush, getting picked up and flying through the air like that. My ears are ringing, but I'm okay. I tell you, it's better than skydiving." Then, as a smile crossed his face, he looked at us, mimicking a little kid as he said, "Look, Mom, no frag!"

We boarded ship and quickly departed. We had clearly impacted the Viet Cong in the delta. Intelligence reports left little doubt they were smarting after the devastation we had dealt them.

We were ready to go home. For our last month in-country, we took the new team out with us, acclimating them. We took them into min-

imally contested areas so they could learn to walk, learn to talk, how
to maneuver, and how to deal with the enemy without getting hurt. We
needed to teach them the tricks we'd learned, so they could take over
for us. We took special care in the introductions concerning our intelligence network. These contacts were critical.

One of the funniest stories involved a new point man, Dicky Cyrus.
Dicky was going to do well, but he wasn't too sure about this hide-
and-seek in the nighttime jungles of Vietnam. We were out on an op
in the middle of nowhere, playing bump-and-run with a company of
VC. We were only supposed to find one or two bad guys—and we ran
into a whole lot of them. A hellacious firefight ensued.

Pete grabbed my shoulder. "Let's get out of here, Harry. We're
outnumbered, outgunned, and they're flanking us. We gotta get to the
river."

"You got it, Lieutenant."

We quit shooting, hoping to break contact. As we ran, there were
several times we had to shoot because they got too close. I was confident we could stay ahead of them. Dicky, on the other hand, was not
so sure. His adrenaline and fear level was maxed out. We got to the
river's edge and Riojas reported, "I cannot make contact with the radio!
I can't make contact!"

Our backs were to the My Tho River. Standing on the bank, Pete
commented, "You know, they're still coming."

"Yep."

Behind us, in the river, about 100 meters away, was an oval-shaped
island approximately 150 meters wide by 80 meters long.

"Let's hit the island. If they want to come out after us, it's a better
defensive position."

I nodded, then looked over at Dicky. "Hey, Dicky, hang your gun
around your neck, blow up your vest, and let's go for a swim."

We hit the water and breaststroked across. As soon as I touched
bottom, I swung my gun around. Crouching, I moved slowly out of the
water, looking for anything that moved. We had no idea who might be
out there. Seeing no one, I motioned for the team to come. As we left
the water, the VC started shooting across at us. Fortunately, they didn't
appear interested in swimming after us.

"Dicky, you are the number two man. You look right and I'll look
left as we go through to the other side of the island. If you see anything,
let me know."

"No problem."

We decided to run to the other side of the island in hopes of gar-
nering time to fix the radio. There were banana groves clumped
throughout the island. We could see, as there was ample moonlight.
We ran right into the courtyard of a deserted hooch. We were faced
with either going through or going around. I slowed, signaling Pete that
I would like to go through the house to see if anyone was home. He
agreed. The trail ran right to the front door and continued out the back.
No one was home. As we continued on, I asked Dicky if he saw anyone
in the hooch.

Dicky paused. ''What hooch.''

''We just ran through a hooch, Dicky.''

''No we didn't.''

''Yeah, we did. You almost hit the table.''

''You mean that dark area back there where the tree limbs were real
thick?''

I chuckled. ''Yeah.''

''That was a hooch? You gotta be kidding me! Man, I'd have never
guessed. How do you guys stay alive out here?''

I heard Riojas behind me. ''Roger that. Got you in sight, zero eight
mikes.'' (See you in eight minutes.)

''Wait a minute,'' Dicky insisted. ''We didn't go running through a
hooch!''

Since we had a few minutes until the STAB was to pick us up, I
leaned over to Pete. ''Pete, can I take Dicky back to show him the
hooch we ran through?''

''Sure.''

''I'm not going,'' protested Dicky.

''C'mon. It's only a hundred yards away.''

''I'm not going. I know it's a trick or something you guys are trying
to pull over on me.''

Finally, I convinced him to patrol back to the hooch. Arriving, we
walked in and I clicked on my flashlight.

''I'll be damned!''

All the way back, he peppered me with questions. ''How do you
guys do this? How do you see when I can't see two feet in front of
me? How do you know where to navigate?''

I just smiled.

Killing is always a gruesome and ugly thing. But, in a war like
Vietnam, body count was the measure of success. I could watch a sad

movie and feel strong pulls at my heartstrings and then, a few hours later, become a calculating, viciously proficient killer. It's like we have become light switches . . . on . . . off . . . at the flip of a finger. We'd been in-country for a little more than 180 days. It changed us, and we were the better for it.

CHAPTER 13

SANDY

ARRIVING WITH TRUCKS FULLY LADEN, WE STOPPED ADJACENT to the runway and waited for our plane to arrive. It was every bit of 110 degrees and 95 percent humidity. We were leaving Vietnam the same way we came in . . . hot and sweaty.

I looked over at Riojas, drenched in sweat, and commented, "It's heat like this that makes you glad to be getting out of here."

"Hummph," grunted Rios in response. "They're short of corpsmen. They want me back over here as quickly as I can get home, processed, and back. You guys all get to have six-month vacations, but me, my ass is right back in the line of fire!"

"Ah, you big baby! Don't give me that. You know it's because they want you to work on your marksmanship," I replied, climbing from the truck.

"I can't believe you're still sore over that. I missed you by at least five or six inches—I mean—that's not even close."

"Yeah. But you were trying to hit me."

"I got them, didn't I?"

"You could've shot an entire platoon with all the rounds you let loose. You were trying to hit me and you know it. The thing that saved your ass is you were lucky to hit those three VC. It's just that they"—

my arm swept in an arc to point in the direction of the Administrative Offices there at Tan Son Nhut—"recognized you can't shoot so you're being penalized. That's why you have to come back early. You got two months yanked for disorderly shooting!"

I smiled. *Better him than me.*

After several stops, we landed in California. We made a stop at Disneyland, especially since they proffered free admission to returning soldiers. After a great time at Disneyland and a short debriefing in Coronado with SEAL Team One, we began our final leg home.

Arriving back at SEAL Team headquarters in Little Creek, our team officially dissolved. After two weeks off, each of us came back and was reassigned to a new platoon. The new cycle began. Having just returned, we were placed at the end of the waiting list of those going to Vietnam. Each of us trained with our new team, traveled to a number of schools for further training, going through the protocols, rules, and regulations before we could head back. It took anywhere from six months to a year to deploy back to Vietnam. I wasn't happy at all with this. I looked forward to going back. There were enough SEALs that, with only three platoons deploying to Vietnam at any one time, there wasn't room to go any sooner. The fight in SEAL Team was to *return* to Vietnam, contrary to the escalating discontent of the American public.

The adrenaline, camaraderie, and personal success I enjoyed stood in stark contrast to the utterly foul mood I ran up against the moment we landed stateside.

"Hey! Sailor boy! How can you assholes fight for such a corrupt government? How can you shoot innocent people in such an immoral war?"

I fought back a rage I hadn't felt in weeks—since last strapping on my web belt. Welling up inside was an anger I thought I'd left behind. My eyes narrowed and my jaw clenched. "I never considered people shooting at me to be particularly innocent." I turned and walked away.

"You are nothing but a puppet. A baby killer."

In the bars in Saigon frequented by U.S. military personnel, we SEALs continually got into one brawl after another. Fights were commonplace as we all looked to blow off steam. SEALs were easy targets because of our reputations and inflated egos. "You guys think you are such hotshot sons of bitches. You . . ." *Wham!* One of us sent him reeling into the next day.

"You SEALs ain't jack shit!" Many jaws, ribs, and bones were broken in barroom brawls. Rarely when the dust settled were any of us roughed up.

Somehow, when we arrived home, it was different. Looking at this sandaled, tie-dyed, long-haired hippie challenging all I was proud of— the essence of what and who I was—I knew better than to smash his sniveling face. It was all I could do to keep my combat attack instincts in check. "I've pissed on better people than you, you two-bit asshole."

What brought this national antiwar sentiment home to us was a letter Curtis received from his girlfriend.

Dear Curtis,

I don't know quite how to tell you this. I suppose the direct approach will be the simplest. I am enjoying college a lot. Many of my classes are exciting and very intellectually stimulating. But the most groovy thing I have ever been involved with is this free speech movement sweeping the nation. It is about time we stand up for what we believe. It is about time we question the lies the government is telling us about the war.

This leads me to the hardest thing I have ever done. I have a friend named Jim who's in my psychology class. He's a pacifist and I have been seeing him. I am sorry, Curtis. But you are a killer and my convictions can't reconcile my love for you and the murderous killing that you do.

I am truly sorry. I know you have a good heart, but you can't kill and not be changed forever.

Make love not war.

Peace,
Cindy

Curtis was devastated. He'd known her since he was a kid, and suddenly it was over. A number of guys got "Dear John" letters while in Vietnam. The guys were brokenhearted for a short time, and then got meaner.

The headlines were crazy. The Chicago Seven. The Democratic National Convention. More antiwar activity. Timothy Leary and Tiny Tim tiptoeing through the tulips. We stayed together—almost sequestered together—away from the nonmilitary outside world. I didn't care for it and really didn't know how to deal with it.

"Eagle, Harry here. Yeah. I'm doing fine. . . . What! You're headed back early? . . . How can I cheat and get back to Vietnam? . . . Oh, come on. There's got to be a way. I don't need any more schools to attend. Not when there's a war going on. . . . You will. Thanks.''

I ran into Gallagher a few days later. "Look, Harry." Gallagher smiled. "I did some checking, and it's going to be a year before your platoon ships out. It just so happens that I have one vacancy left in my platoon. We're outta here in three months. They want me to start training my guys immediately. You want to help?''

"Eagle, I can't believe this! What a great offer!''

I'm going back early! I was honored. When Gallagher had jobs to do, it hadn't taken me long to realize, there were only certain people he wanted with him. It was at this point Roy Dean and I started going in different directions. Things got to be more and more strained between us. Roy Dean had been in Gallagher's squad while I was in Peterson's. Gallagher was setting up his new platoon, and wanted me in it instead of Roy Dean. It became awkward between us.

Shortly after returning from Vietnam, we had an awards ceremony. Many of the admirals, including my father, came down from the Pentagon. We wore our dress uniforms as they pinned medals on us. I was awarded an ample supply: Bronze Star with a Combat "V," Purple Heart, the Vietnamese Cross of Gallantry, the Presidential Unit Citation, Navy Commendation, Naval Unit Citation, and Navy Achievement. These different awards formed an elegant array of three rows of ribbons and medals across my chest. All of which served to announce I had been there and done myself proud. All of my performance reviews were perfect. I had started out in SEALs about as green as I could be. Now I had two chevrons, was close to receiving my third, and was on the fast track of advancement. I was identified as someone the upper echelons wanted to move up. *Good to go!* Life was good.

I was living life like I wanted to, fast and furious. Since we didn't have any kennel facilities on base, Rinny lived with me. While in Vietnam, I'd received tax-free pay, hazardous duty pay, a $10,000 bonus to reenlist, and hadn't cashed a paycheck the entire time. I had money to burn. We never needed money in Vietnam. We lived off the Viet Cong. The USO provided soaps, toiletries, and living essentials while the Navy fed, clothed, and housed us. All we ever spent money on was beer, which didn't cost us much. The Viet Cong provided enough funds to party on.

I spent some of my money on a 440-cubic-inch, Plymouth GTX muscle car. It had a stereo eight-track player with reverberator and a full set of speakers to crank it up. "The Good, the Bad, and the Ugly" was popular, playing on the radio all the time. We SEALs adopted it as our quasi-theme song.

"Hey, Harry," Jack Rowell said, stopping me in the hall after an afternoon meeting. "A friend of my wife's is coming to visit and she likes to party. She's pretty good-looking. You want to go out to dinner with us tomorrow night?"

"Sure. What the hell."

Jack wasn't kidding; she was cute! Blue eyes and blond hair; a petite five-foot-three-inch young gal of nineteen. She was provocatively made up, wearing a sheer top, bare midriff, and tight shorts. Very sexy. *This might turn out better than I expected.*

"Hi, I'm Harry."

"I'm Sandy. Nice to meet you."

"Jack tells me you're a friend of Judy's."

"Yeah," she said, her eyes locked onto mine. Then, with a twinkle in her smile, "I think I'm glad I came to visit."

I felt my heart leap. Sandy was very attractive, dressed to kill, and first impressions were in and looking good. "I'm glad you came to visit, too. So many girls I've met lately, uhhh, I've been uncomfortable discussing what I do and who I am. Obviously, since you know Jack, you have some idea."

"I got an idea as to what you do, but I don't know you. Just who are you, Harry Constance?" she asked with a grin.

"I'm a Navy SEAL who just returned from my first tour in Vietnam. We fought a lot and were successful in killing a lot of the enemy. I'm a soldier, a trained killer, and I'll try to be a perfect gentleman with you." I paused, looking for any hint of disapproval. Sensing none, I continued, "I have a place overlooking Chesapeake Bay—about a half a mile from here. I'm training a new platoon that will ship out to Vietnam in another few months."

"Judy was telling me what Jack had to go through. You guys really put your lives on the line, don't you? What made you decide to become a SEAL?" She asked the right questions.

The entire evening was magical. Dinner was served, I think. I quickly became more and more engrossed in talking, laughing, drinking—totally overcome with feelings I'd not felt for a long, long time. As the sun set, my intoxication at being able to talk so openly with such a beautiful young woman, the buzz of the wine, and my excitement was overwhelming. I poured out my life's story.

"You know, you're sure easy to talk to. It's been a long time since I've had the opportunity to spend time with such a pretty woman."

"Oh, Harry, it's me who's the lucky one. Such a handsome . . ." I took her in my arms and kissed her. Not too long, in case she objected. She squeezed me tight in response. The feel of her firm body against me and the powerful aroma of her perfume washed over me. Passionately, I scooped her into my arms and gently moved onto the sofa. We kissed, her lips soft, anxious, and inviting. My heart was pounding with a familiar rush of adrenaline. What a difference! Tentatively, almost gently, I began touching her. She groaned, her body dancing to my caress. Soon after, we were in bed together. The unbelievable sense of giving and receiving pleasure—her body responding to me and I to her—was such an incredible high.

Early the next morning, I awoke. There she was, lying vulnerable and contented next to me. *This is incredible.* She stirred, rolled over, and looked at me. I leaned over and kissed her softly. "How'd you like to take a walk on the beach?"

"I'd love to. I love the ocean."

I smiled. "That's the right thing to say to a Navy man."

We spent the weekend walking and talking endlessly. She had a way of drawing out thoughts and feelings I didn't realize I felt.

Sunday evening came and she kissed me good-bye. "I hope I get to see you again. I hope you're not like a lot of other sailors, just love 'em and leave 'em."

"No. I'm not. Let me see what my schedule is, and I'll call you this week." As she got in her car to go, I leaned close. "I've never met anyone that put me so at ease so quickly. I promise I'll call. Thanks for coming down."

As she drove away, I smiled. *This could be great. God, that is one hot chick! Whew!* After spending so many months with my emotions all bottled up inside, to be able to express all types of feelings! It was fantastic! The intimacy only further secured something I was starving for. *I have got to see her again.*

Up until then, the only people I could talk to openly about what I'd done and been through were other SEALs. It had been difficult to get dates with some girls because of our heavy training schedule.

Back at work, Jack Rowell was pleased with his matchmaking. "Constance, I guess you and Sandy hit it off pretty well."

"I'll tell you, Jack, I'm really glad you talked me into coming over and meeting her. I never thought I'd let myself get set up for a blind date.''

Sandy was very easy to get along with. Whatever pleased me made her happy. We started dating real steady, real intense, real quick, and real fast. In my mind, those weren't the ''lazy days of summer,'' because I knew I'd soon be heading back to Vietnam. I was on the fast track in all aspects of my life. What might normally take six months to accomplish, I was accomplishing in a matter of weeks. Unfortunately, I extended that mind-set to personal relationships, as well.

''I don't know about you, but this has been the greatest time of my life,'' I said, Sandy's head nestled close against my chest.

''Harry,'' she said, nibbling at my ear, ''what would you think if I were to move down here so we could be together more?''

''What do you mean, 'what do I think'? I think it'd be great! No more driving or flying down from D.C.''

I went to work, came home, and we played. When I arrived home, she was all dolled up, looking hot and sexy. We would go out to eat, dance, carouse around, then go home and make love until all hours of the night. I'd get up the next morning, go to work, and count the minutes until I was home again. It was like a vacation every day with her. Very intoxicating. She gave me whatever I wanted sexually, which, unfortunately, was the only way I knew to express my intimate needs and emotions. In return, I devoted my heart and soul to her.

''Where would you like to be in two years?'' Sandy asked.

''I'd like to be married and have a child.''

''Boy, I can't wait to be married and have kids.''

Grinning, ''Me, too!'' I said.

''Me three!'' she said, emphatically.

I had an uneasy feeling over how hard I operated in Vietnam. The realization I could be killed struck me with greater force from my distant vantage point there in Little Creek, Virginia. Sandy had given me something to live for. Summer passed, the country still abuzz over Richard Nixon and Hubert Humphrey's battle for the presidency and the riots at the Democratic National Convention in Chicago.

''We'll be shipping out soon, probably late January.''

''Don't talk about it. I don't like to think about being without you. These past few months have been the greatest of my life.''

''I know. Our relationship means a lot to me. I don't want things to end between us when I ship out. I'm nervous about just writing back and forth—that I might lose you to somebody else. I wish I could stay longer so we could get on with things."

"Why don't we get married?"

I was stunned. Looking at her smiling face, I was overwhelmed. I'd thought a lot about my desire to achieve life's major experiences, such as marriage and kids. Being a SEAL in Vietnam was hazardous to my life expectancy. "One of my fears is that I could die. I was fortunate—or lucky—several times already. I don't know how long my luck will hold. If I die, that's okay because I will have died for my country and I can accept that. I would love to be married and have kids before I die, but I'm not sure it's fair to you. I would love to marry you."

"Harry Constance, you're worth the risk. Even if you die, I wouldn't want to give up what we have together now just to escape the pain. I've never met anyone like you."

Smiling, "In that case, Sandy, will you marry me? I can only promise you that I will love you the best I can."

"I can live with that. Yes!"

The whole time, it was a party. Sandy met all the guys; we went out as a group, always a party. Go to the beach, shrimp at Duck Inn, drink beer, walk on the beach, sailing, skip rocks. . . . Normally, most people could afford to go out to eat once a week. I could afford to go every night if I wanted. I had thousands in the bank. Unfortunately, I think Sandy felt I was worth a lot more money than I was. It was a delusion I unknowingly created and perpetuated. She would later want a lifestyle beyond my means.

I wanted my personal life to mirror my professional life. Sandy seemed perfect. It was amazing. "I would like to serve, then after the war come back and be an instructor and go into the officer training program."

"You'd make a perfect officer! I'd love to live here overlooking the bay, too. I mean, I love living on the beach! If I could pick anywhere in the world, I'd live right here on this beach."

Whatever I liked, she liked. Foods, styles, vacation destinations, housing architecture, camping, cars, friends—you name it—we were "in sync." The music was playing all the time, and it was just so romantic. We both were willing it to work instead of taking it day by day and really getting to know each other.

"When do we set the date?"

"Well"—she paused—"I don't know. There are advantages and disadvantages."

She grabbed me around the neck. "Let's get married right away then. How about January second, 1969? That has a good ring to it."

"Perfect!"

I called my parents, then living in Florida, to tell them the news. "Dad, I'm getting married. I've found the perfect girl. Her name is Sandy. I want to get married before I ship out. Nothing formal, just a simple ceremony."

There was a long pause. "This is, I have to say, certainly something I did not expect. Son, I really think you'd be smarter to wait until you get back. This is a major decision that you'd better not make in haste."

"Dad, you wouldn't believe this gal. She and I are perfect together. I know it sounds corny, but I think we are meant to be."

"I really think you'd be better off waiting, but Mom and I'll support you in whatever your decision is. I'm proud to stand by you."

"Thanks a lot."

Just before Christmas, we were scheduled to go to Sandy's parents' house. She wanted me to meet her parents and get to know her family.

Her father met us at the door. He was of medium build, with an easygoing, affable personality I readily liked. He ushered us into the living room. "Have a seat. This is quite a shock, but we are excited for the two of you. I understand you're in the Navy."

"Yes, sir. U.S. Navy."

"So what do you do in the Navy?"

"I'm in the Navy's version of special warfare operations, known as SEALs. I enjoy it."

"Sandy tells me that you have already been to Vietnam and that you're going back soon."

"Yes, sir. That's why we want to get married so soon."

"From what I understand, you've seen a lot of combat," he inquired, more as a statement than question. Just then, a baby girl, about a year old, came crawling into the room.

I smiled at the cute baby gazing up at Sandy's father. "Cute kid. Whose little girl?"

"Sandy didn't tell you? This is Marnie, Sandy's little girl."

I felt as if I'd been hit over the head. I wracked my brain, searching to recall Sandy having said anything about a child. *We're getting married in a week. This is a major new development. . . .*

Sandy walked in, looked at Marnie, looked at me, then picked her daughter up. "I'm sorry, Harry. I wanted to tell you at least a thousand different times. But I was so afraid you wouldn't want me once you knew I had a baby.''

''When were you going to tell me?'' I asked, trying valiantly to sort things out. ''Why didn't you tell me?''

''You and I have had so many wonderful times together. You go so fast and crazy. I was afraid a baby would keep us from being able to go out and I would lose you,'' she said softly, tears welling up in her eyes.

Does she really love me, or is she in a really desperate situation with a kid where she needs someone . . . anyone? Wham! It brought me up short. *Well, I guess I do want kids as soon as possible. This doesn't really change things. . . .* Sandy studied my reaction. ''I guess this doesn't really matter that much, as long as we're together.''

She grabbed me and threw her arms around my neck as tightly as she could. ''I knew you'd understand. I just knew you would!''

Later, she talked about how her boyfriend got her pregnant and then split, forcing her to move back home.

I should have asked more questions. We left Marnie with her folks and traveled to North Carolina, where we were married on January 2. We returned to Washington to retrieve all of her stuff, and Marnie, and settled into my beach house in Virginia Beach.

Four weeks later, I was on a plane to Vietnam. Prior to my departure, during the weeks leading up to shipping out, there was a subtle, yet palpable shift in our relationship. Very slowly, the brakes were being applied to my runaway emotions, to my longing for love and intimacy. It was like water dripping onto a fire. All of a sudden, we couldn't do all the partying and frolicking we'd done earlier.

Marnie had her own little room, all neat and decorated. I set up a direct deposit of my paycheck into our bank account.

''I have everything all set up so you'll be well taken care of while I'm gone,'' I reassured Sandy. ''I was sure hopeful you'd be pregnant before I left.''

''Yeah, me too. Sorry, but it just didn't happen this time. I'll tell you what. I'll go to the doctor and find out all I can about fertility and how we can insure getting pregnant.''

''Oh God, I love you!'' I blurted. ''I cannot believe in such a short span of time I now have a wife, child, and am attempting to have my own kids!''

Sandy smiled. We kissed passionately as we stood on the tarmac shortly before I boarded the plane. "You take care of yourself. I want you coming home to me!"

The rest of the SEAL Team wives were doing their kissing and hugging good-bye. It was nice having Sandy there for me. No one had ever shown up for my shipping out. "This really is wonderful, you coming out and sending me off."

"Marnie and I wouldn't have missed this for the world!"

I kissed her once more. We all boarded the plane and flew to Vietnam.

CHAPTER 14

THE CIA'S PHOENIX PROGRAM: PRU OPERATIONS

ONE OF THE PROGRAMS SEALs INHERITED WAS CALLED PRU. Provincial Reconnaissance Unit. Developed by the CIA, it was a top-secret part of their Phoenix Program. The PRU objective was pacification. *Pacification* meaning if you had them by the *huevos,* their hearts and minds would surely follow. It was strictly a program to target for elimination the Viet Cong administrators and the VCI. Couriers, coordinators, tax collectors, planners, politicians, were all included. And "target" was the right word. The CIA painted bull's-eyes on the Viet Cong VIPs. We were given the job of hitting it.

A CIA agent approached Gallagher shortly before our platoon was due to depart. "You're so damn good, and we've got an area in the delta that is *so* damn bad. Your people in the Pentagon tell us you are perfect for this assignment. We need someone who is tough, loyal, honest, fair, and willing to do anything to make this program successful. Can we interest you in this?"

"I'll take it over on one condition," replied Gallagher, "I can bring my own assistant."

"Well," he pondered, "we normally have only one American working on these PRU ops. You don't need an assistant."

Gallagher looked at this guy and smiled. "Let me say it again one more time. I'll take it on the condition you let me bring my assistant.''

The agent frowned. "Who the hell is your assistant?''

"Harry Constance.''

The agents conferred for a few moments, then turned. "All right.''

I flew into Vietnam with my new team. As with my first platoon some months before, we drove to Can Tho for in-country processing.

I said *adiós* to "Big'' Al Ashton and the other SEALs. "Good luck. We'll see you around.''

"I wish you were operating with us, but from what I hear, you'd probably get us all killed anyway. So it's probably just as well,'' remarked Al.

I joined Gallagher in Sok Trang, a province situated right in the middle of the Mekong Delta. It was 160 miles southeast of Saigon and 100 miles from Can Tho, with very little influence from Saigon. There was a small air base located there, with no American troops anywhere close. Gallagher assumed command of 120 PRUs.

"I didn't get to bring my Stoner,'' I groused as we surveyed our new surroundings. "Now I gotta use a CAR-fifteen. Can you imagine me out in the middle of nowhere, the only American, with a CAR-fifteen for firepower?''

"Ah, you had too many bullets to shoot last time. This is more fair. You're now a team leader. You'd kill half your team the first time you got excited if you had it!''

For the PRU program, I was required to wear civilian clothes, sign papers releasing the CIA from liability, and stating that I would adhere to conditions set forth in the Phoenix briefing, and that I would handle responsibly large amounts of cash. I promised not to discuss the program with anyone not associated with Phoenix. I didn't mind, as I figured if anyone knew I was only an E-5, there would have been a lot of unhappy people. Everybody, according to the CIA, who was involved in the program was equivalent to a Naval lieutenant or higher. No enlisted. It obviously took an officer to coordinate helicopters, Naval gunfire, Army howitzer gunfire, to requisition all the materiel, and to pay our units and informants thousands of dollars. They felt you had to be a college grad for that sort of responsibility. Then I came along, a cum laude graduate of Vietnam U.!

Several times, I was flown out to various ships anchored off the coast of Vietnam and was invited for coffee with the Commanding Officer in the Captain's Wardroom.

"Well, sir, what can we do for you?" asked the captain.

"Thank you, sir," I would reply. "I'd like you to bring your ship within this proximity of shore. I'd like to bring a platoon on board your ship three days early. When we get to here," I said, pointing at the map, "I'll lower my boat and men into the water and go to shore. If something happens, I'd appreciate your using your big guns to protect us, and supplying helo support to extract us. Questions?"

"No problem," came the invariable answer. We were busy planning tactically exact operations involving a lot of men and millions of dollars of machinery, all the while being brought coffee by men ranked E-5. I was considered a very knowledgeable, highly placed civilian. Had they found out I was an E-5, it would have destroyed my credibility.

When we arrived in Sok Trang, we were put up in a beautiful French villa. I had a bedroom, my own private bath, and air-conditioning. My room was on one side of the house, with Gallagher's on the other. In the middle of the house was a living room and a dining room, while at the back stood the kitchen. My room was huge, approximately thirty feet by fifty feet. I had a queen bed, couches and chairs, a bureau and a desk, and I was living good. We had tile floors with ornate rugs, hot and cold running water, and maids.

The PRU was made up of 50 percent ex-Viet Cong. The other 50 percent were thieves, murderers, and criminals facing the death penalty. They were offered amnesty if they would agree to work for us. I'm sure they reasoned that conducting daring and frightening PRU operations was better than death. If they participated in this special program they were allowed to live—and carry a gun.

Gallagher and I met in front of the PRU barracks shortly after arriving. "We're going out to the camp and I want you to select twelve individuals. Those you select are to be specially trained in SEAL tactics. There's no hurry. You've got two weeks."

I looked at him, perplexed. "Two weeks?"

Gallagher resumed his dialogue. "At the end of those two weeks, I want them to be able to sneak through the woods, and do everything we are able to do." The only thing I could think to say was "Okay." (This was the first of many two syllable responses to Gallagher's suggestions/orders.)

The majority of these ex-VC and murderers had no idea what discipline in the jungle was. They had to learn to allow something to bite all over them without flinching if they were in a dangerous situation. One of the problems our PRUs had was, when things got tense, they started talking to one another and lighting cigarettes. Unfortunately, those habits could leave you in a permanently horizontal position. They simply lacked the tactical expertise necessary to outmaneuver the bad guys, though. I started training my guys on how to use claymore mines, LAAW rockets, sniping, how to move and be quiet, how not to talk and use hand signs, and how to leave the pigs and chickens alone. All in two weeks.

Walking silently through a courtyard, I stopped abruptly at the high-pitched squeal of a pig behind us. *Weeeeeeeee! Weeeeee!* Turning slowly, my eyes widened at the sight of Hong, the last man in our team, dragging a pig tied to his back. Angrily, I signaled him to let go of the pig. We were in hostile territory and I had guys stealing pigs and chickens! Great for patrolling. On that very same training operation, two of my men put chickens in their shirts. *Bwack! Bbbwack!* "First pigs, now chickens," I muttered. "It's a damn animal farm I'm running."

Unfortunately, part of the reason these men risked taking the livestock was to supplement their income. They were stealing anything they could because they needed it to live. The PRU chief had been taking a percentage of their pay. Everybody was corrupt. Then, for some stupid reason or another, along came Gallagher and I. We determined to treat our men fairly, honestly, and with respect. This may sound noble, but it had more to do with keeping alive in the jungle than high moral integrity. We weren't dishonest or corrupt. We didn't send any unmarked money home like many PRU advisors did. I could name names if I chose to—they bragged about it in the bars in the region.

"How much money are you guys sending home?" came the question. "I sent forty-three hundred home last month alone."

"I didn't send any."

"What? Are you crazy? It's the easiest thing to do. You know the rewards for captured weapons? All you need to do is to claim you captured one hundred AK-forty-sevens instead of the five you actually did. When the CIA calls, ask them if they want you to send them the AKs. They'll invariably tell you just to destroy them—and pay you for what you 'captured.' At twenty-five dollars per AK, it adds up fast. The next day, call and tell them you captured another thirty-five. They'll send you the bounty for thirty-five. 'Hey, what do you want me to do with them?' They'll say, 'Just destroy them. Okay.' You just put the cash in an envelope to the wife and send it. Then skim a percentage of your PRUs' pay—a facilitator's fee, I call it—and it's great income! Get paid fairly for what we do over here. Besides, it's Agency money, so who gives a rat's ass?''

It would have been so easy. All the money we disbursed was cash. It was effortless to change in the Vietnamese currency for U.S. greenbacks. I just felt good about being honest. Our fairness with our men quite possibly saved our lives. There were many who thought it funny, not giving it a second thought. I know of guys who sent home $30,000 over a six-month period. War corrupts everyone in different ways.

What we had were VC and murderers who had a chance to redeem themselves. When presented with professional, honest leadership, many responded by making us proud. The camaraderie among Gallagher, myself, and our PRUs was fantastic. I had twelve "specialists," as did Gallagher, while the rest comprised our infantrymen—our shooters.

(Concurrent with our PRU program was another SEAL program, the Nuyenyai—Vietnamese for frogman—also referred to as LDNN. SEALs trained Vietnamese soldiers to perform like SEALs. They trained them in Saigon and Coronado, California. It was humorous, the stories of flying Vietnamese who had never been out of country all the way to San Diego. They trained in the sloughs between San Diego and Tijuana, Mexico. There were two hundred LDNNs receiving training, some of it from my good friend Gary Chamberlin and my brother-in-law, SEAL Frank Thornton. Our PRU program was identical; we simply didn't have the luxury of taking them back to the States. The Nuyenyai even had access to demolition training and skydiving. Both programs were highly effective.)

The operations we ran were basically our prerogative so long as we stayed within our own district. We had, on any given night, virtually hundreds of targets to go after. My men were excited as they realized what Gallagher and I were designing. Prior to our arrival, they patrolled haphazardly with only M16s. We arrived with a treasure chest of war toys. Like boys playing with BB guns and firecrackers, when we introduced all of our firepower to them—thermite grenades, Willie Pete, fragmentation and concussion grenades, along with claymores and LAAWs—they were delighted. Bringing that kind of force to the battle helped spirits and daring go way up.

We also had colored smoke canisters that we used for guiding in helos and parachute jumpers. Each of us carried two flares, two smokes, and two grenades, at a minimum. New toys for the boys! They liked their gifts.

I had a very good Viet Cong soldier I picked out because of his physical stature, aggressiveness, and apparent loyalty. I made him my number one man at the house. He became my bodyguard. When I came home off of an operation, muddy, wet and cold, caked in mud, stuff all over my gun and bullets, I would come to the back of the house. Old mama san, about sixty-five years old, would start waving her broom at me if I so much as dared to come up the porch steps with my dirty clothes on. She would make me take all my clothes off. Everything. "No, no take swim trunks in . . . they have mud dirt also . . . take off, take off." She was serious, so I complied, wearing only my black and green face paint and a big grin as I headed for the shower.

I returned to my room to find shirt and shorts waiting alongside my flip-flops. After I had dressed, mama san had a rum and Coke waiting for me. Room service, VC-style! When I sat down, my bodyguard came in and presented me with documents we'd captured. My interpreter then appeared, and together we analyzed what we captured. While doing this, mama san was scrubbing my clothes clean.

Another ex-Viet Cong I had guarding the door completely stripped down all my guns, bullets, magazines, and perfectly detail-cleaned them, then put it all back together, came in, and presented them to me. Each "presentation" was almost ceremonial in nature. He would bow and present me with my gun. Every one of my bullets in every one of my magazines had been polished. All the brass shined. My knife was freshly honed daily, so sharp that it would shave the hair off the back of my arm. He'd bow again as he presented my knife. Then I had to tell him whether it was acceptable or not. It was almost to the point that, had I told him it was unacceptable, he would have stabbed himself. It was that personal. He was that proud of his work.

There was one time—and only one time—when I joked with him. Mimicking his broken English with a stern look pasted on, I intoned, "This number ten gun! No workee! This gun no workee!"

He grabbed me, intense alarm clouding over his face. "Get bullets! Get bullets!" He pulled me by the shirt outside to show me just how well the gun worked. He loaded the gun, handed it to me, and said, "You pull trigger. If it no work, you kill me!" He would have handed me his gun to shoot him with. Sarcasm was not a trait he understood or appreciated.

I had to shoot my gun. If I said, "No, no. I trust you," he would have gotten mad. I fired two rounds; then he took the gun back. His response, an approving smile and nod of his head, came as he began the process of cleaning it all over again. Off he went, cleaning it perfectly and bringing it back again. That was the focus of his life, and he took it very seriously.

After checking my gun, mama san would come in with my clothes cleaned, dried, ironed, and folded and place them on my bed. My tiger stripes, bathing suit, T-shirt, socks, and boots were all perfect. A dab of polish on my boots, just the way I liked it. All arranged perfectly at the foot of my bed.

There were three meals I enjoyed that she prepared. Between my Vietnamese and her English, we got along just fine.

"I cook number two tonight. Number two."

"Oh, very good. Very good." Number two was rice and shrimp. (Number one was rice, vegetables, and beef; while number three was fish, shrimp, and rice.) As I finished eating, Gallagher would come in and sit down across from me. We reviewed the documents and what I'd learned from the VC and the interpreter. Later, we filled out our after-action reports, listing how many killed, captured, what we saw, observed, and did. It all had to be recorded.

Captured three people, killed four, nine ran away. Saw jet fly over and blow up. Good supporting documents from the North detailing VCI network in Rung Sat. Etc., etc.

It was important to dot the *i*s, cross the *t*s, and document anything significant. What we did and saw here, coupled with what someone else did and saw over there, allowed those higher up to see the big picture. They took our little piece of the puzzle and added it to other pieces they had to give a better understanding of what was happening. At least, that was the idea.

People read the documents very carefully. Frequently, we had letters like:

Dear honey, Here I am in South Vietnam. I miss you very much. I bet Hanoi is beautiful this time of year. My unit is moving out tomorrow. We're going to go attack the Americans over here. We're going to go here and do that.

Obviously, that letter was intelligence. After we sent it up, we'd hear back that this particular VC was in the 155th Infantry. They'd put a pin in the map. They developed a very good picture about what was going on, based on the information brought in. Frequently, we had intelligence critical to the success of another op we were set to go on, so we kept it to ourselves. It was like finding gold. We didn't want to lose our strategy to the press. If we let it go to NILO, sooner rather than later our information invariably hit the streets. Once it was of no further value to us, we let it go. Initially, we tried passing on information early, and it nearly got us killed in an ambush.

There were a lot of high-ranking South Vietnamese officers who were double agents, or on the take. As I mentioned before—corruption reached all levels. It took exactly one briefing to understand how truly dangerous it was. It went something like this: *The SEALs found this information out. They're going to go in tomorrow to such and such an address and attack the Viet Cong.* The agent(s) would go later that same day to send out an urgent message: *Don't look now, but the SEALs are planning on coming to your location. You were compromised.*

This happened to Big Frank Bomar. Big Frank had made chief and was going to have a big party.

"Congratulations, Frank!" I said, good-naturedly grabbing him around the neck. "When's the party?"

Frank smiled. "Who said anything about a party?" he said, almost innocently. He broke into a wide grin. "It's this Saturday. Be sure and come."

"I'll be there."

That night, Frank and his team went out. Their information was compromised. Stepping from the STAB, Frank wandered right into an ambush. Reacting instantly to the barrage of bullets pelting down upon them from a well-placed ambush, Frank started hosing down the enemy. At six feet four and 260 pounds, he didn't bother to hit the deck. He died, but his gallant effort broke the ambush and spared his team from being entirely decimated. Only one other SEAL was killed. It could easily have been the entire team.

Corruption caused the death of my friend, Frank Bomar. We determined to do everything short of obstructing justice and breaking the law to keep hold of our intelligence so long as it had the potential to come back and hurt us.

I had a PRU whom I entrusted my life with. His name was Biá (pronounced Ba-A), and I quickly promoted him to PRU chief. Biá had been a VC company commander, and his skills and abilities were superb. Our team developed a close camaraderie and dependency on one another. It was a sobering realization when I was the only American fighting in a firefight in the middle of a jungle thousands of miles from home.

One of the ways I protected my men involved health care. I saw to it my wounded PRUs were admitted into American, not Vietnamese, hospitals. Again, corruption was rampant, so medical supplies were sold on the black market rather than stocked for emergency medical treatment. It was a crapshoot as to whether someone would live or not if they had even a moderate wound. When they recovered, I personally returned to the American hospital to pick them up. A few weeks later, they were back to work. Had they been sent to a local hospital . . . who knows?

It was important to me to personally meet with the relatives of my wounded PRUs. Unfortunately, the only person bringing food into their homes were the men who'd just been shot. "Please tell them not to worry about their husbands; they'll be all right," I instructed my interpreter. "Tell them they're being well taken care of at the American hospital, and will be home soon. Also," I said as I reached out with an envelope, "tell them here is their husband's money. This should take care of them for the time being."

Overjoyed, the women thanked me profusely. Before long, the wounded PRUs were back. Because I treated my men like they were "number one," they devoted themselves to me. Their loyalty was beyond question.

My interpreter, a very petite and graceful woman named Kiem, was a fluent translator. She was beautiful, possessing the traits of both her Vietnamese and French heritage. Against my better judgment, Kiem would eventually work with us on a number of operations.

"I need to see the chief," the previously wounded PRU stated emphatically to Kiem.

"Chief, Ko wishes to speak with you."

Solemnly, Ko walked in. He bowed low, handing me his rifle. I took it, unsure as to what to do with it. He went to parade rest. "Sir, I owe you my life. My gun, my life, is yours."

I bowed low and ceremonially handed back his gun. "Tell him it's too heavy for me to carry."

Ko, upon hearing the translation, was pleased. He laughed, smiling broadly.

There was an instant bond, like contact cement. From then on, whenever I went anywhere, my entourage took me. These guys dedicated their lives to making sure my butt stayed attached to my body. Whether we were in the jungle or going downtown for mushroom soup, they stayed close to me. Nobody got in my way.

Some weeks later, we captured documents mentioning me. They were among memorandums sent from one VC unit to another. *There is a blond-headed American working in the area. Whatever it takes, we want him. We want him neutralized—we want him killed.* Since I was the only blond in the area . . . I guess they meant me.

Being mentioned as a target created an element of uncertainty since we obviously didn't live in a teeming metropolis. Furtive glances and overt stares kept me on edge.

By that time, I had five guys with me wherever I went. I was driving my jeep downtown, all six of us squeezed in, when we hit a traffic jam. Two water buffalo, two jeeps, and a bus. No one was able to go anywhere. I looked around and said, in my limited Vietnamese, *"Do myuh I muk low!"* (Son of a bitch!) "Get them out of the way!"

Never say that to bodyguards.

They stood and started shooting. *Bddddap! Bddddap!* At first, over everybody's head, then lower. They could get people out of the way. Suddenly, bullets pummeled the jeep. It was an ambush. I ducked, attempting to reach my CAR-15 while my five bodyguards let it fly. "Go go go!" Biá yelled.

Shifting into gear, I drove right over the top of a water buffalo killed in the first volley of fire. I sped off. "No! Go back! Chief, go back!"

I whipped the jeep around, this time steering with one hand and pointing my CAR with the other. Five automatic weapons trained on one area kept the snipers pinned down. I almost drove on top of them. Biá slammed several shells into the two guys lying there, and the game was over. As word of what happened spread, people in town got to know us real quick. As commonly happens, our reputation preceded us.

Some days later, we came upon another traffic jam—two cabs and a bus—and I stopped. The drivers all looked at me and panicked. The next thing I knew, pedestrians, strangers, people from all walks of life, were out there pushing the bus from the intersection. They didn't want to be part of the next story to go around town.

Here come the PRUs. Watch out! Clear the streets! The stories got taller and taller day by day. "Hey! Let's go in and get us a beer," I hollered above the noise of the engine.

"Yeah!" came the chorus from my guards. I pulled over in front of a bar we'd been to several weeks prior. As we walked in, the place quieted. All eyes looked at the five of us. Whispered conversations quickly gave way to mass exodus. Puzzled, I looked at my men and shrugged, as if to ask, *What's going on?*

"Nobody want get shot," said Ko. "Several VC no want get shot, so they leave."

This happened numerous times. Other times, seeing someone who looked suspicious, my guys approached them ready to shoot. This was a war zone, and they weren't afraid to put a bullet in anyone. One patron decided to be a tough guy, and quickly found the barrel of a gun in his mouth. Excitedly, in a mix of Vietnamese and pidgin English, Biá announced, "Viet Cong. Viet Cong. He looky spy. He VC spy!"

He was certain this was a VC who was spying on us. To him, the easiest way to resolve this was to shoot him. Right there and then, make an example out of him. "Why don't we *not* kill him today," I stated, motioning them to stop. "Send him outside." Then: "Tell him to go back and tell the bad guys I'm right here, come and get me."

They thought that was funny. It was like I was spitting in the face of the Viet Cong. Now it seems stupid—at the time, it was the way we were.

"You're going to let him go so he can go tell?"

"Sure!" I exaggerated.

This met with enthusiastic chuckling. "Go tell them! You better find some VC to tell or we're going to shoot you anyway!"

Off he went, as fast as he could. In the minds of my men and in the village, I was a "great leader." Conversely, the faith and confidence I had in them ran deep.

"We have information there's supposed to be a small cadre of VC moving through with high-level couriers tonight. I want to take them," announced Gallagher at the house.

That night, Gallagher took five guys and I took five. I set up an ambush at the edge of a tree line, while, at another tree line right-angled eight hundred meters away, Gallagher set up his team. We positioned ourselves, spread out over forty yards. We sat there, planning to stay all night if need be. At about two A.M., I heard talking at the back of the team. When it continued, I moved slowly alongside my field interpreter and put my lips to his ear. "You go down there and tell them to shut up or I'm going to shoot every one of them!"

He hurried away. It became silent immediately. Hustling back to me, he whispered, his head bobbing up and down, "Berry sorry. Berry sorry."

Nothing happened the rest of the night. As the sun arose, casting about the first light of dawn, Gallagher called me on the radio. "Did you make contact?"

"Nah."

"Yeah, me either. Bring your team across the paddy at a forty-five-degree angle. Hook up with me and let's go home. What a wasted night."

I stood up and signaled, *Saddle up and let's go.* We all stood up and headed out toward the paddy. I turned to Biá and indicated he was point. I went in the number two team position, with the interpreter third.

"Let's go!" We started marching. I stepped out of line to make sure everybody was there and no one had fallen asleep. We totaled six men, including me.

"Point man, one," I said, quietly counting. "Me, two. Interpreter, three. Four, five six, seven, eight, nine, ten." . . . *Wait a minute. I sat down last night with six. There's now ten.*

"Hold the patrol. Hold the patrol," I said loud enough for everyone to hear. "Stop. . . . Stop!"

I turned to my interpreter. "What's going on?!"

Just then, four guys from the rear of the squad came jogging up. They all fell in, in formation, rigid stance, chests jutted forward and guns held up and down, stiff and very formal. "Where in the world . . ." I stammered. As if someone had said, *Present arms,* each one held out his rifle. AK-47s.

I started chuckling. It hit me funny. All I could think to say was "Cool. Where're you guys from?"

One guy in my team was from the area. He'd grown up there, and recognized the four Viet Cong as friends of his. When he spotted them, he quickly got their attention. "Hey! Come here! Don't look now but there's an American down there who will blow your head off if you walk by."

"We don't want that to happen! We quit. We surrender!"

"Okay. Just sit here. In the morning we'll go tell him. It'd be too confusing if we go to him now, in the dark."

About that time, the interpreter came down. "You two, shut up!"

"Okay."

After the interpreter left, he leaned over to his Viet Cong friends and said, "Sit here next to me. If anyone comes down the trail in front of us, we'll have to shoot them!" They actually prepared to shoot the next group—assuming they didn't know them!

When they presented their rifles to me, I put my arms out in acceptance. Immediately, they stacked their wooden-stock AK-47s in my arms. *Heavy* wooden-stock AK-47s. They fell back in at attention.

"I'm not carrying your guns—they're too heavy." I told the interpreter, ''Tell them to take the guns back.'' The ''heavy'' bit worked before; why not again? Done deal!

After they took back their guns, I turned my back on them and walked away. ''Okay. Let's go! Tell them to fall in! Let's *Di di*!''

After we marched across the rice paddy and hooked up with Gallagher's team, he pulled me aside. ''I watched what took place through my binocs. I think I saw you turn your back on four AK-toting Viet Cong, then proceed to give the *Forward ho!* sign. That had to have been one of the funniest things I've ever seen. Damn!'' He paused, then added, ''I thought you said you didn't make contact.''

I smiled and shrugged. ''Nothing to speak of. Just some *chu hoys* [Vietnamese for surrender].''

Gallagher let out a faint glimmer of a smile. ''Well, I guess they're on the payroll now. Let's go.'' We actually did add them to our PRUs.

The combination of experience gleaned through my first tour, along with the PRUs catching on to our strategies and training, allowed us to start going after bigger targets and undertake more complex operations.

Information came in about a doctor kidnapped by the Viet Cong. He was being forced to work on an island in the middle of a river. Intelligence reports stated that if anyone attempted a rescue, the advanced warning system allowed sufficient time to spirit him away into seclusion. Reportedly, the doctor was anxious to ''surrender'' and return home on the American side. The Viet Cong weren't about to let him go, threatening to kill his wife and family. His daughters were allowed to go to the market, which was how we attained most of our information. He decided that when his daughters were safely out of reach of the Viet Cong, he would bolt for freedom. Unfortunately, while his daughters escaped, the doctor was stopped. He was severely beaten and placed under constant surveillance.

''She's saying her father is treating wounded Viet Cong at their rehabilitation area on an island twenty kilometers from here. He wants to escape and surrender, but he can't get away. She wishes to know if you can help him,'' conveyed Kiem.

After determining his exact whereabouts, it was readily apparent why the Viet Cong used this particular island. With canopy overhead and open expanses of land and water adjacent, their perimeter guard easily detected any movement. At the slightest hint of anything unusual, they'd disappear into the jungle.

''Please tell her I think this is a worthwhile operation for us to undertake. I will to speak with my boss.''

After relaying the details to Gallagher, we devised our strategy. "There's only one way to attack them, and that's with just three of us. We swim in, and they'll never know we're there," concluded Gallagher.

"That's definitely different," I pondered. "I'd much rather take ten or twenty. He's constantly guarded by twenty to thirty people."

Gallagher, furrowing his brow in classic military commander style, stated, "Tell you what. You take your CAR-fifteen, ten magazines, two flares, a LAAW rocket, a couple grenades, and I'll bring the same kinda stuff. That'll even the odds!" You had to love his "kick ass" attitude.

All I could add was "Okay."

We took our best bodyguard, loaded him up—grenades, bullets, claymores, everything—so we all carried a pyrotechnics factory. We had to wear life preservers in order to keep from sinking as we swam. We climbed onto the back of a nondescript local fishing boat that routinely plied the local waterways. It was ten o'clock at night as we eased over the stern when it got into range of the island. The boat never slowed down. We swam, using breaststrokes to not disturb the water's surface, quietly moving to the island sixty yards in the distance.

Halfway to the island, the life jacket the Vietnamese PRU was wearing developed a leak. It rapidly deflated, becoming useless. Thrashing desperately to jettison himself of his gear, he finally was able to drop it all while taking water into his lungs, nearly drowning under the weight. Guns, pistol, rockets, grenades, bullets, all sunk to the bottom of the river.

"Shhh. Hey," I whispered. "Quiet!"

Evidently, the time he spent underwater shook him. He panicked and was in danger of drowning himself. Gallagher was in front, while I swam comfortably right behind him, taking it easy. As he continued thrashing about, I recognized I'd better go help him. His eyes were as big as half-dollars, scared to death.

I swam to him. The first thing he did was to climb right on top of me. In his mind, he was drowning, and I was the life raft. So there I was, trying to hold him up, myself up, and about seventy pounds of gear.

"STOP! Calm down!" I gasped, his hands around my throat. "It's okay. It's all right!"

Suddenly, I'm not sure exactly how he did it, but he broke, ruptured, or bit my life jacket. *Whoosh.* . . . The air rushed out. One hundred ten pounds of Vietnamese, seventy pounds of gear, and no more flotation.

I'm a SEAL, not Superman. Struggling to move him off of me, I finally got the H-harness undone. Now *my* gear plunged to the bottom of the river. There went *my* gun, grenades, bullets, LAAW, everything. I was suddenly one hundred percent unarmed. I held the Vietnamese close in the traditional lifesaving position. He calmed down, and I was able to swim the two of us to shallow water where he stood among the nipa palm. It was a challenge. I was fully clothed, having worn boots—not fins—and dragged this guy to shore. I was ready to abort the mission. The Vietnamese was scared to death. Animatedly, he pantomimed he wanted to leave, now.

Gallagher, fortunately, was the one carrying the radio. It was wrapped securely in several plastic bags. "Let's not undo it yet. Let's wait until morning," Gallagher instructed. "Then you can get on the radio. That'll give us the opportunity to scope this place out, whether we need help or not—see what we need to do."

"Man, Gallagher," I replied, a little unnerved at what had happened and at being in the wrong part of town without a gun or a ticket home. "I don't have a gun, he doesn't have a gun. . . . This sucks!"

Gallagher reached into his shoulder holster and pulled out a High Standard .22 pistol, a silencer screwed onto the end of the barrel. That High Standard .22 held a magazine with all of fifteen rounds in it. Only one magazine. He handed it to me. "There. Don't worry, I've got my M-sixteen."

I stood there, my hand massaging my forehead, thinking this can only get worse. I responded with my well-rehearsed "Okay."

We moved into a canal running east to west that dumped into the river running north to south at the island. Along both canal banks were ample amounts of nipa palm, water lilies, and foliage to hide in. We swam to a point thirty yards up the canal and stopped. Faintly in the moonlight, I could see the house nestled into the tree line on the island. We laid underneath the toadstool lily pads, in the mud, and waited for morning. As the sun came up, I counted fifteen to twenty people coming out of the cluster of houses. *Great! All I have is this lousy .22 pistol. Just enough to make somebody mad.* Some of the men had guns, some didn't. Some wore black pajamas, others not. Clearly Viet Cong.

We watched as they left. The island was roughly a mile wide by ten to twelve miles long. The river actually parted, coming around on either side. On the side we came in at, the west side of the island, the river was 200 yards wide, while on the other side the river spanned 600 to 800 yards wide.

"Get the radio ready," said Gallagher softly.

I tore off the plastic, screwed on the antenna, connected the headset, and checked the battery. I was ready to call.

Through hand signals, Gallagher said, *Set it aside. Lay down and keep an eye on the house. Most've them have already gone. Once I see the doctor, I'm going to rush them. You get on the radio and provide support—cover my back.*

I lifted the .22 and looked at Gallagher. *With this?*

"We've gotta get the doctor. It's important."

The sun came up, brushing aside the shadows in preparation for the day. All three of us concentrated intently on the hooch, trying to catch a glimpse of the doctor.

All of a sudden, I heard a splash right behind me. I was lying on my stomach at about a 45-degree angle, peering through the brush at the hooches in the distance. Another splash. Ever so slowly, I turned onto my right side in order to see what was moving behind us. Four feet behind me was the water's edge. There stood a Viet Cong soldier! He'd stepped over the edge of a sampan and was dragging the nose of the sampan to shore. Right on top of me. He moved closer, barely four feet from me. Fortunately, I was shrouded in lily pads and nipa palm. Moving still closer, he was now at my feet. His eyes came up, locking onto my eyes.

Oh shit!

Slung across his shoulder was an AK-47. I had my trusty .22-caliber. There were another four people in the boat! Quickly, I brought the .22 up. *Boop, boop,* went the gun, the bullets finding their mark in the VC's chest.

Boy, did it piss him off. I quickly discovered, it takes a lot to kill somebody with a silenced .22 pistol. *Boop.* The third round hit him at the base of his throat, right above the collarbone. He collapsed into the water. *That got his attention . . . and, unfortunately, the attention of his friends.*

By then, despite the silencer, the second and third Viet Cong heard the shots. The second Viet Cong now clearly saw me, silhouetted within the lily pads. He brought up his AK-47.

Oh good! What a fair fight. I started pulling the trigger. *I've got three guys to shoot—at a minimum!*

Boop. Boop. Boop. Boop. Boop. Boop. Boop. I shot for all I was worth. I wasn't that far away, I was hitting them, and they acted like they were being stung by a hornet, not shot! They weren't dying.

Bddap! Bddap! Bddap! Gallagher poured three short bursts from his M16 into the sampan. The three VC went helter-skelter out of the boat. Dead.

"Cover me!" Gallagher yelled as he sloshed up the bank and out of the canal. Racing forward, he assaulted the hooch, the PRU right behind him. I was covering him with four .22 rounds. Silenced. If anybody's coming, and they were more than ten feet away, I'd have had to wave at them. The bullets just couldn't go that far.

Hearing the M16 go off, two Viet Cong guards came running out of the hooch. Gallagher buried them both. *Bddap! Bddap!* I grabbed the radio and raced toward the hooches as well. I knelt in the courtyard, getting on the radio. Inside the hooch, I heard fistfights, pots and pans clanging, then the sudden explosion of guns going off.

"Mayday. Mayday! This is Moosejaw Bravo! We need help! We're in a firefight and we need help!"

"No problem. I gotcha loud and clear," came the reply. "Be there in twenty minutes."

This will work, I thought, sarcastically. *Twenty minutes. Flowers could be sprouting from our graves in twenty minutes.* "Could you try to hurry?"

Gallagher ran out dragging the doctor. The doctor had been shot just above the knee and was bleeding profusely. Bodies strewn about, Gallagher set him down, stopping to tourniquet the wound.

My back to the river, I looked across the paddy to my right. I watched all these guys start running down the dike toward us. I hastily counted twenty to thirty guys. Desperately, I thrashed around in the water, trying to kick up an AK-47. *Where is it? I can't find it!* I glanced down at my .22. *Now let's see. Four bullets into thirty guys—how do I do this?*

"Gallagher," I screamed. "Get a move on! We've got company. I've got thirty guys flanking us to the right. Back up to the river now! We gotta back up!"

He replied, "Move down into the mud! I'll meet you there."

I leaped off the bank of the canal into the water. Coming up with the radio held high above my head, I twisted around and plowed back to the muddy embankment. Right after me, Dong, our PRU bodyguard, jumped. Luckily, he kicked up an AK-47 from one of the Viet Cong we'd shot. *That'll buy us time. Maybe.*

Gallagher came over the embankment, sliding in the mud with the doctor. Unexpectedly, from out in the river came the hum of a PBR.

"Moosejaw Bravo. Moosejaw Bravo," came our call sign over the radio.

"This is Moosejaw Bravo. Where the hell are you?" I said, searching the river.

"We're right here. We knew you guys were going to get in trouble," said the PBR radioman. "We've been hiding down here. Only five minutes away!"

"Help's here!" I shouted at Gallagher. "Quick! Move to the river."

I stood up and took my hat off in order to show them my blond hair. I didn't want to go through all we'd endured, only to be shot by our own guys.

"I gotcha! I see you," crackled the radio. The boat turned and headed right at us. I stood up again, motioning to my left at the Viet Cong shooters running toward us. The PBR driver slammed the gears into reverse and revved the engine. This stopped the PBR right in front of me, no more than two to three feet away. Simultaneously, the man on the bow of the PBR, sitting behind twin .50-caliber machine guns, spun his guns toward the oncoming Viet Cong. Bullets started splashing into the water and into the mud around us. No more than two feet above me, the twin .50s kicked off. *BuBuBuBuBuBuBu! BuBuBuBu-BuBuBuBuBu!* Sizzling-hot casings fell into the water around me. He just raked them. Thirty guys. Right there, no more than forty yards away. They didn't have time to run away. He poured it on them.

Gallagher, Dong, and I passed the doctor into the boat, and then followed. The PBR pilot slammed the twin engines into reverse, and we lurched backwards. In almost the same motion, he kept one engine in reverse, and jammed the other throttle lever into forward, spinning the boat around. "Hang on!" he shouted.

Seconds later, both engines were propelling us out of the canal and into the river. Without breaking the fusillade of bullets, the gunner smoothly turned his turret and continued to blast into the Viet Cong position. He expended an easy five thousand rounds. Like that, we were good to go, outta there! You gotta love American firepower!

Arriving back in Sok Trang, Gallagher wrote up an after-action report, for which I received a second Bronze Star.

We went on numerous other little ops over the next few weeks, always making contact. We were pleased at the progress of our PRU. Their discipline, skill, and bravado was vindication for the PRU program. As opposed to ARVN, the PRUs were tough, frontline soldiers. What made it especially enjoyable were the strong bonds developed across cultural, language, and racial barriers. I had the utmost confidence, trust, and respect for these men.

Kiem, my interpreter, had lost most of her family, all murdered by the Viet Cong. A smoldering anger was replaced by overt hatred over time. Revenge was a very strong motivator.

One night, we prepared to go on an op where we had to be at the right place at the right time, interview several villagers, then set up an ambush for an alleged company of main force VC. My field interpreter did not understand the finesse this operation required. The interview process was critical, but his limited command of English had the potential for inaccuracy that could prove deadly. "He says he doesn't understand your questions about bearings, compass locations, and troop strength. He can tell me in Vietnamese, but doesn't know corresponding English words," Kiem reported, in flawless English.

"It's not going to work," I concluded aloud. "I'm not going to chance getting our people killed."

Kiem shrugged. "Well, if it's important, I'll go."

I kind of looked at her with one eye and half smiled, half snorted. *Yeah, right.* I was macho—women didn't do this sort of thing, operating where physical strength and stamina often meant the difference. I dismissed her out of hand. "No. You're a woman. Can't go."

"No, you don't seem to understand," she replied passionately. "Over here, I'm quite capable of fighting. Maybe you should let me go with you once and you'll see how good I am."

Her English was excellent. She could make the operation possible. I wrestled with the decision, then replied, "I'll let you go with us on this one."

She showed up several hours later, wearing tiger-striped clothes, a webbed harness ammo belt, and carrying a M3A1 .45-caliber grease gun. I had no idea where she got all the hardware, but she was definitely ready to go.

Disembarking after the ride upriver, we had a lengthy hike. She stayed right by me, never once backing off. As we entered the village, she went right to work, literally slapping people around and asking questions.

"*Di We* [Lieutenant], follow me!" she insisted after interrogating a number of townspeople. She walked me down the street and around the corner. Pointing at a road leading into town, she said, "They're going to be coming into town on that road in about twenty minutes."

"Good. Set up the ambush." Instantly, everyone jumped to their preappointed tasks. Dong, Ko, and Biá ran down the road, spacing their directional-blast claymores. Ten others moved back into town to keep any possible "heroes" from sneaking out to alert the unsuspecting company. All together, I had thirty guys with me. At the edge of town ran a ditch parallel with the incoming road. We climbed down in the ditch to prepare. They were due to arrive in minutes. We didn't have to wait long. Through my binoculars I spotted the one-hundred-man company coming toward us. *Right on time. No false alarm tonight!* I relayed the information down the line through hand signals. Everyone was ready, locked and loaded. Unfortunately, the company turned and walked in toward town on a dike twenty yards farther away from us. *Even with this change in direction, we should still be able to hit them pretty hard.*

Timing was critical. We waited. They got closer and closer. *BOOOOM!* The claymores went off, ripping through the last fifty to sixty VC. Almost simultaneously, we started shooting. They dove for cover. Kiem didn't waver for a moment. In an instant, she was up on the dike shooting people right and left. She quickly went through her first magazine, deftly discarded it, then locked in her second. *Damn! She's good!* I momentarily paused to watch her ferocity. At that instant, I became a believer. *Welcome to the Team!*

The gun battle raged for thirty minutes before the survivors straggled off into the jungle to regroup. The confirmed body count was twenty-five, with another twenty-five wounded. Not as good as we'd hoped, but still effective. Had they been as close as we originally planned, we'd have annihilated them all.

We promptly sent out our security team after the shooting stopped. Kiem and I ran forward to check out the enemy lying there. She ran in front of me, making sure none of the Viet Cong was still alive. She made sure by shooting them. She was steady, putting it to them. It was such a contradiction. One moment, she was making small talk, asking what America was like, what France was like—I could easily envision her as a secretary in an office. Now she was callously killing the enemy. No remorse, no second thoughts; that was what she was there for. She had the ability to turn it on or off. She did well.

Maybe women and SEALs did mix in battle.

CHAPTER 15

PERUSING THE SKIES

TOWARD THE LATTER MONTHS OF MY SECOND TOUR, HOWEVER, we got involved in more mechanized operations. "Helo-borne assaults" was the term used for lightning-strike missions flown into enemy strongholds to engage them in battle. Typically, we had several helos loaded with troops, flanked by gunships which provided covering fire. Completing the formation was the Command and Control ship (C and C), which flew considerably higher and behind us. We'd received good intelligence regarding one to two companies of Viet Cong moving from point A to point B. They were planning to attack an American military outpost. Gallagher believed the information reliable, so he formulated an assault plan.

"We're going to do a helo-borne assault."

"Okay."

"We're going to need about eighty PRUs."

"Holy crap! That's a lotta guys."

Gallagher smiled sinisterly. In his John Wayne imitation, he drawled, "Yep." Then: "We'll lay on four gunships, a C and C, and ten slicks."

We rehearsed and practiced our assault for the next two days. We went to the airport and prepared to leave. All my troops were loaded down with gear, and we went over one final brief on how to get off the helos, move into the woods, and engage the enemy. We briefed the pilots where we were going and where they were to land. Everybody was ready. We left the briefing room in the early morning light. Out on the tarmac, standing at parade rest, stood my thirty-two PRUs, awaiting my command to board. I placed eight of my men in each of four slicks. We were good to go.

The Viet Cong were to have traveled out of the north, proceeding east along a jungle trail. Intelligence reported the VC would be camped in a two-hundred-meter-wide tree line alongside the trail. This tree line ran for a thousand yards in a north-south direction. My group was to land west of the trees, in a meadow of tall jungle grass, and immediately assault. Gallagher, with his six helos, planned to come in from the north in a flanking maneuver to keep the VC from escaping. This meant my troops should see more shooting initially, while Gallagher needed more guys to flank and mop up along a more spread-out area. Our plan was to come screaming over the treetops at 150 miles per hour, set down a hundred yards from the tree line, scramble off, get on line while the helos left, and attack the tree line. We were to engage the enemy before they could react.

Gallagher's six helos flew in front of us, a gap of several hundred yards between our group and his. All the slicks flew in a straight line. The gunships flanked either side of us, making a V formation like an arrow. As Gallagher continued in a crescent pattern to the left, we were to drop down. About that time, his helos would hook hard right and set down northeast of my position in a right angle. We'd hit the Viet Cong in a crossfire.

This was our first, full, official helo-borne assault with PRUs; where we expected contact the minute we landed. We weren't trying to be stealthy—we were going in and banging on the door.

Screaming over treetops, our helos in formation, we started our high-speed run in. I studied the map, my headset on, in communication with Gallagher. "You see it?" I asked.

"Yep. We identify the tree line. Stand by to set it down. Get your people out and on line."

"You got it, Eagle. I'm off the radio and on line." I threw down the radio helmet and put on my hat in preparation. As if they had slammed on the brakes, the helos literally stopped in midair, a hundred feet up. Down we went suddenly. At fifty feet up, people underneath us, in the grass, jumped up and started running. Without knowing it, we were setting down right on top of them. So much for accurate intelligence! We found out later the Viet Cong companies were behind schedule and hadn't made it to the tree line. They were all together, nice and tight in their little group. While Gallagher's helos flew on past, my helos received a surprise.

Unaware, I commanded, "Load your guns!" As guys were loading their guns, rounds started coming through the door of the helo. One hit right next to my face, striking the splatter shield behind the copilot, splattering lead and hitting me in my face. I thought someone had carelessly touched off a round. I was instantly angry. "Who was it!" I screamed. For an instant, I wanted to shoot someone. I didn't want my own guys shooting me; war was dangerous enough. We got a little bit lower. "Who shot your damn gun?" About that time, the guy next to me pitched over, blood spurting everywhere. I looked out the door of the helo and all I saw were Viet Cong. *They're right there!* In shock, all I could think was, *Oh shit! Look at all the targets!*

Now we were ten feet off the deck and dropping fast. I started shoving guys out the door. It was like being on a galloping horse and shooting; accuracy was impossible. It might work in the movies, but not here. We had to get on the ground—and begin shooting. We desperately needed to return fire to get them to put their heads down, which would cut off the incoming fire. The rounds kept coming. As I pushed people out, they were getting hit. I jumped out. The helo shot up and out of there. I blazed away with my little CAR-15, shooting in a 200-degree arc. VC were all around us! The roar of the helos, the staccato of close automatic weapon fire, all mixed in a hellishly loud cordite haze.

BBDDDAAAP! BBDDDAAAP! BBDDDAAAP! BBDDDAAAP! BBDDDAAAP! I shot as rapidly as the gun would fire. In quick succession, I went through four magazines. Shoot and load, shoot and load. Feverishly, I swung my gun in an arclike motion. All of a sudden, I felt a tug on my pant leg. I glanced down—continuing to fire—at one of my PRUs who'd been shot through the knee. He'd crawled over to me, and was jerking at my pant leg. "What!"

He pointed at his ear. I stopped shooting. From sixty yards away, in front of the tree line, I heard, *Do Do DO DOOP! Do Do DO DOOP!* The Viet Cong had set up a .30-caliber machine gun and were hosing me down. Fortunately, no bullets had hit me yet. I didn't realize they were shooting solely at me. My PRU finally yanked me down. As I hit the deck and surveyed our position, I saw that none of my guys was shooting. The seriousness of our predicament seared into me like a white-hot branding iron. Every one of my men from my helicopter was shot up. The PRU with the radio, bleeding from a jagged wound to his stomach, gasping for air, and ashen-faced, crawled over to me and handed me the handset. I screamed on the radio to the helo pilot who had just let us off. ''We need you to get us outta here!''

''Look! My door gunner is shot. My copilot is shot. I have to med-evac them out, so I'm not going to be able to come in and slick you out. Over.''

My PRUs from the other three helos had gotten on line and began firing at the VC. The math, unfortunately, didn't add up. My eight PRUs were down, dead or wounded. The other twenty-four guys and I were not a good match against a hundred VC. Landing right on top of them forfeited any element of surprise. Our gunfire was ineffective. When I hit the deck upon hearing the .30-caliber, the realization washed over me, *I'm in deep kimchee. We're losing, and the enemy is not running away. The helos have left, and the gunships can't shoot because the enemy is so close to us.* The VC obviously realized their numbers were superior, and began pressing their advantage.

The battle was heated at the right flank. Gallagher, on the left flank, waited to see what was going to happen. His PRUs couldn't shoot, because on my end all my guys were intermixed amongst the Viet Cong.

The .30-caliber machine gun was raking us over pretty good. Bullets were being poured into our position, kicking dirt and mud and plant debris all over us. Ten feet from me was Ko. He'd brought two LAAWs with him. He was shot through the elbow, blood-soaked, his arm swinging uselessly. ''Hey!'' I hollered, getting his attention. ''Shoot the LAAW!'' I pointed to the LAAW and then pointed in the direction of the machine gunner. He took a LAAW off his back and threw it at me, in effect saying, *You want to shoot, go ahead, but I'm not sticking my head up.* I extended the tube, raised up, and touched it off. *Whoosh!* The rocket took off. Unfortunately, I shot way too high. It hit the top of the trees 150 yards away and exploded. *Well, it sounded good. I'd better get it lower or make an appointment with the coroner.* The machine gun, from where they'd set it up, was in a minigrove of nipa palm. The thatch stood 10 to 15 feet high, concealing their location. There must have been a crater there, because they appeared well fortified.

I motioned for him to throw me his remaining LAAW. I stuck my head up, pulled the target into the sights, took a deep breath, and squeezed it off. It jetted across the sixty yards barely six feet off the ground. It hit the nipa palm grove, cutting it like a lawn mower going through grass. *KA-Blooom!* The explosion severed the nipa palm in half. The machine gun went quiet.

"Yes!" I yelled with glee. "Got them sonsabitches!"

I turned to my guys. "SHOOT! Shoot!"

The ones that could . . . did! At what, they didn't know; but they began shooting. As in poker, bluffing and posturing were extremely important elements. The Viet Cong couldn't be certain how many of us were lying in the grass, or how many rockets we had or didn't have. If our resistance fire was weak, their response would have been different. The volume of fire from my guys made all the difference at that moment.

"Keep shooting! Keep shooting! Hooyah, frogmen!"

As enemy fire lessened, I began bandaging my men. I tourniqueted and wrapped the knee and elbow wounds. I dressed and wrapped a direct-pressure bandage to another one of my men, who had taken a bullet through the neck. Still another had two bullet wounds to his chest; fortunately, under his right arm and away from vital organs. Unfortunately, I ran out of bandages after these four men. None of my PRUs had carried first aid kits.

It appeared I had some time. I called my interpreter. "Tell them to shoot over there." I pointed to the left, while the main tree line was directly in front of us. "Slow." This was designed to set up a perimeter fire so the Viet Cong couldn't sneak around to the left and come after us in a pincer-type movement. My men had hunkered down, the VC fire much less effective now.

I got on the radio to Gallagher. "Eagle, I need help."

"What do you need?"

"First aid gear."

"Come and get it."

Somewhat angrily, I replied, "Thanks a lot. I'll be right there."

I put the phone down and looked at my guys. "Don't go anywhere." They looked at me in disbelief. *No problem,* came the message in their eyes. I smiled and patted several of them as I began to run, bent double, two hundred meters to where Gallagher stood. Scattered fire was shot in my direction. I kept running, finally arriving safely.

He loaded me down with first aid supplies, morphine, blood expander, epinephrine, and lots of bandages. "With all the serious wounded you have, you gotta get a medevac in."

Shaking my head in agreement, I said, "You know, I could really use some more shooters. We're in a bad position."

"Tell you what I'll do. I'll move my men up to the northern end of the tree line, at a forty-five-degree angle from you guys. We'll try to suppress the fire. You get a medevac in. When you get your wounded squared away, move up to the tree line, link up with me, and we'll continue."

My two-syllable response was still intact. "Okay." With my shirt serving as a medical bag, I got up and ran back to my wounded guys while everyone was dinging at me. Fortunately, my luck held and I was unscathed.

Upon returning, I got on the radio. "This is Moosejaw Bravo. Requesting medical evacuation. Requesting medical evacuation for eight casualties. Over." For the next forty-five minutes solid, I dressed my men's wounds.

The faint sound of a helo prompted me to stop and grab two smoke canisters. I set them off to mark my position. When the helos landed, I directed two healthy guys to carry the wounded and place them on board.

I ran over and jumped onto the landing skid. I grabbed the collar of the door gunner, pulling him close. "Take them to the Twenty-ninth Evac, Can Tho. This is special ops. Call SEAL Team when you get up there and let them know my guys are coming in. The name's Constance, I'll be up to get them in the morning."

"You got it." The helo lifted off.

I assembled the rest of my guys and we began slowly moving toward the tree line, linking up with Gallagher. I went past where the .30-caliber had been. Lying there, cut to shreds, were three guys. The LAAW rocket, when it exploded, had released enough force and fragmentation to kill all three. That one lucky shot quite possibly saved my life.

Once we got on line, the gunships were able to come in. They fired into the trees as we pushed our advantage, driving farther into the dark jungle foliage. We killed another twenty-five Viet Cong; our basic tactics and firepower proved overwhelming.

The next day, I gave all of the women of the wounded men money and sent them home knowing their husbands were going to be all right. The following day, I took a truck and three of my PRU bodyguards and drove up to Can Tho. My first stop was at the armory for more bullets. I always swiped bullets from the SEALs.

"Who's this for?" they would ask.

"Me."

My problem was that I wasn't supposed to be acting as, or on behalf of, a SEAL platoon. I was supposed to be a mercenary for the CIA. But that didn't get me bullets. I had to go to the guys I knew. I had my rotation of supply centers I'd hit. I went to the Army. There was a Second Class Gunner's Mate I'd worked with, who knew me by face, whether I was wearing civvies, cammies, or whatever. "You need something?"

"Uh-huh."

He'd look over at the truck. Then back at me with an "I ought to know better than this" smile. "You gonna load that truck?"

"Uh-huh."

"You know, we don't have much in there, except for SEAL Team."

"Uh-huh."

"Uh, I gotta go take a leak. Would you mind guarding the door for, say, the next thirty-five minutes until I get back?"

It was my turn to smile. "No problem." A better response than "Okay"!

After we loaded all we needed—LAAWs, claymores, bullets, grenades, and flares—I sent my PRUs off base. I waited patiently for him to return.

"You're still here?" he said with a smile, noticing that the truck was gone.

"I've been watching this door and nobody stole it."

"You know, it's good nobody stole this door."

"Yeah." I smiled, playing along. "By the way, next time I'm buying at the club."

"Cool."

We made little cots on top of the munitions, stacked high in the bed of the truck. Next stop, 29th Med-Evac hospital, Can Tho. My men were all resting comfortably. The doctors and corpsmen in Vietnam were miracle workers. They put a lot of bodies back together. After signing the necessary release papers, I requested medical supplies needed to replenish our stock. Drugs, guns, and ex-Viet Cong. What a crazy combination.

What made it even more humorous was the fact many of my men went into the hospital still carrying their guns, grenades, and bullets. That made the doctors very nervous. They didn't know if they were working on Viet Cong, South Vietnamese, or just who.

I deadpanned. "It doesn't make any difference; he's working for me. Sure, he's Viet Cong, but he's on our side—this week."

The doctors just shook their heads.

We drove on back to Sok Trang. After restocking the armory, we invited everyone to a party. Gallagher and I pulled money out of our own pockets and ordered stuff delivered to the compound. Cases of beer and soda. A couple of one-hundred-pound bags of rice, all delivered to the compound where our PRUs lived.

"Tell them to go get their families. We're having a party!" I instructed the interpreters. It was fun. That party really helped develop the cohesiveness of the entire group. I never worried too much about losing my life out of fear my guys might quit in the middle of an operation.

There were a lot of operations where my field interpreter couldn't go. I'd pick ten guys and say, "Let's go." Solely through the use of hand signals, we were able to communicate effectively. They had no idea what we were going to do. I'd point to my gun and they'd go get theirs. *Te te, beaucoup, Di di*—I knew little more.

"*Te te* VC," meaning "Not too many VC; we can handle them." Or "Oh crap, *beaucoup* VC; let's *Di di*," in other words, "Let's get outta here!"

Gallagher and I were making a name for ourselves with the bad guys. Documents captured, interrogation of prisoners, and intercepted intelligence more and more frequently referred to us.

The Viet Cong determined to stem the tide in Sok Trang. Reports came in telling of increasing troop strength, activity, and threats to locals who were thought to be sympathetic to us. There was an operation carried out by the VC against an outpost at the edge of town. Another project in Vietnam, known as the Cords Project, was "designed to win their hearts and minds through assistance in farming and other basic skills." There were ten Americans and one hundred Vietnamese working to help better the lives of the local populace. The Viet Cong overran the outpost. It was an inside deal. Knowing of the attack, all the Vietnamese disappeared, leaving the perimeter unguarded and the Americans exposed. The Viet Cong attackers basically walked in, shot the place up for good measure, and captured two Americans, a black soldier and a white soldier. The Army asked for help, so we spent the better part of a week attempting to track down the two POWs. We had to try to keep the VC from getting into Cambodia or Laos where they would have an easier time moving the Americans north to Hanoi.

We spent fifteen hours a day, tracking down lead after lead after lead. They were sighted here, then over there . . . it was frustrating. All of it had to be checked out. There was no doubt in my mind but that we were playing bump-and-run with them. After six days, the trail appeared to have gone cold, and, rather than patrolling haphazardly through the woods, we decided to put money in the street to see what developed. On day ten, an old man of sixty, looking like an old gnarled tree, came limping into our headquarters. Excitedly, he tried to speak to me and was not to be denied.

The poor man looked like he'd been ravaged by arthritis at every joint, life certainly having been more harsh on him than others. "Get me an interpreter," I said, not expecting much.

My interpreter began talking with the man. The more they talked, the more excited she got. After a few minutes, she suggested I call Gallagher.

"What is it?" Gallagher asked, impatiently.

The interpreter began, "This morning, this old man had breakfast with one black and one white American." Instantly, things went stone serious. "His story is remarkable."

It seemed the old man had been a prisoner for four years. They'd killed his family—his wife, his sons, and his daughter—and forced him to watch. He had done something to piss off one of the bigwigs in the Viet Cong hierarchy. Rather than kill him, they took pleasure in sadistically torturing him. Every time he was healthy, they'd break something. As soon as the arm or leg would heal, they broke something else. That's why he was all gnarled up. He was a "pet prisoner" for one particular colonel who delighted in torturing the poor man. They didn't tie him up or confine him at night because when he did try to escape, they easily caught up with him and busted him up again. For obvious reasons, he quit trying to escape. For the past two years, he just hung around the camp. He had several thousand meters of open, flat paddies to cross should he try to escape, which had proved impossible.

In the camp were more than one hundred Vietnamese prisoners, mostly city officials and ARVN officers. They were being staged out of there to whatever final destination was deemed appropriate. "Yesterday, he says, they brought in two Americans, one black and one white.

"Yesterday, while they were bringing them in and tying them up and placing them in a ditch, the old man walked up to the colonel and told him, 'I don't want to do this anymore. I'm leaving. You can shoot me, but you can't break anything anymore. I quit.' The colonel thought it real funny and told him, 'You go ahead and go old man. At sunup, my men will find you and kill you.'

"He told the colonel, 'You'll never find me,' and started hobbling off. He hobbled into a canal, swam for a while, got out and hobbled some more. He got to the village where somebody gave him a ride on a water buffalo. He managed to elude the Viet Cong—or maybe they let him go. Interestingly, he said he'd heard about the PRUs. The Viet Cong sat around and talked about Gallagher and you several times. 'Watch out for the Americans and their traitor Viet Cong.' He went on to say the VC encampment is always on the alert, replete with signals, escape tunnels, and armed guards."

We were astonished at all this information. If the old man weren't so believable, especially in light of his deformities, I'd have thought him to be a plant. Plus, all his information regarding the American POWs was completely accurate—what they wore, looked like, who was with them—all this we knew.

Gallagher looked at me. "With this kind of information, the only thing we can do is to react right now."

It was three-thirty in the afternoon. It was essential we attack no later than the following morning or the Americans likely wouldn't be there. Working for the Agency had its advantages. We could get helos or tactical support whenever we needed it. This was one of the real nice things about PRU ops. We didn't have miles and miles of red tape to get past. An operation like this, demanding an immediate response, was one we could pull off.

Gallagher immediately was on the phone to Can Tho. The code name used for liberating captured Americans was Bright Light. When Gallagher used the code name, people got excited. Everyone realized timing was critical. Calls poured in all night long.

"Do you need us to send SEALs?" asked the SEAL lieutenants.

"What do you need?" came calls from the Agency.

We arranged for a "heavy package": ten slicks, four gunships, and a C and C. A hostage extraction had to be a precision lightning strike. With ten slicks, we could bring up to one hundred PRU.

I went to the old man. "How many Viet Cong are there?"

"There are three Viet Cong, and four teenagers who think they are Viet Cong. You know, they walk around with their red scarves, but I don't think their guns work."

"Okay, who else? How many NVA?"

"None."

"Wait a minute, old man. You just said there's seven. Only seven?" I pressed, thinking something must be lost in translation.

"Yeah."

"Uh, how many prisoners?"

"One hundred. I counted them."

"Why don't people try to get away?"

"Oh, 'cause they're all chained together. When you're handcuffed to one another, you can't go anywhere."

"So the Americans are chained?"

"Yes," the old man replied, shaking his head up and down.

Gallagher, who'd listened in on my interrogation, called out, "Constance! Get the Master key out of the closet."

I grinned. We had a big set of bolt cutters, which I promptly grabbed.

Gallagher and I quickly developed a tactical operational plan. At first light, I placed the old man, my interpreter, and myself on a helicopter to scout things out. We flew the mail route, the same route the mail helicopter flew every morning. We deviated just a little bit, flying almost directly over the camp. Nudging the old man, I asked, "Do you recognize any of this?"

At first, he didn't. It was his first time in a helicopter, and he was white-knuckled and scared to death.

"He says he can't tell."

We made a turn and the old Vietnamese man suddenly lit up. "He says he recognizes those three hooches over there," the interpreter relayed. The old man was now beside himself, practically jumping out of his seat. Excitedly with arms flailing, he was practically screaming as recognition and perspective took place. "Yeah! Yeah! Right there!"

The whole time I was asking him, "How many automatic weapons? How many machine guns? How close do the guards sleep to the Americans?"

"If there's a machine gun there, after you have killed all the guards, you get it and use it to kill me. I know there isn't one. There's one AK-forty-seven but it doesn't work; it doesn't have a rear on it."

So, we had seven bad guys who slept in a small hooch, outside of which were three ditches containing prisoners all chained together. Beyond the farthest ditch from the hooch (by another thirty yards) was a bomb crater, thirty meters in diameter, at the junction of two canals. Surrounding all this—the hooch, ditches, canals, and bomb crater—were thick, dense groves of twenty-five-foot-tall nipa palm. The nipa palm groves had perimeter guard shacks and other buildings carved out within the nipa palm canopy. This made entry and exit challenging. The distance from the canals to the nipa palm was about five hundred meters. They moved people by sampan, navigating north, south, east, or west via the canals. Out of fear of being discovered and caught, the job of getting the Americans north to Hanoi went to three "experts." The tired Viet Cong unit, following a week of bump-and-run, surren dered the Americans to the prison camp and disbanded.

"Could you land in that bomb crater?" I asked the helo pilot.

"Tell you what, I could land in the nipa palm if we had to, to save those guys."

I planned to bring my helo into the bomb crater, have the guys jump from about ten feet off the deck, immediately set up, and race toward the first ditch. We had to get in position before any of the bad guys ran out and shot the Americans.

"That should work," concurred Gallagher after I briefed him about what we'd seen.

Gallagher detailed our plans. "I'll land all the PRUs in an arc along here," he said, pointing to equally spaced plots between the canals and the ditches. There will be gunships along the canals to prevent any VC movement, and the C and C will be overhead."

"Harry, your helo will be in front, followed by mine. We'll come in at rice-top level as fast as we can go, bounce up and over the nipa palm, and then land it quick," Gallagher furthered.

Now it was my job to brief the PRUs. I brought in Biá. "We need to get everyone prepared for a quick-strike helo op. I need you to get all the PRUs together in full battle gear. We need to practice jumping from a ten-foot height. This is what we'll be doing as we exit the helos. I need them ready and able to jump the ten feet, get on line, and ready to assault. We'll run to the ditch with the Americans in it, form a circle around them, with all guns pointed out." I paused, making certain Biá understood. "When we jump, don't let me beat you to the ditch!"

"You won't," he replied matter-of-factly.

I needed to move quickly, so I carried only a pair of bolt cutters, my knife, and my CAR-15. No extra bullets, flares, or grenades. I stripped down to running weight. Biá was to carry the bolt cutters and his M16. "Guys, I'll be standing on the skids of the helo. When we're down low enough, I'm going to jump. Try to be close behind. I'm going to get on top of the Americans, signal, then Gallagher and the troops will start assaulting. We'll overrun everybody."

We'd flown the early morning reconnaissance at five-thirty A.M. Now, a little before seven A.M., I'd already briefed all the pilots, had our one hundred PRUs briefed, outfitted, and practiced, and we were loaded up. The old man was in the C and C. I felt good about our Bright Light operation. The old man had also told us, "You know, they don't really get up and have breakfast until seven-thirty." If we could get there before seven-thirty A.M., it would be even more of a surprise. We were good to go.

All fifteen helicopters lifted off, tipped their noses forward, and started up the runway. *Here we go.* Suddenly, the helos leveled off, then set down.

"What the—Why'd we stop?" I demanded, shaking the shoulder of the copilot. He lifted both hands palms up: *I don't know.* The pilot craned his head around to look at me. He pointed to his left, at a jeep sitting at the edge of the runway. As I peered out, I saw Gallagher racing across the tarmac. *He's pissed about something.* I jumped out and ran over.

In an ARVN jeep sat a typical Vietnamese officer. In his starched uniform, cute little silk neck scarf, patent leather belt with his patent leather decorative holster holding his cute little .45, his patent leather boots and his starched little hat, he personified the "all fluff and no substance" moniker. He was a colonel, and he wore a big, pasted-on smile as he looked at two very upset American SEALs.

"Just what are you doing, stopping our operation," demanded Gallagher angrily.

"Not to worry. Not to worry! There are South Vietnamese troops— friendly troops!—four klicks to the north doing a sweeping action in search of Viet Cong," he declared with almost a regal air. Then his face went serious. "Four klicks is too close. Your gunships will shoot up my troops. I am very concerned. Since my troops are already out there, they can sweep down and rescue your Americans. No problem." Then he smiled real big.

"With all respect, sir, the area has so much open space between the nipa palm and the camp, there's no way your men can assault without alerting the Viet Cong," I insisted.

"Your gunships are too close to my men. Do not worry. No problem!"

"Look, if it's your men you're concerned about, how about using one of our helos to make contact with your men so we'll all be absolutely certain our gunships don't get anywhere near your troops? We'd be more than happy to let you fly out three or four minutes ahead of us to get in position. We have to use helicopters. With these helicopters, it'll all be over before they'll know what hit them."

"So sorry, but we will sweep down and rescue our prisoners along with your American soldiers. I personally blocked off this AO. As you know, when an AO is blocked off, no one can go in without my permission. I cannot allow you in. You'll see. It'll all be fine."

I pulled out the map. "Colonel, please look at this. See all this open area. Even if your men were to sprint, they couldn't get there in time to keep the Viet Cong from shooting the prisoners. This is a big open area!"

He was finished talking. He just swung his head back and forth defiantly.

Gallagher was red-faced, veins protruding from his neck. He had us over a bureaucratic barrel. If we would have gone anyway, we could have caused an international incident and been court-martialed. Gallagher looked at me, and, in an instant, it was like something turned off in him. "Take them all back to camp. Now!"

"Yes, sir."

I walked down the row of helicopters giving the signal to disembark. They all piled out and headed back to the trucks we'd come in.

The colonel was trying to say something further to Gallagher. Gallagher was as angry as I'd ever seen him. He was flexing his jaw. *Uh-oh. I think he's going to hit him.* Somehow he didn't. While the colonel was still speaking, Gallagher turned his back on him and walked away.

I took all the PRUs back to base and had them unload their gear, going through protocol necessary to stand down after an operation. My number one guard then took all my gear and put it away. I went into our hooch, and there was Gallagher, stiff drinks made for the two of us, seated there still smoldering. "Sit down and have a drink," he barked.

There was a lot more rum than Coke in it. It was nine A.M. Gallagher sat there and drank a quick four or five drinks. He couldn't sit still and he couldn't unwind. Finally, he said, "Enough of this shit. Let's go over to the club."

He didn't calm down until we were over at the club, had a few more drinks, and talked with a couple of sympathetic Army guys. The specter of knowing—absolutely, positively knowing—that some administrative nonoperator had just caused two American soldiers to forfeit their lives, weighed heavily on the two of us.

Walking briskly into the club and right toward Gallagher and me came a NILO officer, whose job included coordination with the other branches, and his assistant who coordinated U.S. and ARVN activities.

"Sir, we need to speak to you. We understand you were rather rude to Colonel Nyugen Dok Tu this morning. . . ."

"Don't start, slick," Gallagher spat, slamming his fist onto the table. "You assholes waltz in here, worried about civilities, when we just let two Americans take a death sentence. If, and I would lay odds they don't, but if they make it up to the Hanoi Hilton, it will be that little bastard's fault! We had a virtual foolproof operation to free two American POWs and you're worried because I was impolite to an ARVN asshole?"

"Listen here, don't you dare talk to representatives of the U.S. government like that," retorted the assistant, wagging his finger in Gallagher's face.

Gallagher had had enough. Jumping from his chair, he grabbed the officer's neatly starched white collar and jerked him up off the ground. He brought his face to within an inch of his own. "You still don't realize what this asshole has done," he said fiercely. Simultaneously dropping and pushing the guy away, Gallagher hissed, "Get away from me."

"You don't treat me like that!"

"You're lucky you're not dead."

Both officers were by now more than a little agitated. "You haven't heard the last of this!" They turned and walked out.

"Screw it. I've been up all night. I'm going to bed." We walked back to our place.

Several hours later, my field interpreter came rushing in. "They're bringing in some POWs!"

"Really!" I said, jumping up.

"Yeah, but they need transportation."

I thought for a moment. "Take our trucks and whatever PRUs are needed and go get them."

Thirty minutes later, they came back with fifty POWs who'd been liberated from the camp. The ARVN unit had swept south. They arrived at the camp at noon, finding seventy to eighty released Vietnamese POWs. They also found one dead American on the bank of one of the canals.

Our interpreters interrogated the POWs. They all told the same story of how the Viet Cong knew ARVN was coming for over an hour. The

ARVN had walked the four klicks, the last mile and a half in open terrain. The Viet Cong unchained all of the high-level Vietnamese and the two Americans, then herded them to the canal. One of the Americans decided this was his best opportunity to escape, so he dove into the canal and swam across. The guards immediately began shooting at him. Lumbering up the far bank of the canal, he made it to the top. A few feet farther and he probably would have been a free man. Unfortunately, as he crested the bank, an AK-47 round blew through the middle of his back, killing him quickly. The Viet Cong then took their most valuable prisoners and shoved off, leaving everyone else behind. When ARVN arrived, the fox had gutted the henhouse and disappeared.

To their credit, the NILO liaison officers returned and apologized. "We're sorry. You were right. When we got the story from ARVN, it was a lot different from what you were saying. Listen, can we buy you a drink—sorta make up for this morning?"

"Sure," Gallagher replied. "I'd appreciate it."

After being plied with a few more drinks and a little prodding, Gallagher recounted what had happened. "It was foolproof. We had the best, elite team of helo pilots in-country, seasoned troops, and our intelligence of the compound was perfect. Damn shame; what a waste."

After they left, a number of other officials came by with their "condolences" at the bureaucratic snafu.

"Too bad it didn't go down," I suggested. "We'd probably be up in Can Tho partying tonight. At least we got a few free drinks for our troubles."

Almost disgustedly, Gallagher glared at me. "No, you wouldn't be in Can Tho."

"Okay, we'd be in Saigon."

"No, not Saigon."

I was feeling my alcohol a bit. "Ahh, Philippines?"

"No."

"Hawaii!"

"No . . ." We went through this little test, and it got real quiet. Gallagher cleared his throat. "Let me tell everyone here what would've happened. Had we done the op and it went as planned, it would've been a first. There's never been American POWs rescued by any American units in Vietnam. Had we pulled those two out, I have no doubt in my mind Constance here would've been on his way to Washington, D.C., to receive the Congressional Medal of Honor—the CMH—for saving those guys. You all know the deal, the standing invitation stating any American who rescues an American POW gets a CMH. The President personally would pin it on. Tell me, if that had been a successful Bright Light, the word would have flashed to Can Tho, on to Saigon, and then directly to the Pentagon. The President would've been told, and he would've said, 'Get him on a plane. Get him here now.' Anybody care to disagree?''

Everyone nodded agreement. That was what we'd been told through the propaganda mills in July 1969. ''I wasn't going to go,'' said Gallagher. ''You would've been the damn hero, butthead.''

Had it worked, I might well have been wearing the Congressional Medal of Honor and Gallagher possibly a Navy Cross. Unfortunately, we will never know. This time, bureaucracy and ego got in the way and men were killed needlessly. The other American was never heard from again. Corruption kills.

It was a sad day when we had to leave Sok Trang. My second tour was up. Again, the intense bonds we developed with our PRUs were friendships I will never forget. They willingly put their lives on the line for me time and time again. Sadly, I would never see them again. We said our ceremonial good-byes, then boarded the jeep for Saigon and the return to Little Creek. It was what I was trained for. This time, however, I looked forward to getting home to Sandy. *Sorry, guys. I'd love to stick around, but in this case, pleasure before business!*

The PRU program continued for several more years, until it was absorbed into ARVN. Shortly thereafter, corruption and disillusionment decimated the ranks.

CHAPTER 16

GOING HOME, MURDER ONE

I'D WRITTEN SANDY EVERY WEEK. I WAS SO ANXIOUS TO GET BACK to her, to change gears from wild, raging aggression to stability, nonthreatening schedules, some sort of family life like my folks'— and rekindle the passion that had come so easily when we first met.

"Welcome home, Harry. How's my knight in shining armor?" she asked softly, her eyes brimming with tears. We embraced long and hard.

My head reeled at the lingering scent in her hair. I breathed in long and deep. "I can't tell you how I've missed you so." We kissed, entering into a sweet lovers' sanctum.

Arriving home, I was punch-drunk with warm emotions. Marnie, now three years old, jumped into my lap. "There's my girl!"

I lifted Marnie up above me, like many proud fathers before me. "I can't believe I have a family. This is such a rush!" I bumbled.

"It's good to have you home. Now you can get caught up on all the honey-do's," Sandy teased.

"There's a *lot* of things I can't wait to get caught up on," I countered in a low, Lou Rawls-like sexy voice, complete with fiendish grin.

"Harry! Not in front of the children!" she cautioned, feigning indignation.

253

Soon dinner was over and Marnie was in bed. Sandy turned the lights down, then sat next to me on the couch, her hair draped across my chest. "I just never thought you'd get home. Finally, I'll be able to sleep at night without worrying—about you or me."

My hands gently combed through her hair, down her shoulders, and across her chest. She sighed, melting into my arms. We groped and fondled each other desperately, consumed in our passion. My temples pounded in an urgent sensual overload. In a short time, we nestled closely to one another. "Harry?"

"Yes."

"I'd sure like to live in a bigger place than we have here. All your SEAL Team gear and Marnie makes it pretty cramped."

Dreamily, I answered, "No problem. We got plenty of money. I wouldn't mind having a home like my folks. We can start looking, if you'd like."

"I've already found a couple places I like. I just know you'll like them, too."

"Yeah. It'll be nice to have a garage to keep our car in and keep all my tools and SEAL Team stuff. . . ."

In the Navy, enlistment contracts lasted four or six years. During my second tour in Vietnam, mine ran out. As incentive to keeping certain select specialists in the service, bonuses were offered to reenlist. I was deemed valuable enough to offer a $10,000 bonus, tax-free. I re-signed the contract at the admin offices in Nha Be, and was handed a check. My father urged me to send the money to him so he could invest it in mutual funds. Sandy argued we needed the money for "all the things young families need." I decided to hold on to the money. It was a good thing. Of the paycheck funds I'd sent home, very little remained. She also didn't like my GTX, as it was too big and too powerful a car for her liking. So it had to go.

Two weeks later, I'd used much of the $10,000 to help close on a small, three-bedroom, two-bath house. "This feels good. Like Beaver Cleaver or Ozzie and Harriet or something. Man, Sandy, the past few years seem a blur to me. Here I am, one of the best in SEAL Team, married, have a daughter, and now we're moving into our first home!"

"I know! Isn't this wonderful," she beamed.

"I'm gonna be picking up my new platoon next week. There's no pressure. I've got nothing to prove; I've got it all down pat. I'm actually looking forward to training."

The next week was filled with furniture shopping and lots of boxes as we cleaned out our apartment. Boxing, scrubbing, and cleaning to get the place squared away.

As I dumped a trash can into the Dumpster, several letters fell out. I picked them up when, catching my eye, I recognized the name of Marnie's father.

Dear Sandy,

It was good hearing from you. I miss you, too. I am sorry I cannot support you more, but it sounds like your Navy man is getting you through. All I can afford now is the $50 a month, but I want you to know I love you and Marnie very much and look forward to seeing you soon.

Love,
Jim

The other letter read:

Dear Sandy,

I understand you had to get married. I hope you can be happy. Yes, it would've been nice if we could have stayed together. Hopefully, I will be able to afford more after I graduate from school. I do have a job, so I'll try to send $50 a month. I hope I can see you and Marnie soon, I miss you so. Call me.

Love,
Jim

I couldn't believe my eyes. What did this mean? She hadn't said anything about talking to Marnie's father, about needing money, or about her feelings regarding their relationship. All she'd ever told me was she'd been taken advantage of and left high and dry.

"Sandy," I hollered. "Could you come here please."

"Just a minute."

"Ah, could you come in here now."

A moment later she walked in. "Yeah?"

I held up the letters. "What're these?"

Her eyes widened as her face went serious. She paused, quickly regaining her composure. "Well, ah, I meant to talk to you about that.

I felt it was fair that you shouldn't have to pay for all of Marnie's expenses, so I called him. He agreed to send fifty dollars a month. That's pretty much all it is. No big deal.''

"No big deal? . . . No big deal? I accidentally find these,'' I chided, holding up her letters and shaking them, ''and you never said anything. Then he talks about wishing you were still together, and something about when he could support you. . . . No big deal!''

"Oh, Harry. You have to believe me. I, ah, I had to tell him something. I couldn't very well say, 'Look, you jerk, send me money.' I just said something nice like, 'Too bad things didn't work out.' But, I thought I owed it to Marnie for her father to pay something. You gotta believe me,'' she implored.

"When were you planning to tell me—or were you ever planning to say anything? This really hurts.''

"Harry, calm down,'' she said gently, clutching my arm. "He doesn't mean anything to me. I should've said something to you. You have to believe me! Then came the house, the furniture, being with you—honestly, I forgot all about it. That's why I threw the letters away.''

I wanted to believe her. I *needed* to believe her. "Okay. I guess it's not that big a deal.''

"By the way, did you know I met your sister Madjie? We've been getting together lately when Frank's out training. She's a nice person.'' (My sister had married a fellow SEAL, Frank Thornton.)

The heat of the moment dissipated. I smiled. "You met Madjie? That's good. Frank's a good man.''

Shortly after moving, the passion between us really began to wane. Upon my return from Vietnam, I immediately found that the intensity level had declined markedly. Now, it was worse. A series of events then transpired that seriously undermined our marriage.

"Harry, I haven't had a period for two months now.''

Excitedly, I broke out in a wide grin. "Do you think we're pregnant?''

Cautiously she said, "Well, no. I hoped so, too. I went to the doctor today. He's pretty certain I have an ovarian cyst. To treat it, he'll have to do a hysterectomy and remove the ovary. That'll mean no more children.''

My excitement shattered into glum silence. *No kids? That was part of the dream, part of who I want to be.*

"Harry . . . Harry . . . Imagine how I feel. I've been totally depressed about it. Surgery is tentatively scheduled for next Monday.'' She broke into tears. ''I hope you still love me.''

''Of course I do,'' I mumbled. *Come on Harry. You're a SEAL; you can handle it.* ''I'm sorry, Sandy.'' I grabbed her and held her as she sobbed in my arms.

The surgery was successful. I tried not to let it affect me. I fully realized a hysterectomy was a life-altering change in a woman's life. Like everything else painful to me, I was trained to block it out.

Sandy and Madjie set up a double date to go to a movie. On Friday night, Frank and Madjie picked us up. We were exchanging small talk as Frank drove, when, all of a sudden, a woman, oblivious to traffic, stepped from the curb right in front of the car in front of us. Her body caromed off the front fender. Frank slammed on the brakes. She was lying alongside the road right next to our car. Both Sandy and Madjie went white with shock. Frank bounded from the car over to her. I sat in back, drumming my fingers on the door panel armrest.

Madjie turned, looking at me with some sort of alarm. ''Harry, aren't you going to go help her?''

''No. She's making us late to the movie.''

Now it was Sandy's turn to look at me. The look on her face pulled me up short. She was appalled, unbelieving that her husband would say such a thing. ''Harry!''

Instantly, I realized the impact of my comment and got out. *Maybe that's why we're not getting along so well. Maybe I'm just too hard and unfeeling.*

The ambulance came and took the young woman away. Frank and I climbed back into the car. Hoping to show my remark was nothing more than a momentary lapse, I stated, concerned, ''She's going to be all right. Her leg's broken, and maybe a rib, but it doesn't appear she has any internal injuries and she was awake and alert.''

Sandy was cold and quiet.

Two weeks later, I headed out for training. Union Camp, outside of Petersburg, Virginia, is a camp used for live weapons firing and run by the Army. Seemingly every type of ordnance imaginable was there.

Our platoon was shooting when Gallagher received a radio message to contact SEAL Team immediately. He jumped in the jeep, ran into town.

When he returned, he summoned me over to him. ''Harry, there's a problem at SEAL Team. Get your gear and go.''

I drove back to Little Creek. Upon arriving, I was met by one of the chiefs, "Harry, you're to see the CO at 0900 tomorrow morning. Be in uniform."

Promptly the next morning, I reported to the Commanding Officer. "Harry," he said a little more seriously than I had expected, "you have to go over to Naval Investigative Services this morning at 1000 hours. They want to talk to you about some stuff."

"What do they want to talk to me about," I pressed, concerned.

"I'm sorry. I'm not at liberty to say. They'll have to brief you."

I had no idea what was coming. I walked over, a little past 0915 and they were ready for me. For the next three hours, they grilled me—interrogated me—rigorously.

The first thing they did was to read me my rights. My heart quickened in alarm. "Walter Harry Constance, you are being formally charged with first-degree murder of innocent Vietnamese civilians, women, and children."

Totally taken aback, I blurted, "What?" I was so stunned. "Ah . . . Ah . . ."

"Let's begin. Would you mind having a seat here while we ask you a few questions?" he said, more as a command than a question. The two NIS agents began with general questions: When were you in Vietnam? Where in Vietnam? Who were you with? Were there any particular operations you'd like to talk about? Finally: "Thank you. You're dismissed," he said, the clock striking one P.M. "Don't leave the area."

I went home shaken. *What could I have done? Everything has been written up properly. Murder? Of who? I'm a trained professional. The only people I killed were authorized and in the line of duty.*

Because I was nervous and clearly agitated, Sandy knew something was bothering me. "Harry, what's wrong?"

"I don't know. I was called in from Union Camp, you know, to see the CO. Well, it wasn't about any special assignments or awards. You're not going to believe this. I had to talk to NIS. They're accusing me of murdering civilians. I honestly have no idea what they're talking about."

I waited, hoping she would come to me. Instead, she walked over and sat on the couch. "Murder, huh? That's pretty serious."

Later that night, shortly before eleven P.M., the phone rang. "Hello," I answered.

"Hi, Harry. This is Pete Peterson. I need to talk to you tonight. Real hush-hush, though."

"Yeah, sure. No problem," I said, knowing already why he had called. "You want to come over here? Okay. See you in a few minutes."

Pete had transferred to SEAL Team One in Coronado. He arrived shortly after the phone call. Pete appeared shook. "Harry, something's up. And it's big. They flew my ass back here from California. I even got a call from Riojas in Saigon. I mean, someone's hot for one of us in Seventh Platoon. From the looks of it, I think it's you they're after. All the guys are in town, except Riojas and Charlie Watson."

Pete continued, "Someone has made an allegation over an operation you and I went out on. They read me the riot act. They told me I was at least a key witness, if not an accessory to murder." Disgust clipped Pete's every word. "They're questioning me about an operation where you supposedly killed all sorts of women and children. I'm having an in-depth interview tomorrow morning. Harry, level with me, man. Do you know what's going on?"

"I have no idea what's going on! Pete, we—I—didn't do anything wrong!"

"Good. That's what I wanted to hear. Start thinking, and try to get all your ducks in a row." We spoke for a while, playing out several plausible scenarios before Pete left.

I walked into the bedroom. Sandy was scared and visibly distraught. I'd talked with her about killing people, but only in general terms. We'd never sat around and discussed any of the gruesome details. Listening to Pete and me coldly discuss various operations and the grotesqueness of some of the assassinations we carried out shook her deeply.

"Harry, I had no idea."

"Sandy, don't worry. This really isn't anything."

The next morning, there sat Roy Dean, Mikey Boynton, Jack Rowell, Ashton, Keener, everyone. Each waited their turn to be interrogated by NIS.

Roy Dean walked over to me. "They wanted to know all about the op where you went in after some Viet Cong sector chief—remember the one where you were all bloody after you knifed those guys in that hooch?"

"Okay. But what's the big deal?"

"I don't know."

Mikey Boynton walked out. "You know what it is? Remember that night when you guys went into that hooch? When Pete was beating the guy up in front of the hooch because you were making so much noise inside?"

"Yeah," I responded.

"Well, that's the op they're talking about."

Puzzled, I shook my head back and forth. "That's stupid."

Then it was my turn. "Constance, we've been drawing together statements from all the SEALs who were with you in Seventh Platoon. It is apparent that you murdered a Vietnamese woman, her children, and, further, you brutally dismembered these innocent civilians. We know you cruelly cut off body parts. We have an eyewitness who can attest to these allegations, along with corroborating statements from most of your team."

I began to get angry.

"Please sign here, and we will expedite things as fairly and smoothly for you as we possibly can."

I carefully read the legal document set in front of me, saying I affirmed that I did, in fact, cruelly and willfully brutally murder innocent civilians. "There's not a chance in hell I'm signing this."

Fortunately, we'd had training in NIS interrogation techniques, which I recognized immediately. They started in on me again. This time, however, the picture came into focus. They tipped their hand when they changed tack, explaining how it had all come about. They thought it would help me confess and fill in the blanks.

"We received an extremely detailed, in-depth letter telling how you did, in fact, kill the civilians in question and, further, how you cavalierly bragged openly about it. The letter was sent, due to the serious nature of the allegations, straight to D.C., to NIS headquarters."

A burning rage flamed in my gut. There was only one person who could have written that letter. Then, besides writing it, he completely went over the heads of SEAL Team leadership to NIS. Never said a word to the Commanding Officer of SEAL Team. Never said a word to anybody at SEAL Team. He obviously never wanted it to be investigated by SEALs first. He skipped right over them, to D.C.

"I'm sorry, gentlemen, but the party's over. You don't have any eyewitness. I was the only one there. Secondly, the incident in question was fabricated just to harass one of my teammates. It never happened. I'm getting a lawyer."

Their faces drawn and coldly serious, they hardened. "We know you did it. If you don't sign, I guarantee you we have enough proof to lock you up for a long time. By not signing, you leave us no choice but to throw the full weight of the law at you. I'll tell you again. Your best chance is to sign here."

"Talk to my attorney." I walked out.

Quickly, word spread nationally. The brass at Special Warfare in the Pentagon were briefed. Calls came from the West Coast and many points in between, all asking the same thing. *Hey! What about Harry Constance? Did you hear he's being brought up on wiping out a whole village of women and children?*

In less than thirty days, the first topic in any bar any Navy SEAL was seated in was "Did you hear about Harry Constance being charged with multiple murders? Massacre of hundreds of innocent civilians— kids even."

Gary Chamberlin called from Coronado, one of a number to do so. "Hey, Harry. You can't believe what's going around out here."

"Let me guess. It has something to do with murder and involves me, women, and children."

"Yep!" He spun an even more outlandish distortion.

"Man, I'm getting better every day. Of course, it's total bullshit. The problem is I'm being tainted. The attorney met with them last week. Of course, the charges are completely groundless. Once he met with them, they dropped all charges."

"That's it?"

"Yeah, that's it. It's over. Could you do me a favor and let people know the truth of what happened?"

"Sure."

A short time later, Gallagher called and offered his support. "Eagle, I can't believe what's going on. I was being railroaded into something I absolutely, positively did not do. Now my reputation is trashed. You know the old adage—where there's smoke, there's fire—I can't believe the stuff I'm hearing."

Gallagher assured me he would do all he could.

The accusations took their toll on me. Sandy heard the rumors through the Navy wives. I clammed up, bitter and angry at the world. She became more distant each day.

Finally, I was permitted to resume SEAL Team duties. Back at Union Camp with my new platoon, I was approached by the rest of the team, each of them curious. "Is it true what they're saying? Is it true you're a killer—as in, murderer?"

I hoped they believed me. It's not a good idea to go into combat with someone having a huge question mark and murder rumors swirling over his head.

Roy Dean, Mikey Boynton, Hooker, Chuck Jesse, Jack Rowell, Gallagher, and others came to visit me at Union Camp.

"You know, Harry, that's the same story you told in front of us all that night we were on the boat—you know, where we got Chicken Charlie sick."

Roy Dean started laughing. "Harry, I was the one who egged you on."

"No kidding, Roy Dean! Boy, has that cost me."

"That's it, huh? Man, I really helped you embellish the story. *Did you cut that part off?*" Roy Dean shook his head and frowned. "Why didn't he write to SEAL Team Two command rather than going all the way up to NIS?" He paused, grinning at the recollection. "I'll never forget Charlie running out."

Mikey Boynton chimed in. "That was the whole point. We talked about a lot of gross shit 'cause it was fun to get Chicken Charlie sick. I can't believe that's what this is about. Come to think about it, Charlie Watson is the only one no one's heard from."

Months earlier, I was the fair-haired, can-do-no-wrong, kick-ass, take-names, SEAL. The sun shone brightly on me. I was married to a wonderfully sexy wife. Now, everything was in disarray.

Gallagher kept me above water. He campaigned with the power structure on my behalf for months. Pete, Gallagher, Riojas, and others in the platoon, when asked whether I was a killer, adamantly defended me. "That's bullshit. I was there. It never happened."

Others were less helpful. "Hey. Who knows what Harry did? I wasn't there." Unfortunately, an answer like that left questions lingering.

By now, it was Christmas 1969. In less than two months, I was set to ship out once again for Vietnam. The bright lights and festive atmosphere were in distinct contrast to my world. *What did I do to deserve this?* I kept thinking back to advice my dad had given me. "Keep your head up, do your job, and be a man."

"Sandy, are you coming to the airport to see me off?" I asked, as I readied for my third departure to Vietnam.

"No. I can't," she informed me, throwing her arms around me and giving me a kiss. "See you."

I found myself headed for Vietnam one more time, with many significant issues still unresolved. My relationship with Sandy was, at best, "troubled." I'd been in tougher spots than that. Things were bound to right themselves. At least, I hoped so.

CHAPTER 17

THE TIMES, THEY ARE A-CHANGING: THIRD TOUR—RULES FOR WAR

GALLAGHER AND I WERE TOGETHER YET AGAIN—SOMETHING never done before or since—three tours with the same tandem. We had a new team consisting of Frank Moncrief, Lieutenant Dicky Moran, Little Mike McDonald, Bobby Osborne, Tom Keith, Dick Cyrus, Jack Squires, Bob Neidrauer, Gallagher, and myself. Our team hadn't had the opportunity to train together as long as we had before. We'd had a grand total of three months together.

I was, despite the potential derailment of my career over the murder allegations, still on the fast track for meritorious promotions, thanks largely to Gallagher's active campaign to save my neck. The only reason the two of us were allowed to stay together was our effectiveness. Quick "field meritorious promotions" were available during wartime. Normally you had to wait a year or longer to advance to the next Navy grade. On the battlefield, you got promoted or you got dead. Living and advancing suited me.

Most of the guys were senior to me in pay grade, yet junior in combat experience. It was never a problem. I was in charge of the operations until they had enough experience to take over. As soon as we came out of the battle zone, Dicky was in charge. If he wanted something done, he'd tell me to do it, and I complied. But, when it came to combat, we were all equal. Since I had more experience, I frequently told the team how and where to set up.

We reported to Can Tho as our base of operations. The first thing we noticed was a profound change of attitude. Around town and in the clubs, during my first tour, there was a camaraderie and sense of shared purpose amongst the troops—Army, Navy, Marines, and Air Force. There honestly was, in 1967, patriotism, flag-waving, and fun-loving guys. My second tour was hard to gauge due to where Gallagher and I were stationed. The difference in March 1970 was substantial. No sooner had we arrived than we were struck by the somber moods—depressed people, grumbling people, "give a care" people; it seemed all the servicemen we came in contact with were demoralized. The politics of home had completely overshadowed our presence in Vietnam.

It must have been similar to the French back in the 1950s. Vietnam was a French colony for many years. During World War II, France had been decimated by Germany. A simple way to rebuild the French economy after the war was by milking their colonies for all revenue possible. Vietnam buckled. The Soviet and Chinese Communists supported a Vietnamese rebel leader, Ho Chi Minh, as he rallied a segment of the population against the French. Soon, many French installations in Vietnam were the victim of sabotage. The war-weary French sent in troops, who soon were bogged down in an escalating war they were reluctant to fight. The French government pleaded with the United States for support. Presidents Truman and Eisenhower wrestled with a dilemma: support the imperialism of French colonization (which they were dead set against) or contain the ongoing expansion of communism. Finally, by 1954, the French had had enough. They renounced their colonial hold on Vietnam, packed up, and left.

Almost immediately, the United States moved to prop up the newly formed South Vietnamese government. The Communists moved to try to exploit the power void left by the French exodus. The CIA set up "advisors" and others to respond with the same terrorism the Communists used against the French and South Vietnamese. Presidents Kennedy and Johnson moved to increase American involvement.

To me it seemed that four factors collided together to divide the American people over the war: bad U.S. government politics, color television satellite broadcasts illuminating the horrors of war on the nightly news, budding cultural schisms occurring at American colleges, and a drug culture that affected troops and antiwar protesters alike. By 1970, President Nixon had a war the American people were ashamed of. He spoke eloquently about ending the war with a negotiated settlement. If you were the Communists of North Vietnam, wouldn't you be thinking all you had to do was hold out while the Americans self-destructed and exited like the French? The Paris Peace Accords were convened, dragging on and on. This was the reality we found in Vietnam in 1970. We barely had time to pick up our bags when significant rules and well-defined boundaries were explicitly outlined out for us.

"Gentlemen, there've been some serious changes in the war," opened the captain at our initial briefing in Can Tho. "We have new rules. You cannot fire upon the enemy unless you are fired upon. If you see the enemy walking by, even if they are wearing black pajamas and carrying an AK-forty-seven, you are to let them go and not shoot at them. Chemical grenades are forbidden for use any longer." (This was significant since the CN helped drive people out of hooches. The alternative was to shoot or toss a fragmentation grenade in, indiscriminately killing or maiming women and children along with the bad guys.)

He cleared his throat and continued. Gallagher and I quit listening, instead talking quietly about where we wanted to go for dinner. "Now, there are no longer any free-fire zones. Instead, there are a number of sectors we have negotiated with the North where we will not, I repeat, not operate."

Gallagher started laughing. "How the hell do you have rules in war? Isn't that the point? 'Rules' and 'war' don't fit in the same sentence."

The captain's eyes narrowed; a flash of anger lit across his face. "Listen, Chief, you'd best keep your comments to yourself during this brief. Is that understood?"

Now it was Gallagher's turn to be angry. "I understand perfectly, Captain. Tell me, before I shut up—because I've been here for two tours already—have you ever once been pinned down, lying in the mud, bullets popping the trees and ground around you, hoping against hope you'll somehow find a way to see the sunrise? These so-called rules are going to get my men killed, dammit!"

"Calm down. Abide by the rules, serve your country, and you'll be fine. They're negotiating a peace treaty in Paris as we speak. I'm not at liberty to discuss all the particulars, but we're not to create an incident that could derail the peace process."

As we offloaded our gear, the seriousness of the changes hit home.

An official document from high command was delivered to Lieutenant Moran.

To: Lieutenant Moran, Ninth Platoon

From: Commanding Officer, SEAL Team Two

It is in the best interests of the war effort that we must order your platoon to split in half. Half of your team is to report to Ha Tien on the Cambodian border. The other half is to be stationed due south, in Hi Yien, at a small American position close to Square Bay.

Further, we must inform you that fixed wing, tactical support will no longer be available. Other support will be restricted, allocated through official channels only.

The new SEALs had no idea anything was amiss. I quickly explained it to them. "This is absolutely terrible. We're having our hands tied. It's essential we have the ability to lay on support, call for helicopter support, maybe fixed wing jets to fly over and drop napalm, howitzer coverage, whatever. We've always called for that sort of support put on alert. Now it's apparently not available."

Sure enough, on our very first op, Gallagher called for helicopter support. "We're sorry. Helo support is unavailable."

"Well where the hell is it," Gallagher demanded. No answer was given.

Obtaining materiel was more difficult, too. We'd request one hundred grenades and they'd give us ten. Fifty LAAW rockets and receive two. It was like they didn't want to help us, nobody wanted us to go, and everything was being played down. By then, the intelligence networks should have been well developed and extremely productive. Several ops required intelligence beyond that available in our immediate area. When asked for critical intelligence, the response was "I'm sorry, but we don't have much."

We split the team. Gallagher and I took three SEALs (Dicky Cyrus, Bobby Osborne, and Mike McDonald) and moved south to the Square Bay region. The worst possible thing happened to us. We found where the Viet Cong were hiding. We chose to ignore the nonengagement rules. "They might work," Gallagher explained, "in the pacified areas of the country, but for damn sure they don't work out here in enemy country."

It got their attention. Rumors drifted in that the Viet Cong were preparing to mount a full-scale, battalion assault on our little outpost village.

The province we were assigned to encompassed the tip of South Vietnam. The province chief was a Buddhist monk named Father Wa. He was well respected, and well connected, to both the North and South, and was, for a long time, able to keep the province neutral. Unfortunately, his health failing, he had to step down. Immediately, the area became rife with Viet Cong, seeking to fill the power void. The village complex we lived in was Father Wa's former home. Although somewhat overgrown and in need of repairs, the compound was ideally suited to our needs.

Our village was a rectangular compound 600 meters long (running east-west) by 300 meters wide (running north-south), housed 400 people, 150 of whom served in the ARVN. The perimeter was ringed by dikes and concertina wire, with the housing complex located in the center of the compound. A series of dikes and rice paddies filled in the remainder of the area, with a stream bisecting the entire 600-meter length. At the eastern end, beyond the dike by about 100 meters, stood jungle vegetation. We were 10 to 15 miles from the ocean. In the bay were anchored several Navy ships. They were logistical ships, replete with all sorts of materiel.

The village was served by one gas-powered generator that ran for just fourteen hours a day. Helicopters flew in every few weeks to bring in a barrel of diesel and various supplies. Sampans navigated the streams and canals bringing in local produce and foodstuffs. The soldiers didn't do any sort of patrols, but were charged simply with guarding the perimeter. I had to wonder what strategic value the place held prior to our arrival. We, on the other hand, went out and handed it to Charlie every night. Two weeks after arrival, we were already having trouble getting resupplied. Not just military hardware, but even food ran low.

I started ragging on Bobby Osborne. The SEAL prototype was roughly five feet, eleven inches to six feet, two inches, and 200 pounds. Bobby was at least six-four and 250 pounds. He was so strong, he'd carry twice what everybody else could carry. "Man, Bobby, you guys are bad luck. I don't know what it is about you guys. Last tour, Gallagher and I had maid service, personal cooks, and bodyguards. We get hooked up with you guys and end up here in this cesspool. What'd you guys do to get us assigned to this hellhole?"

Bobby didn't miss a beat. "It wasn't me who was charged with murder."

"Bobby, you stay close to me, and I'll get you kill—I mean, I'll *keep* you from getting killed."

He smiled. Bobby was right behind me when we operated. He was on his first tour, and everything was a new experience. "You know how we're running low on food?"

"Yes," he said, already wary of leading questions from me.

"How'd you like to go with me to get some more? Gallagher and I were thinking of going out to the ships and taking along several AK-forty-sevens and a few of the Viet Cong flags we've taken from some of the dead VC. It's great trading material."

We had a STAB with twin 110 Mercury outboards that would flat fly. Gallagher, Bobby, McDonald, and I jumped into the boat. Traveling up and down the river meant being sniped at. Fortunately, their snipers weren't very good. Occasionally, they got a few rounds close to where we had to get our heads down, but that was rare. What made it interesting were the canals we had to navigate in and out of. Thirty to fifty yards wide, twisting and turning. I had to leave the throttle wide open. With the many turns, we missed the canal banks often by barely a foot. Fortunately, the snipers couldn't get up alongside the canal because there wasn't any cover. They stayed back behind the tree line out of respect for the .60-caliber machine guns mounted on each side of our boat. The two gunners, taking no chances, opened up on anything close to the canals' edge, strafing back and forth. Several times black-pajama-clad men pitched from the trees. At fifty miles an hour, in no time we were out of range.

On this particular night, we ran the "gauntlet" with Bobby at one of the .60s. He went through a case of M60 ammo on the way out to a Navy LST. "Bobby, did you take into account we might want to do some shooting from your side of the boat on the way back?"

"I didn't get us shot, did I?"

We approached the LST. After signaling that we were Americans, we went on board. Gallagher started into his well-honed routine of building rapport. He gave the officers' mess an AK-47, the chief's mess a gun, and put a Viet Cong flag in at the enlisted mess. They were impressed.

"What can we do for you guys?" the captain asked.

"We've had a hard time getting American food. We've been having rice for breakfast, rice cakes for lunch, and vegetables and rice for dinner. If we're real hungry, we have a little rice for dessert," informed Gallagher. "We need some real food."

"That's what we're here for," the captain proclaimed, smiling. "Don't worry, we'll load you up."

Load us up they did! We had a case of steaks, three five-gallon cartons of ice cream (vanilla, strawberry, and chocolate), ten pounds of shrimp, potatoes—great food!

"One last thing, if I may."

"Sure, what is it?"

"We're running low on M-sixty ammo for our trip back." They included some M60 bullets.

We ran the gauntlet again, shot at the bad guys, then loaded all the food into the refrigerator. We had a steak cookout that night. We all sat around in our swim trunks and enjoyed a good ol' American barbecue!

"Boy, is this good!"

"Steak and potatoes! Ice cream for dessert! This is the life," enthused Dicky Cyrus.

One week after replenishing our food supply, the refrigerator went on the fritz. "Back to the ship," I suggested. "They've got to be able to help us fix this stupid thing!"

We got back into the boat, loaded on .60 bullets, and ran the gauntlet again.

"Hey, it's us! We need help!" We all motioned like we were overwhelmed by a dire emergency.

"Permission to board granted. What's the problem? Did you eat all that food already?"

"No. Worse. Our refrigerator went out yesterday. All our food is melting. Melting! We won't have anything to eat! What do we do?" The ensign laughed.

Gallagher went to the master chief on board. "What we really need is an ACR [air-conditioning repair] man. If you have an ACR volunteer, we could run him in, have him fix it, and have him back out by tonight."

"Let me see if I have any volunteers."

The master chief asked for a volunteer, and one hand went up. He was a young kid, a second class (translation: real green). He'd never been in-country—he'd never left the ship. Never been with SEALs. Never been in combat. Gallagher looked at me with a twinkle in his eye.

"Son, I appreciate your volunteering to help us out. We'll have an adventure you can write home about—how you fixed a refrigerator in Vietnam."

"No problem. I'm really good with refrigerators," he said, enthusiastically.

By this point, Gallagher had broken into a smile. *Poor kid. He has no idea.*

"What am I going to need?"

"Well, it doesn't work," I stated. "I have no idea what's gone wrong."

He had us load a full set of tools, an oxyacetylene torch, Freon kit, and more food.

We accidentally neglected to tell the kid about what to expect. I hit the canal full bore. At first, he was impressed I could drive the boat and miss the sides of the canal as we slid around the corners.

Gallagher sat at the back of the boat on a crate we were bringing back, relaxed and smoking a cigar. Mike McDonald and Bobby Osborne, as if on cue, got up and took their position at each of the M60s. "It's getting close," commented Gallagher above the roar of the engines.

"What's going on?" asked the ACR kid innocently.

As we came around the next bend, Gallagher suggested, "I would get my head down if I were you."

"Why . . . ?" The tree line burst with sniper fire. It was the most we'd seen. All hell broke loose. The .60 guys were kicking it back. Thunderous jarring of the boat mixed with such a deafening barrage sent the kid reeling.

"Holy shit!" he screamed as he dove onto the deck.

Gallagher said, "You don't have to get that low. They're not that good a shot."

"Oh, man!" he wailed. "I'm gonna die! Oh my God! We're in an ambush. We're gonna die!"

Next thing he knew, things quieted down and I slowed the boat. We'd arrived at our outpost. "You can get up now."

Beads of sweat coursed down his face. The poor kid was scared to death and still quivering. "You guys are crazy! I want to go back to my ship."

Gallagher shrugged. "Okay. See ya."

I put my hand on his shoulder. "If I take you back right now, it'll be just you and me. The other guys have work to do. But, if you stay and take care of the refrigerator, we'll take care of you."

He contemplated the situation for a moment. "Oh, great. I get to live awhile longer," he said, managing a weak smile.

He worked all day. Just before sundown, he got the refrigerator fixed, the generator that supplied power to the outpost running better than it ever ran, and he fixed the movie projector. Now we could watch movies!

We had a great dinner of salad and shrimp, followed by big bowls of ice cream. We set up the projector to shine the movie onto a sheet we hung up and invited the local villagers to watch. They didn't really care that it was in English; it was just such a novelty to watch a Hollywood action movie out in the middle of nowhere.

"Well, it's time to go back."

"I don't think I want to go back in the dark."

I put my arm around him. "Hey, no problem. We do it all the time."

We loaded all his tools and equipment back into the boat. I handed him a helmet. "Here. Put this on, and stay really low. We've all been impressed at how brave you've been, coming out here and helping us."

I was serious. The young sailor came around and really was brave about the whole thing. By the time we reached his ship, his entire demeanor changed from fearful and apprehensive to courageous warrior. *He'd been with the SEALs. We'd all been ambushed, fighting valiantly to stay alive—and he was part of it.* He couldn't wait to get down to the mess deck and start telling the stories. *Ran the gauntlet. In a firefight. With SEALs. Fightin' the deadly Viet Cong.* He had his war stories ready to go. But, bless his heart, he'd been brave to come with us.

Like we'd done in our first two tours, we began paying for intelligence with SEAL Team Two funds, working to develop a reliable intel network. We learned about a high-level Viet Cong security chief and where he lived. "Should we go snatch him?" I asked.

Gallagher nodded. "I think so."

Once dusk descended, we traversed through the jungle to a house we'd been told about. Sure enough, the hooch was guarded. We quickly deployed into the assault plan we'd used effectively time and time again. Shoot the guards, rush the hooch, set up a perimeter, jerk the guy out of bed, then disappear into the jungle. No problem.

Dawn was slowly breaking on the horizon when we fired the volley that cut down the two Viet Cong guards. Gallagher and I raced into the hooch. As I smashed my way through the doorway, I caught sight of the security chief disappearing into a bunker inside the house. Resembling an igloo in appearance, the bunker took up most of the interior space. At the first sound of trouble, the chief rolled out of bed and into the bunker. It was very unusual. The "igloo" led to a series of tunnels. It was clever. As we searched for him, he would escape through a secret exit and be long gone into the jungle. I yelled out to the guys in back. "He's gone into a tunnel! Watch for him! He's trying to get away!"

Unfortunately for him, Dicky Cyrus was standing on top of the secret escape door/trash pile. Dicky recognized it, dug through, and found the opening. "I'll throw in a smoke!" We had learned. Not *gas,* smoke. He didn't come out. Dicky peered in through the haze. "It didn't go all the way in! The tunnel appears to turn back on itself, making a couple of U-turns."

McDonald, frustrated, yelled, "Now it's all smoky. We gotta wait until it clears! We can't see anything!"

Gallagher said, in a low tone, "Harry."

"Yeah, Eagle."

"Put your gun down. Go get that man. I want him."

Thrilled, I frowned. "Okay"—here we go again.

I was a big American. He was a little bitty Vietnamese guy, in a little bitty tunnel. I went into the tunnel on my hands and knees, barely fitting. I had maybe an inch clearance going up, and an inch clearance on each side. I went in four feet, made a U-turn, came back four feet, made another right turn that led into a damp and clammy room. A candle was burning, so I had light as I made the second turn. *He's got to be in here. He's probably hiding in the corner.*

CLICK! An American-made .45 pistol slammed into my temple. Blood pounded in my ears. I turned my head slowly, expecting any moment to be blasted into oblivion. He was immediately to my right, and I found myself staring down the barrel of the .45, barely an inch from my nose. *Oh, shit! Wrong thing to do!* I eased backwards. Inch by precious inch, I backed up. I backed all the way out.

"Gallagher, the man's got a .forty-five!" I blurted, clearly shaken.

Shaking his head disgustedly, he walked over. "Here." *Chu-chik.* "Take mine. Now go get him, I said!"

I exhaled long and slow. "Okay." This was getting old, real fast. I must've been stupid. I went back in. On my hands and knees, the .45 in my left hand, I crawled back in. Just before turning the final corner, my heart was pounding audibly. I lay down on my side, inching forward like a worm, gun extended in front of me. *If he hasn't moved, he'll still be against the right wall.* I squirmed forward, peering at the wall through the gunsight. *He's not there!* I looked across the room. He was on the other side. I had my gun pointed at the right wall. He had his .45 pointed at me. *Oh, shit!* I pointed my gun at him.

We stayed there, motionless and staring down the barrel of each other's gun. The distance between us was six feet. Although I was intensely focused, it seemed our worlds were in slow motion. The smoke, darkness, dank, musty smell, and flickering candlelight all impacted my perception. *C'mon! Keep focused.* My trigger finger spasmed lightly. We're both dead if either pulls the trigger. Seconds continued to pass. I studied his eyes. *He doesn't want to die, and he doesn't want to kill me.* I put my gun down. He lowered his slightly.

"Khong co chay."

He got onto his hands and knees and started crawling toward me. I started backing up. We exited the tunnel, him with his gun and me with mine.

I looked over at Gallagher. "Here's your gun."

"Where's the guy?"

"Right here," I said as the Vietnamese chief exited the tunnel. I held my hand out. He handed me his gun. "Here's his gun," I said, almost flippantly.

Gallagher's jaw dropped. "How'd you do that?"

"Oh, no real problem. We understand each other."

Suddenly, the other Vietnamese we had with us grabbed the chief and began beating him, hitting and kicking him to his knees. I leaped to his defense. "Stop! Stop!"

I helped him to his feet. "Tie him up. I'm taking him back. He's mine. You can't play with my prisoner. Only I can beat up my prisoner. Anybody have a problem with that," I said, making eye contact with each one. "Does anyone want to argue?" They understood.

"Papa san, you sit right here," I said, motioning to the VC chief.

"You want to keep this .forty-five?" asked Gallagher.

"It probably doesn't work. That's probably the reason he didn't blow my head off."

Gallagher, standing out in front of the hooch, pointed the gun across the field. *Boom!* "No. It works real fine. Do you want it?" I'd been very fortunate.

The chief had been pressed into service with the Viet Cong and forced to do some very bad things to the local populace in order to keep himself and his family from being killed. He readily agreed to provide us valuable information if we could round up his family. He appreciated the fact I treated him kindly, not allowing the other Vietnamese to cut off his ears or his nose, or perform other forms of customary torture. Once we'd safely placed his family in the complex, he gave us very timely and damaging information. To this day, I wonder why he didn't pull the trigger. SEAL Team luck.

We used his information to go out every night and devastate the Viet Cong in the region. We hit them hard and furious. We picked up details on the Viet Cong area infrastructure, the routes, times, and itineraries. We hit them in their sampans as they crossed the rivers. We hit them in their beds. We set up claymores along a trail we knew a VC company was moving across.

As we were interrogating several prisoners not long after our capture of the VC chief, the interpreter became excited. "He say very important VC near Square Bay. Very important. Run entire district! He know where they live, and he tell me."

We put an operation together and left for Square Bay, a few miles east of Hi Yien. The only detail we had not accounted for was the tide. We planned to extract shortly before dawn, and it didn't exactly jive with the tide. Unfortunately, the tidal difference there was fully thirty feet! We took longer to get in than we planned, so we ran late. On point, the last hundred meters to get onto the beach was in eight inches of water. We half crawled, half breaststroked through soft, deep mud. We were caked in mud by the time we hit the beach.

"Move in and pick up the trail," ordered Gallagher.

Right at first light, we finally found the hooch complex described by our captive. There were two hooches on one side of a twelve-foot-wide canal, three hooches on the other. A large coconut tree had fallen across the canal, between the hooches, making a nice bridge. The canal was five to six feet deep.

We assaulted the first hooch. The sole resident was a mama san. She was scared to death and was not a threat. As we ran out the back, Gallagher leaned over and whispered, "I need you to stay over here and provide security. I'm going to take the new guys [McDonald and Cyrus] and hit those hooches across the canal. You keep Bobby Osborne over here with you."

"All right. I'll keep Big Bob with me."

I looked over at Bobby, seated on the ground across from me outside mama san's back porch, he on one side of the coconut tree bridge, myself on the adjoining side. I thought back to how I felt on patrol two months into my first tour. As the sun was coming up, I examined my

Stoner, caked in mud. Bobby was carrying an Ithaca twelve-gauge pump shotgun with a duckbill modification and a tubular extension affording a nine-round capacity. "Bobby, keep your eyes open for any movement and stuff. I'm going to tear my Stoner apart because it's full of mud, and I'm sure it's not working."

Poor Bobby. He searched the shadows for VC. He was deathly quiet, unsure whether the mama san we'd just left was the enemy, whether the people near Gallagher were the enemy, whether we'd been compromised because of the noise we'd made running through the hooch—and now his partner wanted to take his gun apart. In enemy country.

"Man, don't tear your gun apart! We're going to need your Stoner!"

"Not if it doesn't work."

Mama san had a little crockery urn setting near us, collecting rain. I grabbed it, using the water to scour the components. I was halfway finished with cleaning my gun when I heard wood knocking against wood. Oars hitting the side of a sampan. I was sitting cross-legged on the ground. *Uh-oh!* I stopped and listened. I glanced over at Bob. His eyes were the size of silver dollars. He was staring at the canal.

I gave the signal of index finger to the lips—*Be quiet.* I slowly placed my arms on either side of me and pushed up so I could lean my head forward enough to look into the canal. Fifteen feet below me, in the canal, were four black-pajama-wearing, AK-47-toting, main force Viet Cong. The one at the front of the sampan was standing, looking at Gallagher, taking his AK-47 off his shoulder. Because the tide was out, their heads were level with the embankment and Gallagher couldn't see them. I was behind the crockery urn, unseen by the VC. They floated slowly towards us and the coconut bridge, separated by barely ten yards.

I leaned back, pantomiming to Bobby that I would shoot the first one. *You shotgun the rest. One round in each guy. No problem,* I assured him. *We can kill all four of them.*

Bobby had never killed anybody. In effect, I was saying, *You'll have no problem*—easier said than done on someone's first go-around. I gingerly pulled out my 9-millimeter pistol. Looking into Bobby's eyes, I questioned, *Are you ready Bobby? They're only fifteen feet from us.*

Bobby was ready to go. He'd been vaccinated with adrenaline so deep his eyes were saucers and every muscle tensed.

Ready. Set. Go. I moved my legs around to get into position. The lead Viet Cong quickly picked up my movement; they were now a scant twelve feet below us. The first VC had brought his gun around to port arms, intent upon Gallagher. Number two man had taken his gun off his shoulder, the third man was sitting down, and the fourth man squatted at the back of the boat, balancing the sampan with his paddle.

I raised up. *Bam! Bam! Bam!* I plastered three shots into the first VC's chest, picking him up and splashing him into the canal. "Get 'em!" I shouted.

Bobby, like a snake striking, jumped up, the sampan barely eight feet from him. *BOOOM!* Bobby blasted the second guy right in the head. He was so excited, he emptied the shotgun. *BOOOM! BOOOM! BOOOM! BOOOM! BOOOM! BOOOM! BOOOM! BOOOM!* Into blank water.

After we shot, the remaining two Viet Cong dove for cover in the canal. With their AK-47s. Bobby, in the meantime, now had an empty gun.

"Bobby, we gotta go get 'em!" I screamed, knowing we could be dead in moments. They still had guns. The next thing I knew, this big 250-pound human projectile went flying through the air into the canal below us. "Yaaaaa!" he yelled as he cannonballed into the water. There came two VC, AK-47s in front of them, out of the water. Simultaneously, there was Bobby Osborne, unarmed, body-slamming across the sampan, arms extended, corralling the both of them. As he sank the sampan, he gripped tightly the two VC. Bobby's left hand found one man's throat and clamped down, drawing him to him, the AK-47 harmlessly turned sideways between them. The second Viet Cong slipped from Bobby's grasp. Bobby focused his attention on the VC he had in hand. He started pounding the VC in the face with his fist. Fortunately, the second VC, his gun shoulder-harnessed across his chest, disappeared under water.

I can't believe he did this! I dove down the embankment, right behind Bobby. All I could think to do was to try to get my pistol positioned to shoot the VC before he surfaced with his AK. All at once, the VC popped out of the water directly in front of me.

"Oh, shit!" Reflexively, I rapidly squeezed three shots off at point-blank range.

Meanwhile, Gallagher, hearing the shooting, came racing towards us. Bobby was still pummeling the poor Viet Cong in the face. His left hand clenched in a death grip around his throat.

"Osborne," Gallagher said slowly and deliberately. "You can quit that now. He's . . . surely dead."

I can attest. That man was surely dead. Bobby looked up. Plastered across his face was fear, adrenaline, excitement—and blood. *Welcome to combat, SEAL-style.*

Our shooting woke everybody up. "That's it. Let's pick up all our stuff and get out of here."

"Okay, Eagle," I acknowledged. "Bobby, quick, reload your shotgun and cover me. I have to put my Stoner back together."

The first Viet Cong I shot wore a pistol belt and resembled the man we were looking for. Generally, Viet Cong with pistol belts were highranking. "I want to take his body with us so we can get him identified," Gallagher commanded.

"Man, I don't want to drag his body," I whined.

"I know, but we didn't bring a camera."

"You sure you want him?" I persisted.

"Look, if you don't want to carry him, put him back in a sampan and float him out. I want him brought back."

"Good idea," I reasoned. "I don't know why I didn't think of that. I guess that's why you're the big boss!"

"Cut the crap. We gotta get going."

I fished the sampan out of the canal, poured out the water, and placed the body in it.

Mike McDonald took over on point so I could float the sampan. We followed the canal on out into the bay. The tide continued to drop. By the time we reached the bay, there was no more than three inches of water. From the mouth of the canal out to the middle of the bay where our boats were was two hundred yards. I threw my muddy, inoperable Stoner into the sampan and began the trek out. Force my leg forward a step, push the sampan, force my other leg through the mud, push the sampan. I glanced at my watch. "Damn, 0830! We gotta hustle. We're sitting ducks out here now that it's broad daylight. Its taken us a half hour to go only a hundred yards in this hip-deep mud."

"What would you think if we left the sampan here and made a beeline for the boat?" asked Bobby.

"Bobby, we're halfway there. Keep dragging."

"I know, but now we're carving the sampan through the mud. There's no water left to float it in. It's taking forever."

A Viet Cong company heard gunshots and came to investigate. It was readily apparent from the trail we left in the mud where we went. By following it, they arrived at the bank overlooking the bay. There we were, literally bogged down in front of them. Hastily, they set up. They opened up, bullets splattering the mud all around us.

Gallagher was the last guy, positioned closest to the shoreline. While the rest of us scurried—in slow motion—to hide behind the wooden sampan, he had no cover. Bullets hit the sampan. Mud kicked up all around Gallagher. They never hit him!

Gallagher lay, partially submerged, on his stomach, shooting his M16. Bobby squeezed off his shotgun. "Ah, Bobby," I chided. "Use your pistol. A shotgun doesn't shoot that far."

Bobby and I were shooting 9-millimeter pistols; the corpsman's gun had gotten muddy and quit functioning, so it too was in the sampan. Mike McDonald and Dicky Cyrus were to our left. They held their M16s up and blazed away, ineffectively. We kept pushing to get out to the water.

Thump! Thump! Thump! Shells ripped into the sampan. "Call them again!" I shouted at the corpsman, who was carrying the radio. "Tell 'em to get those helos here now!"

Over the crackle and static of the radio, we heard, "This is Sea Wolf twenty-three. We've scrambled to your emergency. We'll be inbound to your location in ten minutes. Over."

"Corpsman, tell him two minutes or the battle's over. Gallagher's running out of bullets, we'll be out of bullets, and the VC are gonna smoke us. Two minutes!" I emphasized, as fear, apprehension, and adrenaline flooded over me.

The corpsman had been on the radio for the past ten minutes as we tried to group everyone together behind the sampan and move farther out. Gallagher was trying to catch up with us while we attempted to provide some sort of cover for him. We all lay down and sank in, level with the mud. "Maybe this can buy us time until the Sea Wolves get here," shouted Bobby.

I had to laugh. "Look! We are one with the mud!"

Nobody thought it funny at that particular moment. The corpsman was trying to talk above the static on the radio to the weak signal of the inbound Sea Wolves. Nine minutes. We lay there looking up. *A clear blue sky, nice and warm, a little breeze, and bullets all over the place.*

Suddenly, the radio went silent. I jerked my head. Usually, when a radio went silent, it meant somebody with a big powerful radio had keyed into your frequency.

A deep resonant voice with a Texas twang spoke clearly from the radio, "Moosejaw Seven Bravo, this is Pony One thirteen. Have you in sight. We're coming inbound hot. Suggest you get down."

"Pony" was the code name for a fixed wing aircraft, the OV-10. Unlike Sea Wolf helicopters, which carried only 2.75-inch rockets, the fixed wing aircraft carried big 5-inch Zuni rockets and miniguns.

Big guns! Big bullets! Big rockets! We might pull out of here, after all! "Where the hell did he come from," I wondered aloud. "There aren't supposed to be friendlies anywhere near us!"

From five thousand feet, circling in the sun, these guys had been monitoring the radio traffic, and knew we were there. When the shooting started, they looked down and saw us trapped out in the mud. They listened as we talked to the Sea Wolves about how we were pinned down and taking heavy fire. The two OV-10s went into a side-by-side dive.

I was out of bullets, so all I could do was lay there and watch. Faintly, high above us I picked out two tiny dots. Two planes materialized out of the sun, streaking straight down. All of a sudden, they started releasing all these rockets, fire plumes thrusting the rockets forward toward the Viet Cong positioned on the bank. Then the miniguns opened up. The next thing we knew, the whole tree line and bank just started exploding. Fireworks-like flames burst fifty, sixty, even seventy feet into the air! The air exploded with the ear-shattering reverberations of the bombardment.

"YES! We win!" We all were shouting and hollering at our good fortune.

The Ponies made two runs and expended all their ammunition, which was an awful lot! They made one oval, low-level loop around us, gave us a wag of the wing, and flew off. "Moosejaw Seven Bravo, it's been a pleasure. We're heading back to Can Tho. Have a good day. Out."

We worked to get out to the waterline while the enemy was busy. With ten yards to go, the boat in as close as it could come without being stuck itself, we saw coming from over the horizon two Sea Wolves, racing toward us, still several miles off. Quickly, we loaded the dead Viet Cong, us, and our gear into the boat. The STAB roared to life, spun around, and headed out. Seconds later, we started taking more fire from the embankment on the west side (to our right) of the bay. Perfect timing for the Sea Wolves' arrival. They shot up the second group of Viet Cong, allowing us to escape.

As we arrived back at camp, the new guys were beside themselves with what had just transpired. I thought back to Fraley's death, to the battalion op where we'd been pinned down in the bomb crater. By the time we got back, I'd pretty well shaken it off and was ready to move on to whatever was next. The new guys, on the other hand, continued to replay and rehash each minute detail. On and on they went, dissecting every aspect over and over again.

Gallagher, like me, moved on to things more pressing. "The helicopter's coming in this afternoon. I need for you to go with them back to Can Tho and get me these items." He handed me a list of radio parts, guns, rockets, bullets, and electronic components we needed. "One more thing. I have a little present I want to give you to wear when you go."

"What's that?"

Gallagher reached over and handed me some lieutenant bars. "When you go up to Can Tho, I want you to go over to supplies and see Chief Johnson. Tell him that you're Lieutenant Arne Johanssen and sign accordingly. We've got to have the radio gear."

"Don't worry. It shouldn't be any problem."

The radio equipment would allow us to encrypt our messages. Our message traffic was being intercepted by the NVA, who had English-speaking interpreters telling them what we were doing.

Off I went up to Can Tho. I traveled to the various supply stations obtaining what we needed and staging it all at the Admin building. "Thanks a lot for your help," I said, after receiving the last of what I needed. I turned to leave, then stopped. "Isn't there a contingent of Pony and Sea Wolves stationed here?"

"Yes, sir. There are. In fact, they just returned this morning from an operation down south where they saved some SEALs. They're over in the officers' club."

I walked into the officers' club, happy for my lieutenant's bars. Over at a table were four guys in flight suits, drinking beer. I had my camouflaged clothes on, which indicated I was a SEAL. I walked over. "Anybody here Pony One thirteen?"

One of the men turned and stared at me. "Yeah, I'm Pony One thirteen."

"I'm Moosejaw Seven Bravo."

He lit up. "No shit!"

"Really."

"Sit down, buddy! Have a drink. Tell me, how good did we do?"

We relived the battle. One of the things we found was that pilots never knew the extent of damage they caused. They zipped in, dumped their load, and zipped out. They didn't know if they scared off the enemy, shot a water buffalo, or decimated a VC battalion. They loved getting direct feedback. We sat there for an hour and a half, buying each other drinks, reliving the entire mission. We cleared the table, making marks. *I was here, they were here, you were there. . . .* We were into it, having a close-knit, combat camaraderie sort of good time.

An ensign had joined us, and it was his turn to buy drinks. We were still swapping stories, when an admin commander in charge of the supply buildings walked over behind the ensign, demanding he step aside in deference to his rank.

I stared over at the ensign. "Hey, Joe, bring the drinks!"

"Go back and tell your friends no more drinks, and tell them to quiet down," the commander ordered.

The ensign stood there, unsure what to do. I thought he was waiting for the order to come up, so I got up to help. "Hey, I'm here to help you carry."

The commander stepped in front of me. "You'll wait your turn, Lieutenant. Rank has its privilege."

"No, the ensign was here first. We'll get our drinks and get out of your way."

"No. You'll do as you're told."

Joe the ensign, trying to keep the peace, interjected meekly, "Commander, there's no reason to get upset. We're all just a little excited."

The commander shoved the ensign out of the way, then stood defiantly in front of me. "Just who in the hell do you think you are?"

His arrogant, unabashed throwing his weight around hit a raw nerve. I hauled off and hit him with a solid left hand to the jaw, laying him out cold.

Everything stopped. The pilots jumped up and grabbed me, hustling me away. They knew I was in very serious trouble—brig time, court-martial, possibly dropped from SEAL Team. They ran me over to their Sea Wolves barracks. I took off my lieutenant bars and stashed them in my pocket. The ensign ran me into a room where four Sea Wolf aviators sat playing cards. "You guys, hide him! There's been a fight over at the club. Take care of him."

It was readily apparent I was a SEAL due to my clothes. "Guys, I could really use a flight suit."

The Sea Wolf closest to me grinned. "I could sure use a set of cammies."

"Great!" I exclaimed. "Let's swap."

I put on his flight suit, and he put on my cammies. There was no chance he'd be mistaken for me, since I was blond and he was taller and had dark hair. No sooner had I sat down when in came the Military Police and the commander I'd flattened.

"You guys see a Navy SEAL come in here? He struck the commander here in the face—totally without provocation."

As they came in, I grabbed a flight helmet and put it on. I picked up a hand of cards and pretended to play.

"Did you see a guy in cammies?"

We all pointed toward the back door. "I think he went that way."

"Thanks!" Off went the Military Police. Off went the commander.

"Good luck. I hope you find the bastard," one of the guys yelled after them.

"Not me," I whispered, shrugging sheepishly.

The Sea Wolf I'd swapped my cammies with ran across the runway, then over to the mess hall, and then back to the dorms, which kept the MPs busy.

"It's too late for you to get your helo back to your home base and it's not a good idea to try to get a room over at the visitor barracks. Why don't you sleep in Washburn's bunk. He's in Australia for some R and R," informed one of the pilots. "What happened, anyway?"

"I don't know; maybe its a character fault in me or something. I nearly got killed this morning. We were stuck in the mud in Square Bay. Pony One thirteen and you Sea Wolves bailed our asses out of the ringer. I'm respectful of rank, don't get me wrong, but war's serious business. Then a rear-echelon, admin puke started throwing his weight around, pestering this poor ensign just to show he's a badass. I hauled off and hit him. I know I shouldn't have, but it sure felt great."

The next morning, I rounded up all the things I'd procured, got on the helicopter, and flew back.

"You did what?" Gallagher demanded when I told him what had happened. "I give you a set of bars, send you to the real world to get a drink, and what do you do? You abuse the privilege! I don't know, Harry. I just don't know. I thought I trained you better."

Perplexed, I offered, "Well, Eagle, I hit him as hard as I could."

"That's the problem, not hard enough. He got up and came after you, right?"

"Yes."

"Well then, you didn't hit him hard enough. A real SEAL would have hit him another time when he was going down. He'd have been out for five minutes and that would've been all the time you needed." It was both funny and stupid at the same time. No flag, no penalty . . . on with the war!

We were striking terror into the local Viet Cong establishment. Unfortunately, there was a downside to our successes. The local Vietnamese inside our complex had grown lax in their patrolling of the perimeter, and we weren't aware of it. *The Americans are going out to find the VC. Why should we worry about VC coming here?*

One of the Americans who visited us regularly was Father Mac. Father Mac was a Catholic priest who cared equally about the troops and about the Vietnamese. His background was fascinating. He'd previously served in Africa before volunteering to chaplain in Vietnam. While in Africa, he was picked up by a local native force because they didn't understand the difference between missionary and mercenary. They were going to barbecue him at sunrise but he managed to break out the back window of the little hooch they had him in and escaped. We all respected him a lot. "My place is here. You guys are fighting and you need spiritual comfort." His passion was in helping the local Vietnamese children, however.

He'd come in and out with the delivery helicopter. Father Mac was light complected, with sandy brown hair. He was slender, standing about five feet ten inches tall. He enjoyed visiting us since, for some reason, he liked SEALs. He set up and ran an orphanage in Can Tho, working throughout the countryside, going from installation to installation. Whenever he was with us, after dinner, we'd play blackjack. It was ten cents a chip, five chips maximum. Father Mac beat the pants off of us. He was the dealer, and we lost tons—a good three to four dollars a night. The only time we held was at twenty. Father Mac put all the money into the orphanage, so it was fun losing to him. If he came away after a week's stay with us with fifty bucks, that was a lot of money. He teased us relentlessly.

"God knows what you have; that's why I win and you lose." Or "God doesn't want you to win, Harry. Double down."

"Okay, Father Mac. Give me a card." At which he invariably dealt me a card I didn't need. "Oh no! Busted again!" I lamented with a laugh, as Father Mac raked in the chips. Father Mac called it divine guidance.

There was an old Vietnamese guy, seventy years old or so, withered and wrinkled, bent from his years of hard work. His name was Mr. Tran, and he'd fought with the French against the Viet Minh. He was very proud of his military record. Most every one of his neighbors in the village thought him *dinkidao* (Vietnamese for crazy or nuts). The military command had taken away all his guns because they felt he was a hazard. He came to us a few days after I returned from Can Tho, asking the interpreter for an audience. Standing as tall and erect as he could, he saluted proudly. "I am a soldier. I've been a soldier all my life. I have been shamed by my people after years of service. The lieutenant confiscated all my guns and bullets. I want to help fight against the Viet Cong. Would you please consider giving me a gun and some bullets so I can fight once more?"

The Vietnamese lieutenant walked in and, standing behind him, pantomimed *dinkidao* by circling his index finger around his ear while making a clownish face. It was hard to keep a stern face as this solemn and proud old man stood in formal ceremony, while a dignified, uniformed lieutenant behind him was making faces.

Talking further with the old man, I determined he was definitely eccentric, but not *dinkidao*. Gallagher and I looked at each other. *What do you want to do?*

Gallagher and I just couldn't say no to the old man. "Why don't we give him a carbine and a couple of bullets. The worst thing that could happen would be he shoots one person. He'll run out of bullets before he can shoot anyone else," I suggested. "We'll tell Mr. Tran he can pick the gun up here in the evening and he must patrol all night, then return it in the morning. We really could use his assistance on night patrol," I said, nodding my head in an attempt to try to convey respect to the poor old man before me.

After relaying our decision, the old man beamed proudly. "Mr. Tran says, Perfect! That's the duty he wanted, and he's very happy you will allow him to serve his country. Exactly what he wants to do."

"Okay, here's your gun. Start patrolling," I said, handing him an M1 carbine. You'd have thought I'd given Mr. Tran some priceless treasure the way he gingerly took and admired the gun.

The next night, his second night on duty, he reported for his gun. It was a little ceremony to him. He bowed low. He then proceeded to show how he'd cleaned it up, then demonstrated his insertion of the bullets, safety off, safety on—that he was good to go. It was nice to see how happy he was. He bowed. I bowed. He bowed. I bowed again. He bowed once more. "Off you go. Get out on patrol," I said, smiling broadly. We'd been there two months without a problem. What harm could he cause?

We went back to playing blackjack and drinking a few beers, Father Mac attempting to steal all our money for the orphanage again. It was going on midnight and everyone was tired.

"All right, cash in your chips. Everyone give Father Mac your money," instructed Mike McDonald. We put the beers away and cleaned the room, turned the lights out, and went to bed.

Before playing poker, I just happened to clean my Stoner, assemble ten 100-round belts, and set my cammies at the end of my bed, ready to go. I rarely did that, but I'd reasoned we might be operating either that evening or the next, so I might as well be ready.

I was just about asleep when I heard a single shot. *Bam!* Then another. *Bam!* Two shots—then I heard some other shots. Quickly, I threw on my clothes, crisscrossed my ammo belts across my shoulders, grabbed my Stoner, and bounded out the door into the courtyard. Gallagher emerged from his room, armed and ready.

"What's going on?" Gallagher asked.

"I don't know." Several more gunshots rent the night sky. "Something's happening out on the perimeter." More gunfire went off. *Bddddd-Dap! Bddddd-Dap! Bddddd-Dap!*

"What time is it?"

I glanced at my watch, "It's one A.M."

"We're getting hit, Harry. We're getting hit! Get the radio going! Get the generator back on and up, on the double!" Gallagher rubbed his temples in contemplation as the rest of the SEALs and Father Mac appeared. "McDonald, you and Dicky Cyrus come with me. I'm going to check the perimeter. I'll grab this radio. Harry, you get our frequency up and stay here. Break out all the gear."

I nodded acknowledgment.

"Bobby, go unlock the bunker. Get me a case of LAAWs and a case of claymores. Grab a case of .sixties. Get them in here and set up the M-sixties," I commanded.

What had sounded like individual guns going off was now a pretty good sounding firefight.

The radio cackled to life, Gallagher screaming, "We're being assaulted! I need you out here! We're being assaulted! I need you out here immediately!"

"Okay. I'm on my way."

"Bobby, we gotta go!" I yelled, as he carried more claymores into the courtyard. "Gallagher needs us on the perimeter pronto!"

"But I don't have the .sixty set up."

"That's all right. We gotta get out there!"

The corpsman, Bobby Osborne, and I raced to the perimeter, carrying five LAAWs, four claymores, and our usual assortment of guns and grenades. After rendezvousing with Gallagher, we set up along a hundred-yard stretch under heavy assault. It was at the northern end, bordered by jungle.

I had a hasty meeting with the Vietnamese soldier in charge of the twenty Vietnamese assembled there. "We'll take care of this stretch. Move your men down the line."

As they ran off, I noticed Mr. Tran hunkered down with his carbine in a ditch. I grabbed the interpreter and ran over to him.

"The old man would like to know if he can have some more bullets," asked the interpreter.

"Sure. What happened?"

"He was patrolling, walking the rectangular perimeter, when he got to the back corner. Looking down, he saw where somebody who was wet (having swam through the perimeter canal that completely surrounded the complex) had cut the wire and come through, going over the berm and into the complex. He says he saw three zappers come through the fence and they're hiding in the grass somewhere. He shot at one of them, but he's not sure he hit anything."

Oh great. Three zappers behind us in the tall grass. And we don't know where they are.

We positioned ourselves at a 45-degree angle on the inside rim of the berm, facing outward. Suddenly, we were hit by a hellacious firefight from beyond the perimeter. The next thing we knew, the three guys on the inside opened up on us from about sixty yards behind us. The concussive sound-wave of artillery reverberated through us, our ears ringing to the point of hurting.

We threw four grenades and fired a LAAW at the Viet Cong outside the compound. Temporarily, their firing died down.

"Over the berm!" I screeched, bullets hitting all around. We dove over the berm and began firing toward the inside of our compound.

Then the Viet Cong outside the wall started firing again, so we leap-frogged back to the inside part of the berm. Back and forth we went, leapfrogging and shooting in both directions. Whichever side was taking the least fire was the side we jumped to. On and on it dragged, going on for an hour straight.

"We gotta knock this off. We're running out of bullets," said Gallagher. "Send the corpsman back to call for helicopter support, and send someone for more bullets."

I looked around and there sat Father Mac. "Father Mac, what're you doing?"

"I'm out here to help."

"Tell you what. Come with me, we gotta get more bullets."

Soon, we were headed back out. Father Mac carried a case of Stoner and a case of .223 for M16s! Each case weighed about fifty pounds. Father Mac took it upon himself to distribute the ammo. Everybody was reloading, shooting, then calling for more shells.

"Father Mac, throw me down some more Stoner," somebody would holler.

"Praise the Lord and pass the ammunition!" He'd run the ammo can down to the guy and feed it out to him.

"Hey, Father Mac, bring me down some grenades!" Father Mac would run grenades down. He ran the hundred yards, back and forth, delivering whatever we ordered. He never seemed to tire, despite the hours wearing on.

"Father Mac, it'd be fantastic if you could drag up two of the M-sixty machine guns and ammo for them. That'd help us a lot."

"Okeydoke, no problem. See you in a minute." Out he came with the machine guns.

We set the two M60s at each end of our defensive position. The corpsman and Dicky Cyrus started pulverizing the Viet Cong positions, weakening their fire upon us greatly.

We continued taking fire from both sides, however. In addition to the M60s, we kept two of our six SEALs continually firing into the zapper positions, regardless of which side of the berm we were on. We didn't seem to be making any headway. They continued pounding our position, as we did to them. Still no helicopter support.

"Harry," Gallagher called over the radio, "we've got to take out these zappers behind us. This is ridiculous. I want four of us to position evenly and assault into the reeds and go after these guys."

Bobby, Mike McDonald, Gallagher, and I set out. We thought the zappers were, from their firing at us, about 150 meters away from us, in a 30-meter-wide by 5-meter-deep area. Bobby, Mike, and I ran toward a dike that headed straight to their position. "No, no, no!" I cautioned. "I'm walking the dike." The two of them had to walk in the reeds, in knee-deep water.

"Let's assault!" yelled Gallagher above the din.

We started moving forward. I shot the Stoner in bursts, as I had only a two-hundred-round belt and couldn't afford to run out. We kept shooting in order to keep their heads down, hoping to move right to them. Steadily we moved in on them. Sixty yards. Fifty yards. Because I was on the dike, I was slightly ahead of the other three. Thirty yards from their position.

I fired a short burst, then paused momentarily.

Ping! to my immediate left. "Grena—" I screamed. The grenade landed right next to me. I turned to dive to my right, but I couldn't move fast enough. A bright flash, then concussive force slammed me, picking me up and tossing me high into the air, doing somersaults. "AHHHH!" I shrieked, searing pain burrowing into my face, neck, and arms. *That must be fragmentation from the grenade coming through my body.* Funny how you really can experience time slowing down at critical moments. It was like everything was in slow motion as I realized I had time to feel the pain while flipping through the air. I landed near Gallagher twenty-five feet from where I'd been.

As the Viet Cong released the grenade toward me, Bobby Osborne and Mike McDonald returned the favor, lobbing two grenades into them. It wiped them out.

I was unconscious. Quickly, they gathered around. "Harry. Harry."

I came to, fading in and out. "Yeah . . ." My head hurt bad, as if in a burning vise. The world was spinning, all the colors of a kaleidoscope brightly flashing through my head.

Gallagher shined his red-light flashlight on me. "Where're you hit?"

"Man, I'm burning all over my face, neck, and arms. I think I'm covered in frag," I said, somewhat incoherent, having a hard time telling him how I felt.

Gallagher couldn't see anything, so he switched the red filter away, going to clear light. "Holy shit!" he exclaimed as he pored intently over my wounds. "All over your arms are red welts. Red, third-degree burns. But I can't find any holes anywhere."

What had happened was that while I tumbled through the air, my red-hot Stoner barrel had repeatedly hit me, each time searing my skin wherever it touched. As I regained composure, Gallagher had Father Mac and two others gingerly carry me back to the team house. Father Mac stayed with me while Dicky Cyrus and Bobby Osborne grabbed more bullets and headed back out. Father Mac called for a medevac.

"The medevac will be awhile. We have inbound helos coming to shoot for you. Once we have a clear LZ, we'll bring in the medevac chopper. Over."

Father Mac provided first aid, giving me pain pills and a stirrette of morphine. Right away I began feeling better.

"I'm feeling pretty good. We gotta go get back in the war. It sounds like it's still going something fierce out there."

"What? God can perform miracles, but you still seem quite debilitated to me."

"Father Mac, if we lose, it doesn't matter how bad I feel; it'll only get worse."

I put my clothes back on. "All right," Father Mac reluctantly agreed, "I'll follow you back out."

Disoriented and dizzy, I moved slowly out the back door of the team hooch. We walked toward the perimeter we'd been battling to maintain. The shortest way was walking on the dike along the creek passing through the middle of the compound, directly underneath our team hooch. I held my Stoner in front of me, Father Mac helping me from falling over.

The path wound past a grove of banana, mango, and coconut trees. Suddenly, climbing out of the canal behind a coconut tree came a Viet Cong. Less than ten yards in front of us. *Bdddd-dap!* "You're dead," I said dreamily.

Father Mac ran over to where the man lay. "He's dead, all right." Father Mac unstrapped the man's knapsack and opened it. Explosive charges, detonators, blasting caps, and wire. Father Mac's face went blank. "Praise the Lord! Harry, he was headed to your SEAL Team hooch to blow it up, I'd bet. You and I could've been in there when it blew! Thank God we came out here!"

We kept going, finally reaching Gallagher. "What are you doing out here? Get back to the team hut! Now!"

So we turned and went back.

A half hour later, the helicopter gunships arrived, tipping the battle finally into our hands. Flares went up, lighting the early morning sky. Six gunships poured sheets of lead into the VC along the perimeter.

The following morning, I was medevacked to the hospital in Can

Tho. The doctor came in and quizzed me as he looked me over for frag wounds. "Where does it hurt the most?"

"I don't know. I have a monster headache, and my teeth hurt. They're loose."

After my burns were dressed, I was pronounced whole and sent over to the dentist. "Your teeth are loose and they obviously hurt, but they're going to be fine. Just don't chew on anything hard."

The helicopter gunship pilots estimated we'd been up against a main force VC battalion consisting of around three hundred men. Six SEALs, one hundred South Vietnamese, and Father Mac had withstood tremendous odds. The only reason we lived to tell about it was because of a bent, wrinkled old man who still had his pride and wanted to maintain his value to the community despite being told he was all washed up and *dinkidao.*

Days later, a representative from Naval Command flew in. "We're moving you SEALs to another AO. Please get your gear squared away and be prepared to leave within the week," he informed us.

"Wait a minute!" Gallagher protested. "We've only now begun to figure out this area. Our intelnet is functioning, and the area is rapidly becoming pacified. How the hell can you move us now? Why the hell would you want to?"

"I'm sorry, Master Chief. Orders are orders. They're coming down from above."

"Where are we going?"

"Can Tho for now."

"For now? What do you mean, for now?"

"Well, we're waiting for final orders. All we know is you're to report to Can Tho on or before next Monday."

No sooner had we arrived than we were being informed we were moving to the border region, to Ha Tien, to join Lieutenant Dick Moran and the rest of our Ninth Platoon. We had just started really mixing it up, observing where main force NVA were moving. We'd had five hard-hitting ambushes where we called in helicopter gunships and just demolished NVA companies. Suddenly, it was time to move again.

The Paris Peace Accords were in full swing. President Nixon was talking about peace with dignity. To us, this meant we were trying to figure out a way to retreat without it looking like a unilateral surrender. Our next assigned area of operation was . . . back to Can Tho. Every few days, new restrictions were issued. It was difficult not to be cynical.

"Your next assignment is up in Nha Be, in the Rung Sat Special

Zone just outside of Saigon. You'll be there for the remaining two and a half months of your tour.''

Nha Be had traditionally been a West Coast SEAL Team One area of operation. Now we were all, both Teams One and Two, stationed at Nha Be. Off we went. On our way, we ran into two other teams also being staged there. Two platoons were never put together—now we had three. Our effective range of operation was clearly being limited. Rather than adding more platoons to flank enemy strongholds, someone made the decision to cram us all together in an out-of-the-way, desolate region.

We ran a convoy from Tan Son Nhut Air Base down to Nha Be. Everybody who'd been in-country awhile seemed to know where the fun places to stop and have a beer were. One such place was Tammy the Troll's. It was no problem convincing this group to stop for a beer break.

We came down this little bit of a hill and stopped under a bridge, hence the "Troll" title. The area consisted of a row of shacks, most of which were bars. The most popular was Tammy's. Maybe it was because the temperature was cooler sitting under a bridge, maybe it was something else, but guys liked to drink beer there for one reason or another, and SEALs definitely preferred Tammy's. As we pulled into the parking lot, we all started laughing. It was like having an impromptu SEAL convention. Almost all the vehicles in the parking lot belonged to SEALs.

Walking in, I asked, "What're all you guys doing here?"

"What're you guys doing here?" came the response back.

We all sat down and started discussing various top-secret ops we'd been undertaking while Tammy brought us beers. Better than twenty of us crowded together. One chord resonated throughout the room: We all were being jerked to and fro, kept from doing what we were assigned.

"There's a whole country here, and we're all restricted to Nha Be."

The first guy I saw when I walked in was Gary Chamberlin. Every SEAL knew him, calling him "Chambo." He stood five feet ten inches tall, and was a stump. Muscle upon muscle, strong as an ox. He was part Cherokee Indian, with dark complexion, jet-black hair, and brown eyes. After a few beers, I went over and sat down next to him.

"So what've you been up to?" I asked.

"Hell if I know. We've been all over the countryside. We ran all sorts of surgically precise, finesse ops—just kicking ass. Especially with my LDNNs, we went all over, liquidating the Viet Cong."

"Oh yeah?" I bragged. "On my last tour, I ran a group of PRU. Your LDNNs all went to Coronado for fun and games. My guys, nothing but a ragtag group of ex-VC and murderers, had to be trained in-country. We whipped them into shape in two weeks. You think you ran some hot ops. I'd bet money our PRUs ran circles around your guys. We passed ourselves off as Viet Cong and just toasted the day-lights out of them. I'm sure there's regulations prohibiting it now."

"Yeah, I know. We danced over and back across the Cambodian border so many times it's not even funny. I mean, it was dark out and I can't read Vietnamese. How'd I know where the border was?" Chambo paused, then sneered. "Man, one time our intelligence network clued us in on an NVA battalion coming to hit an Army outpost. They traveled through this corridor," Gary explained, drawing it out on a napkin. "We set up claymores, all wired together along a hundred-fifty-foot stretch. They were all walking together . . . click . . . half their battalion went down!"

"That sounds too easy. We flew in on a helo-borne assault, ready to hit a VC company in the tree line—only they hadn't gotten there yet. We landed right on top of them. Boy, did that piss 'em off." I recounted the rest of the story. Since it was my "enhanced" version of the story, it had plenty of "timing and finesse"!

We got serious. "What do you think they're doing with us? You think we'll be able to go back to operating?" Gary asked.

"I don't know. I doubt it."

"Probably right. We were doing a lot of operations along the Ho Chi Minh Trail and in the North, outside Hanoi. The admin pukes sure clamped a lid on that. Did you do much along the border?" asked Gary.

"Yeah, some."

Chamberlin took a long hit on his beer, leaned back on his stool, balanced on two legs. His eyes flashed excitedly. "I'll tell you something that might really impress you. Do you know where I spent the first part of this tour when I got here?"

"No, not exactly," I replied.

"You know where the DMZ is?"

"Yeah, north of here. My brother Charles has been stationed there with the Marines."

"I was operating with LDNNs on some top-secret, covert special ops."

"What were you doing?"

"Downed pilots."

This meant he was spending more time on the other side of the DMZ than he was on our side. "Find any?"

"No, but we smoked a lot of NVA. I also almost got Salt and Pepper. I trailed them for weeks, getting really close but never quite catching up to them."

"Oh, no kidding. That's too bad." Salt and Pepper were the names given to two American GIs, one black and one white, who defected over to the NVA. After being turned, they lured other Americans into ambushes by pretending to be lost or hurt. When an American jeep or deuce-and-a-half stopped, they dove for cover while the VC or NVA shot them up. "Have you had *any* luck?"

"I've been getting to know a lot of people."

"Really," I responded, knowing he meant he'd been through some of the villages of North Vietnam.

"You won't believe this. I was in Hanoi three months ago. You know that actress—you know—Henry Fonda's daughter, the one who's gone stupid and was saying all that idiot antiwar stuff we read about in the Philippines? I got within ten feet of her."

"That's gotta be bullshit! How the hell could anyone, especially someone as ugly as you, get that close? There's no way I'm buying this."

Chamberlin smiled wryly. "No, man. It's true! Here's what happened. There's this bridge that connects North Vietnam to China across this river. The bridge is a major, major supply route into North Vietnam. The Air Force has tried for months to knock it out, to no avail. There is a cliff jutting out above the bridge, providing a natural shield; and, if you wanted to take it out coming up the river, you'd be shot down by antiaircraft batteries positioned there. They tried and tried and tried. Several planes were shot down; they just couldn't get it.

"So word came to me that they wanted me and my LDNNs to carry explosives up, get past the perimeter defenses, set a charge, and blow the damn thing up. Typical admin assholes. We busted ourselves to get all the way up there, only to discover they finally found a way to bomb it while we were en route. So we shucked our gear, leaving the explosives with a double agent who'd housed us. We couldn't pass up the opportunity to go on in to Hanoi.

"You wouldn't have believed it! There were so many international people there, it was incredible. All sorts of languages being spoken—Chinese, Vietnamese, Russian, Italian, French, German, Spanish, several Middle Eastern dialects, a whole bunch, along with English. You wouldn't have believed how easy it was to walk around Hanoi and fit in. It's really a very nice city.

"Our contacts told us about this parade that was about to start, so we decided to watch. One of my LDNNs was originally from the North, somewhere outside of Hanoi, and, as luck would have it, knew two of the guards. He told them I was a Serbian advisor, about to go on some top-secret mission, and we wanted a better view of things. So we went right up to where all the military big wigs were. I kid you not! I walked right up behind Jane Fonda. I could've gotten wet with her! [translation: Gary could have stabbed her.]"

"No shit!" I marveled. "So what'd you do?"

"I quickly got us the hell outta there, back to where we had the radio and our guns stashed. I radioed Da Nang to see if they wanted me to take her out. It sure ruffled feathers. How long does it take you to get a response from command when you radio in an inquiry?"

"Not too long. Two minutes, five minutes or so at the longest."

Gary proceeded: "I didn't hear back from him for, get this, over an hour. Over an hour! It obviously went way up the chain. When our ranking SEAL commander responded back, the decision was not to do it. It was too bad. I had a perfect spot with a clear view of the missile site inspection. We could've pulled it off and disappeared.

"When I got back, my lieutenant bawled me out, telling me never to put him in a position like that again. He wasn't happy. But that's the truth, I got that close." Gary paused as he gulped down the last of his beer. "Now, we all get to camp out together at Nha Be."

Arriving at Nha Be, we all participated in mostly "idiot ops." We didn't have enough bad guys to go around. About the only thing they found for us to do was to ferret out zappers placing underwater charges for our big ships to hit.

Everything was grinding to a halt. While I was going out almost every night in Hi Yien, at Nha Be I got in just ten ops in my final sixty days in-country. They'd finally corralled us into an area where we couldn't find the enemy.

As we drove to Tan Son Nhut for the final time, I couldn't stop thinking about how much everything had changed. How different attitudes were. There were no more discussions or false hopes of winning. Everyone saw the handwriting on the wall—in bold print—leaving a very real sense of frustration. We'd come for a purpose, in support of all the proud traditions that defined the United States of America's armed forces: upholding the security interests of our country; championing the cause of freedom throughout the world; battling the spread of communism amongst the poor, third world countries; assisting implementation of programs such as Operation Handclasp and the Peace Corps around the world. Instead, we became increasingly cynical as reports of vacillation over our national purpose resulted in loss of support, stringent rules and regulations, and the demoralizing realization that there was no intention of winning. So many things went haywire. Defense contractor companies were coming in, with their experimental weapons systems, callously using the war to test things out. A lot of good friends died. We weren't fighting offensively any longer.

"I guess it's a good thing we're going home. I really don't want to be here for the bitter end," I commented to Gallagher as we waited for our plane.

"It burns me to the core to think we're losing this war despite having the capacity to win it." Gallagher sighed. "The world's changing. The thing scaring me the most is there's a vacuum now where the admirals and generals no longer have decisive control over what we do and how we do it. I hope to never be sacrificed by some admin puke or political asshole. I mean, you don't have to look any further than the PRU and LDNN programs."

I nodded knowingly. "I was thinking about that. Just as we got those programs off the ground, they get canceled, or, more correctly, 'scaled back' to the point they no longer work effectively. Damn it! We had them fighting effectively for their own country. Boom! Gone."

We boarded and flew from Saigon to Anchorage, Alaska, on to Travis Air Force Base in California, then back to Virginia Beach. With our demoralization over the war, instead of coming home on a high, we were quiet and somber. *Oh well. I can't wait to see Sandy. We'll get our marriage squared away and everything will be good to go!*

"You going to try for a fourth trip?" I asked Gallagher after we'd landed.

"Nope. It's no longer worth it. I've been asked to take over the training platoon at SEAL Team Two. Training new guys is what's going to be important from now on. I expect you to come with me."

"A teacher, huh? I could enjoy that. I do have a lot of experience." I thought it over for a moment. "Okay!" It was settled.

CHAPTER 18

SOUTHERN EXPOSURE

"**W**HERE'D ALL THESE GUYS COME FROM?" KEENER ASKED AS we sat eating lunch at SEAL Team Two headquarters in Little Creek, Virginia.

"It's funny, isn't it?" I replied. "It's like they're coming out of the woodwork."

"I don't understand it. Jim over there," he said, gesturing toward a man two tables over, "he was telling me, 'I had to go up to Annapolis to teach the students there.' Bob over there, he and Smith went back to UDT to train recruits, and now they're back in the Teams. It's like all of a sudden, we're getting this big influx of guys back into SEAL Teams just as Vietnam is slowing down—ending any meaningful SEAL deployment assignments."

I smiled, nodding my head in agreement. "I think the deal is guys enjoy the status, the money, and the challenge of being in SEAL Teams. But they aren't like you and me, wanting to go into combat."

"I know, Harry. The problem is, because of their rank, they're pulling admin assignments directing training. We learned a lot over there in combat. You remember how we changed a bunch of things from training because we found ways to do it better? How're these guys, without combat duty experience, supposed to direct training?"

"Ah, I don't think it's that big of a deal. Guys like you and me and Gallagher—there's a lot of us going into team leadership and training. I don't think we'll have any problems. They're SEALs, too. I think it'll be like it was in Vietnam. Guys with experience were listened to and followed until the officers and ranking team members got acclimated. I don't think it'll be any different."

Keener grinned. "I hope you're right."

Just then, Al Ashton sat down next to us. "You see who's here?"

"Yeah, we were just talking about the very same thing," I replied.

Big Al shook his head disparagingly. "You know, it's really funny, Harry. The cockroaches are all coming out of the woodwork and all the wood's floating to the surface. Look around! Look at all these guys returning to SEAL Teams." He then mimicked in a sissy, singsong voice, " 'Excuse me, there's a war on; gotta go. Sorry.' Then: 'Hey guys, war's over! I'm back!' "

Keener and I, along with several other combat vets handpicked by Gallagher, were assigned to train new SEAL Team recruits in how to survive and flourish in stealth warfare. Initially, we were to train guys going to Vietnam, but that soon evolved into a program where we took a new platoon from their infancy up until they were ready to fly to their assigned destination. Hot spots all over the world—Soviet-dominated Eastern Europe, South America, Northern Ireland, the Middle East, North Korea, the Philippines—were quickly home to SEALs deployed in undercover clandestine operations. "Technical advisors" were little more than what PRU advisors had been. Vietnam had been great training for counterterrorist insurgency deployment.

From 1970 through 1975, we were allowed to train unencumbered by bureaucratic meddling. Unfortunately, little verbal jabs, innuendo, and snide remarks from combat-hardened veterans directed at those who'd skirted combat duty, began creating a larger and larger chasm between the two. I certainly did my share of harassing.

One development that split the two factions even further apart was that instead of working together, we had gravitated toward separate objectives. In fact, a new headquarters was formed to oversee SEAL Teams, including new quarters for officers to be billeted to, so that in addition to the leadership hierarchy at Little Creek, there was also the *new* headquarters, known as Naval Special Warfare, to oversee the overseers and SEALs stationed around the world. For a while, we coexisted pretty well.

There were, including myself, about a dozen East Coast SEALs and a dozen West Coast SEALs who delighted in really giving these new admin officers the business. We were arrogant, macho, young, brash, invincible "warriors." We had respect for anyone who had slogged through the rice paddies and endured the hellish crucible of war in Vietnam. On the other hand, we didn't appreciate what we felt were misguided orders from guys who flexed their level of rank in our face. We would run into an officer who had not been to Vietnam and had not seen combat, he'd say something to us, and our expression would be a blank, challenging stare. *Who are you?*

On the other hand, if the officer had operated in Vietnam, our response was always a quick salute and a respectful "Yes, sir!" The difference was simply that he'd built his credentials. The other admin officers were met with derision because they had "not made their bones." They'd not led by example. It was a shame that bridges were not established to quell the developing rift that had festered for years at both SEAL Team One and SEAL Team Two. Month by month, the rift grew wider, more obvious, and more vicious. This "insubordination," as the admin guys aptly described our insolence, was tolerated—until we got into positions where we were vulnerable. While we were in our various platoons preparing trainees for life-and-death, antiterrorist situations, we were sanctioned. If we moved too high up the ladder, letters of accusation and innuendo would pour in to command. Unfortunately, that's what admin guys are the most proficient at, writing letters.

Fortunately, I was a good instructor. I easily developed good rapport with my men. I did my best to train them, diagramming in detail how to respond to various enemy actions.

It was now late October 1972. I'd been out for six weeks with my training platoon when we returned to Little Creek. "Hi, honey, I'm home."

"Harry, we have to talk."

"Sure, what's up."

"I'm leaving. I'm being picked up by Jim, you know, my former boyfriend."

My heart fell. I could handle a lot. I understood the stark and hostile world of combat, and could handle it. Although not enjoyable, I brushed aside the admin officers' insults. In my own home, where I let my defenses down and bared my soul, I was caught off guard. It cut deep.

"There's got to be a way to work this out. C'mon. . . . I'm not going back to Vietnam; I can try to keep from any long-term assignment. . . ."

"Harry, let it be. These things happen to good people. Give me some time." Sensing someone driving up in front of the house, she pulled away. "There he is now. I have to go. I'll call you later." That was it. She simply left.

Days stretched into months, and I kept trying to convince Sandy to come home. Slowly her resolve lessened. I determined to rebuild and improve our communication. Whatever it took to make it better.

Finally, she relented. Our marriage was on again.

"Getting away gave me a lot of time to think things over. I've dealt with a lot of things, and I want things to work out between us. If we can be together—if you stay around—we can be happy. When you're gone all the time, I'm lonely and I'm miserable," Sandy explained softly.

"No problem," I said, hopefully.

While I was willing to bend over backwards to put our relationship back together, I wasn't about to put up with assholes giving me orders. I unconsciously infused my frustration into my work and developed a shorter fuse. Fortunately, before it got me into any real trouble, I was placed in a new operational platoon with an officer named Iron Mike Cadden. He was a very good officer. He'd not been to Vietnam, but his instincts and insights as to how SEAL Teams operated—and how to lead effectively—preceded all the "empower your employees" management strategies that later came into vogue.

"I want the platoon in this room. Everyone in here. Close the door."

Quickly we filed in.

"All right, gentlemen. I'm the officer, Constance is the chief." Then, pointing at each man individually, he detailed their responsibility to the team. "Is there any question on anybody's position?"

No one said a word. With a name like Iron Mike, we anticipated more of a my-way-or-the-highway approach.

"We have an operation coming up. We're going to go on a long-range E and E survival mission. It's going to take extensive logistical requirements—planes, trains, and automobiles—we're going to need it all," he said, pointing to the list typed neatly on the manifest. "We have an op order that is difficult at best, and I expect us to shine every moment." He leaned back in his chair, kicking his feet onto the desk, "Okay, Chief. What do you want to do? It's your ball game."

I'd been on this path before. "You're the lieutenant."

"You're the chief. You have the experience. I expect you to make it happen. Make me look good."

"You got it," I assured him.

Rapidly, Iron Mike gained our respect and loyalty. Here was an officer who was willing to listen to us and work as a team to get the job done.

We ran flawless operations. One such op involved parachuting into Vermont in the dead of winter, snow silently swirling around us. We ran a cross-country winter warfare operation that dazzled our opponent, Army 5th Special Warfare out of Fort Devens in Massachusetts. We totally dominated them in every way. Word of our successes reached Naval Special Warfare as well as SEAL deployments around the country.

"Hello, Harry? This is Lieutenant Cadden. Guess what? We've been assigned special duty in South America! You kept abreast of all that's going on down there?" he inquired.

Security briefs were one of the things I grew to enjoy. After several years, the compilation of what I read in the papers and what was disclosed of top-secret operations and intelligence helped me piece together an understanding of world politics. Information about political power brokering, corruption, multinational business interests, CIA and other U.S. Special Forces clandestine operations, and shadowy terrorist organizations—all joined together to yield an amazingly clear picture.

"Sure have. Where're we going? Venezuela, Brazil, or Bolivia?"

"Chile."

This was like saying we were headed into the Soviet Union. U.S. relations with Chile had chilled substantially. "Are we taking United or American Airlines?"

Cadden laughed. "Actually, we're headed to Bolivia. Get squared away and prepared to go in a week."

Going to South America meant an opportunity to implement new technology and methodology forged from our experiences in Vietnam. That aspect was exciting. Telling Sandy was not.

"You've got to be kidding me! What's there to do in Bolivia? How long do you think you'll be gone?"

"I don't know. Probably six months."

Silence ensued as she mulled over my announcement. Slowly, I stood by and watched her temperature rise. Anger flashed in her eyes. "No sooner do we get back together, work hard to rebuild things between us, and you're off and running. Again."

"This is what I do . . . who I am. Besides, a billet to Coronado is supposed to come open about the time I get back. You want more money? It's a great assignment that'll help me make chief."

"I just want you around."

Immediately, her cold shoulder reappeared. My reaction was one of bewildered anger and frustration. "Dammit! I'm leaving for a hazardous mission, and, instead of sending me off with a kiss like everybody else, all I get is this 'poor me' bullshit. I can't believe you."

"You'll be lucky if I'm still here when you get back. I'm telling you, Harry, I just can't take this loneliness anymore. I had no idea what I was getting into when I married you." Her tone of voice rose a little higher.

I'd had enough. "You're never happy! I'm not home enough, I'm not making enough, I'm not this, I'm not that. . . . How about, I'm not here?"

Few words were spoken over the days leading up to my departure. "See ya," was all she said.

It was early 1972, and Latin America was one of the world's hot spots. In the United States, the law stated that fishing rights began in international waters, twelve miles off the coast. A large number of U.S. tuna fishing boats were being seized as countries asserted a *two-hundred-mile* limit. Simultaneously, announcements of kidnappings of foreigners, businessmen, and politicians seemed to be coming in weekly. Argentina, Bolivia, Brazil, Chile, Colombia, Ecuador, Uruguay, and other countries in the region were rife with political unrest, coups d'état, and foreign policy at odds with that of the United States. The governments were being systematically destabilized, seemingly drifting toward leftist and Communist agendas. This alarmed the U.S. government greatly. Argentina had just gone through a bloody military coup d'état. Bolivia, under President Alfredo Ovando Candia, was carrying out a leftist agenda of the Nationalist Revolutionary Movement (MNR). This included nationalizing Gulf Oil Corporation holdings. Gulf screamed bloody murder, as the displaced Bolivian military and civilian elite actually were murdered. We'd been at odds with Ovando since his accusations in 1970 alleging an attempted coup orchestrated by the CIA, Gulf Oil, and a group of military leaders. In October 1970, Ovando was forced to resign and General Juan Jose Torres stepped into the presidency. In August 1971, the leftist Torres was overthrown, putting into place a very right-wing government supported by the United States. Chile, in 1970, had put into power a Marxist, Salvador Allende. Allende had also begun nationalizing foreign (many being U.S.-owned) and domestic companies. American relations with Chile went through the floor when an executive of the Chilean Telephone Company, a subsidiary of ITT, was exposed by American news correspondent Jack Anderson as having written to John McCone, head of the CIA, to encourage military opposition to Allende's inauguration. By then, Allende was battling for his country against rebel insurgents, inflation, unrest, and popular opinion. This stroke of ugly American imperialism, true or not, was the sword he needed to tame public opinion.

We fell into this spiderweb of special interests. Of all the platoons in either SEAL Team One or SEAL Team Two, Lieutenant Cadden's was selected. SEAL teams were placed all over the world, but this Bolivian charge was one of the top assignments.

Due to the rightist regime in place and its proximity to its neighbors, Bolivia was a perfect base from which to operate. Cadden selected me, Manuel Perez, Mike Smith (an eventual representative and deputy treasurer from the state of Vermont), Warrant Officer Paulsen, and Butch Baylett. Manny was a corpsman, spoke Spanish, and was fearless. Mike Smith was a young, polite, and well-liked SEAL who was bright and hardworking. Warrant Officer Paulsen was multitalented and devoted to detail, while Butch Baylett was from the "know no fear, go anywhere, do anything" school. We jelled as a team.

We touched down in La Paz, the capital city of Bolivia. La Paz was a city situated at an elevation of sixteen thousand feet, where nothing really grows except barren rocks. I glanced over at Manny Perez. "¿*Qué pasa, amigo?* Now we can put our Spanish to good use."

"*Sí.* The Vietnamese sure didn't *habla español.*"

"Different country, same smells. Jungles all over the world have a similar feel to them!"

"What jungle smells? Maybe high Andes Mountain smells. Or something."

More familiar odors tingled my senses. "Yeah. Look at the squalor," I said, gesturing in the direction of muddy dirt roads irregularly lined by shanty after shanty, "the stink of raw sewage quickly overpowers everything else."

We settled into our motel rooms, tired after a fourteen-hour flight and the altitude-induced exertion. Quickly, we fell asleep. Suddenly, we were rudely awakened. Almost to a man, we awoke abruptly, feeling as if we were being choked. The air seemed to be about as thin as I'd ever encountered, even worse than the air we dealt with in high-mountain, cold-weather training in Alaska.

La Paz was a city located in a crater between mountain peaks. There was a stark, windswept harshness to the landscape and a lot of filth. Lake Titicaca, on the other hand, lay just a few miles west of La Paz. A gorgeous expanse of water, it was framed against azure blue skies, varied hues of green vegetation, and steep mountain peaks reflected in its mirrored water. Two totally conflicting environments spaced very few miles apart.

We were transported southeast to the town of Cochabamba. Cochabamba was considered the garden city of Bolivia. Where the capital city of La Paz had a desolate, austere appearance, Cochabamba was the exact opposite. Many, if not most, of the foreign dignitaries and ambassadors lived and worked in Cochabamba because of the resortlike, Mediterranean flavor.

Cochabamba was a small mountain city of perhaps 350,000 people. AK-47-toting police and military guards kept the peace. The town nestled against a mountain, and was served by efficient roads and rail transportation. It had modern conveniences and a stable flow of electricity and running water. Our hotel was quaint, merging Bolivian (Aztec) cultural architecture with modern design. The food was excellent, the scenery beautiful.

"Damn!" I blurted, feigning disgust. "It's places like this that makes me long for arctic training in Alaska, or duty in Iceland. Someplace! Anywhere but here!"

Mike Smith didn't miss a beat. "Yep. Sunburns'll kill you."

"Listen up," instructed Lieutenant Cadden. "We have a reception tonight with the Bolivian Special Forces leadership. As you know, part of our responsibilities are to train them in diving, stealth, reconnaissance, demolition, and parachuting. We also might be doing a little border patrol along the Chilean/Bolivian frontier."

All of us enjoyed working with the Bolivians. They seemed genuinely pleased we were there, and worked diligently to learn the techniques we taught them. One of the men I hit it off with was Captain Raul Bonilla. He was from a well-to-do family in La Paz, and his uncle was a high-ranking official in the new Bolivian government. Captain Bonilla enjoyed parachuting almost as much as I did. We'd go up in old, rickety DC-9s with well-used parachutes. As jumpmaster and rigger, I studied every parachute for even the slightest deficiency. Captain Bonilla would join me, bird-dogging my every move.

Water diving in Bolivia was not without its thrills, however. "Raul," I asked as we surfaced, holding onto a tree branch jutting out of the

Río Ichilo, a tributary to the Amazon River, "what's the name of those red-bellied fish? The ones the kids are catching on the riverbank?"

"Piranha," he replied, matter-of-factly.

My eyes widened in disbelief. "Piranha?"

"*Sí,* piranha."

"The same type of piranha that eat every last ounce of a cow or horse or person in a feeding frenzy?"

"*Sí,*" Raul said coyly, measuring my reaction. Suddenly, diving in Bolivian rivers lost a lot of its appeal. Getting wet was one thing. Getting eaten was another!

For some reason, they weren't bothering us, so I loungingly floated on the surface. *If Raul, who obviously knew they were thick here in the river, wasn't kept from diving, then neither would I be.* All of a sudden, a school of perhaps a hundred or more red piranhas came darting in our direction. Raul decided to get out. I was right behind him.

Cadden called us together. "Guys, I've received intel reports of an increase in Communist insurgent activities because of us. Harry, you and Manny are to talk to people around town and let me know if anything comes up."

"Can do, boss," relayed Manny.

Manny and I enjoyed roaming the streets of Cochabamba, as the people were always friendly and the action lively. The rest of the guys had a harder time of things since they didn't speak Spanish very well. They didn't venture too far from the hotel. Manny and I went out again, and it was about eleven P.M. when we returned. The street was totally deserted. "Manny, something's up."

"I noticed. Where is everyone?"

Alarmed, we walked quickly to the bar/grocery store around the corner. As we walked in, a hush fell over the normally boisterous room. Manny and I warily moved to the bar, our senses on edge.

"*¿Qué pasa, mi amigo?*" I asked the barkeeper. (What's happening, my friend?)

Armando, a normally friendly man with a quick wit and ready smile, nervously shot furtive glances toward the door. Hurriedly, he explained that rumors had spread through the area of men asking about Americans. The men asking the questions were known members of the *comunista* movement. "It only means one thing, my friend. Watch your back."

We alerted the rest of the team and made provisional plans. Mike Smith devised and implemented our defensive strategy. We contracted with the Bolivian Special Forces to provide guards, while mattressing our windows. We were escorted to and from our training operations by armored personnel carriers. It was an odd feeling to have trained and perfected cloak-and-dagger techniques only to find ourselves sticking out like sore thumbs.

Nothing ever happened. Preparation was the key to our safety, I was certain. Kidnapping and assassinations continued in the news in South America and throughout the world. We never became headlines. Six months got chewed up in a hurry, as we ran numerous border ops.

"It's hard to believe it's been six months. This last month we've been in so many countries you'd have thought we were travel agents or something."

"We sure saw an awful lot of action. It'll be good to get home and see the family," I concurred. And home we went.

Sandy and I had been together, on and off, for six years. She wasn't home when I got back, so I unpacked and waited expectantly. It was ten P.M. when she got in.

"Hi, honey," I said, hoping for some type of excitement, some type of positive response.

"Hi. I thought you were getting home tomorrow. Good to see you."

She came to me and gave me a peck on the cheek, saying, "It's been a long day and I'm tired. Marnie's been sick. I'm sorry, but I'm going to have to get to bed." She walked across the room, then paused. "Glad you're home."

Gee, what a homecoming.

The next morning, Gallagher called to talk. "Harry, there's an opportunity you need to take advantage of. There's an opening for an instructor in Coronado with SEAL Team One in BUDS (Basic Underwater Diving/SEALs). If you want to make chief early, it's good to be either a recruiter or a training instructor. You won't get independent credit for being a training instructor so long as you stay under anyone's umbrella. If you go to BUDS, it's an actual, independent training. It's a good billet."

"You're probably right."

I told Sandy the opportunity in San Diego was available. She was ecstatic. "San Diego! California! Oh, Harry," she said, throwing her arms around my neck and squeezing tightly. "This could be perfect for you and me. How soon until you find out?"

"I'm not sure. Maybe three to six months."

Finally, maybe things were righting themselves between Sandy and me.

CHAPTER 19

UNRAVELING

"So, HARRY, BEFORE YOU GO TO BUDS, WANT TO GO WITH ME to Europe?" asked Gallagher as we walked into SEAL Team Two headquarters in Little Creek, Virginia.

It was now September 1974. President Richard Nixon had resigned in disgrace from the presidency of the United States. The final Americans had (or would be shortly) returned from Vietnam. A tremendous sense of disenchantment cast a pall over the nation. We had lost an extremely divisive war—America's first loss. From my perspective, we lost it from within, not from having been bested on the battlefield. Nowhere (except perhaps at the more liberal college campuses that gloated at our nation's "comeuppance" at being thwarted in some sort of "ugly American imperialism") was there a more profound impact than in the military. A once proud and noble tradition of military service was being routinely questioned and its shortcomings exposed.

Congress overrode the presidential veto and decreed that only they, not the President as Commander in Chief, were legally able to send the country into war. And, since they were now the purveyors of military sword-wielding, committee after committee was formed to oversee military operations and budgets. Hoops and more hoops, reports and forms and detailed analyses; they were all continually being required to be filled out. This made for more and more admin positions within the Navy and within SEAL Team hierarchy. The bureaucrats had decided to play war and I began to feel I was on the losing team.

I was delighted to spend some time in Europe with Gallagher. Traveling in civilian clothes and performing undercover ops was exciting after trudging through the jungle for so many years. Terrorist activities all over Europe—kidnappings, hijackings, bombings—and, of course, the boiling cauldron of Arab-Israeli discord, made this a plum assignment.

"Listen. Before you go with me, you need to know what's been going on here."

What's going on here? I'd been back for weeks, and had already been briefed and brought fully up to speed as to Team Two happenings. "I'm all ears."

"It's about your wife. She's been hanging around the O club. There's talk she's been sleeping around. I wanted you to know, so you weren't left wondering why everyone's looking at you funny."

I swallowed hard. Sleeping around? *I've been gone for a long time. Maybe it's my fault. Dammit! Not my wife.* A swirl of emotions and a thousand different thoughts poured through my head.

"Harry, I knew you'd take it hard. Look, whether you want my advice or not, I'm giving it to you now. My wife, she understands and accepts who I am and what I do. She lights up when I get home, and teases me about getting out of her hair before I ship out. Sandy's not cut out for this. Here's my advice: Cut your losses. And hers. Then make your decision as to what's best for your career." Gallagher squeezed my arm as he walked off, and smiled. "Do the right thing."

I reeled at the news Gallagher brought me. I could understand how maybe, out of loneliness, an affair could develop. Now I understood that, despite my trying to warm things up between us, it had been to no avail.

I went home and poured myself a stiff rum and Coke. At least I think there was some Coke in it. Then another. Sandy got home late.

The next morning, I awoke early. "Sandy, we need to talk."

Not yet awake, she replied, "Yeah, what is it?"

I got up and made some coffee. She wandered into the kitchen. "Sandy," I stammered, deciding to not hold back, "there's talk around here about you sleeping with other men. Not just an affair, but several men! Spending time at the officers' club. What the hell's the matter with you? Why didn't you talk to me? Do you have any concern over our relationship? Any concern for what I might think?''

"Don't start this shit with me! Here you've been gone all over the place, year after year, leaving me and Marnie to fend for ourselves.'' Instantly, she was wide awake, a fire in her eyes. "But that's besides the point.''

"What do you mean, 'that's beside the point'? That *is* the point!''

"Harry, this is 1974! The whole world is passing you by. Haven't you heard all the leading psychiatrists and psychologists talking about free love and open marriage? It'll blow your mind. And we'll have a much stronger marriage to show for it.''

"Sandy, this is bullshit and you know it! Here you are, screwing not just one guy, but several, behind my back, and—''

She broke into tears. Blindly she shook, tears streaming down her face. "You, you, you don't . . . know . . . you don't know how this has helped us stay together. It has helped me love you more . . . and . . . and . . .'' Stopping to gather herself, she paused, then continued. "You've got to open your mind.''

"How can you say this?'' I protested.

"I thought you would understand. I've heard stories about what went on—what goes on—in Vietnam, the Philippines, Korea, and Europe. All the whores and one-night stands!''

Angry and confused, I went to work. Over the next weeks and months, I battled over and over in my mind what I should do. *Take Gallagher's advice and let her go? Stay the course and deal with "open marriage"?*

Commanding Master Chief Rudy Boesch called me to his office. "Constance. Congratulations! You've been selected as a BUDS instructor beginning ten January.''

"Thanks for letting me know, Rudy,'' I beamed.

"Be there a week early, by three January.''

I had three months before heading to BUDS, so I joined Gallagher in Europe. First we went to Holy Loch, Scotland, where we were housed at a nuclear submarine base. We ran a number of nuclear sub operations, mainly playing cat-and-mouse games with the Soviets. We also did a quick-strike series into northern England with SAS commandos.

We next spent a few weeks in Suda Bay, Crete, before moving into Germany. There we worked with the German Kamphschwimmers (frogmen), doing parachuting and some underwater scuba operations.

The placement of SEALs all over the world led to an escalation in the number of SEAL platoons and trainees. It was a fun time, traveling around the world.

BUDS was a pleasurable assignment. Teaching was something I enjoyed, and I seemed to have a natural knack at rapidly developing rapport with new SEAL recruits. I enjoyed conveying my experiences in the context of teaching how to deal with every possibility that could arise. I was also reunited with my good friend Gary Chamberlin. I was in Coronado for three years, from 1975 through 1977. During that time, I'd maintained my motivation, had received excellent marks in my evaluations, and my ranking within the Teams was high. By 1976, I'd made chief.

At BUDS, the focus was on UDT-style amphibious assault training, land warfare, and underwater scuba training. We had a tight-knit group of combat veterans running training. George "Pigpen" Hudak was there, as were Billy "Bambam" Cheathem, Donny Crawford, "Cowboy" Hayden, and a few other guys who came in and out.

"Harry, are you going to go for the officer training program?" asked Chief Kelley late one evening. "You need to apply. There aren't many guys more deserving than you."

"Thanks," I said, smiling. I received calls from both coasts, all saying, *Do it Harry, do it.*

Each year, three candidates were selected and sent to officers training school to become officers in SEAL Team. They were known as limited duty officers (LDO). They were also called "mustang" officers, since it was their expertise and abilities that gained their advancement, not an academic degree. I put in my paperwork, was evaluated, and was ranked number two in the nation. Everyone congratulated me, knowing my selection was assured. The only man ahead of me was fellow BUDS instructor Billy Cheathem (Cheathem went on to be Commanding Officer of SEAL Team One). Unfortunately, due to budget cuts, the program was only able to fund one position in 1977, thus denying me the opportunity. I was disappointed, but wasn't overly concerned since I would simply reapply the next year.

My time as a BUDS instructor was coming to a close. The normal course of action was to return to a platoon, and I decided to return to SEAL Team Two.

My marriage had dissipated into an uneasy truce. My next career move came down to two choices. One was to move back to Little Creek and resume working with Gallagher. Doing so would virtually guarantee my selection into the LDO program. The other possibility was to run an advanced training base at a forward operating unit in Puerto Rico.

"Harry, take the position in Puerto Rico! You know how our marriage suffered in Virginia. Puerto Rico is warm, exciting, and romantic! All Little Creek offers is divorce. Take Puerto Rico! The sun, the water; we can really get to know each other and put our marriage on the right track," Sandy reasoned.

Puerto Rico it was.

No sooner had I signed the orders to go to Puerto Rico than I received a phone call. "Hello, Harry? Harry Constance?" said a familiar voice on the other end of the phone.

"Yeah. This is Harry," I responded.

"Rudy Boesch here."

At once recognizing the voice, I blurted, "Hello, Rudy! Great to hear from you. What can I do for you?"

Rudy was steadily working his way up the ladder, taking more and more sensitive and critical roles within the Teams. What he said carried a tremendous amount of weight. "Harry, don't go to Puerto Rico. You need to come back to SEAL Team Two. You'll lose everything if you go to Puerto Rico. There's guys there who'll destroy you."

Confused, I said, "But I've already signed the orders of intent."

"Don't worry. You can get out of it. Call your detailer."

"Thanks. I'll think about it."

"Seriously, Constance, think long and hard."

"I will. Thanks for calling."

Rudy and I were never close, but I admired him and he seemed to have taken a liking to me after I hung in and made my SEAL qualifications. I mulled it over for several days, before deciding to stick it out. *Who could he mean when he said "guys who will destroy you"? Everybody seems nice enough—and I can get along with most anybody.*

It didn't take long to recognize what, and who, Rudy alluded to. There were two officers who didn't like me from the day I arrived. My combat experience and attitude drove a wedge between us. I had the experience; they didn't. I had the medals and ribbons to show for it; they didn't. I was the one guys were always buying drinks for; they weren't. I was the one receiving the calls requesting special duties abroad. I was the one who had first-name communication with many of the Special Warfare officers in the Pentagon.

I walked right into a hurricane I didn't see coming. Shortly after Vietnam, I'd had a run-in with a Lieutenant Meese. We'd argued over tactics, it became heated, and I'd shown him up. I'd just returned from war, having practiced and perfected quick-strike attacks, and I had it down. Meese was absolutely certain his strategy was superior. I had been a little too young, a little too brash, and a lot too vocal in my contempt for his arrogant insistence that his untried strategies were superior to battle-tested strikes. Instead of an objective debate over merit, our disagreement escalated into a high-stakes standoff. It never should have. My methodology went like clockwork, quick, lethal, and clean. His stratagem misfired. Grudgingly, he had shaken my hand and mumbled something about there being benefits to being in combat. I had forgotten the incident. Lieutenant Meese had not. My new bosses were mad and about to get even.

I was supposed to take over training for the SEALs detailed there. The unit in Puerto Rico was perfecting deep-water diving, utilizing barium chambers for pressure research, and working with underwater submarine operations.

"Constance."

"Hello, Lieutenant," I replied. "Good to see you again."

"Likewise. Your job is to oversee engineering. You are responsible for keeping the boats operational, as well as the jeeps and trucks in running order. Got that?" Meese instructed.

"The job details I put in for involved advanced training tactics. That's what I'm here for."

"No. Things have changed. You can train the motor pool," Meese said, a sarcastic grin across his face.

Lieutenant Quist, his assistant, chimed in, almost gloating, "We can't function if the boats and trucks aren't working. That's your only job. Glad you're here."

Obviously, I'd made a mistake. I sat down on our sofa and gazed out over the turquoise-blue Caribbean ocean. *How could I have been so stupid? I even got a call from Rudy—a warning—a clear wake-up call.*

Thus, my primary duty was as chief of the motor pool. My secondary responsibility was as a Diving Supervisor. I had gone through school outside of Washington, D.C., specifically to augment my diving credentials and to receive my Hyperbaric Chamber Operator/Supervisor credentials so I could provide these services in Puerto Rico.

Another duty I worked at after working hours was with the skydiving club. I was voted in as president by the members because of my certification as jumpmaster and rigger.

Sandy walked through the door. "Oh, hi hon," she said, busily headed toward the bedroom.

"Sandy, can I talk to you?" I asked, wanting to discuss my predicament and get her thoughts.

"Um, not now. I've met some girls and we're going out. I've got just enough time to change my clothes and get out of here. I'll talk to you tonight. See ya."

Night after night, Sandy came home late. She loved visiting her circuit of clubs and friends. More and more she was gone.

"I have to admit, it sure isn't what I signed up for," I confided in Donald Weightman as we sat drinking a beer in the hot, humid Caribbean swelter.

"You're getting screwed, you know it? I can't believe the way those assholes are treating you," Donald charged.

Donald Weightman was all of six feet four, and 240 pounds. Blond-haired and blue-eyed like me, he could have passed for the bronzed and chiseled poster boy of SEAL Teams. He was a SEAL Team corpsman, so we all called him Doc. In Vietnam, he fought bravely with his SEAL comrades. The two of us became friends.

"I know, Doc. It's crazy. I feel like I'm being pulled apart. The primary reason I came here was to attempt to salvage my marriage. I feel like I am being torn on the one hand by Sandy, and on the other hand by Meese and Quist."

"What are you going to do?"

"About the only thing I can do, just suck it up and try to catch a break until I can get back into the platoons."

Later, after I returned home from work, Sandy informed me, "By the way, tomorrow I've been invited to a Tupperware party at my friend's house."

"That's nice."

"You want to go?"

"Tupperware party? I don't think so."

Rumors began filtering in about Sandy and her girlfriends getting together for luncheon dates. They would invite one guy to join them. After eating, they drew straws to see who got to have sex with him as the others watched—or joined in. *Puerto Rico was supposed to help our marriage,* I thought, angrily.

A new platoon arrived with fourteen SEALs ready for training in underwater demolitions. Two were old friends of mine, Bobby Osborne and Butch Baylett.

Pulling me aside, Bobby, Butch, and another SEAL by the name of Joe Camp wanted to talk with me. "Harry, a certain three-letter agency has hired us to provide training in insurgency and guerrilla warfare techniques to a few subjects in Venezuela," reported Bobby.

Butch cut in excitedly. "We need someone like you, Harry. Someone well versed in combat skills. I assure you, it's well worth your time! We need you for about a month."

Bobby lifted his beer as if to emphasize his point. "This is worth several thousand dollars to you. As a matter of fact, how does five thousand dollars in a month's time sound? Plus expense money, a plane ticket, and all that hotel stuff. The Agency will take care of you. I'm on my way down to Caracas to set things up."

I related what I'd been through and my frustrations. "Count me in for this!"

"Good," Butch said, smiling. "You'll get detailed instructions, money and tickets delivered here sometime next week. All you have to do is to make sure you can get the time off, have your operating gear ready, and make sure your passport is good to go."

Three weeks later, my gear was packed, leave approved, and tickets from San Juan to Miami to Caracas, Venezuela, were in hand. I told Sandy, Doc Weightman, and Dave Paaaina what I was up to. Paaaina was a huge mountain of a Hawaiian man, a legend in martial arts. Dave was scary, he was so good. I'd helped him get into SEAL Team.

Doc was the first to respond. "No kidding! You're going to work in the same project as Bobby? You couldn't have picked a better time to get out of here, the way Meese is on your ass."

"No kidding."

Paaaina, always quick with off-the-wall one-liners, stated, "Don't forget to sharpen your knife, stupid!" (Translation: Be careful and watch your back.)

Three days before I was to set out, on Tuesday morning at two A.M., the phone rang. Groggily, I picked up the receiver. "Hello, Constance."

Even half asleep, I recognized the voice on the other end of the line immediately. "You'd be real smart not to go. Something's gone wrong—you'd be smart to bow out," Gallagher intoned cryptically.

Instantly, I was wide awake. I grappled with Gallagher's words over and over in my mind for hours. By seven A.M., just before leaving for work, I called the number Butch had given me in case I couldn't go. "Butch, Harry. Sorry, can't go." I hung up the phone, depressed.

A little more than a week later, I was in my office when SEAL Chief Charlie Bump walked in, a pained expression on his face. "You won't believe the phone call we just got. Remember that op Bob and Joe were on? In Venezuela? Well, they just got toasted. It seems they were being chased by the hoard [government troops from Venezuela]. They radioed for extraction and the Agency left them hanging out to dry. The hoard overran them. End of story. Everyone to the bar and have a drink on them."

Stunned, I wandered from the office, a numb realization of why Gallagher had called.

"You mean to say they were just left behind?" inquired Big Gene Gardner, one of several new SEALs present.

Bump shrugged. "Just another snafu. You know how it is."

Paaaina was puzzled. "What're you saying? Was it a bureaucratic screwup, or was it deliberate?"

Tom Keith, who served with me in my second platoon in Vietnam, replied, "They should've picked the guys up. I'm sure the Agency said, 'To hell with them.' It probably went something like, 'We could get our plane shot down and it'll look bad. We can't let people know where we are and what we're doing. How could we explain our being some-place we're not supposed to be to a hostile Congress. Turn off the radio and let's go have a drink,' is probably accurate."

Gardner still had a hard time grasping that an American government agency would not do everything in its power to save American lives. "You really think the government conspired in this case?"

"Gene," I started, "almost all of us have worked for the Agency at one time or another. There are unwritten codes of conduct each of us will attest to based upon our experiences. The Agency only takes care of their own. Any contract agents, for example, us, are considered expendable. They were obviously doing things they weren't supposed to be doing. When the heat went up, they refused to take the risk of being found out. They probably said something to the effect, 'Besides, if they're really SEALs, they'll get themselves out of trouble.' "

Bump furthered, "They just didn't want to expend any assets. They figured wasting them was easier." He shrugged. "They cut their losses."

A pained sense of loss hung over the room. We all knew Bobby and Joe. Doc Weightman, trying to loosen us up, decided to let me have it.

"You could've been there. You could've been toasted and gone out in a blaze of glory. Since you're not, how about buying another round of drinks!"

Meese continued to pull the rope tighter around my neck. I was being jerked around on a routine basis.

"You are not to take the boats out. Don't tell me you need to test them! I want you, being the chief, to stay at the docks and at the motor pool yard. You are diving far too much. We have plenty of work needing to get done without you running around. Got that?" he asked, pushing my buttons. "By the way, I am not at all pleased with your performance. I'm sorry, but you leave me no alternative but to lower your evaluations."

"You lousy son of a bitch! Do you realize what you're doing? No wonder they plunked your sorry ass down here in this rat hole. All you admin pukes care about is your cutesy little games and politics. My orders were to provide advanced training, deep-water dive training, and not motor pool duty!"

"Your duties are to do whatever the hell I tell you they are!"

"Harry, what's wrong with you?" inquired Doc Weightman as we sat at the bar. "Do you think drinking yourself into oblivion will make it better? Where's the 'Hooyah, frogman!' can-do, go-through-walls SEAL I know?"

"This is my career they're screwing with. It's been spotless up till now! It's out of my control. Up until this point, my evaluations were perfect. I was proud to accept whatever happened—even the screw-ups—because it was me pushing the buttons. You see what's going on."

"You aren't powerless. A lot of what's gone on is your fault! You've lost your sense of humor. You're snapping at everybody—biting their head off at any little thing."

"You're right," I mumbled, recognizing the obvious. "Thanks for the pep talk, Doc." I left the club and went home.

Unfortunately, I was too late. My boss got madder and madder, delighting in my destruction. If I didn't do anything, something would happen. The end result was my boss fired me, and my wife left me. What a month!

I was ushered into Lieutenant Meese's office. "Have a seat, Constance."

I sat, knowing full well what was about to occur and powerless to stop it.

"We no longer think you can perform the minimum duties of a SEAL. We're converting you back to regular Navy, dropping your quals as a frogman. That'll be all."

Solemnly and heavily, I departed. I'd gone, in less than eighteen months, from the top of SEAL Team ratings to being released. I had been in the top five in the nation. Now I was being terminated, in early January 1979, because I "didn't know what I was doing." I'd descended from perfect 4.0 ratings to zero.

Well, at least I have some time off now prior to my new assignment. I need to get away. I think I'll go sailing.

It was an eight-hour sail from each island in the Virgin Island chain. I rented a twenty-seven-foot sailboat and set out. Leaving early, I sailed to St. Thomas. The warmth, water, sun, and tropical sea breezes intermingled in a peaceful respite after so many months of turmoil. For ten days, I sailed from island to island. I anchored in pristine lagoons, completely uninhabited.

After going through the checklist of boat system shutdowns, it would be midafternoon and I'd swim ashore. My clothes, food, and wine were wrapped in plastic bags. Once ashore, I took my diving gear and dove for lobster. Next, I foraged through the deserted, lush idyllic garden area for freshwater to rinse the salty ocean brine off of me and to fill my lobster pot. I then gathered branches and twigs for a fire.

I cannot begin to describe how mentally soothing it was to sit there on a gorgeous sandy beach, turquoise water shimmering before me, warm and gentle breezes softly moving through the leaves, delicious lobster and sourdough bread, a glass of wine. . . . I watched the sunset until all that was left was the flicker of the firelight dancing among the shadows. Day by day, my bearings and perspective returned. Life would be all right. I decided I could handle things in a dignified and controlled fashion. It was a defining moment for me. I would not let the recent events destroy me.

When I returned home, Sandy was set to leave. I was surprised she was still there. "We'll be leaving within a couple of weeks. It's for the best. Too bad things between us didn't work out," she stated, flatly. "I tried. You have a problem. You have to learn to let go. Anyway, I'll see you. I'm moving back to Virginia to stay with my parents for a while until my things arrive."

The next morning, the Naval detailer called. "Where would you like to go, Chief?"

"I really don't care," I responded. "What's available?"

"How about we give you a ship out of Hawaii?"

"That'll work," I said, surprised. *This could be a good assignment.*

"I got my call from the Naval detailer today," I informed Sandy. "It looks like I've got another stint in paradise. They're sending me to Hawaii."

"Hawaii? Hmm. Really?"

It didn't take long for Sandy to realize Hawaii was too alluring a place to pass up. "Harry, I've changed my mind. I'd like to give things another try. We're both older and wiser now. I think we'll go with you."

"Whatever."

It was March 1979 when we arrived in Hawaii. I was assigned to the USS *Whipple*. It was a whole new experience for me. While I was learning my position, Sandy wasn't doing much more than hanging out at the house. As a result, we really did make progress. We went out and had many great times together. We loved going to the beach, taking a bottle of wine, and watching the sunset. She even did some snorkeling, hiking, and diving with me.

Work went well, as I moved from being someone who basically hadn't been on a ship to qualifying as Engineering Officer of the Watch, then Officer of the Deck, in less than a year. It was record time. I received all the qualifications I could possibly attain for a surface sailor. When we shipped out overseas, I put long hours in, motivated to make the most of where I was. I was accorded respect as chief and as a former SEAL.

I had an excellent first class petty officer by the name of Phil DeSoto. He taught me what it meant to be a chief in the Navy (compared with being a chief in SEAL Teams). We became fast friends. In turn, I taught Phil to scuba dive and skydive.

On weekends, we skydived from ten thousand feet. Playing, we would fly apart, then back together, bump, bump, bump. Skydiving was an incredible experience, and we went whenever we could.

About this time, I received an urgent call from Puerto Rico. "Chief Constance? Harry Constance?" came a voice on the other end of the line.

"Who wants to know?" I said, warily.

"I regret to inform you, but you must return immediately to the Naval Station here in Puerto Rico. You're accused of stealing a parachute."

"What? Stealing a parachute? You've got to be kidding me!"

"Sorry, Chief. I'm not. Talk with a lawyer if you want, but be here in four days—by next Wednesday, twelve August 1981."

I grabbed my gear, made a few phone calls, got a lawyer, and caught the next plane headed to the mainland. By Monday evening, my attorney and I were back in Puerto Rico.

"Hello, Jorge?" I inquired, "It's me, Harry Constance. Yeah, right, the blond-haired guy. Hey listen, remember the parachute I bought from you? Good. No, nothing's wrong with it. My problem is the Commanding Officer here at the Naval Station is claiming I stole it from him. I know I bought it from you, but that's what he's saying. I need for you to try to find your receipt from when I bought it, and to testify on my behalf that I did buy it from you. I'm sorry to involve you in all this, but it's very serious. You will? Great! Thanks a lot. I'll be by tomorrow to see you after I get more information as to what's going on. Bye."

I spent Tuesday getting my documentation and witnesses together, then had dinner with Doc Weightman. We reminisced about the past few years. "Great to see you again. I didn't think I'd be still facing Meese with three thousand miles between us! I appreciate your support."

"No problem," Don commented. "What're corpsmen for, anyway? By the way, are you still married to that same gal?"

"Yes, believe it or not, I am."

He shook his head and smiled. Changing subjects, he inquired, "Remember when you were helping us with the hyperbaric chamber testing and the deep-water dives?"

I nodded. "Yeah."

"We've gotten very good with it. We're saving lives all the time for a lot of Navy guys, as well as many local divers who get bent. Remember that first guy we tried to save in there, the guy with his lungs bulging out his chest? We've had a bunch more of those, and we've figured out how to save them," Doc recounted proudly.

"Ah, that's great," I agreed.

"Harry, I've never seen someone go through more garbage than you. What's the story? Are you one of those guys who run around with a big Hit Me sign all over him?"

I shrugged, then shook my head from side to side. "I've wondered about that myself—a lot lately."

The next day, Wednesday, I took my place before a court martial tribunal consisting of three military judges. After my being sworn in, the CO, Lieutenant Meese, submitted the allegations against me.

Glaring at me with an arrogant, "I'm going to destroy you" look in his eyes, Meese began. "Harry Constance willfully and in full knowledge, did break into my office on or about twenty-three July 1979 when he was stationed here as Motor Pool Chief. The most valuable item stolen was a bright yellow parachute." He went on to describe the parachute in great detail.

He walked casually over to the parachute, clearly enjoying his buildup to his coup de grâce—his conclusive, damning proof. Slowly and deliberately, he pulled out the parachute from its backpack. "Please note the yellow coloration of the parachute. You can see for yourself that this is clearly the parachute I described." He turned to his Administrative Assistant. "Does this look identical to the parachute stolen from my office?"

Lieutenant Quist nodded. "Yes, sir."

"In addition to the parachute, there were several other items missing. I cannot prove he took those. But, I can prove Harry Constance also used the phones here at the station to make personal calls totaling at least, but not limited to, one hundred and fifty dollars!" He carried a dossier of documents I assumed contained the phone bills to the bench.

"The evidence is, in addition to the fact Walter Harry Constance stole these items, he also was stripped of his SEAL qualifications due to inept performance and dereliction of duty."

This angered me. Meese was relishing recounting how I'd been disgraced. "Objection, Your Honors!" my lawyer barked. "That has nothing to do with the parachute, and is clearly an attempt at discrediting Chief Constance!"

"Sit down, Lieutenant," the judge to the right insisted, pointing at Lieutenant Sunday, my attorney. "This is not *Perry Mason.* This is a military tribunal."

Lieutenant Meese stared at me, a faint smile pursing his lips, then continued, "Unfortunately, these actions, relieving Chief Constance of his SEAL Team qualifications had to be administered by me. It is my feeling that Walter Harry Constance retaliated by stealing the items in question. I think you'll have to agree." Satisfied, Meese sat down.

The judge in the middle looked at Lieutenant Sunday. "Lieutenant, would you care to respond to the allegations?"

"Yes, Your Honor, I would. First of all, let me call Jorge Gonzales to the stand.'' Jorge stood and walked to the witness stand, the parachute on the evidence table in front of him. ''Could you state for the court your name and occupation, please.''

''My name is Jorge Gonzales. I run a jump and dive shop here in San Juan. I sell all types of parachutes and skydiving equipment: helmets, goggles, boots, scarves, you name it. I also have a full-service dive shop.''

''Do you recognize the parachute in front of you?''

''Yes.''

''Do you have a receipt from when Chief Constance purchased a parachute from you in August 1979?''

''I do. I have it here with me.''

''Would you care to read off the serial number from the receipt, please.''

''Uh, yes, it is D4475R957F.''

''Your Honors, I wish to admit this into evidence at this time.'' He retrieved the receipt from Jorge and handed it to the judges, then turned his attention back to Jorge. ''Would you care to show where the serial number of the parachute in front of you is located?''

Jorge turned the harness upside down and pointed to the metal plate with the engraved serial number on it. ''The number is D4475R957F.''

''I appreciate the CO's description of the parachute. They are obviously similar. However, he has the wrong serial number. Further, Mr. Gonzales here swears under oath—and has the receipt to prove it—that he sold my client the parachute in question.''

''Your Honors!'' demanded Lieutenant Meese, visibly outraged that we were able to produce Jorge and the receipt nearly two years later and in such a short time. ''I am certain, if we recheck our records, we will find that same serial number within our records. That parachute was stolen from me!!''

Now it was the judges' turn to reprimand Meese. ''Please sit down, Commander.''

''Would you care to comment on the phone usage?'' inquired the judge on the right as he looked at me.

I walked to the bench and was handed the phone bills, with my calls highlighted. They were calls to a Long Island, New York, number. Then it dawned on me. *Oh, yeah! I remember these.* ''Your Honors,'' I responded confidently, ''these calls were, in fact, made by me. The number is to a mail order skydiving shop with great pricing and availability for equipment. I assisted the SEAL detachment here in Puerto Rico as a rigger and as jumpmaster on a number of occasions. Most of these calls were to obtain equipment, for the skydiving club, quicker and at prices cheaper than anywhere else. My understanding is that the rules clearly state that there is a clear directive allowing for the utilization of military assets for an approved recreational activity. I was president of the skydiving club here. If you call that number there,'' I said, pointing at the phone bill, ''you'll reach the company. Those calls are not in any way personal calls to friends or family.''

The judges considered my explanation. ''We will take a fifteen-minute recess while we determine our decision. Everyone is to be back and seated in this room at eleven-twenty-five A.M. prompt.''

After deliberating, the judges solemnly stood to address me. ''Chief Constance, you have been charged for the very serious claim of theft of government property. Based upon the evidence presented, we find you not guilty.''

I let out a huge sigh of relief, shook Lieutenant Sunday's hand, then glanced over at Meese. He refused to look at me, instead staring, stone-faced, straight ahead.

''However,'' the judge implored as he continued, ''with regards to the charge of misuse of government property, we find you guilty as charged. You are hereby fined the sum of one hundred fifty dollars. After paying the fine, you are free to go. Case closed.''

Doc Weightman waited at the back of the room with Dave Paaaina. Both of them never lost faith in me. As we walked out, they congratulated me. ''You should've been totally cleared of everything. They knew you were being set up! You shouldn't have even gotten a fine!''

''Ah, it's just a slap on the wrist. It could've been much, much worse. With the way my luck's been going, I could've been thrown in the brig for who knows what. Damn the evidence! A hundred fifty bucks to fly all the way from Hawaii to Puerto Rico to see my friends Doc and Paaaina? What a deal,'' I said, chuckling.

A few weeks after returning from Puerto Rico, I received a call from Frank Thornton, now a lieutenant in SEAL Team One. ''Hello, Constance. Thornton.''

Surprised and pleased at hearing his voice, I said, ''Great to hear from you! What's up?''

''Well, Harry, I always felt you were worth something. I couldn't believe what occurred in Puerto Rico. From what I understand, though, you shouldn't have gone there in the first place. Do you want reinstatement back into the Teams?''

I was stunned. No one had been thrown out of SEAL Teams and returned. "Damn right I do! But how?"

"Write me a letter about why you want to come back, and attach it to a special request chit."

"Okay. Then what?" was all I said, overwhelmed at the impossibility being tendered to me. "I can't believe this!"

"Send it to me and I'll personally take it to Uncle Dave."

"Thank you, Frank. You think seriously it'll do any good?"

"Uncle Dave's the one that wants you. I'm counting on you not to let us down. Uncle Dave'll be glad you want back in."

Stunned and overjoyed, I felt reborn, like I'd been granted a new lease on life. *Nobody gets back in!*

When I returned from my final cruise aboard the USS *Whipple*, Sandy was waiting for me. "Harry, I want a divorce."

I looked at her long and hard, then asked, "Is there someone else again this time?"

"No. It's for the best. There's no one else in my life. It's time. It's over. Here's the papers. I need for you to look them over and we can sign in a couple of days. I want fifteen thousand dollars and I'll waive any and all other requests."

We arranged to meet at a small café in downtown Honolulu, near Waikiki. I walked in, handed her a copy of the judge's decree, her copy of what my lawyer said, a copy of the agreement on what she was to receive, and a check for $15,000. "The divorce is final. This is all yours," I said, gesturing at the check. "I'll agree to take Marnie and raise her as if she was my own because I love her."

She carefully folded the papers, then placed the check in her purse. Sipping on her piña colada, she smiled. "Well, I just want you to know that I am now going with an Air Force officer who's a pilot. Him and I are going to fly around the world on this fifteen thousand. We're going to party for the rest of our lives. You can't believe how well we match!" Sipping the last drops from her drink, Sandy stood and walked out, leaving me with the tab.

I went home and tried to explain to fourteen-year-old Marnie why her mother wasn't coming back. She cried on and off for most of the evening. *I just hope I can be a good parent to her with all the demands of SEAL Team One.*

CHAPTER 20

IN AGAIN

UNCLE DAVE SCHAIBLE WAS THE ORIGINAL SECRET AGENT man. He taught some of this country's best spies invaluable techniques. He showed us, as young SEALs, how a SEAL took it in the face and kept going. Obviously, I am biased in my admiration for Uncle Dave, but his exploits and expertise were legendary. In November 1981, he was Commodore of all Naval Special Warfare Units (including SEAL Team operations) in the western United States and Far East. For him to take interest in me was gratifying, to say the least.

The *Whipple* was anchored in Pearl Harbor when I got the call. "Chief Constance, lay to the quarterdeck. You have a phone call."

Arriving, I picked up the phone. "Hello."

"Constance, this is Uncle Dave," said the voice on the other end.

"As in Schaible?"

"As in no shit," he said. "What the hell are you doing in Hawaii?"

"Guarding our coast, sir."

"Why don't you grow up and come to work for me?"

"Sir, I got beat up and thrown away. I opened my mouth and probably got what I deserved. I don't want to tarnish your reputation."

"You never will," he confided. "I know you too well. That's why I'm calling you. I want you to come back to work for me. No one else.

I've got the paperwork you sent me." Commodore Schaible stated, "I want you to know, I took your paperwork to Washington, D.C., and your request has been approved."

My loyalty to Gallagher was beyond question. Uncle Dave was the only other man I would willingly take a bullet for. "Whatever you want, I'll go through hell to accomplish." Uncle Dave would back me up and make sure that I and my men had whatever we needed to per- form the duties I knew were coming. The Venezuelan disaster was just one of many examples that underscored the perilous world we operated in. Uncle Dave fully understood this. "Report to my office on ten November."

"I'll be there."

As ordered, I walked into Commodore Schaible's office at exactly eight A.M., November 10. "Who are you?" asked the secretary.

"I'm Chief Constance. I'm here to see the Commodore."

The security guard quickly got in front of me. "Excuse me! You'll have to back out of the room," he stated authoritatively.

I turned to him. "No. I don't think so."

He got real excited, thinking he had a fight on his hands. "Don't make me have you thrown out of this room," he insisted.

"Don't try."

He moved toward me. I lifted my hand and pointed at him. "You're going to get hurt, slick. I'm here to see Uncle Dave."

"Uncle Dave?" Then it registered with him, and his face brightened. "Uncle Dave?"

"Ask," I pressed. "He's expecting me."

The guard opened the inner door leading to Commodore Schaible's office. "Excuse me, sir. I'm sorry to bother you. There's a Chief Con- stance here who says he's going to kick my ass if he can't see you."

"Send the asshole in here!" he bellowed loudly.

As I walked in, Uncle Dave smiled warmly. "Hey, dickhead! Didn't I ever teach you anything!" For the next five minutes, he gave me a tongue-lashing only a SEAL could appreciate! Vintage throwback to training days.

After we discussed old times, the talk changed to what he wanted from me. He detailed his objectives along the Pacific Rim, what was occurring politically, along with his realistic expectations for the next twenty-four months. I was to develop a platoon for quick-strike tactics.

"Because of your combat experience, we have selected you to run a contingency platoon."

"Been there, done that."

"You and Gary Chamberlin are going to be leaders in counterterrorist training for SEAL Team One."

It was great to be paired with Chambo. We quickly got caught up on what we'd been up to. Gary had just returned from an advisor role in Afghanistan. "I'm glad you're back!"

"This should be fun," I remarked, "finally getting an opportunity to work together." Over the next few years, Gary and I devised a whole new training program for SEAL Team One for counterterrorist operations. I was in constant, weekly communication with Uncle Dave.

The team I was assigned to train consisted of some of the finest men I'd come across. We worked together for several years, with almost all of the men going on to the newly formed SEAL Team Six. SEAL Team Six was Captain Richard Marcinko's creation of the "next level" of SEAL Team operators. They were the specialist's specialist. Marcinko wanted his men to go deep undercover, with resources to operate in Middle Eastern, European, and South American countries to gain acceptance in the circles of drug kingpins and warlords who were coming to prominence as the terror power-brokers. Demo Dick also, rightly, believed you needed to train in the Middle East for the Middle East, and not in the Arizona or Nevada deserts. He fought against rules and regulations, time and time again. He made a lot of people angry, but he was on the mark.

Regardless of dissension surrounding Marcinko, SEAL Team Six was there to stay. In fact, Six was plucked away from the Navy and placed under operational control of Joint Special Operations Command at Fort Bragg, North Carolina. This unit was deemed by the Pentagon necessary to coordinate a joint response of the elite teams—Delta Force, SEALs, and Green Berets. To be chosen for SEAL Team Six was a coveted assignment. I had Dave Taquard, Dan Plussard, Ted Traver, Dan O'Toole, Jerry Manning, all promoted on to Six.

In counterterrorism, quickness and precision were paramount. We developed techniques never used before. Some were hybrid techniques we'd learned from the Israelis, while others were a response to current necessity. We utilized state-of-the-art electronic and satellite surveillance intelligence.

There were three specific kinds of ops we trained diligently on. The first was how to conduct a short-airfield, Entebbe-style raid on an aircraft to neutralize the terrorists inside. The second operation involved how to board a ship at sea and take it over.

The third kind of operation, known as desert missile ops, involved long-range raids into desert environs. It was in this particular phase of training that we undertook some interesting missions. We used satellite photos to identify missile batteries. That was easy enough. The hard part was destroying those batteries. If we used aircraft, we had two problems to contend with. First, the country would scream bloody murder over violation of sovereign airspace. The second problem was penetrating the air defenses set up to protect their sovereign airspace. Our charge was to figure out a way to sneak in, blow up the missile batteries, then extract without it being a "suicide op." We became proficient in traversing across the desert to the missile base. After breaching perimeter security and setting the charge at the site, we lit up the night sky. Quickly, we left everything we'd brought, stripped down to T-shirt, running shorts and shoes, and a web belt with lightweight supplies. We ran for three hours straight, then stopped. This was our window of opportunity. At that point, we dug foxholes in the sand, covering ourselves with reverse-detectable blankets. What those blankets did was to shield the infrared radiation our bodies gave off. This hid us from low-flying reconnaissance aircraft searching for our heat pattern in their infrared-detection scopes. The next night we arose and ran for hours, until we reached the border. Several times, we ran for more than a week, covering one hundred miles or more.

An offshoot of this mission involved placing homing devices on key installations for smart bombs to hone in on. A lot of cruise missiles and smart bombs are only as smart as the object they're homing in on. Many, if not all, of the missiles we watched strike buildings in Baghdad, Iraq, during the Gulf War struck buildings with homing devices placed by SEALs.

Yet another outgrowth of this special training op involved nuclear weaponry. We studied the defenses of the Sandia Nuclear Lab, located in Albuquerque, New Mexico, on the premises of Kirkland Air Force Base. The Department of Energy consulted Special Operations and our contingency platoon regarding the safety of their nuclear stockpile. We conveyed our belief that they were vulnerable.

Concerned, the DOE asked us to attempt to prove our assertion that we could, in fact, steal a nuclear warhead. We met with Sandia officials to outline the details.

"You men don't have a prayer," the CO of Sandia's defense forces said confidently. "There's no way in hell you can breach the perimeter, get past the bars and chains, and hope to get to the warheads—let alone try to escape with one.''

"Tell you what," I replied, equally confident. "We think you have a flaw in your defenses. I truly hope you don't. For the sake of this exercise, let's use a fifty-five-gallon drum since it's about the same size as a tactical nuclear warhead. Fill it with sand until it weighs the same as a nuke. Then clearly mark it as 'TRAINING,' so we'll know it's the one to grab.''

"I don't know why we have to play this idiotic game. There is no way! You're wasting our time.''

"We'll see.''

They knew we were coming, and still we pulled it off. Our unit, black-faced and shrouded in black, silently penetrated the outer perimeter. We "took out" several key guards, installing members of our team in their place. Next, we exploded a hole into the warhead depot. It was an eerie feeling, staring at real nuclear warheads, knowing the awesome destructive capabilities sitting before us. Immediately, we located the "TRAINING" fifty-five-gallon drum and hoisted it onto the shoulders of two of our men. Out we went, less than two minutes after entering, well before Sandia's Reaction Force could respond. We'd set up a number of training delaying devices (had it been real, modern-generation claymore mines would have been used). The benefit of these was that when the Reaction Force was diving for cover, they couldn't be running after us. For those who continued running, we had two snipers set at 45-degree angles. Armed with night scopes effective at from 800 to 1,000 yards away, they easily deterred the remnant force that made it past the delaying devices. We vanished into the pure New Mexico night air.

As is always the case, we were accused of cheating. I relished hearing the admin report blasting our attack as being outside the rules, outside the boundaries of fair play. Typical admin reaction at being bested. As if terrorists were going to announce they were coming, play with non lethal weaponry, and otherwise "play fair.''

To my chagrin, Uncle Dave was reassigned to the Pentagon, picking up his fourth star in the process. Gone were my day-to-day conversations with him. This bode poorly for me, as Uncle Dave shielded and supported the training activities Gary and I were conducting. Several of the senior officers under Uncle Dave resented our circumventing rank and working directly for him. They resented that we didn't have to answer to them. Exit Uncle Dave; enter conflict. They didn't like me, and they didn't like Gary.

Marnie and I were settled into a house, and she was registered at school. I had arranged with neighbors for her after-school care while I worked. I had done my best to provide some sort of father-daughter stability in the few minutes and hours we had together. Then the phone rang.

"Mom! Hi! Where are you? You are! When do I get to see you? Good! Yeah, here's Dad."

As soon as I held the phone to my ear, Sandy launched into an account of what had happened to her and how sorry she was for leaving me. "We had a great time traveling all over. We went to all the major countries in Europe. The money flowed like water. We went back to Hawaii. After the money was gone, you know what he said to me?" she queried, somehow thinking I'd feel bad about her squandering $15,000.

"What did he say?"

"You won't believe what a louse he is! He said, 'I don't date single chicks, and I don't date chicks without any coin.' Can you believe he would treat me like that after all the money I spent on him? Harry, I've thought a lot about what you said before I left. I'm sorry I was so stupid. I guess I didn't realize what I had until seeing you from a distance. James, the Air Force pilot, swept me off my feet. The longer we were together, the more I realized what a good man you really are." She changed her approach. "You know, Marnie really needs a mother—she needs me. With you gone as much as you are, I'd really like to be there for her. And for you. If you could find it in your heart to forgive me, I promise I'll be the wife you need me to be. No more affairs. Please, Harry, I'm begging you."

She pushed all the right buttons. Soon she was in Coronado. Things went well—for about three weeks. Yet again, she was gone.

Gary and I took our contingency platoons to Subic Bay, Philippines. The two senior officers in the Philippines were Lieutenant Theodore Grabowsky (nicknamed "Grub"), Detachment Commander, and Lieutenant George Worthington (nicknamed "Gorgeous George" because he used hairspray and worked on his tan), the Air Operations Officer.

Not long after we arrived, I was in trouble. Lieutenant Grabowsky instructed my platoon officer, Lieutenant Nash, that this evening we were to assault a destroyer anchored in the harbor taking on fuel. When Lieutenant Nash suggested he consider something else, since being underneath a ship taking on fuel was in clear violation of Naval safety regulations, Grabowsky replied, "You'll dive on that ship taking on fuel! Period."

When Lieutenant Nash recounted the instructions to me, I couldn't believe my ears. "No we're not!" I insisted.

"Grub says we do. I went over this with him. He was firm."

"Somebody has to tell him," I responded. Lieutenant Jack Nash was the right person to speak with Grub. From the look in his eyes, I realized he was reluctant to approach Grub again. "I'll do it," I said.

I walked over to the admin offices. I knocked and was shown into Lieutenant Grabowsky's office. Politely, I said, "Sir, Lieutenant Nash just came in and said something about diving on a ship uploading fuel in the bay. If there's any way possible, I'd like to see if we could work out a better plan."

The reason for my concern was that Navy regs were in place for a reason. When a ship took on fuel, mishaps often occurred. Due to the volatility, should a problem arise, the ship was to disengage and propel itself away from the fueling station. If we were swimming underneath, someone would get hurt.

Grub looked at me like I was chopped liver. "You are ordered to dive!"

"Bullshit! It's against every safety regulation the Navy has. If you call the Naval Safety Center hot line, they'll tell you there's no way they'd authorize that op."

Grub's eyes flashed angrily. "Bullshit! You'll do what you're told!"

"C'mon, Lieutenant! It's not worth getting men killed over. I'll call the Safety Center."

Lieutenant Nash had been in the lobby, overhearing our conversation. I walked into the lobby and dialed the hot line number. Lieutenant Nash dipped his head into Grub's office, said a few words, then came over to where I stood and pushed the button down, disconnecting the call. "Grub said we can do something else."

Walking out, Lieutenant Nash, whom I liked and respected, concurred, "I know you did what was right. But, I think you just ruined yourself in SEAL Teams."

"I can't believe this is happening to me again!" I lamented. "I'd be okay if I still had Uncle Dave to back me up."

Gary and I were running hot platoons. Grub and Worthington began slamming their "my way or no way" commands in my face. I, in turn, went out of my way to show them they weren't combat capable. I knew better, but I continued to arrogantly, and with disgust, weigh in on their designs. "Now that's stupid . . ." I'd state, in front of everyone.

Through it all, Lieutenant Nash and I got along well. Grub asked him to fill out an op order to take our platoon to Malaysia to train their Special Forces in intensive counterinsurgency training. An op order involved extensive documentation, similar to a detailed pro forma business plan. He came to me because he hadn't done an op order, and it had to be done in four days. I'd done them repeatedly when I was with Gallagher in Vietnam. Manning and I designed and typed the operational details, including half of the team parachuting with a large rubber raft and outboard motor while the other half landed in Kuala Lumpur and transported eastward to our staging area. We laid on logistics, laid on materiel, and detailed cost analyses. I later received a commendation in my evaluations from Lieutenant Nash for my efforts. I didn't mind being a team player.

After returning from Malaysia to the Philippines, it was soon time to head back to SEAL Team One. "You will receive an evaluation when you return to SEAL Team One in Coronado," reported Grub.

"Great," I commented, thinking it was a determination on my skills. Instead, he was alluding to a decision on whether I stayed in SEAL Team One at all.

When I returned to Coronado, the new Commanding Officer called me in. "We have reviewed your evaluation. The decision has been made that you are no longer needed in SEAL Team." His words came out of the blue. Just prior to my shipping out to the Philippines, Uncle Dave had been the CO's boss. Now he was gone, and with him, my protective cover. Now my head had rolled, and soon it would be Gary's turn.

I was numb. "Damn! This is a real surprise to me. I thought I was doing good!"

"Nope. You gotta go. You're a pain in the ass, you're arrogant, and you're a problem child."

I had had Uncle Dave serving as the best flak jacket in the world. Now, I had no one to protect my back, and politics said I had to go. This time I knew it was over for good.

Captain Richard Marcinko had worked hard to set up an elite SEAL Team. He'd taken his contingency platoon and elevated it to the next level, replete with their own budget, authority, and specialized authorization and assignments. He was dismissed from SEAL Team Six, but soon resurfaced in another platoon known as Red Cell. As an officer, he was much further along than I was, but soon his chain got yanked. Hard. There was discernible apprehension, grudges, even fear, that Marcinko had gotten beyond the control of those up the chain of command. By May 1986, Captain Marcinko was interrogated by NIS with his ouster their clear cut goal. On charges many feel were a setup, he was convicted of conspiracy, bribery, conflict of interest, and making false claims against the government. They wanted him badly, with officers even writing letters to then-President Reagan contesting promotions for Marcinko. At times, he clearly bent rules, but he brought SEAL Team Six up to a par with the Israelis and British SAS.

Uncle Dave had attempted to mimic Marcinko's SEAL Team Six, to a lesser degree, with Gary and me, by asking us to do ops he requested, and supplying the necessary elements. We were, at pay grades far less than those around us, vulnerable to senior officers. While Uncle Dave was around, however, we were left alone. When he left for Washington and we left for the Philippines, the support from Uncle Dave disappeared. There is documented apprehension concerning SEALs like me, trained soldiers and, sometimes, ruthless killers. The uneasiness came from fear that we were "amoral"—some sort of ticking time bomb ready to go off.

I was two years away from the twenty-year mark, so I opted to stay in the Navy to garner retirement benefits. Whereas last time I received Hawaii, this time the detailer sent me packing to Great Lakes, Illinois, just north of Chicago, beginning six weeks later, in September 1983.

Chamberlin and his platoon returned from the Philippines. He came by to see me. After a few comments about times spent in the Philippines, Gary remarked to me, "I can't believe your buddies did that to you."

"What do you mean?"

"Well, you heard about the chiefs' meeting," he presumed.

"No."

"You didn't hear about the secret chiefs' meeting?"

"No."

"You remember Roy Dean Matthews?"

"Of course."

"He and Herschel Davis, and a couple of other chiefs all got together with the new Commanding Officer, and they all voted to get rid of you. They all voted that you were detrimental to SEAL Team. And that's what the Commander used to drop your qualifications and get rid of you, so Uncle Dave couldn't do anything about it."

"You're kidding me!" I challenged. "Not Roy Dean! Not Herschel Davis! I went through training with them." I was beside myself.

"Yeah. Because you and I did things outside recognized authority, it was decided the easiest thing to do was to get rid of you. So they lied, said what each other needed to hear, documented what they needed to document, and kicked your ass out. Totally illegal, but totally effective."

That was a bitter pill to swallow, yet it answered questions and brought closure to what transpired prior to my dismissal. I'd been at a loss as to why I was dropped. The writing was on the wall when I was dropped in Puerto Rico, but this time the ax came at me from left field.

"I thought you knew. I mean, with all your men moving on into SEAL Team Six, you certainly weren't a failure at doing your duties with the platoon. Your drinking, your showing up some of the officers, but, most of all, the loss of support from Uncle Dave, was what combined to wipe you out."

"But why Roy Dean and Herschel?"

"I don't know," Gary returned.

In the final analysis, I had no one to blame but myself. Maybe I drank too much a time or two. Maybe it was the periods of clouded judgment as I agonized over my marriage to Sandy. Maybe it was my disrespect and intolerance at nonoperators' comments that were ignorant at best and deadly at worst. It was probably a combination of all these. More than anything, it was not being a good politician.

Before leaving for Great Lakes, I attended a party. Uncle Dave was there, and came over to talk to me. He was upset. "You know, Harry, had your future been planned better, you'd have been Naval Special Warfare Commander. You're the only one that I knew that had both the good and the bad. You could've gone all the way up this ladder. Your career in SEAL Teams is over." He paused, contemplating his words carefully. "Move on. Do something else."

He swirled the beer in his glass, disappointment clouding his face. "You damn stupid asshole! You had it all. You could have been the poster boy for SEAL Teams. I've never seen potential in anybody else like I've seen in you. Your intelligence, your ability, your deadliness, your thought, your compassion—I've never seen it in anyone!" He took a half step away, then turned around and looked at me, his eyes blazing. "It shouldn't have happened. I'm sorry."

After I returned from the Philippines, Sandy and Marnie were living at my place. Since I was gone, I let Sandy stay for Marnie's sake. I stayed with my friend and fellow SEAL, Dave Mitchell, who lived in Imperial Beach, until I transferred to my next billet. Sandy drove my BMW, while I drove an old VW van I picked up for a hundred dollars. It might have been simply the path of least resistance or an emotional lull, but I saved some money and called to ask Sandy out. "You want to go see the Coasters? I was thinking maybe we could go out to dinner and then see the show. Good! Pick you up Friday night at six. Sound all right? Great! See you then."

The evening went well. Dinner was good and the show entertaining. We'd been together, on and off, for twelve years, and the time together that evening was relaxed and comfortable. She didn't seem disappointed I was out of SEAL Teams.

"Would you mind if I came in?" I asked as I drove her home. "It's been a long time."

"Oh, Harry. It's been a wonderful evening. I'm sorry, I have a headache. I need to get to bed. I've had a great time. Maybe we can get together in a few days. Okay?"

"Sure, no problem," I said, disappointed, but encouraged at the thought of maybe getting back together.

After dropping her off at the house I relinquished to her, I left in my "beater" VW van. Low on gas, I pulled in at a self-serve service station to fill up. Just as I was cleaning the windshield, I recognized my BMW driving by.

A headache, huh? I'll bet I know where she's headed. As quickly as I could, I finished up, jumped in, and took off. I followed her for several blocks. Sure enough, she pulled into the officers' club at the Amphib Base.

Something welled up inside me. Then it snapped. It was over. It was September 1983, and after fifteen years, it was over. A profound sense of sadness gave way to subdued relief as it flooded my mind. *We're finally through. Probably ten years too late.*

Though divorced, I'd given up my house and my brand-new BMW to Sandy. I grappled with what to do about Marnie, the only bright spot from our years together. Even though I was not her father, she and I had a warm relationship. I decided I would support her until she graduated from high school. As far as Sandy was concerned, I was done. No more car payments, no more insurance payments, no more house payments. She had taken me to the cleaners long enough.

"I'm leaving for Denver, to visit my sister," Sandy informed me, certain my resolve would crumble should she need me. "Take care of the kid."

"Later," was all I said.

Before leaving for Great Lakes, I had a long talk with Marnie. "I'm going to give you a choice. I have to go to a Navy base near Chicago. It'll be an eight-to-five job, so I'll have a lot more time to spend with you. On the other hand, I know what it's like to be uprooted and be the new kid without any friends at a new school. I've checked with the Fitzpatricks, and they're willing to let me pay for you to stay with them and their daughter so you can finish high school here in Coronado."

"You mean I could stay with my best friend Jennifer—at her house?"

"Yes."

"That'd be so cool if I could do that. I mean, I love you and all, but I wouldn't know anybody. . . . You mean it? I could stay here?"

I smiled. Marnie was a great gal, caught in such an unstable household. I'd always felt bad about that. "You can stay. Just think it over carefully."

"Thank you, Dad."

Unfortunately, Uncle Dave Schaible suffered a stroke, forcing him to relinquish control of strategic placement and design of Naval Special Warfare operatives. SEAL Teams lost a great man. I lost a friend. Good-bye, Teams. I left for my final duties in Great Lakes.

CHAPTER 21

OUT FOR GOOD

O UT OF MONEY, HAVING FEW POSSESSIONS, AND IN DEBT TO THE IRS, I reported to Great Lakes to conclude my military career. No one called me any longer, and the finality of a bright career flickering out hit home. I was embarrassed and humiliated. I smiled wryly to myself. *Amazing, the twists of fate. It's over. No one knows where I'm at. It's done.*

It was November 1983, and I had a little more than a year left of service to reach my twenty-year career. My task was as an instructor teaching engineering systems to sailors. I was buried on the graveyard shift—working from ten at night until six A.M.—through the winter and until my retirement on October 31, 1984.

Normally, when an individual who was a "war hero" retired, he was accorded what is known as full military honors. There's a parade, a formal ceremony, and the drum and bugle corps shows up. Soldiers were to stand in formation as the ceremony was carried out. I rated all of that due to my combat services. Par for the course, I received none of it.

On the afternoon of my final day, I got a call from the school director. "Your paperwork's ready."

I walked across the base wearing my engineering jumpsuit, stepping into his office with a couple of the other engineers. "Hello, sir," I acknowledged.

Gaining the attention of the other engineers, the director stated, "You guys may not realize it, but Harry here is a Navy SEAL. Looking over his paperwork here, he's done more than most of you guys could think of."

I stood before him for at least some semblance of an "official" retirement. The director continued, "I worked with some of you SEALs in Vietnam, piloting PBRs. Sorry you're where you are now, but you still have my respect for your years of service to our country and the U.S. Navy."

I shook his hand formally; he then handed me my plaque and twenty-year retirement certificate. I was through. "That's it. Tomorrow you'll go on admin leave, and on December thirty-first, you'll retire to the Fleet Reserve. You may start your leave as of now."

(This was comparable to having vacation and sick leave built up, so I was out October 31, rather than December 31.)

"Thank you, sir."

I returned to the barracks. I'd chosen the Chief's Barracks because I sent much of my money home to Marnie and couldn't afford off-base housing. I did, however, receive word Sandy had returned to Coronado and was going to provide for Marnie, especially since I had paid up her schooling and living expenses through the end of the school year.

I packed up my new Ford Bronco and left. *I'm free and clear! I have a retirement check coming in, which should cover bare necessities. I love the great outdoors! As a SEAL, I could live off the land.* I'd thought long and hard about what I wanted to do. I determined to go live in the national forest in Montana. *Big Sky country, here I come.* I headed the Bronco westward as I pulled through the gates of Great Lakes Naval Base.

As I entered Montana on Interstate 90, I came to the junction of I-15 near Butte. It was late, so I pulled off the road, climbing into the back to sleep. I breathed in deeply the cold, November night air. *I'm free and I'm happy,* I thought as I gazed sleepily at the stars overhead. *It's nice when you make a decision like this. Nobody expects jack from me. I can do whatever I want, whenever I want! Just think, I can't get in trouble anymore!* As I drifted off to sleep, two thoughts began nagging at me. *You're not a quitter! Who says you're a screwup? You're not a quitter! Who says you're a screwup?* I wrestled with this all night long, tossing and turning.

I awoke at dawn. It was frosty cold, weather I really liked. Boots, jeans, wool sweater, and cap, I was out wiping the ice from the windshield. There was a lightness to my spirit. Then my thoughts from the night reappeared. Again, I wrestled over what to do. *Why am I even thinking about this? I've made up my mind, I'm headed for the mountains!* Then, as if from the back of my mind came, *If I go to the mountains now, everyone will have assumed they won, that they were correct. I will have quit, and no one will have any reason to doubt that what took place wasn't right.*

Why fight it anymore? It's over. Let it go—be happy for once.

No! I'm not going to give in. I'm not going to let it happen. I'll go back down to Coronado and at least have my two cents' worth.

I turned my Bronco south on I-15 and headed for San Diego. When I arrived, I stopped by to see Marnie.

I also decided to go back to school, enrolling first at Mesa College and then continuing on to San Diego State University. I was determined to start all over again.

I had to sell my Bronco, but I was determined to get myself squared away. *Forty isn't that old,* I told myself. I paid rent with monies from the GI Bill school funds and my retirement check.

Dingdong. It was Sandy. She'd been kicked out by her sisters in Denver, and needed a place to stay. I said no.

Gary and I got together. "So you got canned, I see," I said, stating the obvious.

"Yeah. Not long after you left. I stayed here because of my wife Nelda's job."

We talked about old times and not so old times, about friends and current events. I told him I was going to school and what my plans were.

"I'm now with NIS. There's an opening for an NIS Training Agent. You'd be perfect! You'd be training law enforcement, Department of Defense personnel, and Naval personnel in the safeguards of nuclear weapons. What do you think?"

I applied as soon as I could. In no time at all, I was making money, got a nice place, and was back on some sort of upwardly mobile track. Soon, the Navy had Gary and me traveling around from base to base. After two years, in 1987, the Navy felt what we were doing was important enough to set up a permanent training course at the Fleet Training Center, Naval Station, San Diego. NIS wanted to keep a traveling program going, while the Navy wanted the permanent facility. As is frequently the case with the government, they chose to do both. The Navy came to Gary and me and asked if we wanted to go to work in their permanent detachment, or continue with NIS.

The head of the Naval program was an old Navy salt by the name of "Gunner" Rickman. "Harry, come to work for me. I'll let you run the program, and I'll promote you to GS-eleven [civilian, government service pay grade]. You'd develop all the tactics that Marine and Navy security personnel will utilize in the safeguarding of nuclear weapons."

"Okay—I accept!" My previous conditioning at short answers seemed appropriate. It was an easy decision.

I began in September 1986. Several months later, Sandy called. Marnie probably relayed to her that I was making money again. "Harry, now that you're back on solid ground, it seems to me you finally have your head on straight for the first time in a long time."

"Thank you very much," I cut in, figuring what was coming.

"I'd really like to see if we could start new and afresh. We've always made a good couple, and Marnie's been asking about you. We could be a family again."

"Sandy, let me be real plain. We are done. No more. *Nada*—as in *nada* chance," I said flatly.

"I can't believe you feel that way! Especially after all I've been through because of you. Now I'm nearly broke and they're threatening to repossess the car. The least you can do is to send me a little money so Marnie and I can get around. Don't tell me you're that cold and heartless!"

This had worked in the past, but it wasn't working now. "I *am* that cold and heartless."

Angrily, she slammed down the receiver. A few minutes later, she called back. "Listen, if you don't send me some money and soon, I'm going to call your CO and let him know you're doing drugs."

An irrational fear crept up in my throat. I desperately did not want to be embarrassed and fired again. The where-there's-smoke-there's-fire pain I went through during and after the first-degree murder allegations was awful. I'd never done any drugs beyond alcohol, but I didn't want Gunner saying something like, "Sorry Harry, we just can't take the chance. Think of how it would look—former wife details drug use by nuclear weapons and shooting specialist." I sent her the money.

A month later, she called again, reaching me at work, threatening me further if I didn't send more money. "I'll ruin your career!"

"Let me see what I can do."

I told Gary of my quandary. He glared at me. "Go up and tell the CO first."

Doubtful, I replied, "I don't want to be rocking the boat with my personal problems."

"If you trust me, you'll do it. Then, she'll have no more black-mailing leverage over you."

I went to the CO. "Commander, I need to talk to you about a personal matter."

He invited me into his office. Quickly, I detailed my dilemma. He listened attentively, then asked, "Do you mind if I have Gunner Rickman in?"

"No, not at all." *Great, now even more people are going to know my problems.*

After Gunner arrived, I reconveyed what was occurring. They asked questions, we discussed the possible ramifications, and then the CO said, "Harry, we know it took guts for you to come up here and tell us. We also want you to know we think you're an outstanding training officer, you don't have any problems, and you haven't exhibited any signs or indications of drug use. You've passed all your drug tests. It's obvious to me she's just trying to hook you. I want you to go to work and—do me a favor—don't talk to her anymore. Just tell her to go to hell. That's my two cents!"

Gunner chimed in, "Yeah! You can't use my phone to talk to her anymore!"

Grinning, all I could say was a simple "Thanks, guys." I was grateful.

Three days later, she called. Reaching the switchboard operator, Sandy insisted, "I want to talk to Constance!"

"I'm sorry, he's busy. May I take a message or have him call?"

"Bullshit! I know he's there! Either I talk to him, or I'll call the CO! Get him on the line!"

"Paging Chief Constance. Paging Mr. Constance."

As I came to pick up the phone, the operator rolled her eyes. "There's a madwoman on the phone for you."

I smiled worriedly. *Great. It's gotta be Sandy.*

The operator knew what was going on. She held her hand up. *Wait!* We worked in a small office complex. She quickly signaled Gunner to come out of his office. At once, we had eleven people gathered around the speaker phone.

"Where's my money?" she snarled, her voice resonating through my office. "They've come and repossessed the car!"

"I don't have any money for you."

That launched her into a tirade. "What the hell do you mean you don't have any money! I know you're making enough money to take care of things! You'd damn well better drop off some cash tonight— tonight!—or I'll make you wish you were still in Great Lakes! I can ruin you! You know that, don't you! I go to your CO and tell him about how you were kicked out of SEAL Teams, and that it was all from drugs!"

"Sandy. It won't work. We're through. Don't bother me anymore," I said calmly.

"It will too work!"

"Tell you what," I said, somewhat embarrassed at having everybody listening to me arguing with my ex-wife, "you call the CO. I had a long talk with him after you called the other day. I told him everything. So go right ahead. I just don't give a shit anymore."

At that, my coworkers started clapping.

"What's that!" Sandy said, alarmed.

"Oh, you're on speaker phone."

Flustered and upset, Sandy started to say something several times, then shrieked and slammed the phone down. She never demanded money again.

With her out of my life—*finally*—my life was smoothing out. I had stability, I had friends, and I had some degree of self-respect. Our training program was working. It was fun designing and creating something new and different.

Since it was a training course, it was determined that we needed to have materials—notes, handouts, and manuals for the students. Educational curriculum specialists were hired to help with the didactic paperwork. It also allowed for standardization, so the Navy knew exactly what was being taught from one instructor to the next.

One of the Educational Specialists I worked with was a tall, willowy blonde named Barbara. She'd come in and sit at the back of the classroom to listen. I tried to convince her that this was a combat class for men. "Look ma'am, I use a lot of four-letter words, it's rough, and there's an emphasis on killing. It's not the place for a woman."

Firmly rejecting my sexist slight, she said, "You do what you have to do—use the words and pictures you have to use—I'm just here to make sure you do it right."

We talked a number of times about the program and where it was headed. *She's beautiful,* I thought, *and smart, too.*

Gary came to me. "What do you think of the blond-haired woman in your classes?"

"What do you mean?"

"She's been asking about you. She told me she thought you were cute."

"Really?" I said with a start. There I was, forty years old, feeling like I was in high school again. Then reality set in. "I've got nothing. What could she possibly see in a guy like me. I really don't care to get hurt again. I've never been good with women."

"She likes you. You ought to at least ask her out."

"Yeah, right," I quipped sarcastically. "I pick her up in my VW and we go out for Taco Bell. She'd probably tell me to take her home immediately. There's no way she'd be interested in a guy like me and, if she were, once she figured out who I am, she'd drop me so fast it'd make your head spin."

She was a classy, well-dressed, and well-educated lady. I couldn't see her having any future with a guy like me, broke, discredited and disgraced, not once but twice. A strong self-image was in short supply at that point.

"You don't think she's cute?" Gary persisted.

"I didn't say that," I replied uncomfortably. "She's cute."

"Well, ask her out!"

Barbara and I continued to exchange pleasantries in passing, but that was it for months. Finally, Gary, who was as diametrically the opposite of a Casanova as could be, took it upon himself to be a matchmaker. He had Barbara switched to my course as Educational Specialist again.

Slowly, I fell in love with her. It was an entirely new experience for me. I was drawn to her, finding excuses to discuss the smallest details with her.

She came to critique another of my classes, when an overwhelming urge to kiss her came on me. *What the hell is wrong with me? Look at you, a SEAL, and you're scared of this woman. Everybody's told me she's interested in me. What's the big deal? Why am I so afraid!*

I was teaching the group how to do a room entry, SWAT assault. The technique was to come busting through the door as quickly as you could to catch the criminal off guard, much as we did in storming through hooches in Vietnam. "Barbara, would you care to see what it looks like, the ferocity of the assault I was talking about in class? What it's like from the enemy's point of view?''

''Yes,'' she replied.

I said, ''Fine. Step inside.''

We went into the room and closed the door. The only lights were from large flashlights set on a countertop. Theoretically, the power had been cut. One of the lights shone on Barbara, illuminating her golden blond hair.

I walked beside her and kissed her gingerly. She smiled and kissed me back! My heart was pounding! The adrenaline flowed almost as much as it did in combat. My head swam. . . .

Suddenly, the door burst open and six guys exploded through the door!

Caught, all I could offer weakly to the dozen eyes looking intently at us was ''Uh, don't you guys ever bother to knock?''

CHAPTER 22

BARBARA

WE BEGAN DATING IN SEPTEMBER 1986, SEEING EACH OTHER more and more. She liked me for who I was. She was only interested in me, not busy checking out other men around us. We spent hours talking about anything and everything. My most interesting discovery was that she made me a better person. Her humor, intelligence, and ''being there'' for me supported me in a way I'd never known.

It wasn't nearly as difficult to ask her to marry me as it had been to kiss her and ask her out! We were married a year later, in November 1987. Next to joining SEAL Teams, marrying Barbara was the best decision I'd ever made.

She had two kids, Carrie and Darren, so it was instant family all over again. I was catapulted to a middle-class station in life overnight. It wasn't that much earlier I was starting over, broke. I'd owed the IRS $2,000 and undergone bankruptcy. Now, I had a wife, two kids, and a nice home.

Our friendship grew deeper and deeper with the years. Had we met and dated in the sixties, it wouldn't have worked. I was too coarse, as I prepared and then went to Vietnam. At the same time, she went to Kent State during the height of the antiwar movement and was there for the National Guard incident that rocked the nation in 1970. I don't think we would have dated much!

She married and underwent a divorce that left her changed. The heartaches of life helped evolve both of us, allowing us to focus more upon the enjoyment of life.

In 1989, an opportunity came to move up the ladder, with a position in Sacramento, California, as Director of Security at the Sacramento Army Depot. It was an enjoyable assignment, since it afforded me a chance to broaden my skills further. Barb and I were climbing the ladder together. Slowly, the feelings of rage, anger, distrust, suspicion, and sense of persecution subsided. I quit smoking and my drinking fell off.

I did well enough to warrant a promotion, to GS-12, equivalent to the beginning officer rankings, comparable to that of lieutenant. I was finally accorded officer status and privilege. Performance skills and increased job responsibilities brought with them a GS-13 ranking. It is comparable to lieutenant commander.

Things went well in Sacramento. I had a good home life, my good friend Gary Chamberlin had moved to Sacramento as well, and work was enjoyable.

One area of my life that caused me concern was my dad. He had some health problems, suffered from high blood pressure and had had several small strokes. He was nearing seventy, but seemed to be doing fairly well given his age. Early in February 1991, as I was about to leave for an executive management conference in Albuquerque, New Mexico, I called and spoke to my mother.

"Hello, Mom. I'm headed to a conference in Albuquerque. I'd like to get together. How about Barb and I come down in two weeks and visit you and Dad there in Austin?"

"That'd be great, son."

They really liked Barbara, and were pleased to see me happy. Several months earlier, my dad said as much when he and Mom visited us. "You did it, son," he related. "All those years in Teams, all the ups and downs. I always wondered how it was going to end. Were you going to end up in jail, end up dead, or end up rich? I suspected one of the first two. With Sandy, I never expected more than that. But I had to let you make your own decisions and go your own path." He gave me a hug, something my father rarely did. As we climbed into the pool in the backyard, he smiled contentedly. "You have a winner in Barbara and you seem to be on the right track. I'm proud of you, son."

His sentiments meant a great deal to me. I don't know if it's innate or not, but there is for a son a strong yearning for approval and acceptance from his father. That moment was especially meaningful. It was to be the last time I saw my dad alive.

When I returned from the Albuquerque conference, Barb picked me up at the airport and we drove home. Happy to be home, I grabbed Barb and gave her a hug. Suddenly, tears ran down her face. Her lips were quivering and she cried convulsively. "Harry . . ."

I knew what she was going to say. "My father's dead, isn't he."

She nodded her head. I assumed Dad had had another stroke or heart attack. I brought Barb to me, holding her close. She pushed away. "You have to know what happened."

My eyes widened. "Uh-oh! What happened?"

"Dad took his .thirty-eight service revolver, put it in his mouth, and pulled the trigger."

Barb collapsed onto the bed, crying bitterly. I gently pulled her to me, my mind not yet registering the pain creasing my heart.

The phone rang. It was my brother Charles, calling from his post in Saudi Arabia during the February 1991 Gulf War. "What's happened? The Red Cross says I have an emergency and I need to call home. I called you."

Charles and I had grown closer since I married Barb. He suspected something with the family, so he called me. "Charlie, Dad has died."

I heard my brother inhale suddenly, as the news hit him forcibly. He paused a second, then asked me the question I was praying he would not. "How did it happen?"

I wanted so badly, because he was fighting in the war, to say, *He died of another heart attack,* but I couldn't. *Charlie's a Marine; he'll hold it against me if I don't tell him the truth. I'd expect it of him; he expects it of me.* "Dad shot himself."

The news so shocked Charles, he literally dropped the phone, turned, and walked away. The guy behind him had to hang up the phone.

Fifteen minutes later, he got on the phone again and called his wife for more details. Then he called me back. "I can be on a plane and home in three days."

Clearly asking my opinion, I responded. "Let me tell you something, Charlie. One thing you and I both know about our dad; he wouldn't want either one of us coming home because of what took place. If you feel the need to come home, do so. But if you're over there to kick ass and take names, then kick ass and take names. Do it for Dad."

"Okay. Call me when the funeral arrangements are made."

"I will."

I flew back to Austin the next morning. Charlie's wife, Kathy, and my sister, Madjie, also flew in. I consoled my mother. I went through, with Kathy, all my father's papers in order to make certain my parents' affairs were in order. It was a heavy loss for me. My dad was a rock. I was proud of him, I looked up to him. I valued his counsel, and I valued anything and everything he valued. Suicide. My tall, proud, successful, thrice-shot-down-in-World-War-II-war-hero father, dead of a self-inflicted gunshot wound. *Why, Dad? Why!*

I spent hours pacing the floor, soaking up the feeling of his presence in his home, gazing intently at the many time-worn photos gracing the walls. He'd been ill, and had been feeling he was becoming a burden to my mom.

I'd killed and seen a lot of death. No one's death, not Fraley's, not Curtis Ashton's, came even close to affecting me like the death of my father. It altered my perception of family, and thrust the issue of death—real gut-wrenching death—to a level of awareness I'd not known before. I lay on the floor with a pen and a piece of paper writing my father's eulogy, trying to sum up in five minutes the essence of his life. It was good therapy for me.

He'd wanted to be cremated, so his wishes were fulfilled. I was given the urn in a brown pasteboard box. I put Dad in my suitcase and left for home. The airline promptly lost my luggage. I know this sounds funny, in a macabre sort of way, but I was furious. "You either come up with my father, or I'm going to start beating up on people," I said angrily to the poor Delta agent, whose fault it obviously was not. Security was called. "Don't you come near me! You tell them to go find my dad!" I explained why I was so distraught. They found my suitcase in Salt Lake City.

I kept Dad in my closet for about a year, until Charlie returned from Saudi Arabia. Charlie and I went out on the point overlooking the ocean at the Naval Air Station in Coronado. I opened up the piece of paper I'd written Dad's eulogy on and read it to Charlie. Both of us cried together for the first time in our lives. Taking out the urn, we spread his ashes partly in the ocean, and partly on the jetty. Buried on land and sea. For me, it symbolized closure on an important part of my life.

In 1993, the Sacramento Army Depot unfortunately hit the Base Realignment and Closure list. It was slated to close in 1995. I put in for a job transfer. This time, two opportunities came available. The first was to Rock Island, Illinois, as the Senior Security Officer responsible for all of the Army's arms, ammunition, and explosives. A national responsibility. It was a plum assignment, clearly the best position available. But, after much consideration and hand-wringing, Barbara and I decided not to leave California. I turned it down and took a position as Chief of Police at the West L.A. Veterans Affairs complex. It is the largest VA complex in the country.

I was making a living doing something I enjoyed. The West L.A. VA hospital has the largest population of PTSD (post-traumatic stress disorder) veterans in the country. I'd danced at the precipice and lived to tell about it. I realized there were others, especially veterans, who had been dealt an unfortunate hand and hadn't made it over the "hump" of life. I decided to do what I could, if only through the recounting of my story. Life can be so sorrowful and so bitter that the easiest thing to do is to quit, to end it, to give up, back up or reject it. What's hard is to carry on and overcome those obstacles. It can be done. I'm no better than anybody else. I'm an average individual who found, through SEAL Team training, that you can do whatever you put your mind to. Some people just need more help than others.

A close friend whom I met while in Sacramento is my eye doctor, Randy Fuerst. We were neighbors and did a lot of things neighbors do. We went hunting together, fishing, camping, and I helped Randy with landscaping. Over a campfire, Randy remarked, "You know, Harry, you've been through a lot! A bad marriage, unwarranted and unfair murder charges, court-martial charges, fired twice, bankrupt, stabbed in the back by friends, and then, to top it all off, your dad commits suicide. You've got quite a story. Have you ever thought about telling it?"

Randy kept after me, pushing me to tell my story. Finally, I relented, realizing that God had kept me alive on numerous occasions, and that there are people, especially veterans, who might benefit from some of the experiences I've been through. "I don't know why. I don't think it's any big deal, but if you want to write it, go right ahead."

"I'd like that," said Randy. "What should we call the story of your life?"

With little more than a moment's hesitation, I responded, *"Good to Go."*

Randy responded the only way he could—"Okay!"

It couldn't be more fitting.

EPILOGUE

THIS STORY REPRESENTS MY BEST RECOLLECTION OF THE EVENTS that have shaped my life. I apologize for any anguish my life's story may cause anyone. I feel I am a better man for having told it.

Time has a way of healing old wounds. With the unwavering support of family and friends, what seems impossible becomes doable. You accept where you're at, not in resignation, but in honesty, and move forward. I hope in some small way the telling of my story gives others the courage to endure whatever hardships they may encounter. The ability to believe in yourself and try again will definitely make you . . . *Good to Go.*